THE VERNACULAR SPIRIT

THE NEW MIDDLE AGES

BONNIE WHEELER, *Series Editor*

The New Middle Ages presents transdisciplinary studies of medieval cultures. It includes both scholarly monographs and essay collections.

PUBLISHED BY PALGRAVE:

THE VERNACULAR SPIRIT

ESSAYS ON MEDIEVAL
RELIGIOUS LITERATURE

Edited by

Renate Blumenfeld-Kosinski,
Duncan Robertson, and
Nancy Bradley Warren

palgrave

First published 2002 by PALGRAVE™
175 Fifth Avenue, New York, N.Y. 10010 and
Houndmills, Basingstoke, Hampshire RG21 6XS.
Companies and representatives throughout the world.

PALGRAVE is the new global publishing imprint of St. Martin's Press
LLC Scholarly and Reference Division and Palgrave Publishers Ltd.
(formerly Macmillan Press Ltd.).

ISBN 0–312–29385–2

Library of Congress Cataloging-in-Publication Data
The vernacular spirit : essays on medieval religious literature / edited by
Renate Blumenfeld-Kosinski, Duncan Robertson, and Nancy Bradley
Warren.
     p.   cm. – (New Middle Ages)
  Includes bibliographical references and index.
  ISBN 0–312–29385–2
  1. Literature, Medieval—History and criticism.   2. Religion and
literature.   I. Blumenfeld-Kosinski, Renate, 1952-   II. Robertson,
Duncan.   III. Warren, Nancy Bradley.   IV. New Middle Ages (Palgrave
(Firm))

PN682.R4 V47   2002
809'.93382'0902—dc21

                                                        2001056147

A catalogue record for this book is available from the British Library.

Design by Letra Libre, Inc.

First edition: June 2002
10 9 8 7 6 5 4 3 2 1

Printed in the United States of America.

CONTENTS

GERMAN AND FLEMISH

SPANISH

SERIES EDITOR'S FOREWORD

The *New Middle Ages* contributes to lively transdisciplinary conversations in medieval cultural studies through its scholarly monographs and essay collections. This series provides focused research in a contemporary idiom about specific but diverse practices, expressions, and ideologies in the Middle Ages. *The Vernacular Spirit: Essays on Medieval Religious Literature*, a collection of essays edited by Renate Blumenfeld-Kosinski, Duncan Robertson, and Nancy Bradley Warren, is the twenty-eighth volume in this series. Scholars from several disciplines here ask what it meant for believers to experience the divine through language, especially through the potentially fragile medium of a developing vernacular. These essays range widely over various genres of later medieval Christian religious expression, locating each in its particular space and linguistic inflection. As we read these essays, we become more keenly aware of ways people locate the divine not only within their political, national, and ideological constructs but also within their own local language.

Bonnie Wheeler
Southern Methodist University

INTRODUCTION

*Renate Blumenfeld-Kosinski, Duncan Robertson,
and Nancy Bradley Warren*

Christian religious writers have struggled at all times with the mediation of language. The fathers of the Church sought to break through the written text of the Scriptures—the *littera,* metaphorically conceived as an outer shell—to reach the spiritual meaning residing inside it. "An angel is nourished with the richness of wheat," wrote St. Bernard, "but in this life I have to be content with the husk, as it were, of the sacrament, with the bran of the flesh, with the chaff of the letter" (*Sermons on the Song of Songs,* 33.3). Even so, commentators nourished in the Latin tradition were able to move effortlessly from reading to prayer to writing and back again, unhindered by problems of translation. After 1200 however, Latin literacy becomes increasingly problematized, as laymen and, significantly, lay and religious women demand access to the domain of spirituality, previously monopolized by the clerical elite. In the new "textual communities," an urgent need is felt to develop the spoken vernacular as an idiom capable of conveying doctrinal complexities and affective experience.[1]

The immediate response to this demand is a flowering of religious poetry and prose in all the European tongues. The pioneering role falls to religious women, notably Hadewijch of Antwerp, Beatrice of Nazareth, Mechthild of Magdeburg, Marguerite Porete, and other thirteenth-century beguines. Their movement is taken up thereafter by English visionaries, such as Julian of Norwich and Margery Kempe; by Catherine of Siena in Italy; by Margarete Ebner and the anonymous authors of the *Sisterbooks* in Germany; and by many others throughout Europe. Extending further into Spain in the fifteenth and sixteenth centuries, the movement may be said to culminate in the writings of Teresa of Avila.

Throughout this period, questions of gender inevitably accompany questions of language. The often negative association of the vernacular with the feminine—the "mother tongue"—is frequently invoked to stigmatize both the vernacular and the feminine/feminized readers or speakers of it, as sources of social and spiritual disorder. Clerical authorities perceived the linguistic "inferiority" of the vernacular in relation to Latin as mirroring the spiritual and intellectual inferiority of women in particular and uneducated laypeople generally. This linkage provided a convenient rationale for preserving the Latinate clergy's monopoly on religious knowledge and its privileged authority, in the political as well as ecclesiastical realms.[2]

There are, however, other ways in which questions of gender come into play. Vernaculars have a Janus-faced quality for the ecclesiastical establishment; they appear both as potentially threatening sources of disorder and as valuable tools for inculcating desirable ideologies, especially in the very women whose independent spiritual advances were such a source of anxiety. Women like Beatrice of Nazareth and Margery Kempe embraced vernacular languages to craft sophisticated theologies all their own, winning acceptance and turning the negative associations of the vernacular and the feminine into assets.

The rubric "vernacular theology" (independently proposed by Bernard McGinn and Nicholas Watson) brings these diverse writings together. Surveying the field as a whole, McGinn places vernacular theology in relation to monasticism and scholasticism as one of three forms of medieval religious thought, to be considered on a comparable footing.[3] Each of the three would be defined by its distinctive goals and methodologies. Monasticism centers, as McGinn recalls, on the *experientia amoris,* sought over centuries in meditation on the Scriptures. Scholasticism would be defined by Anselm's program of *fides quaerens intellectum,* and by the pedagogy of the *quaestio* and the *disputatio.* Vernacular theology resists summary characterization, but might perhaps be globally identified with the dialogic form that structures many late medieval vernacular writings, arising from encounters between clergy and laity, men and women, teachers and disciples, patrons and writers—and most generally of course from the encounter between written and spoken languages.

The concept of vernacular theology embraces the diversity of the field, and bridges the divide that had been previously placed between "feminine" affective or embodied mysticism and the "masculine" domains of abstraction and intellectuality. Laying aside such "essentialisms," we are now more able to acknowledge the speculative character of mystical writings, as in the case of Marguerite Porete. Striking individualities have emerged: Hadewijch and Catherine of Siena come immediately to mind. New interpretations can be presented concerning the relations between male figures such as Richard Rolle and Heinrich Seuse and the women religious with whom they were respectively associated. It is now possible to trace connections that had not been previously perceived, for example, between the beguine movement and Meister Eckhart.[4]

This rich domain has attracted a prodigious surge of interest over the past three decades. The initial impetus to renewal was given by feminist scholars such as Caroline Walker Bynum and Barbara Newman.[5] In more recent years, historians and theologians have integrated the feminist studies into a broadly inclusive overview of religious doctrines and experience, summarized in Bernard McGinn's encyclopedic history of mysticism;[6] this latter work has all but replaced that of Bouyer, Leclercq, and Vandenbroucke,[7] and it has been supplemented in turn by the researches of McGinn's students and associates, notably Ellen Babinsky,[8] Amy Hollywood,[9] Saskia Murk-Jansen,[10] and Michael Sells.[11] Nicholas Watson's book on Richard Rolle and his other studies of the late medieval English context have also generated a scholarly following;[12] this current is most recently represented by an anthology, *The Idea of the Vernacular* (1999).[13]

The above references evoke what has become an active, populous, and fast-changing scholarly environment. Earlier studies had sought to clarify the psychological-theological nature of the mystical writers' experiences, and had documented the histories of the movements in which they participated. More recent research has shifted emphasis from questions of content to those of linguistic and literary mediation. Convinced, indeed, of the need to focus primarily on the texts themselves, we have turned our attention to the markings of genre, the implied or explicit relations between writers and audiences, and the manifestations of language-consciousness in narrative technique, rhetoric, and poetics.[14]

Among the themes that unify the contributions to this volume, the most general is that of the construction of the vernacular, particularly (but not solely) in relation to Latin. This issue, which touches directly or indirectly all the works here discussed, is perhaps most visibly present in the amplified French translations of psalms discussed by Morgan Powell and Lori J. Walters, and in the fifteenth-century English translation of Archbishop Thoresby's *Injunctions* studied by Moira Fitzgibbons. Fiona Somerset's study of late medieval "excitative speech" contributes directly to the same discussion, as does the analysis of the Latin/Flemish textual tradition concerning Beatrice of Nazareth by Else Marie Wiberg Pedersen.

An important dimension of the vernacularization movement is the diversification of literary genres beyond the range of expository forms established in the Latin tradition. That the vernacular saint's life (a novice-level didactic form in Latin) could convey sophisticated doctrinal issues is demonstrated by Pedersen's essay on Beatrice of Nazareth. A further transformation of the saint's-life genre is performed in the "autohagiographies" of Richard Rolle and Heinrich Seuse, as studied by Lisa Manter and Ulrike Wiethaus, respectively. Werner Williams-Krapp's survey of the genres of German vernacular religious writing in the fifteenth century includes catechetical texts, narratives (especially saints' lives), and contemplative literature. Many of the writers examined in this volume creatively adapt "worldly" genres to the concerns of spirituality. Barbara Newman describes Marguerite Porete's use of allegory inherited from the *Romance of the Rose;* Guillaume de Digulleville's *Pèlerinages* draw abundantly on the same courtly tradition, as Maureen Boulton's study demonstrates. Carole Slade recalls that Teresa of Avila's childhood reading of the novels of chivalry influenced her religious vocation, inspiring her to adopt active as well as contemplative roles.

The dialogue between men and women is of course a major theme, which informs almost all of the essays collected here. In the fourteenth-century German Dominican milieu Ulrike Wiethaus discovers complexities of relationships linking female visionaries and male clergy; these in turn shape the female-gendered construction of the vernacular language. Similar issues are raised by Ronald Surtz with regard to the relations between prominent women in fifteenth-century Spain—Queen Isabella the Catholic and Countess Leonor Pimentel—and the clerical writers who penned treatises under their respective patronage. Other male-female dialogues arising from the circumstances of literary patronage include Adam of Perseigne, the (presumed) author of a twelfth-century translation of Psalm 44, addressing the countess Marie of Champagne; and Christine de Pizan, in her allegorized translation of the seven penitential psalms, advising her patron, Charles the Noble of Navarre. Elizabeth Teresa Howe studies a similar, implied patronage relationship linking the cardinal Jiménez de Cisneros to two early-sixteenth-century Spanish visionaries, Sor María de Santo Domingo and Madre Juana de la Cruz.

The essays in this volume are presented by languages, in alphabetical order, and in chronological order within each language group.

Lisa Manter's essay, "Rolle Playing: 'And the Word Became Flesh,'" treats Richard Rolle's self-authorizing strategies in his Latin and Middle English writings. She explores the ways in which Rolle, in his Latin texts, shapes a saintly persona for himself that authorizes his Middle English writings and helps to create an audience for these works. Mobilizing Jacques Derrida's theories of signification, she argues that in Rolle's writings the humanity of Christ becomes a linguistic sign, and that the signifier "Christ" is conflated with the signifier "Richard Hermit." In his vernacular writings, "Richard Hermit" becomes a model of piety whose Passion is interchangeable with that of Christ.

Moira Fitzgibbons's chapter, "Disruptive Simplicity: Gaytryge's Translation of Archbishop Thoresby's *Injunctions*," examines Gaytryge's translation methodology in *The Lay Folks' Catechism.* While the *Injunctions* exhibits a conservative outlook, enjoining Christians to follow Church principles and practices without much independent thought in order to avoid damnation, Fitzgibbons argues that Gaytryge takes substantial liberties with his Latin source, envisioning a more active role for laypeople in their own salvation and highlighting the potential for lay learning and knowledge. He sees religious instruction in the vernacular as providing laypeople with greater authority and with the license to question the clerical magisterium while remaining good Christians. In spite of its seemingly rudimentary nature, the *Catechism* thus merits inclusion in the body of literature known as vernacular theology.

Fiona Somerset's chapter, "Excitative Speech: Theories of Emotive Response from Richard Fitzralph to Margery Kempe," analyzes the development of later medieval ideas about the dangers, benefits, and consequences of emotionally provocative language in Fitzralph's *Quia in proposicione nuper facta* (a reply to objections made by friars to his *Defensio curatorum*) and in the vernacular writing of Margery Kempe. She argues that Fitzralph's text provides a remarkably detailed treatment of possible types of speech and of criteria for determining whether a given statement is expositive, assertive, or excitative, ideas that have important implications for authorial accountability. Kempe, in turn, as a vernacular theorist, uses some of the same tools to examine the consequences of excitative expression, envisioning ways in which lay devotional emotion may be not simply socially disruptive but in fact socially beneficial.

Morgan Powell's essay, "Translating Scripture for *Ma dame de Champagne*: The Old French 'Paraphrase' of Psalm 44," discusses a twelfth-century French verse paraphrase of the psalm, *Eructavit cor meum*. The poem amplifies its rendering of the psalm in the form of a narrative that recounts how "David," a *jongleur*, comes to perform his song at the marriage of Christ and the Church. The French poem, attributed to Adam of Perseigne, is dedicated to Marie, the countess of Champagne, and patroness of Chrétien de Troyes. It presents itself as a reperformance, as it were, in which the roles of David and the bride/queen are taken by the poet and the countess, respectively. The poet offers spiritual instruction to the lady, who also represents the wider courtly audience. Within the entertainment space of vernacular poetry, the poet is able to provide a lay reading of scripture, a fully realized alternative to clerical *lectio* and exegesis.

In "The Mirror and the Rose: Marguerite Porete's Encounter with the *Dieu d'Amours*," Barbara Newman traces a connection between the *Mirouer des simples ames*, by Marguerite Porete, and its famous "unlikely intertext," the *Romance of the Rose*, subtitled le *miroer as amoreus*, by Jean de Meun. Newman situates this interaction within the thirteenth- and fourteenth-century culture of *mystique courtoise*. She cites the *Five Incitements* to the *Ardent Love of God*, by Gérard of Liège, and the anonymous beguine *Règle des fins amans* [Rule for True Lovers]—two works that Marguerite might easily have read, which exemplify the influence of courtly themes upon religious writing. Marguerite certainly knew the *Romance of the Rose*. Her general allegorical strategy, the debate she constructs between Lady Love and Reason, and several of her more controversial propositions, draw her into a paradoxical association with Jean de Meun's sexual naturalism, a linkage that contributed doubtless to her condemnation by the Church authorities.

Maureen Boulton's chapter, "Digulleville's *Pèlerinage de Jésus Christ*: A Poem of Courtly Devotion," examines Guillaume de Digulleville's trilogy of pilgrimage texts as a unified cycle, focusing particularly on the *Pèlerinage de Jésus Christ*, the least studied of the three. She analyzes the texts' relationship to the *Romance of the Rose* and explores the literary innovations present in the *Pèlerinage de Jésus Christ*, particularly its incorporation of elements of dream vision, allegorical personification, lyric, and direct discourse. She argues that this text provides an important example of the ways in which authors of religious texts appropriated secular literary techniques, considering in particular the significance of devices from the courtly *dit* in enhancing the affective aspects of Digulleville's life of Christ.

Christine de Pizan's relationship with her patron, Charles the Noble of Navarre, informs her construction of the vernacular, as Lori J. Walters demonstrates, in "The Royal Vernacular: Poet and Patron in Christine de Pizan's *Charles V* and the *Sept psaumes allégorisés*." Charles the Noble was a descendant of St. Louis, who had initiated the *Grandes chroniques de France*, a history of the royal house written in French prose. Christine, writing in French, associates herself with the ideological promotion of this "royal vernacular," as Walters calls it: a language that could function as a living social and political bond, expressive of the mission of the monarchy. Through the vehicle of an "allegorized" translation of the seven penitential psalms, Christine conveys to Charles the Noble an interpretation of his role, by identifying him as David, or alternatively as Solomon, called to make peace among the warring factions and nations occupying the early-fifteenth-century political scene. Christine's French prose takes on, moreover, a prophetic dimension, in that she purports to render not merely the Vulgate, but rather the original, "Hebrew" speech act of which the Latin had been itself a translation, an original meaning that she conveys for her own, present time.

Else Marie Wiberg Pedersen's chapter, "Can God Speak in the Vernacular? On Beatrice of Nazareth's Flemish Exposition of the Love for God," presents Beatrice of Nazareth's *Seven manieren van heiliger Minnen* as a work of vernacular theology about the nature of God and divine love. She considers this work in the context of other *vitae* of religious women, which, she argues, should also be viewed as theological and doctrinal texts rather than simply biography/autobiography. She examines the roles of such texts in the development of new ecclesiastical paradigms for the education and control of the laity, especially in relation to increasing anxieties about heresy and women's spiritual practices. In the process, she explores the contradictions inherent in the Church's attitudes toward vernacular religious texts, which were perceived as both useful and dangerous.

In "Thieves and Carnivals: Gender in German Dominican Literature of the Fourteenth Century," Ulrike Wiethaus situates vernacularity within the parameters of gender and power relations, at a time when access to Latin was carefully monitored by male elites. Focusing on Heinrich Seuse's *Life of the Servant* and Margarete Ebner's *Revelations*, Wiethaus describes a complex web of relationships between female visionaries and male clerics in the Dominican milieu. Seuse translated his *Life of the Servant* from German into Latin to ensure its scholarly reputation. But the text is haunted by the nun Elsbeth Stagel, who may or may not be the author of substantial passages. Ebner's revelations (an autobiography) show her attachment to her female community, though Heinrich of Nördlingen also played an important role in her life. In these texts, Wiethaus stresses the coexistence of Latin and vernacular literacies, each with its own community-appropriate functions. In female writings, family concerns surface more strongly than in male texts; there is also a greater sense of enclosure in female texts, as opposed to the more open spaces in those authored by males. Through the act of writing in the vernacular, however, women were able to advance their spiritual autonomy and sanctify their daily routine.

Werner Williams-Krapp's chapter, "The Erosion of a Monopoly: German Religious Literature in the Fifteenth Century," studies the dissemination of German fifteenth-century religious literature, with particular attention to the diversity of genres. These include catechetical writings, collections of sermons for reading, narrative literature such as saints' lives, and mystical/contemplative texts (Eckhart, Seuse, etc.). Surveying this field, Williams-Krapp stresses that religious and laypeople read essentially the same works. High Church officials wrote in both Latin and the vernacular, the latter in order to promote a pastoral theology that would address people's desire for piety in everyday life. Despite cautionary notes concerning the need for pastoral supervision and warnings against excessive emotionality, vernacularization and printing led to a democratization of knowledge, eroding Church authority. A well-read (especially urban) audience, critical of abuses in the Church, proved receptive to humanism and Luther's reform.

In "Female Patronage of Vernacular Religious Works in Fifteenth-Century Castile: Aristocratic Women and Their Confessors," Ronald E.

Surtz examines the gendered distinction between Latin and the vernacular in fifteenth-century Spain. Surtz focuses on several vernacular treatises commissioned by female patrons: a revised sermon and a treatise in praise of St. John the Evangelist, which Queen Isabella the Catholic commissioned from her confessor, Hernando de Talavera, and several works written by the Dominican Juan López for Leonor Pimentel, the countess of Plasencia. These texts show an interesting mixture of flattery and reprimand, in which the traditional hierarchy between teacher and student is both maintained and subverted. From this material we gain a detailed view of the activity of aristocratic women, who gave a powerful stimulus to vernacular religious writing in Spain and throughout Europe.

In "Cisneros and the Translation of Women's Spirituality," Elizabeth Teresa Howe surveys the influence exerted by a male patron in early sixteenth-century Spain, Cardinal Jiménez de Cisneros. Cisneros founded the university at Alcalá de Henares, where he assembled a group of scholars to prepare a Polyglot edition of the Bible. Under the cardinal's direct sponsorship were published a number of devotional texts in Spanish translation, including writings of Ludolph of Saxony and John Climacus, and biographies of Angela of Foligno and Catherine of Siena. Directly and indirectly, Cisneros also encouraged the vocations of two visionary women, Sor María de Santo Domingo and Madre Juana de la Cruz. His endorsement of affective spirituality opened the way for the next generation of religious, that of Teresa of Avila and the Carmelite reform.

Teresa of Avila's awareness of "secular" vernacular literature is the subject of Carole A. Slade's essay, "'Este gran Dios de las cavallerías' [This Great God of Chivalric Deeds]: St. Teresa's Performances of the Novels of Chivalry." Teresa was initiated into the reading of *libros de cavallerías,* such as *Amadís de Gaula,* by her mother, when she was twelve or thirteen years old. Despite the moral ambiguity of these fictions—repeatedly denounced, of course, by the Church authorities—Teresa was able to apply her early reading experience to her own spiritual development, in enactments of male as well as female roles. In the alternatively martial and nuptial imagery she deploys in her autobiography and in *The Interior Castle,* the lingering influence of the romances continues to manifest itself. Not without some difficulty, however, did her literary spiritualization proceed, for she expresses frequently a certain envy of men, of the relative freedom of action they enjoy, as well as much frustration at being compelled always to operate through them in her own active work.

The essays in this volume describe sharply individuated literary situations spread geographically across western Europe, and temporally from the late twelfth through the late sixteenth centuries. Struck as we are by the diversity of the material, we discern also a common intent among our contributors to test frontiers, question received generalizations, and dismantle categorical oppositions, in the light of insights gleaned from each given case. Sacred and secular, spirituality and theology, action and contemplation, clergy and laity—the familiar binarisms, scrutinized in context, open into rich complexities and nuances. The unifying concept of the vernacular is constantly renegotiated across this field: Resisted or embraced, it is experienced as the future of medieval religious culture—heralding the discourse of the Reformation—and also as its past, as the recovery of a sacred speech preceding the Vulgate translation.

The prevailing literary orientation of this collection offers terms of comparison among medieval writers who justify their linguistic choices in diverse, distinctive ways. The self-construction of the writing subject is at issue in many of these essays, as are the engagements of that subject and the writings produced in the overlapping spheres of ecclesiastical, national, and international politics. The consciousness of genre is another constant, expressed in the writers' adaptations of "worldly" lyric and narrative forms, and implicit in translations of Scripture or instructional material. Rhetoric, poetics, and techniques of composition come to the fore in close readings of texts that mediate between medieval spirituality and our own. The texts may or may not be transparent records of lived experience; but taken as literary artifacts, they become accessible as objects of study to our view.

Literary-critical caution—our hesitancy to read "behind" the texts—has resulted in a new determination to understand vernacular writings as statements of theology. Reaching beyond discussions of "affective" or "embodied" spirituality, receptive at present to the writers' intellectual ambitions, we remain conscious still of the interflow among reading, writing, and subjectivity, which distinctively defines the religious domain. Elements of mystery persist, and command our respect. These have prompted literary scholars to deepen and widen their questioning, in collaboration with medievalists in history, theology, and other research fields. It is a lively, ongoing conversation, overheard throughout this volume, which will continue to challenge participants for many years to come.

Notes

1. Brian Stock's studies of "textual communities" describe interrelationships between orality and literacy in religious movements through the end of the twelfth century. See his *Listening for the Text: On the Uses of the Past* (Baltimore: Johns Hopkins University Press, 1990), especially the introduction and chapter 1, and *The Implications of Literacy: Written Language and Models*

of Interpretation in the Eleventh and Twelfth Centuries (Princeton: Princeton University Press, 1983).

2. On the association of gender and the vernacular, especially in England, see Nicholas Watson's influential article "Censorship and Cultural Change in Late Medieval England: Vernacular Theology, the Oxford Translation Debate, and Arundel's Constitutions of 1409," *Speculum* 70 (1995): 822–64.

3. Bernard McGinn, *The Flowering of Mysticism: Men and Women in the New Mysticism (1200–1350)* (New York: Crossroad, 1998), pp. 17–20; see also his introductory essay, "Meister Eckhart and the Beguines in the Context of Vernacular Theology," in Bernard McGinn, ed., *Meister Eckhart and the Beguine Mystics: Hadewijch of Brabant, Mechthild of Magdeburg and Marguerite Porete* (New York: Continuum, 1994), pp. 4–14.

4. See especially the essays in McGinn, *Meister Eckhart and the Beguine Mystics.*

5. The now classic references are to Caroline Walker Bynum, *Jesus as Mother* (Berkeley and Los Angeles: University of California Press, 1982), especially the essay, "Women Mystics in the Thirteenth Century," pp. 170–262, and *Holy Feast and Holy Fast: The Religious Significance of Food to Medieval Women* (Berkeley and Los Angeles: University of California Press, 1987). See also Barbara Newman, *Sister of Wisdom: St. Hildegard's Theology of the Feminine* (Berkeley and Los Angeles: University of California Press, 1987), and her recent *From Virile Woman to WomanChrist: Studies in Medieval Religion and Literature* (Philadelphia: University of Pennsylvania Press, 1995). Significant in the same scholarly context are the anthology edited by Elizabeth Avilda Petroff, *Medieval Women's Visionary Literature* (Oxford: Oxford University Press, 1986), and the study/anthology by Peter Dronke, *Women Writers of the Middle Ages: A Critical Study of Texts from Perpetua (d. 203) to Marguerite Porete (d. 1310)* (Cambridge: Cambridge University Press, 1984). Concerning the pioneering role of medieval women, the feminist scholars of the 1980s refer frequently to the "Grundmann thesis," in Herbert Grundmann, *Religiöse Bewegungen im Mittelalter* (Berlin: Emil Ebering, 1935), especially pp. 452–75.

6. Bernard McGinn, *The Presence of God: A History of Western Mysticism* (New York: Crossroad, 1991-). Three of the projected five volumes have been published so far: vol. 1, *The Foundations of Mysticism: Origins to the Fifth Century* (1991); vol. 2, *The Growth of Mysticism: Gregory the Great through the Twelfth Century* (1994); and vol. 3, *The Flowering of Mysticism: Men and Women in the New Mysticism (1200–1350)* (1998).

7. Louis Bouyer, Jean Leclercq, and François Vandenbroucke, *Histoire de la Spiritualité Chrétienne* (Paris: Aubier, 1961–1966).

8. Ellen Babinsky's studies of Marguerite Porete include a translation, *Marguerite Porete: The Mirror of Simple Souls* (New York: Paulist Press, 1993).

9. Amy Hollywood, *The Soul as Virgin Wife: Mechthild of Magdeburg, Marguerite Porete, and Meister Eckhart* (Notre Dame: University of Notre Dame Press, 1995).

10. Saskia Murk-Jansen, *The Measure of Mystic Thought: A Study of Hadewijch's Mengeldichten* (Göppingen: Kümmerle, 1991); see also "The Use of Gender

and Gender-Related Imagery in Hadewijch," in *Gender and Text in the Later Middle Ages,* edited by Jane Chance (Gainesville: University Press of Florida, 1996), pp. 52–68.

11. Michael Sells, *Mystical Languages of Unsaying* (Chicago: University of Chicago Press, 1994).

12. Nicholas Watson, *Richard Rolle and the Invention of Authority* (Cambridge: Cambridge University Press, 1991). On vernacular theology, see especially Watson, "Censorship and Cultural Change."

13. Jocelyn Wogan-Browne, Ruth Evans, Andrew Taylor, and Nicholas Watson, *The Idea of the Vernacular: An Anthology of Middle English Literary Theory, 1280–1520* (University Park: Pennsylvania State University Press, 1999).

14. Bernard McGinn's history reflects this programmatic emphasis: "Greater attention to the role of genre, the anticipated audience, the styles of representation, and especially the possibilities and limits of the nascent vernacular languages, in comparison with Latin, will help us appreciate more fully the hermeneutical situation within which medieval mystical consciousness is textually mediated to us" (*Flowering of Mysticism,* pp. 29–30).

ENGLISH

CHAPTER 1

ROLLE PLAYING:
"AND THE WORD BECAME FLESH"

Lisa Manter

> *More yit, swet Ihesu, þy body is lyke a boke written al with rede ynke: so is þy body al written with rede woundes. Now, swete Ihesu, graunt me to rede vpon þy boke, and somwhate to vndrestond þe swetnes of þat writynge, and to haue likynge in studious abydynge of þat redynge, and yeve me grace to conceyue somwhate of þe perles loue of Ihesu Crist, and to lerne by þat ensample to loue God agaynward as I shold. And, swete Ihesu, graunt me þis study in euche tyde of þe day, and let me vpon þis boke study at my matyns and hours and euynsonge and complyne, and euyre to be my meditacioun, my speche, and my dalyaunce.*
>
> *[Moreover, sweet Jesus, your body is like a book written entirely with red ink: just so is your body entirely written with red wounds. Now, sweet Jesus, allow me to read upon your book, and to understand somewhat the sweetness of that writing, and to enjoy that reading continuously and studiously, and give me grace to understand somewhat the peerless love of Jesus Christ, and to learn by that example to love God in return as I should. And, sweet Jesus, grant me this study at all times of the day, and let me study this book at my matins and hours and evensong and compline, and to have it always be my meditation, my speech, and my conversation.]*
>
> —Richard Rolle, *Meditation B*

Vividly in this epigraph,[1] but also throughout his Latin and Middle English writings, Richard Rolle, self-proclaimed mystic and hermit of fourteenth-century Yorkshire, exploits the interplay of text and identity by rendering the humanity of Christ as a linguistic sign. Christ's body literally becomes the body of the text; he is transformed into a particular assemblage of words whose meaning must be interpreted through careful reading like any other text. No longer a figure outside the text but rather a particular type of writing, Christ exceeds his usual function as a model for lived behavior. He represents a mode of thinking, a type of speech, and finally a particular pattern of discourse—Rolle's dalyaunce. Moreover, Rolle's texts conflate the signifier "Christ" with the signifier "Richard Hermit" so that Rolle's textual persona shares the transcendental authority of Christ's name. "Richard Hermit," thus elevated, becomes the guarantor of the Rollean text—the focal point around which Rolle spins his web of authorial privilege in his Latin writings. As a result of the success of the former, Rolle becomes the beneficiary of the pious devotion that Richard Hermit's authoritative Middle English works of spiritual guidance evoke. In other words, Rolle's textual maneuvers in his Latin writings gain him vernacular disciples by creating a saintly persona that authorizes Rolle's Middle English writings as authoritative guides to understanding the "loue of Ihesu Crist" [love of Jesus Christ]. In this way, Rolle makes sure that the route to God passes through his own corpus, creating an audience not only for his Middle English works but also for the vernacular translations of his Latin writings.

Writing as Self-Definition

Rolle's Latin writings, especially the sections of spiritual autobiography, invite readers to fashion a personality out of the textual traces that provide evidence of Rolle's individual calling and distinctive gifts.[2] Like the figure of "Ihesu" in Rolle's Meditation B mentioned in the epigraph, "Richard Hermit" functions within the texts as an idealized, yet singular, model of spiritual development. Rolle's bid for spiritual authority depends upon his reader's belief in a hermit whose personal life history deserves imitation and upon the ability of the manuscripts bearing his name to convey transparently the hermit's identity. If the texts do not add up to a "Richard Hermit" for the reader, they have failed. But it is the seductive invitation of Rollean writings to reconstruct the hermit as a person that must be resisted if we are to examine critically "Richard Hermit" as a textual creation. This is not because the only evidence of the persona "Richard Hermit" is textual, nor even because we cannot claim that Rolle's text corresponds with his life; rather, it is because the conflation of Rolle and "Richard Hermit" is the basis for the textual game that is played in Rolle's writings.[3]

My approach to Rolle depends upon the recognition that "Richard Hermit" is a product of both his autobiographical narratives and the style of the text itself.[4] For this reason, Rolle's textual patterns, especially the systematic use of language to elevate the sign "Richard Hermit," take center stage in my analysis. Rolle's identity and his reputation as a mystic depend upon his textual play with writing. His texts encourage the reader to confuse Rolle, the historical figure, with "Richard Hermit," the textual persona. If the reader buys into the textual economy that glorifies "Richard Hermit," Rolle gains prestige and authority in two spheres: first, in the strictly textual, that is, for the "I" of the text and, in a circular fashion, for the concepts associated with that "I"; and secondly, by transference, in the interpersonal or material realm, that is, for the once living author who shared the same appellation and for those who embrace that name as a locus of authority for their own causes.[5]

But the question remains, why create a textual self in written form if one's interpersonal creation of self is likewise within language? What success can autobiographical writing offer that the spoken word cannot? The impetus behind Rolle's works is the need for an arena of self-representation under authorial control. In order to advance his own identity narrative, Rolle embraces the written text as the authoritative realm, arguing that "whoever it is that you find described or written about, you can always reckon that he is incomparably more worthy than yourself. It is such people who are called the lovers of Christ . . . they live as solitaries, for God's sake. . . . I myself fled to the wilderness when it proved no longer possible to live harmoniously with men, who, admittedly, were a frequent obstacle to my inner joy."[6] Rolle describes society as a realm of possible failures and denied pleasures beyond his control, but once society is placed within writing it becomes subject to his authorial definitions and descriptions. He recognizes that dialogic encounters with others do not represent him to his best advantage, and he embraces the written text as a place where the author can represent himself as he "should have been" to counter the possible misinterpretations of his identity in spoken exchanges. This attempt to reappropriate through writing what he perceives to be lacking in speech points to the dilemma that drives Rolle's textual maneuvers: Attempts to present oneself to others in the dialogic space of speech never measure up to the imaginative constructions of identity that are available to the author in the monologic terrain of the written text.

To contain the possibility of other discourses, Rollean texts seek to bind his readers to an idiosyncratic textual system by exploiting their connection to the sign "reader" within the text. The "reader" is pictured as one who has already submitted to the author's textual system and is set in opposition to those who reject Rolle's construction of "Richard Hermit." While the reader's refusal to accept the validity of the text may not be completely eradicable, it can at least be contextualized to Rolle's profit by placing a resistant reader within the evaluative web created by the author. Rolle's Latin texts, in particular, serve to gain him historical readers who

will fulfill the role of "the good reader" who understands the author fully
and rightly.[7] In this sense, writing, for Rolle, acts as ideal speech—a
scripted pseudo-dialogic exchange that validates the set of linguistic con-
stellations associated with the author's name.

Playing with the Word: Transforming Christ into the "Name of Ihesu"

The transformation of "Richard Hermit" into a transcendental sign—equal
to the "name of Ihesu"—begins by offering the reader a guarantee that
"Richard Hermit" has a legitimate claim to such a position. Rolle's attempts to gain authorial validity occur mainly in his Latin works, addressed
primarily to a learned audience of religious. This audience holds the ability
to confirm or deny Rolle's claims to being a hermit, a mystic, and a saint.
For this reason his Latin works generally differ in tone and function from
his English writings.[8] In the former, he is defensive, almost confrontational,
seeking to convince or bully his readership into accepting him in his self-
defined role of the Hermit of Hampole. In the latter, he is authoritative,
providing commentary on Latin texts or guidance to his female disciples.[9]
In this sense, Rolle's Latin texts serve as midwives to his more authoritative
Middle English works and, ironically, to their own translations into the vernacular. Latin is indeed, as Nicholas Watson notes, the language "in which
all the major literary and personal struggles of his career had to be played
out. In the first half of the fourteenth century the spiritual *auctoritas* to
which many of his works lay such aggressive claim was only available to a
writer of Latin; the canon of *auctores,* ancient and modern, was, and was long
to remain, a Latin canon."[10] Nevertheless, it is the vernacular that allows
Rolle to lay claim to his hard-earned authorial rewards.

In both his Latin and vernacular writings, Rolle is careful to build his
textual *bricolage* out of the privileged narrative of the humanity of Christ,
in particular the Passion and Resurrection.[11] Since "Richard Hermit"
must gain its authority through the play of signs in Rollean texts, Rolle
depends upon the reader's knowledge and acceptance of the authority of
the narrative system of affective piety. Rolle is able to make use of these
Christocentric narratives to glorify both his authorial persona and his
writings by exploiting the metaphysical view of language expounded by
medieval theologians; his readers are encouraged to accept the hierarchy of
signs laid out in his texts as fixed and natural. As Derrida notes at the beginning of *Of Grammatology,* such a metaphysical view of language is
"grounded in a pure intelligibility tied to an absolute logos: the face of
God."[12] In Rolle's texts, "Ihesu" functions as the absolute logos, or what
Derrida calls "the transcendental signified," for the reader. It is "implied by

all categories or all determined significations, by all lexicons and all syntax, and therefore by all linguistic signifiers, though not to be identified simply with any one of those signifiers, allowing itself to be pre-comprehended through each of them, remaining irreducible to all the epochal determinations that it nonetheless makes possible, thus opening the history of the logos, yet itself being only through the logos; that is, *being nothing* before the logos and outside of it."[13] No signifier can be equated with this transcendental signified, which is thus unrecoverable through signs. Rather, all signs gesture toward that originary meaning and its sign system is "guaranteed" by that unrepresentable signified.

The *Oleum effusum*, the often excerpted and translated fourth section of *Super canticum canticorum*, provides an example of how Rolle sets up the name of Jesus as an originary and transcendental term in such a way as to prepare his reader to be taken into his linguistic system.[14] In this text, Rolle, building on the popularity of affective piety, creates a new devotional mode—veneration of the "name of Ihesu." Traditionally, a transcendental term such as "Ihesu" is meant to stop the chain of signification by positing a meaning or referent that would stand outside the particular discursive economy of the text. But Rolle plays fast and loose with his absolute logos, treating it more as a transcendental signifier than as a transcendental signified. The concept of Jesus is transformed into the "name of Ihesu," allowing Rolle to liberate "the signifier from its dependence or derivation with respect to the logos and the related concept of truth or the primary signified."[15] The "name of Ihesu" is a sign subject to its relationship to other signs. True, the name of Jesus remains a privileged signifier—"þo name þat es aboue al names, name alþer-heghest"[16] [the name that is above all names, the highest name of all]—but its power comes from its placement in the Rollean textual system, not from its ability to transcend language. "Ihesu" thus becomes the touchstone in the Rollean economy, not as a signified that stands outside the system but rather as a privileged signifier to which other signs can be linked.

Rolle establishes this role of the name of Jesus at the beginning of the *Oleum effusum*. The text is devoted to glossing a single phrase from the Song of Songs—"Oleum effusum nomen tuum" [Oil outpoured is your name]; this phrase acts as a forum for Rolle to expound the virtues of the name of Jesus. Rolle opens his analysis by equating *oyle* with *saluacion* and *Ihesu* with *hel[e]ful* or *sauyour*: "Oyle, þat es taken for ay-lastande saluacion es hopyd. Sothle Ihesu es als mykel to be-mene os sauyour or hel[e]ful" [Oil, which is taken to mean "eternal salvation is hoped for." Truly "Jesus" is as much to say "savior" or "healthful"]. From this he concludes: "Þarfor qwat menys it 'Oyle out-ȝettyd es þi name' bot 'Ihesu es þi name?'" [Therefore what does it mean to say "Oil outpoured is your name" but

"Jesus is your name"?]. *Oyle* and *saluacion* become interchangeable with or are reducible to *Ihesu*. The Rollean text is willing and even eager to exploit this metaphoric quality of writing: "Sothle þo name of Ihesu es in my mynde Ioyus sang, in my nere heuenly sounde, in my mouth hunyful swetnes" [Truly the name of Jesus is in my mind joyous song, in my ear heavenly sound, in my mouth honeyed sweetness (186)]. However, the text must preserve a distinction between those signs that are interchangeable with Jesus and those that are not in order to create a coherent textual economy: "Þerfor Ihesu es noght funden in ryches bot in pouert, noght in delites bot in penance, noght in wantone Ioyng bot [in bitter] gretyng, not among many bot in alon[n]es" [Therefore Jesus is not found in riches but in poverty, not in pleasure but in penance, not in wanton joyfulness but in bitter weeping, not among many but in solitude (190)].

Finally, however, it is not the things to which the name of Jesus refers that offer salvation but the very name itself: "Þerfor many wretches of þo world trowand þam to Ioy with Cryst, sal sorow with-outen ende, & þat for þei lufed noght þo name of Ihesu. 'What so ȝe do, if ȝe gif al þat ȝe haf vnto þe nedy, bot ȝe lufe þe name of Ihesu], ȝe trauel in vayn'" [Therefore many wretches of the world, believing themselves to rejoice with Christ, shall sorrow without end, and the reason is because they loved not the name of Jesus. "Whatsoever you do, if you give all that you have to the needy, but you love not the name of Jesus, you travail in vain" (189)]. Though Rolle's "Ihesu" operates as a sign among other signs—able to be replaced by other signs in a chain of signification—it must at the same time retain its extratextual efficacy in the mind of the reader if Rolle's textual system is to succeed. The value of the name exists in what it can accomplish for those who are "wyse" enough to embrace it:

yf þou wil be wyse & noght vnwyse, yf þou wil stand & noght falle, haue in mynde bysele for to halde þe name of Ihesu in þi mynde . . . & if þou wil do lele þis, far fra [drede] þou sal be [a] gloriouse & a lowabul ouercomer. Seke þerfor þo name of Ihesu, hald it, & forgete it noght. Sothle na thyng slokuns sa felle flawmes, destroyes alle ille thoghtes, puttys out venemus affections, dose away curious & vayn occupacions fra vs. Also þis name Ihesu lele halden in mynde, draghes vpe be þo rotes vices, settes vertues, insawes charite, [in]-ȝettis sauour of heuenly thyng, wastes discorde, reformes pees, gyfs in-lastand ryst, dose away vtturle greuousnesse of fleschly desyres, turnys alle erthle thyng to noy, fylles þo lufand of gastle Ioy; so þat wele it may be sayde: *Et gloriabuntur omnes qui diligunt nomen tuum, quoniam tu benedices iusto.*

[If you would be wise and not unwise, if you would stand and not fall, have in mind actively to hold the name of Jesus in your mind . . . and if you would do this faithfully, far from dread you shall be a glorious and praiseworthy victor. Seek therefore the name of Jesus, hold it, and forget it not. Truly, nothing slakes so well the fierce flames, destroys all ill thoughts, puts out venomous affectations, does away with curious and vain activities. Also this name Jesus faithfully held in mind pulls up vices by the roots, sets virtues, sows charity, instills a taste for heavenly things, devastates discord, restores peace, gives inner rest, utterly does away with the grievousness of fleshly desires, makes all earthly things noisome, fills the desire for spiritual joy; therefore it may indeed be said: And all who love your name shall be glorified, since you bless the just (188)].

The extratextual benefits Rolle promises seem endless. The Word as word is the answer to all one's problems and desires.[17]

More importantly for Rolle's textual project, the emphasis on the name of Jesus creates a void of meaning that Rolle can then fill with a chain of signifiers of his own choosing. In this way, Rolle draws in the reader by playing upon the power of the name of Jesus within the larger network of Christian discourse, while simultaneously transferring the authority of that discourse to his own writings. Christian readers, at least those "couetand saluacion" [coveting salvation (190)], are thus encouraged to love the name of "Ihesu" and to embrace the texts of the hermit famous for his devotion to the name.[18] But before Rolle can claim the full benefits of his textual labors, he must firmly establish the link between "Ihesu" and "Richard Hermit." To this end, Rolle's well-known Latin work the *Incendium amoris* continues the project initiated by *Oleum effusum:* Christ's name is poured out in an endless signifying chain providing the fuel for Rolle's self-aggrandizing system. In this longer work, he makes an even more audacious bid for authority: he encourages readers to transfer the sanctity of the name of Ihesu to the name of Richard Hermit.

The Passion as Contract

In order to achieve this transfer of holiness, Rolle plays upon the discourse of *imitatio Christi,* with a special focus on the economics of the Passion. The Passion is transformed into a structural contract that promises special rewards to those who suffer for Christ's sake. And since Rolle is in charge of the exchange rate of this textual economy, it is not surprising to find that in the hierarchies of the blessed, solitaries are awarded the highest position. Solitaries, like Richard Hermit, "who for His [Christ's] name get the knocks and blows of the world; [who] despise wealth and all empty glory; [who] are subjected to contempt, insult and slander"—these saints "whose very praise is torture to them"—are rewarded by being "taken up to the company of angels in their fatherland!"[19] The rejection of worldly rewards

for the name of Christ fulfills their half of the heavenly contract: As outlined in Rolle's text, the narrative of the Passion serves as the guarantee
that their imitation of Christ's suffering will earn them the promised eternal glory.

The idea that Christianity inverts secular values is, of course, not a new
one, nor is Rolle's account of the transformation of earthly suffering into
heavenly bliss. The Rollean textual economy makes use of these common
tropes in order to transmute future heavenly glory into glory for "Richard
Hermit" in the eternal present of the text. Heavenly glory, indeed, depends
upon earthly glory, for it is only in inverting the system of earthly values
that Rolle is able to define spiritual success. Rolle's heavenly glory is surprisingly similar to its earthly namesake but is awarded according to the
economy of his Passion, not through unfettered social discourse. Rolle embraces affective piety to provide a fitting alternative to the faulty economy
of worldly glory: By imitating Christ in his humanity, the lover of Christ
is able to claim personal glory in the face of social rejection. What better
model for Rolle to imitate, since anxiety over the world's misrecognition
and rejection of him motivate his textual project?

In Rolle's system, Christ, by embodying an inversion of worldly values,
serves as a corrective model to faulty human judgment: "Christ, though he
was rich, for our sakes became poor, and we, though we are poor, want
nothing so much as to be or seem to be wealthy. Christ, though he was Lord
of all, was made the servant of all: and we, though we are worthless and useless servants, nevertheless want to rule over all? He, though he was the great
God, was made lowly man: and we, though we are merely lowly exiles, are
puffed up with pride as if we were gods."[20] Rolle reworks the paradoxes
that typically surround the mystery of Christ's humanity into juxtaposed binaries that are used to dismiss the validity of a system that bestows worldly
rewards based upon the questionable evaluations of the world. The Rollean
contract, however, never abandons the worldly terms of "worth," "honor,"
and "respect" but rather ensures the acquisition and continuance of these
gains against the vicissitudes of earthly discourse. If Richard Hermit receives praise, the world has given him proper recognition; if, however, the
world rejects him, his lack of temporal success reinforces his spiritual superiority: "If temporal honor can be destroyed by shame and earthly glory fin-
ished by confusion, it seems to be undoubted that an insult is better than
honor, confusion than success, grief than glory, because anyone who often
falls into empty glory through these, if he has habitually faced the former
with patience he would learn humility in this present life and escape punishment in the life to come, because God does not punish the just twice.
More, he would be crowned in splendor . . . To be despised or to be made
a fool of in front of others helps a man rise to the joy of the angels!"[21] The

contract that Rolle sets up is not a renunciation of glory and recognition but a deferral of temporary honor and success in favor of an even greater, more permanent glory. Lack of temporal honor and glory is perceived as a punishment, not as a blessing; it is clearly marked as something that must be suffered in order to attain honor and glory in another realm. Furthermore, the rejection endured by "Richard Hermit" is embraced as not only a sign of heavenly approval but as a necessary step to earn his place among those "perfect souls" who "think it not unfitting to endure a few years' hardship in order to be raised to heavenly thrones."[22] Suffering is the dues that must be paid for this glory so the lover of Christ can claim what should have been his if earthly judgment were reliable.

Since worldly values are not what they should be and holy folk are generally rated "pretty low among men,"[23] Richard Hermit asks to share Jesus' Passion to ensure his future glory:

> O good Jesus, scourge me, wound me, pierce me, burn me, here and now; do with me whatever in your goodness you decide, that in the future I may not have evil, but I may feel your love now and for eternity. For your sake, to be despised, harassed, and insulted by all, is sweeter to me than to be called the brother of an earthly king, or to be honored among men and praised by all. May misery rush in upon me in every place in this present life, and may God spare me in the other! It is here I would suffer and be put right; Christ grant me this now in the present, if I may not otherwise escape punishment in the future![24]

Richard Hermit embraces scorn and suffering not because he is careless of his earthly state or because he seeks to crush the power of the flesh, but because it is better to embrace the possibility of earthly failure if it serves to guarantee joy. The pattern of Christ, who endured suffering here and was resurrected in glory, can be followed by the lovers of Christ, such as Richard Hermit, to claim their rightful recognition as the perfect.

In his imitation of Christ, Richard Hermit is set up as a model of piety who, in turn, can be imitated, like Christ. Rolle's vernacular writings, in fact, depend upon the interchangeability of Christ's Passion and Rolle's Passion. Christ and Richard Hermit obtain the gains described above for their followers by revealing the flawed hierarchy of human judgment and offer salvation through another binary system, that of the Passion. Through the contract of the Passion, Rolle creates a discursive game where "no lover [of Christ] can be the loser, but rather he stands to gain much."[25]

By emphasizing that his own *Incendium amoris* mirrors the Passion in its inversion of worldly values, Rolle is able to truncate the larger cultural discursive system by selecting those attributes that are aligned with his textual persona and placing them on the side of "good." Rolle's binary system, once established, allows him to demonize the existing discursive system that threatens him and rehierarchize it to his own advantage. "Indeed, this lying world has its delights of miseries, its riches of vanities, its hurtful charms, its pestilential pleasures, its sham happiness, its insane love; its mindless, hateful affection, the darkness of its high noon which ends in eternal night . . . its twisted honors, its horrible friendliness . . . its joy that weeps, its melody of sadness, its approval of contempt . . . and its sneering praise."[26] The paradoxes of worldly power and pleasure reveal a strict dualism that pits two chains of signifiers against one another—the signifying chain of the transcendental good (Christ—heavenly saints—solitaries—Richard Hermit—Rolle's *Incendium amoris*) and its opposite ("a perverted fire of love, which both devastates virtue at its source and encourages the growth of all vices").[27] These binaries are then paired with obsessively hierarchical language, for example: "They consider themselves to have reached the top when in fact they are well down the scale."[28] This pairing not only undoes the system of secular punishment and reward but ensures that Richard Hermit comes out on top within the logic of his text.

Rolle's portrayal of his world in binary hierarchies is not original, for "Western thought, says Derrida, has always been structured in terms of dichotomies or polarities: good vs. evil, being vs. nothingness, presence vs. absence, truth vs. error."[29] But embracing a binary economy does provide Rolle some room to maneuver, for the two elements of such a binary system are never "independent and equal entities"; one is instead defined as the failure of the other.[30] By playing with binary inversion, therefore, Rolle does not reject the worldly values of glory, success, and gain but creates a space for himself to control these terms and the means to attain them, so that those who get the glory are people who, not surprisingly, resemble Richard Hermit:

> Because for the sake of the Savior the holy hermit has made solitude his home, in heaven he will receive a dwelling, golden and glistening, and in the midst of the angelic orders. Because for love of the Creator he dressed in filthy rags, his Maker will clothe him in brightness in an ankle-length tunic. Therefore, because he, in order to conquer the flesh, did not blush to have features wan and lean, so now he receives a countenance that shines with wonderful glory. In exchange for his revolting garments he will wear raiment glorious and resplendent with precious stones, forever in the midst of those who dwell in Paradise. And truly because he has purged himself from vices and avoided all ostentation and has done with all appearance of filth, in his heat of love for the Almighty he receives a most sweet and heavenly song within. And he has deserved to have his mind filled mellifluously with the melodies of those chanting rhythmically in charitable song.[31]

By merging the dominant discourses of affective piety and worldly success, Rolle is able to set up his own economies of glory within his text. In Rolle's system of binaries, the earthly glory he has been denied is itself denied the position of glory, replaced not by shame but by heavenly glory, which is both an inversion of the original and a replacement for it. Rolle's textual economy places Richard Hermit in the privileged position in a signifying chain,[32] one that is, of course, safely removed from social discourse and protected from the realities of the everchanging historical present. It is Rolle's textual system that claims priority of place in defining glory, setting up the steps to attain it, judging the worthy and unworthy, and bestowing the rewards.

Cashing in on the Rollean Textual Economy:
Imitatio Ricardi

But what good is it to come out on top, to redefine glory, success, honor, if suffering in imitation of Christ in this life is to be rewarded only in the next, or worse, only in the text? What of recognition, authority, power, privilege, and joy in the present? Despite repeated requests to share in Christ's earthly suffering, Rolle asserts that "God (and, for that matter his creature, too) is not above or averse to being loved: rather everyone admits to liking being loved, and finding pleasure in others' affection."[33] Rolle clearly would like to claim future glory now and displace his suffering altogether, especially since he fears that "what I am loving will not love me in return."[34]

Although writing has served him well, there are only limited returns within the text itself. Although his Latin texts use the play within language to construct an authoritative identity—"Richard Rolle, Hermit of Hampole"—Rolle does not content himself with play for the sake of play. He is playing to win, and his Middle English works allow him to do just that. Not only is he able to address a larger vernacular audience, he is also able to cash in on his textual investments in Latin. His writing strategies move away from defensive apologies (e.g., *Judica me deus*) and carefully constructed written economies of sainthood (e.g., *Incendium amoris*) to making use of that textual persona to gain living disciples. With his Passion meditations and his works of spiritual guidance (for women religious in particular), he gains a set of readers who validate his authoritative position as spiritual advisor just by reading and using these devotional texts. The readers for whom these work were written—"ad Margaretam reclusam de kyrkby" [to Margaret, recluse of Kirkby]; "to a good ankeresse" [to a good anchoress]; "cuidam moniali de ȝedyngham"[35] [to a certain nun of Yeddingham]—may or may not be the original historical addressees, but they clearly function as signifiers of devoted disciples, which by their very presence in the *incipit* mark Rolle as spiritual advisor, with all its attendant authority. The description of *The Form of Living* as a work written for Margaret, "suam dilectam discipulam" [his beloved disciple], further suggests that these *incipits* are meant to signal Rolle's position as *magister*.[36] Although Rolle takes advantage of the opportunities offered by Derridean play, he also takes advantage of the expectation that his readers will not—that, in fact, they will anchor the sign "Richard Hermit" to the historical writer Rolle, who writes authoritatively about his own persona in Latin and who generously provides his disciples with Middle English texts of spiritual instruction.[37] Sutured to the saintly figure "Richard Hermit," Rolle is able to claim the role of spiritual advisor and writer of meditative material; he is thus able to influence the responses of historical readers by directing their devotions and giving them models for their spiritual images of Christ.

Whatever the actual benefits accrued by the historical Rolle during his lifetime, the number of extant manuscripts, the false ascriptions, portraits of the hermit, medieval debates over his form of mysticism, attempts at canonization, and nineteenth- and twentieth-century critical interest all suggest that the author's project was a success.[38] Rolle's move away from Latin treatises to vernacular devotional literature helped secure him this widespread popularity. The carefully constructed authorial identity of his autobiographical Latin works gave him a basis from which to claim his authority as a spiritual guide. In his English works, he resurrects the Passion narrative, using affective piety's emphasis on *imitatio* to draw others into imitating not only Christ's example but also Rolle's by conflating Rolle's Passion with Christ's.

The *Ego dormio*, an epistle of spiritual counsel, opens with a bid to persuade a female reader to equate Rolle and Jesus. To establish this connection, Rolle first firmly places himself as the intermediary between the woman reader and Christ, as Christ is the intermediary between God and the soul:

> Mich loue he sheweth þat neuer is wery to loue, bot euer, standynge, sittynge, goynge, or any oþer dede doynge, is euer his loue þynkynge, and oft sithe þerof dremynge. Forþi þat I loue þe, I wowe þe, þat I myght haue þe as I wold, nat to me, bot to my Lord. I wil becum a messager to brynge þe to his bed þat hath mad þe and boght þe, Crist, þe kynges son of heuyn, for he wil wed þe if þou wil loue hym.

> [He shows much love who never is weary of loving, but always—standing, sitting, going, or doing any other deed—is always thinking, and often dreaming, of his love. Because I love you, I woo you, that I might have you

as I would, not for me, but for my Lord. I will become a messenger to bring
you to the bed of the one who has made you and bought you, that is Christ,
the king's son of heaven, for he will wed you if you love him (26).]

Rolle becomes the authorized wooer, sublimating physical desire between
himself and women into a more appropriate advisor/initiate relationship
via metaphor. This relationship neither taints his identity as chaste hermit
nor threatens his authority (for an equal might challenge him), and it
clearly establishes Rolle as the way to Christ.

Rolle as wooer in Christ's place leads to Rolle's and Christ's "wil" becoming interchangeable: "He asketh þe no more bot þi loue, and my wil
þou dost, if þou loue hym. Crist couaiteth þy fayrnesse in soule, þat þou
gif holy þi herte, and I prech noght elles bot þat þou do his wille" [He asks
for no more than your love, and you do my will if you love him. Christ
desires the beauty of your soul, and that you give your heart completely,
and I preach nothing else but that you do his will (26)]. Rolle positions
the woman reader—"or another þat redeth þis" [or another who reads this
(31)]—as the disciple of both Christ and himself. Along with prose requests that she love the name of Jesus and think on it continuously, he provides her with a meditation on the Passion in poetry paired with a love
song "þat þou shalt haue delite jn w[hen] þou art louynge Ihesu Criste"
[that you shall have delight in when you are loving Jesus Christ (32)]. The
love song that ends the epistle answers the disciple's plea—a plea scripted
for the reader by Rolle at the end of the verse meditation—"to hyre þe
songe" of "þi [Christ's] loue" [to hear the song of your (Christ's) love (31)].
If the reader uses this epistle as a devotional text, as the text prescribes, she
not only engages in worshiping Christ but also accepts Rolle's Passion narrative as a worthy meditation and embraces his love poetry as a sample of
the "melody" of Christ (31).

Although Rolle sets up the basis for the connection between imitation,
love, and becoming one with the beloved object in his Latin works, the
enactment of this process of imitation and conflation is fully achieved only
in Rolle's English *Meditations*. These *Meditations* establish a parallelism between *imitatio Christi* and *imitatio Ricardi*. In *Ego dormio*, Rolle explains that
meditating on the Passion is the way to "[k]yndel me fyre within" [kindle
a fire within me] and hear the "melody" of love (31). The implied promise
to the reader is that, by meditating on Rolle's Passion narratives, she will
find herself following Rolle's own mystical path. As Rolle has imitated
Christ in his suffering on earth to achieve glory, so will the reader imitate
Rolle's devotional patterns to achieve the same heights. This process is laid
out most explicitly in Rolle's lyrics to Margaret of Kirkby—"If þou wil
loue as I þe say, thou may be with þe beste" [If you will love as I tell you,

you may be with the best (42)]—but is exercised most overtly in his disciple's meditation on Rolle's Passion, which, as the epigraph suggests, becomes the textual equivalent of Christ's body, the "swetnes" [sweetness] of which is written in Middle English.

While critics have noted that much of Rolle's *Meditation A* and *Meditation B* lack the originality of his other works,[39] this, in part, can be explained by the existence of these *Meditations* as items of exchange between a historical Rolle and his historical disciples. With the emphasis on textual persona and the Rollean economy already in place, the texts become items of exchange both within this economy (operating on the assumption of its validity) and outside of it (in the dialogic world of speech and material exchange). The shorter *Meditation A* clearly fits into the category of conventional Passion meditation, with its repetitive structure ("Thinke than . . ." [Think then] and "Sithen how . . ." [Afterward how]). *Meditation B,* however, is more clearly identified as part of the Rollean mystique by its colophon: "Here begynneth a deuout meditatcioun vp þe passioun of Crist, j-made by Richard Rolle, heremyt of Hampolle" [Here begins a devout meditation on the passion of Christ, made by Richard Rolle, hermit of Hampole (69)].

In her contemplation of Christ's Passion, the reader of the *Meditations* indirectly honors Rolle as the writer of this devotional material. The texts encourage admiration of the wondrous suffering of Christ as a Rollean creation that can be appreciated "studiously, in al my lif" [assiduously, throughout my life (83)]. The reader is not only called upon to engage in her own *imitatio* of Christ's Passion but also to see Rolle's text as an *imitatio* of the Passion. As one who imitates Christ himself, who acts as His saintly surrogate in wooing the reader, and who shapes the Passion narrative in Middle English prose and verse, Rolle encourages the reader to see Christ in Rolle's image and Rolle in Christ's image: "And thynke on me, þat I be nat foryeten in þi praiers . . . And thynke o[f]t þis of his passione" [And think on me, so that I may not be forgotten in your prayers . . . And think this often of his passion (*Ego dormio,* 30)]. Thinking of Christ becomes interchangeable with thinking on Rolle.

The good Rollean disciple, produced or anticipated by the text, is also called on to recognize these texts as stylistically representative of Richard Hermit. This assumption that the textual style is the man is what Rolle has been working toward. Even in the fairly conventional *Meditation B,* there are moments of Rollean virtuosity, such as the anaphora (the first four paragraphs open with some variant of "Lord, þat made me") and the emphasis on Christ's antithetical positions ("fro so heigh to so low, fro so heigh lordship to so low pouerte, fro so heigh nobeley to so low meschief, fro so . . ." [from so high to so low, from so high a lordship to so low a poverty, from so high a nobility to so low a misfortune, from so . . .]) in the opening prayer (69). These moments of rhetorical and poetic virtuosity signal that Rolle is interested not just in relaying the events of Christ's Passion but in showing off his writing style, a style that signifies "Richard Hermit." But Rolle's project does not end with producing a distinct style; the text continually works to assimilate "Richard Hermit" into the position of "Christ" by playing with the Word.

The most spectacular examples of playing with the Word are Rolle's comparisons of Christ to a heaven "ful of sterris" [full of stars], to a net "ful of holys" [full of holes], and to a honeycomb "ful of cellys of deuocioun" [full of cells of devotion (74)]. With these poetic similes, Rolle emphasizes the endless chain of signification of which he is the master in his own text. Christ, as the transcendental signifier of the Rollean text, can be and is equated with any number of other signifiers in the text. In the excerpt from *Meditation B* quoted in the epigraph, Rolle makes his most daring substitution: his text for Christ's crucified body. If Jesus is like a book, then that book is Rolle's *Meditation.*[40] It is to be studied, learned, meditated on, and shared with others, for it "is hool medicyne for euche desaise of soule" [is healthy medicine for every disease of the soul (74)].

Meditation on Rolle's texts will not only gain the reader a heavenly reward but will also make her a worthy companion for Rolle. As she is drawn into the Rollean economy, where *imitatio Christi* is inextricably linked to *imitatio Ricardi,* she, too, becomes one of the elect. As suggested in *Ego dormio* and the Rollean lyric "Thy ioy be," perfection comes through continuous meditation on Rolle's Passion narratives. Once perfection has been achieved, "When þou art as I [Rolle] say, I pray þe thynke on me. / Our þoght shal [w]e sette togedyre in heuyn to dwelle, / For þer þe good ben mett, that Crist holdeth fro helle" [When you are as I say, I pray think on me. Our thought shall we set together in heaven to dwell, for there the good meet, whom Christ keeps from hell (48)]. By shaping historical readers through the process of *imitatio,* Rolle is finally able to extract "gret delite and swetnesse" [great delight and sweetness] from Christ's Passion outside the text;[41] he gains for himself the sought-after lover, friend, and disciple described in capitulo 34 of the *Incendium amoris:*

Then where is the one who will sing me the music of my songs, the joys of my longing, the fervor of my love . . . so that from this fellowship of love and song I might at least search out my inmost being? So that the measure of music for which I was thought worthy might be made known to me? So that I might find myself freed from unhappiness? . . . O that I could find a man who was a supporter of that melody, who could sing to me of my glory, if not in spoken words then in writing, and produce those flowing notes and

songs, which in the Name above all others, I have not been ashamed to set
before my Beloved. I would love such a one above gold, and none of the
precious things we have here in our exile would I deem his equal. For the
beauty of virtue would dwell with him, and he would thoroughly search out
the mysteries of love.[42]

From the description given, it appears that such a friend could only be one
who conformed to all the requirements that Rolle has laid out in his writings. He or she must understand the *incendium amoris,* which produces the
three signs of love—*feruor, canor,* and *dulcor*[43] [heat, song and sweetness]—
that Rolle has been describing. This someone becomes the embodiment
of the text itself, "Richard Hermit" incarnate, the person the author would
like to be.

If the Rollean text can create such a being, Rolle has succeeded in finding himself, in creating himself, through this alter ego: "In short, I would
love him as I love my heart, nor would I dream of hiding anything from
him because he would reveal to me the song I long to understand, and he
would make plain and clear my joyous shout. The more I understood, the
fuller would be my exultation, and surely the more fruitful my emulation
of him."[44] The author has created a mirror that reflects back not his own
image, but his ideal image. By being able to mold readers into his textual
image, as the modest success of the Rollean mystique suggests, Rolle has
succeeded in writing himself into being through this reader-as-alter ego.

The requirements to become Rolle's friend, however daunting they appear at first glance, are ultimately nothing more than becoming a devotee
of the Rollean text: "The fire of love would be shown me, and my joy and
song would shine out for all to see. My confused thoughts would then lack
no one to put them into praise, nor would I toil to no purpose."[45] In praising Rolle's writings, the reader acknowledges the persona the author has
attempted to create, and in doing so, he or she disseminates this persona to
the world.

Richard Misyn's well-known fifteenth-century translation of the *Incendium amoris* and *De emendatione vitae,* and the translations of Rolle's vernacular works into Latin, though fewer than the Latin-to-English
translations, suggest the importance of Rolle's vernacular success for his
reputation as an author. Even more suggestive of the triumph of Rolle's
authorial persona with his vernacular audience are his medieval portraits,
the most famous occurring in three manuscripts of the Northern poem
Desert of Religion.[46] In these portraits, Richard Hermit appears with the Sacred Monogram on his chest, which not only attests to readers' association
of him with devotion to the name of Jesus but also suggests that the two
are so intertwined as to be inseparable. One could even claim that the au-

thority Rolle has gained through his Latin and vernacular texts has inverted the authority of "Ihesu" over Rolle, for now the name of Jesus is made famous by being written about by Rolle. In a similar inversion of traditional hierarchies, in Rolle's corpus, authority has been transferred from the Latin to the vernacular: Rolle's Middle English works embody the attainment of his authorial goals. The simultaneous authorizing of Christ by Richard Hermit and Richard Hermit by Christ and of the Latin by the vernacular and the vernacular by the Latin is the victory of Rolle playing—Christ's flesh has become Rolle's word, and that word has taken flesh in the vernacular.

Notes

I would like to thank Christopher Bettinger for reading and responding to the very rough early drafts of this essay and Will West for his help in polishing this piece for publication. Further thanks go to Saint Mary's College of California for funding the presentation of an earlier version of this essay at the 1999 conference of the Group for Early Modern Cultural Studies.

1. Richard Rolle, *Meditation B, Richard Rolle: Prose and Verse,* ed. S. J. Ogilvie-Thomson, EETS o.s. 293 (Oxford: Oxford University Press, 1988), p. 75. All citations from Rolle's English works are from this edition and are hereafter given parenthetically in the text.

2. As Nicholas Watson has aptly pointed out in *Richard Rolle and the Invention of Authority* (Cambridge: Cambridge University Press, 1991), Rolle "campaigns to establish his own *auctoritas*" (p. 264); the majority of texts traditionally placed in his canon are overwhelmingly concerned with his own spiritual status and convey a tone of self-aggrandizement as he attempts to establish his own sanctity through his textual productions.

3. The popularity of Rollean texts during the Middle Ages and the time spent reconstructing a "real" Rolle in nineteenth- and twentieth-century studies attest to the success of this textual game. See my dissertation "Passionate Imaginings: The Mystical Remythologies of Richard Rolle, Julian of Norwich, and Margery Kempe" (Ph.D. diss., University of Michigan, 1998), pp. 20–35.

4. This may be an uncomfortable step for some medieval critics because this separation of textual figure and author has been reserved for writers of fiction. The function of the author's persona in mystical texts has been passed over because critics have been eager to equate the author with his or her textual persona. For a rare discussion of distinctions between author and authorial persona in medieval mystical writings, see Lynn Staley Johnson, "The Trope of the Scribe and the Question of Literary Authority in the Works of Julian of Norwich and Margery Kempe," *Speculum* 66 (1991): 820–838.

5. For example the Cistercian nuns at Hampole, who were most likely the instigators of his Office, or twentieth-century critics seeking to validate the

authenticity of a text based on its connection to this conflated figure of author and textual persona.

6. The English translations of Rolle's Latin are from *The Fire of Love* (trans. Clifton Wolters [Harmondsworth: Penguin, 1972; reprint, 1988], p. 128). On occasion, I silently emend the translation to make it more accurate. "Quia cuiuscumque uitam scriptam inueneris uel relatam audieris, semper incomparabiliter illam uitam te digniorem existimabis. Tales enim Christi amatores dicuntur, qui pro eius nomine aduersa et aspera mundi suscipiunt, prospera et omnia uana gaudia contempnunt, despeccionibus, opprobriis et scandalis saturantur, in suis laudibus torquentur, qui pro Deo solitarie uiuentes, in uia morientes, ad consorcium angelorum assumuntur in patria. Ego enim in solitudinem fugi quia cum hominibus concordare non potuim me nempe a gaudio sepe impediebant" (cap. 27, p. 220). Rolle's Latin text is from *The Incendium amoris of Richard Rolle of Hampole* (ed. Margaret Deanesly [Manchester: Longmans, 1915]; hereafter, in these endnotes, chapter numbers are followed by page references to Deanesly's text in parenthetical citation form.

7. Rolle writes of his anxieties over this possibility of misinterpretation most overtly in *Judica me deus*. See Manter, "Passionate Imaginings," pp. 45–56.

8. Watson outlines Rolle's movement from self-apology, in an attempt to establish his spiritual authority, to more "self-assured writings" (*Invention of Authority*, p. 196).

9. For a discussion of the use of vernacular devotional texts by women readers during this period, see Anne Clark Bartlett, *Male Authors, Female Readers: Representation and Subjectivity in Middle English Devotional Literature* (Ithaca: Cornell University Press, 1995).

10. Watson, *Invention of Authority*, p. 222. Watson goes further to argue that the English works were meant for "a narrower, not a wider, section of the Church than . . . his Latin writings . . . [H]e is not likely to have anticipated the scale of their popularity, or to have realized that they would make so important a contribution to his reputation" (p. 223).

11. See John Alford, "Biblical *Imitatio* in the Writings of Richard Rolle," *Journal of English Literary History* 40 (1973): 1–23, for a discussion of Rolle's habit of borrowing from biblical sources.

12. Peggy Kamuf, ed., *A Derrida Reader: Between the Blinds* (New York: Columbia University Press, 1991), p. 32.

13. Jacques Derrida, *Of Grammatology*, trans. Gayatri Chakravorty Spivak (Baltimore: Johns Hopkins University Press, 1976), p. 20.

14. Also known as the *Encomium nominis Ihesu*, this particular selection from Rolle's commentary on the Song of Songs appears in Latin in ten manuscripts and in Middle English in four. See H. E. Allen, *Writings Ascribed to Richard Rolle, Hermit of Hampole, and Materials for His Biography*, MLA Monograph Series, no. 3 (New York: D. C. Heath & Co., 1927), pp. 66–68, where she notes the popularity of this work. It appears to have appealed to a wide audience, and its popularity is evidenced by Rolle's reputation as

"the foremost exponent of the popular devotion to the Holy Name of Jesus" (Watson, *Invention of Authority,* p. 55). Although Watson disagrees with Allen's labeling of this work as juvenilia and places it firmly within his middle period (along with *Incendium amoris*), there is little external evidence for dating. Whatever the date of its composition, it provides a condensed example of Rolle's typical transformation of "Ihesu" into the "name of Ihesu," which serves as a cornerstone for his textual economy. This work, along with his other Latin works of the early and middle period, are part of his overarching project to build textual authority, authority that can be exploited during the vernacular writing of his late period. For a discussion of the chronology of the works, see Watson, *Invention of Authority,* pp. 273–278.

15. Derrida, *Of Grammatology,* p. 19. Nonetheless, Rolle does not intend that play to extend "infinitely," as Derrida would have it; he extends the possibility of play only to himself. His readers are expected to accept the written system that he has constructed as the truth.

16. *Yorkshire Writers: Richard Rolle of Hampole, an English Father of the Church, and His Followers,* ed. Carl Horstmann, 2 vols. (London: Swan Sonnenschein & Co., 1895–1896), 1:186; the text is from London, British Library MS Harley 1022. Although it is unlikely that the Middle English translation is by Rolle, the Middle English text was clearly circulated as a Rollean text (see Allen, *Writings Ascribed,* p. 67). Horstmann provides the only edition of the *Oleum effusum* (which he labels the *Encomium nominis Ihesu,* following the example of later printed editions); he includes text from both the Harley and Thornton manuscripts, but the former provides the better text.

17. Malcolm Moyes, in his "The Manuscripts and Early Printed Editions of Richard Rolle's *Expositio super novem lectiones mortuorum,*" in *The Medieval Mystical Tradition,* ed. Marion Glasscoe (Cambridge: Brewer, 1984), pp. 81–103, notes some contemporary testimonies to the power of this sign within the Rollean textual economy: "In the eyes of some medieval readers, the mere repetition of the word 'Ihesu' in the context of a Rolle work evoked a response denied to the same words in another writer's work" (p. 91). He draws these conclusions from annotations in several Rolle manuscripts that mention the Holy Name.

18. At the end of *Oleum effusum,* Rolle makes another bid for eremetical self-definition based on his connection with the name of Jesus: "Sykerle may he chese to lyf anele þat has chosin þo name of Ihesu to hys special" (p. 191).

19. See note 6 for the complete passage from the *Incendium amoris.*

20. Wolters, trans., *Fire of Love,* p. 104. "Christus cum diues esset pro nobis factus est pauper: et nos, cum sumus pauperes, nihil est quod tantum cupimus sicut esse uel apparere locupletes. Christus cum esset omnium Deus, factus est omnium seruus: et nos cum simus indigni et inutiles serui, uellemus tamen omnibus dominari? Ipse cum esset magnus Deus, factus est humilis homo: et nos, cum simus infimi et exiles homines, in tantum pro superbia nos extollimus, quasi Dii essemus" (cap. 18, p. 199).

21. Ibid., p. 69. "Si temporalis honor dedecore destruitur, et mundana gloria confusione finitur, constat procul dubio quod melius est opprobrium quam honor, confusio quam culmen, luctus quam laus; quia per ista sepe quis in inanem gloriam labitur, per illa semper si pacienter tulerit, in presenti ad humilitatem eruditur et in futuro penam non patitur (quia Deus iustos bis non confundet,) et sublimius coronatur . . . Despici . . . ac confundi in conspectu hominum facit hominem ascendere ad gaudium angelorum" (cap. 9, pp. 167–68).

22. Ibid., p. 52. "[N]on apparebit ipsis inopportunum, ut hic affligantur per aliquot annos, qui ad subsistendum inseparabiliter in celicis sedibus sustollantur" (cap. 2, p. 152).

23. Ibid., p. 54. "[A]b hominibus minores estimantur" (cap. 3, p. 153).

24. Ibid., p. 69–70. "O bone Ihesu, hic flagella, hic seca, hic percute, hic ure, immo facias de me quicquid placeat bonitati tue, dummodo in futuro malum non habeam, sed tuam amorem senciam hic et in eternum. Pro te omnibus esse despeccio, confusio, et opprobrium dulcius est mihi quam si uocarer frater regis terreni, et inter omnes et ab omnibus honorarer ac laudarer: ut irruat super me undique miseria in hac uita, et parcas mihi Deus in alia. Hic uolo tribulari et corripi, et hoc concedat mihi Christus in presenti, si aliter non euadam futuram penam!" (cap. 9, p. 168).

25. Ibid., p. 187. "[N]ullus amans amittere potest sed oportet multum lucrari" (cap. 41, p. 274).

26. Ibid., p. 171. "Habet enim mundus mendax delicias miseriarum, diuicias uanitatum, blandimenta uulnerancia, delectamenta pestifera, felicitatem falsam, uoluptatem insanam; dileccionem amentem odibilem, tenebrosam, in inicio meridiem, in fine noctem eternam[,] . . . decorem deformem; amiciciam horribilem[,] . . . gaudium lamentacionis, melodiam mesticie, preconium despeccionis, . . . et laudem ludibrium" (cap. 38, p. 259).

27. Ibid., p. 49. "[N]isi excecarentur peruersi amoris igne, qui cuncta deuastat germina uirtutum, et augmentum iugerit omnium uiciorum" (cap. 1, p. 149). Rolle claims in this opening section that those who reject his true fire of love could not possible do so "unless they were made quite blind" (*nisi excecarentur*) by its very opposite (*peruersi amoris igne*).

28. Ibid., p. 90. "Putant se summos cum inferiores sunt" (cap. 14, p. 186).

29. Barbara Johnson, Introduction to *Dissemination,* by Jacques Derrida (Chicago: University of Chicago Press, 1981), p. viii.

30. Ibid., p. viii.

31. Wolters, trans., *Fire of Love,* p. 88. "Sanctus quidem solitarius quia pro Saluatore sedere sustinuit in solitudine, sedem accipiet in celestibus auream et excellentem inter ordines angelorum, et quia uilibus uestibus pro amore Auctoris induebatur, tunicam talarem et eternam in claritate Conditoris confectam induet. Accipiet itaque splendorem in facie premirificum quia carnem domans faciem pallidam et macilentam habere non erubuit; palliumque pulcherrimum lapidibus preciosis intextum pro despectis pannis inter paradisicolas potestates portabit in perpetuum. Uerum et quia uicia

euacuans, ac in uenustate uisibilis uite non uiuens, species spurcicie pror-
sus abiecit. In ardore amoris omnipotentis sonum in se suscipit suauissi-
mum et celicum, et mela modulancium in caritatiuo canore meruit menti
eius melliflue inmitti" (cap. 14, p. 184).

32. John McGowan, in *Postmodernism and Its Critics* (Ithaca: Cornell University
Press, 1991), perceptively comments on this sort of play: "What gets placed into
play is never random, nor are the ways it can be played. But the introduction
of play does unsettle the dominant order by supplementing or exceeding the
determinations that order has tried to make stable and permanent. Play points
to other (suppressed or unacknowledged) possibilities" (p. 105).

33. Wolters, trans., *Fire of Love*, p. 100. "Amari autem nec Deus nec aliqua crea-
tura dedignatur uel respuit: immo letanter se diligi omnes fatentur, et
amore iocundari" (cap. 17, p. 195).

34. Ibid., p. 181. "[T]imeo ne id quod amo non ita me reamet" (cap. 40, p. 269).

35. Ogilvie-Thomson, ed., *Prose and Verse*, pp. xlix, xxxvi, xliv.

36. This *incipit* occurs in MS ULC Dd v 64 III (see Ogilvie-Thomson, ed.,
Prose and Verse, p. xxxvii).

37. For example, in the *leccio nona* of his Office, the *Incendium amoris* is cited as
both the ruler of perfection and the proof of Richard's attainment of that
perfection: "It is not unknown to men, and especially to those who seek
by devout and attentive studies to learn perfection of life, how and by what
means this blessed zealous hermit of God, Richard, reached the state of
perfect love and charity so far as is possible to mortals. He himself in the
thirteenth chapter of his *Incendium Amoris* says thus (the famous description of Richard's attainment of 'calor, canor, et dulcor' . . . then follows)"
(Allen, *Writings Ascribed*, p. 60).

38. Allen and Watson attest to the success of his writings, as evidenced by his cult,
his Office, and the number of extant Rollean manuscripts, manuscript ascriptions, adaptations, compilations, and translations. Watson notes that "during the fifteenth century he was one of the most widely read of English
writers, whose works survive in nearly four hundred . . . manuscripts, almost
all written between 1390 and 1500" (*Richard Rolle*, p. 31). The fascination with
Rolle's life and character, discussed above with regard to modern criticism,
extends back to at least the years immediately following his death. Numerous
manuscripts offer commentary on the Hermit's life and teachings, and more
than a few refer to him as a venerable hermit known for his works of contemplation. He is alluded to in the well-known devotional works of Walter
Hilton, in *The Cloud of Unknowing,* and in *The Book of Margery Kempe,* and
one late-fourteenth-century supporter, and fellow hermit, was so taken with
his work that he wrote a defense of Rolle against his detractors. His influence
on the priory at Hampole is noted by Horstmann: The nuns regarded [Rolle]
as a saint and their patron. Not long after his death his name began to be celebrated for miracles, especially of healing, and pilgrims flocked there not only
from the neighbourhood, but from distant counties" (Horstmann, *Yorkshire
Writers,* 2:xxxvi).

39. See H. E. Allen, ed., *English Writings of Richard Rolle, Hermit of Hampole* (Oxford: Clarendon Press, 1931), who writes: "In spite of the perfect external evidence for Rolle's authorship of the present work, his signature, as it were, is not so clear as in other writings; that is, we miss the usual reminiscences of his actual mystical experience. The few references to 'heat, sweetness and song' are colourless and academic. On the other hand, the addresses to the Holy Name of Jesus are ardent and personal, and the ecstatic style of the work suggests Rolle" (p. 17). While she notes that there is "nothing original in Rolle's treatment of the Passion" (p. 18), she also points out that Passion meditations were recommended for beginners and not likely to contain the more idiosyncratic thematic elements of Rolle's writing. Sister Mary Felicitas Madigan, *The Passio Domini Theme in the Works of Richard Rolle: His Personal Contribution in its Religious, Cultural, and Literary Context,* Salzburg Studies in English Literature: Elizabethan and Renaissance Studies, no. 79 (Salzburg: Institut für Englische Sprache und Literatur, 1978), argues for the originality of the *style,* if not the themes, of his meditations on the Passion that appear not only in these specific texts, but elsewhere in his works of spiritual guidance.

40. This metaphor of Christ as book is underwritten by a tradition of referring to Christ's crucified body as a charter or book. See Nicholas Watson, "Conceptions of the Word: The Mother Tongue and the Incarnation of God," *New Medieval Literature* 1 (1997): 85–124. In section 4, "Kenosis and the Preacher: The Vernacular as Christ's Flesh" (pp. 104–112), Watson discusses the charter image in particular, giving examples from *Pore Catif* and Nicholas Love's *Mirror of the Blessed Life of Jesus Christ.* See also Adrian James McCarthy's discussion of the Christ/book metaphor in the introduction to his edition of *Book to a Mother,* Salzburg Studies in English Literature: Elizabethan and Renaissance Studies, no. 92 (Salzburg: Institut für Anglistik und Amerikanistik, 1981), pp. xxviii–xliii.

41. This "gret delite and swetnesse" is the reward promised by Rolle for those who "festyn in þi hert þe mynd of his passioun" [fasten in your heart the thought of his passion] (*The Commandment,* in Ogilvie-Thomson, ed., *Prose and Verse,* p. 38).

42. Wolters, trans., *Fire of Love,* p. 153. "Quis ergo mihi modularetur carmina cantuum meorum, et gaudia affectuum cum ardoribus amoris, . . . ut saltem ex canticis caritatis sodalis subtiliter indagarem substanciam meam, et mensuram modulacionum, in quibus prestabilis putarer, mihi innotesceret, si forte ab infelicitate exemptum me inuenirem. . . . [U]tinam et illius modulaminis inueniam auctorem hominem, qui etsi non dictis, tamen scriptis mihi gloriam meam decantaret, et pneumataque nexus in nomine nobilissimo coram amato meo edere non erubui, canendo ac pneumatizando depromeret. Hic etenim esset mihi amabilis super aurum: et omnia preciosa non adequarem ei que habentur in hoc exilio. Uenustas namque uirtutis cum ipso habitat, et amoris arcana perfeccius inuestigat" (cap. 34, pp. 243, 244).

43. See *Incendium amoris,* cap. 14, for a description of these gifts from Christ.

44. Wolters, trans., *Fire of Love,* p. 153. "Diligerem denique illum sicut cor meum nec esset aliquid quod ab ipso occultare intenderem, quia canorem quod cupio intelligere mihi exprimeret, et iubilum iocunditatis mee clarius enodaret. In hac equidem apercione exultarem amplius, aut certe uberius emularem" (cap. 34, p. 244).

45. Ibid., p.153. "[Q]uoniam mihi ostenderetur incendium amoris et sonora iubilacio euidenter effulgeret. Clamosa quoque cogitacio sine laudatore non laberetur neque si in ambiguis laborarem" (cap. 34, p. 244).

46. A full-color picture of the portrait from London, British Library MS Cotton Faustina B.vi can be found in the frontispiece to *The Fire of Love or Melody of Love and the Mending of Life or Rule of Living, translated by Richard Misyn from the 'Incendium amoris' and the 'De emendatione vitae' of Richard Rolle, Hermit of Hampole,* ed. and trans. Frances M. M. Comper, 2nd ed. (London: Methuen & Co., 1920). In this illustration, "Richarde heremite" is sitting, a position he defends vociferously in the *Incendium amoris,* with a book in his lap, in a hermit's white habit, with "IHC" (Ihesu) written in red letters on his breast. Whether this is a label that identifies the figure as Richard Rolle, the hermit devoted to the name of "Ihesu," or refers to Rolle's claim that he experiences the love of "Ihesu" as a palpable burning in his chest, the illuminator has literally inscribed "Ihesu" upon "Rolle." For a further description of this and other portraits, see H. E. Allen, *Writings Ascribed,* pp. 308–310.

CHAPTER 2

DISRUPTIVE SIMPLICITY: GAYTRYGE'S TRANSLATION OF ARCHBISHOP THORESBY'S *INJUNCTIONS*

Moira Fitzgibbons

Recent studies of vernacular religious writing have demonstrated that medieval English instructional texts often contain lively discussions of authorial methods and motives. Despite, or, perhaps, because of, their didactic goals, pastoral writers of the Middle Ages expound at length upon such issues as the benefits of writing in English, the needs of their intended audiences, and their works' position relative to other literary genres.[1] In addition to the historical context they provide, these self-reflexive passages offer considerable entertainment value to modern-day readers. Robert Mannyng's chatty enumeration of his friends and travels in *Handlyng Synne,* and the rousing advocacy of English for Englishmen in *Cursor Mundi* ("Selden was for any chaunce / Englis tong praysed in Fraunce!" [The English tongue was seldom praised in France for any reason]) provide salutary reminders of the rewards of delving into these ostensibly sober-minded texts.[2]

Compared with these works, *The Lay Folks' Catechism* initially seems a bit disappointing. Translated in 1357 from the Latin *Injunctions* (compiled that same year at a council convened by Archbishop John Thoresby of York), the *Catechism* is circumspect about its origins.[3] Its translator divulges nothing in the way of personal information: Even the name generally attributed to him, Gaytryge (or some variation thereof), stems from external evidence rather than from anything he says within the text.[4] Gaytryge does not address his work's potential relationship to secular romances or songs. Moreover, he identifies his audience only obliquely. The beginning of the *Catechism* indicates that he addresses himself primarily to uneducated clerics: He alludes to

ecclesiastical decrees that enjoin parish priests and "all that haues kepyng or
cure undir him" [all those who have keeping or cure of souls under him] to
acquire sufficient knowledge to educate laypeople in the fundamentals of the
faith (60). Throughout the text, however, Gaytryge employs an unspecified
"we," making the work sound less like a preacher's handbook than a sermon
directed toward a congregation encompassing laypeople as well as priests. Indeed, in his conclusion he switches to the second person, telling his audience
that "ye er al halden to knawe, and to kun" [you are required to know and
to learn] the material he has presented (563).

Compounding the ambiguity surrounding the work's authorship and
audience are Gaytryge's terse and indirect references to his use of English.
Instead of explaining his own choices as a translator, he briefly makes note
of ecclesiastical decrees mandating vernacular instruction for laypeople.
Fifty lines into the work, he explains that parish priests must: "Openly on
Inglis opon sononndaies / Teche and preche thaim, that they haue cure of,
/ The lawe and the lore to knawe god all-mighten" [Teach and preach,
openly in English on Sundays, to those of whose souls they have cure, the
law and the lore to know God almighty (49–51)]. He revisits this idea at
the end of his prologue: "Our fadir the Ercebisshop of his godenesse / has
ordayned and bidden that [Christian precepts] be shewed / Openly on inglis o-monges the folk" (74–6) [Our father the archbishop of his goodness
has ordained and bidden that Christian precepts be shown openly in English among the people]. Gaytryge makes no further comments about the
presence of English in his work.

As I shall demonstrate, however, these allusions to "openness" accurately
reflect the provocative ideas operating in the *Catechism* as a whole. Far from
a throwaway phrase, "openly on inglis" reflects both Gaytryge's own
methodology and his vision of the greater authority afforded to laypeople
by religious instruction in the vernacular. Taking substantial liberties with
his Latin source, Gaytryge presents Christian precepts in a manner that encourages laypeople to assume a new and more active role in their own salvation. Whereas the *Injunctions* enjoins Christians to follow the Church's
principles and practices in order to avoid damnation, Gaytryge tells his audience that learning doctrine can facilitate a more positive achievement—
direct and personal knowledge of God. Within the *Catechism*, the
commandments, sacraments, virtues, and deadly sins function not just as
defenses against punishment, but as elements of a kind of "cultural literacy," through which laypeople could perceive themselves as interpreters of
Christian behavior and principles, as well as believers in the faith.

In transforming a text centered around lay obedience into one highlighting the potential for lay knowledge, the *Catechism* exposes the substantial gap separating episcopal theories of vernacularity from the

practices of individual translators. Even as Gaytryge complies with the archbishop's request for a simply written text, he situates Christian precepts within a new context, which transforms their meaning. The *Catechism* never directly challenges the goals set forth by Thoresby, but it does carve out a space from which laypeople could question clerical authority while still thinking of themselves as good Christians. In so doing, the *Catechism* demonstrates that even seemingly rudimentary texts merit a place in the body of literature that Nicholas Watson has called "vernacular theology"— works written in English in the later Middle Ages, that engage with a broad range of religious issues in sophisticated and subversive ways.[5] In fact, I would argue that simple works like this translation deserve our particular attention: They prove palatable to fourteenth-century ecclesiastical leaders at the same time that they advocate a new form of spiritual authority for laypeople.

The *Catechism*'s close ties to its source make its innovations particularly noteworthy. Records of Thoresby's tenure (1352–1373), including a letter brought to light by R. N. Swanson in 1991, indicate that the archbishop explicitly commissioned the translation and oversaw its dissemination throughout his diocese. References in the York register to a close associate of the archbishop named "J. de G." raise the possibility that Gaytryge interacted with Thoresby on a personal level; however, there is not yet any firm historical evidence to confirm that J. de G. and Gaytryge were one and the same person. But the letter from Thoresby and the presence of the translation within the register do allow us to be reasonably certain of the *Catechism*'s temporal and geographic proximity to the document developed at the 1357 council.[6]

Perhaps influenced by these findings, contemporary readers of medieval religious literature have had little to say about the *Catechism*'s departures from its source. G. R. Owst contents himself with a passing reference to the *Catechism* as "a very free translation," and Henry Nolloth, one of the *Catechism*'s editors for the Early English Text Society, asserts that "the translation is really a very wide expansion of the original text," but does not pursue the matter beyond suggesting that Gaytryge made the changes in order to achieve "fuller explanation and clearer understanding by the layfolk."[7] More recently, Anne Hudson has pointed out the wider range of the English text, but characterizes its content as "simple and straightforward."[8] Jonathan Hughes goes so far as to describe several of Gaytryge's specific changes to his source, but he too concludes that the translation's "originality lay not in its content, but in its simplicity and conciseness."[9] In a more extreme version of this argument, N. F. Blake characterizes the text as a purely transparent presentation of doctrine: "Although [the *Catechism*] contains a few literary flourishes, it is designed as a straightforward text containing plain statements of belief. No attempt is made to cajole, to threaten or to persuade; fact is here all-important."[10] Critical attention to the *Catechism* has been so sporadic that scholars have never reached a consensus regarding its title—and the "debate" on this subject has been strikingly dispassionate and desultory.[11]

Exceptions to this indifference emerge in the work of David Lawton and Sue Powell. By examining the elements of alliteration and rhyme present in the translation, Lawton concludes that Gaytryge's work represents an attempt to adopt the rules of the *ars dictaminis*—the Latin art of "persuasive letter writing"—within a vernacular text.[12] For her part, Powell traces the complex textual history of the *Catechism* from its ecclesiastical origins to its presence in secular manuscript collections, as well as its citation by heterodox writers in the fifteenth and sixteenth centuries.[13] Building upon both Lawton's interest in Gaytryge as a writer and interpreter in his own right and Powell's account of the *Catechism*'s role within late medieval religious controversies, I will explore how Gaytryge's seemingly straightforward translation actually revises the archbishop's main message. If it is true, as Nicholas Watson has suggested, that both writers shared a sense of themselves as "innovators," it seems equally clear that the *Injunctions* and the *Catechism* present two very different conceptions of laypeople's roles within the Church.[14]

Thoresby's Theories of Translation

The career of John Thoresby, archbishop of York, demonstrates the soundness of William Pantin's reminder that "fourteenth-century men cannot be neatly divided into radicals and reactionaries."[15] An energetic administrator who spent his tenure trying to reorganize a diocese thrown into disarray by the effects of the Black Death, Thoresby demonstrated a remarkable commitment to the religious instruction of clerics and laypeople.[16] He had ample precedent for mounting an educational initiative: from the Fourth Lateran Council onward, bishops such as Robert Grosseteste, Walter Cantilupe, and Richard le Poore stressed the importance of knowledgeable lay participation in Church rituals. As Judith Shaw has written, these leaders manifest a pronounced "tendency . . . to borrow from each other."[17] Indeed, Thoresby's *Injunctions* relies heavily on an earlier text, the influential Lambeth *Constitutions* produced in 1281 under the auspices of Archbishop John Pecham. Many aspects of this educational movement seem quite progressive from a modern-day perspective: While D. W. Robertson may overstate his case when he writes that thirteenth-century bishops sought "to bring the fruits of scholastic synthesis to the people," these programs undeniably paid tribute to the intellectual and spiritual potential of lay men and women.[18] As the initiator of what may well have been "one of the first examples of a major vernacular publication project" in medieval England, Thoresby played a pivotal role in rendering religious knowledge accessible to the laity.[19]

But the archbishop does not promote education for its own sake, or even exclusively for the sake of laypeople's salvation. Instead, he uses it as a means of controlling his flock. Certainly, Thoresby had ample reason to pursue this goal: Jonathan Hughes's study of the York diocese during Thoresby's archiepiscopate paints a vivid picture of understaffed parishes, despoiled churches, and violent attacks on clerics by laypeople.[20] As we shall see, Thoresby also considers his diocese to be jeopardized by less tangible threats, including ignorance and lassitude. Although making a wholesale evaluation of the archbishop's responses to these circumstances is beyond the scope of this essay, I will explore how his *Injunctions* situates lay education within the context of obedience and submission. Andrew Taylor has pointed out the textual constraints imposed by Thoresby's distribution of the *Catechism:* Rather than creating their own translations, clerics in the diocese would henceforward be required to use material produced under the archbishop's supervision.[21] Thoresby's writings indicate that he sought to place limitations around the content of religious knowledge as well. By exploring Thoresby's statements in his letter to Gaytryge and within the *Injunctions* itself, I will demonstrate that the archbishop possesses an essentially restrictive conception of spiritual instruction. He anticipates that with the help of a simply written vernacular text, laypeople will apprehend fully and unambiguously their subordinate position within the Church.

Nowhere does the archbishop suggest that this will be an easy task. Throughout his writings, he makes clear that he perceives problems far more complex than the simple absence of knowledge—he knows his diocese too well to envision laypeople as blank slates. Neither does the archbishop harbor any delusions about the clerics under his authority: He acknowledges that priestly incompetence plays a significant part in the sorry situation he describes. As his prologue and letter to Gaytryge reveal, however, Thoresby displays far more reticence toward this latter issue than he does toward laypeople's shortcomings.

Thoresby's understanding of ignorance as a complicated issue derives at least partly from the Fourth Lateran Council itself, and from other texts generated by the council's decrees. In his introduction to the *Injunctions,* for example, the archbishop highlights the ways in which ignorance can serve as a screen for resistance to the Church's authority. Thoresby writes that he will set down Christian precepts "so that no one on these things has the power to excuse himself through ignorance" (26).[22] Thoresby was far from the first ecclesiastical leader to remark upon recalcitrant Christians' use of ignorance as a strategy for avoiding punishment: His reference to this issue follows Pecham's *Ignorancia sacerdotum* almost word for word, and the Lateran bishops themselves mandate that the twenty-first decree of the council "be frequently published in churches, so that nobody may find the pretence of an excuse in the blindness of ignorance."[23] The specific target of this admonition varies according to context: The Lateran decree seems aimed primarily at parishioners, while Pecham tailors the warning to remind priests of their duty to teach the fundamentals of the faith to their flocks. Within this passage, Thoresby does not specify whether he refers to laypeople or parish priests.

The archbishop's letter commissioning the translation provides a fuller view of his individual preoccupations. Thoresby explains that he and the other Church leaders who attended the provincial council had agreed about the dangers posed by overly elaborate sermons: "By the excessive subtleties of preaching (which we hold to be vain and superfluous, while being tolerant of many) which for the most part assert contradictory matters among themselves, both the laypeople and others of mean learning have not merely fallen so far into errors, but are inwardly ignorant of the basis of our faith, which is intolerable ignorance."[24] Somewhat convoluted in its own right, the passage highlights a number of different problems. Once again, Thoresby describes ignorance as something more complicated—and threatening—than a mere lack of learning; here he defines it as incorrect knowledge gleaned from sophisticated sermons by unqualified listeners. Combined with his prologue, the letter reveals that Thoresby regards the potential recipients of the *Catechism* as a blend of the disobedient (those who use ignorance as an excuse) and the confused (those who misconstrue intricate sermons). In the archbishop's view, proper Christian indoctrination involves a careful matching of content to context: Highly embellished sermons offer too much material for the unlettered to handle. Although Thoresby does not mention any works by name, several scholars have posited that he had in mind works like *The Prick of Conscience* and William Nassyngton's *Speculum vitae,* which contain extended categorizations and illustrations of Christian principles.[25] In any case, the archbishop's assertion implies that clerical writers bear some responsibility for the widespread misunderstanding of the faith.

The passage's allusion to "others of mean learning" outside the category of laypeople highlights another group of clerics. In addition to writers besotted with theological arcana, Thoresby perceives difficulties caused by priests on the other end of the spectrum—those whose schooling did not enable them to teach the fundamentals of Christianity to their flocks. His prologue makes indirect reference to this problem as well. Describing the failure of rectors, vicars, and other clerics to properly instruct the laity, Thoresby writes, "[L]et it be said to come about through neglect: we will not say ignorance" (7–8).[26] Despite the archbishop's naysaying, insufficiently educated clerics constituted one of Thoresby's most pressing problems; as Hughes describes, the plague took a terrible toll on clerics throughout the York diocese and made qualified replacements hard to find.[27]

In both his letter to Gaytryge and his prologue, however, the archbishop stops short of directly pointing out the ignorance of priests. Given that he is writing in Latin (and, in the case of the letter, addressing himself to a fellow cleric), the archbishop's delicacy seems rather unusual. As its title indicates, Thoresby's source text, *Ignorancia sacerdotum,* certainly had no qualms about baldly naming the problem at hand. I think this aspect of the *Injunctions* is commensurate, however, with its primary focus. Although the archbishop recognizes priestly shortcomings, his text as a whole works to establish an authoritative pastoral presence in laypeople's lives. Well aware that the *Injunctions* will be translated, distributed, and presented to lay audiences, Thoresby takes care to ensure that his text will not fan the flames of anticlerical sentiment.

A reluctance to undermine priestly prerogatives might also explain the tortuous wording found in Thoresby's disparagement of intricate sermons. Even as he characterizes complicated arguments as "excessive," "vain," and "superfluous," the archbishop leavens his critique by pointing out that he and the other bishops are "tolerant toward many" of these sermons, and that these works contradict themselves not completely, but "for the most part." The presence of these qualifiers suggests an unwillingness on Thoresby's part to reject sophisticated theological texts outright (or to cede such ground to the friars). Whether the priests in question are undereducated or overly abstruse in their arguments, then, Thoresby attempts simultaneously to address clerics' deficiencies and to uphold their authority over laypeople.

The archbishop treads a similarly fine line when he describes the solution to his diocese's problems—a program of indoctrination centered around the basic tenets of Christianity and facilitated by the distribution of the translated *Catechism.* At least once a week, Thoresby declares in his prologue, each priest should instruct his parishioners in such precepts as the articles of the faith, the Ten Commandments, the virtues, and the sacraments. Moreover, clerics should remind parents to instruct their children in these matters. In some ways, this instructional paradigm establishes parallels between the capacities of laypeople and clerics. Just as parish priests should master Christian principles and then pass that knowledge along to their congregations, so should laypeople teach their sons and daughters the precepts they learn at Church. But the archbishop does not encourage free-floating exchange among the various levels of teachers and learners. Indeed, his stipulations make clear that priests should adopt a sternly paternalistic attitude toward their parishioners, investigating "whether they have learnt and got to know these things, and have instructed their children in this way, firmly imposing upon those who do not obey in this respect a healthy penance which they should be sure to increase to suit the circumstance, as their disobedience requires."[28] The archbishop's vision of religious instruction is essentially coercive. Lay men and women should "compel" their offspring to absorb Christian knowledge; parents failing to fulfill their duties should themselves be treated like recalcitrant children.

Not satisfied merely to set forth such requirements, Thoresby takes the extra step of attending to the manner in which his decrees are presented. Although the archbishop does not conceive of his text as a full-scale sermon in its own right (as David Lawton has written, the *Injunctions* functions more as "a memorandum to the clergy than . . . a practical preaching implement"),[29] Thoresby addresses "writerly" issues with great care. When outlining priests' instructional duties in his prologue, the archbishop specifies that clerics should present Christian beliefs "without ornate subtlety of words" (14).[30] This statement echoes Pecham's text, which warns against using "fancifully woven subtleties" in front of a lay audience.[31] Thoresby goes beyond his source, however, by drawing attention to his own use of simple prose. At the end of his prologue, he explains that he will write "in words plain and coarse, so that they will be drawn down more easily into public knowledge" (27–8).[32] Clearly, Thoresby seeks to produce—and by implication, to generate in others—a mode of writing that will complement his "back-to-basics" approach to Christian theology. His letter explicitly requires Gaytryge to adopt this method: The monk should translate *in grosso modo*—a phrase that R. N. Swanson translates as "roughly," and which also connotes crassness and rudeness.[33] Thoresby takes pains to assure Gaytryge that this policy does not constitute a reflection on the latter's abilities as a translator—indeed, the archbishop heaps praise on Gaytryge for being "endowed with the flowers of eloquence."[34] According to Thoresby, the need for simplicity results solely from the limitations of the *Catechism*'s intended audience: Gaytryge should pursue "clarity of meaning rather than stylistic elegance" only because the work "is intended for the informing of the laity."[35]

Given the archbishop's concerns regarding the ignorance of clerics, this statement seems somewhat disingenuous. As we have seen, Thoresby has several reasons for attempting to distill Christian precepts down to their doctrinal and linguistic essences: He needs to curb the excesses of some clerics and elevate the awareness of uneducated priests as well as of laypeople. But explicitly associating the vernacular only with laypeople allows

Thoresby to uphold the special, superior status of the clergy. The fiction of a Latinate clergy remains, even as the reality recedes.

The ambiguities and evasions prevalent in Thoresby's writings seem incompatible with the clear, open meaning (*intellectum patulum*) he asks his translator to produce. In reality, the archbishop seeks to render some ideas perfectly plain—namely, that ignorance is "intolerable" and that a "healthy penance" awaits the disobedient—while at the same time obscuring the problem of clerical incompetence, and closing off justifications for lay resistance and dissent. In commissioning a vernacular text to further these goals, the archbishop manifests a desire to use translation as a means of "containment." As Tejaswini Niranjana has written, translations can serve as a defense against certain ideas, even as they allow other concepts to pass from one language to another. Specifically, Niranjana points out the role translations can play in bolstering institutional authority. The social instability and ideological inconsistency that often threaten one group's domination of another can be masked and/or suppressed by translated works, which offer the illusion of "coherent and transparent texts and subjects."[36] Thoresby seems to adopt this strategy when he arranges for a translation that advocates laypeople's submission to clerical authority, even as it implicitly addresses problems prevalent in both groups.

Of course, translations need not always serve this purpose. Indeed, Niranjana suggests that "translation, from being a 'containing' force, [can be] transformed into a disruptive, disseminating one," if postcolonial readers are willing to investigate, expose, and revise the assumptions operating in translated texts.[37] The mode of analysis advocated by Niranjana might benefit readers of medieval works as well, according to Ruth Evans. Arguing that translations operate within "various kinds of border zones (between medieval and modern, orthodox/nonorthodox sensibilities, and masculine and feminine)," Evans calls for "a complex view of that interstitial space as *not necessarily* producing containment of the (medieval and modern) subjects located there."[38] I believe that Gaytryge's work provides one example of a translation that consistently undercuts the "containment" tactics at work in its source.

Gaytryge's Practice

Gaytryge's references to Thoresby are unvaryingly positive. In his prologue to the *Catechism,* Gaytryge expresses his hope that God will save "oure fadir the Ercebishop" [our father the archbishop (42)] and attributes the new educational initiative to Thoresby's "godenesse" [goodness (74)]. Even as he compliments the archbishop, however, Gaytryge displays his willingness to alter the vision of vernacular instruction operating within the *Injunctions.* As mentioned above, within the *Catechism*'s prologue Gaytryge writes that priests must "Openly on Inglis opon sononndaies/ Teche and preche thaim, that they haue cure of" [Teach and preach to those of whose souls they have cure openly in English on Sundays (49–50)], and asserts that Thoresby "has ordayned and bidden that [Christian precepts] be shewed/Openly on inglis o-monges the folk" [has ordained and bidden that Christian precepts be shown openly in English among the people (75–76)].

It is difficult to pin down the exact meaning of "openly" as Gaytryge uses it here. Since one definition of "openly" in Middle English is "plainly, clearly . . . so as to be readily understood," we might say that these passages recall Thoresby's statements regarding the need for simple language and the production of "openness of understanding" within the laity.[39] Alternatively, or additionally, Gaytryge may be emphasizing the communal way this information will be presented: "Openly" can also mean "generally" or "publicly."[40] (Written approximately fifty years before the Catechism, the biblical paraphrase Cursor Mundi repeatedly uses the word in this sense: Jesus "openly bigan to preche" [began to preach publicly] after choosing the Twelve Apostles, St. John set out "openly . . . to teche" [publicly . . . to teach] the people of Galilee, and so on.)[41] It is also worth noting that Gaytryge elsewhere uses "open" to mean "honest" and "frank"—like many medieval pastoral writers, Gaytryge employs the phrase "open shrift" [honest confession] to indicate that penitents should reveal their sins completely rather than holding them back (312).[42] From Gaytryge's perspective, the forthrightness required of laypeople within confession may dovetail with priests' own obligations as preachers and teachers.

By virtue of its very ambiguity, Gaytryge's use of "openly" illustrates the extent to which he is willing to recast his source's ideas. In addition to neutralizing the patronizing tone of the archbishop's instructions (e.g., his association of a "plain and coarse" style with the laity), the word shifts the focus of the Catechism from a product to a practice. To Thoresby, "openness" constitutes the intended result of the Catechism: By means of a plainly written text, the laity will achieve a clear understanding of their religion. For his part, Gaytryge uses "openly" to describe the process of presenting Christian principles. His prologue injects an element of flexibility into religious instruction. Depending upon his predilections, a priest could interpret the passage not simply as a mandate to employ an accessible style, but as a license to speak in a candid or expansive manner. In so doing, Gaytryge allows for the very kind of overly elaborate and/or inappropriate religious discourse that Thoresby explicitly seeks to eradicate. Moreover, the passage extends the possibility of openness to the preaching situation itself; when Gaytryge refers to precepts shown "o-monges the folk" rather than to them (76), he intimates that information could be conveyed within a give-and-take discussion, rather than a one-way lesson.[43]

Even more important, Gaytryge demonstrates throughout the *Catechism* that he has applied the idea of openness to his own practices as a translator. His prologue's other allusion to the archbishop exemplifies the decisions he makes throughout the work. Having prayed for Thoresby's salvation, Gaytryge claims that the archbishop shares Christ's desire "that al men be saufe and knawe god almighten" [that all men be safe and know God almighty (44)]. As we have seen, however, neither the goal of universal salvation nor the possibility of knowing God emerge as concerns in the archbishop's writings. But the latter idea emerges as a central theme within Gaytryge's *Catechism*. In linking vernacular instruction with the capacity to know God, Gaytryge not only reveals his willingness to adapt the *Injunctions* to suit his own interests, but also provides laypeople with a basis for using religious information in similarly individualistic ways. If they possess the ability to gain knowledge of God—indeed, if an archbishop considers them duty-bound to do so—why should laypeople feel compelled to accept without question the interpretations of priests? Although Gaytryge himself never disparages clerical authority, throughout the *Catechism* he insistently links learning the fundamentals of the faith to the attainment of more profound knowledge. Within this context, priests function not as the indispensable mediators and disciplinarians envisioned by Thoresby, but as facilitators of the all-important bond between the individual believer and God.

Gaytryge invokes this relationship well before he mentions the archbishop's decrees. Drawing primarily from the second book of the *Sentences,* Peter Lombard's epochal 1157 compendium of theological insights, Gaytryge begins the *Catechism* by establishing the centrality of knowledge to every Christian's salvation.[44] According to Gaytryge, God's reason for making all the creatures of the world "was his owen gode will and his godenesse" [was his own goodwill and goodness (6)]. Benevolently wishing to share the joys of heaven, God endowed some of his creations with the capacity for knowledge:

> And for no creature might come to that ilk blisse
> Withouten knawing of god, als that clerk techis,
> He made skillwise creatures, angel and man,
> Of witt and of wisdome to knaw god-almyghten,
> And, thurg thair knawyng, loue him and serue him;
> And so come to that bliss that thai were made to. (10–15)

[And since no creature might come to that same bliss / without knowledge of God, as that clerk teaches, / He skilfully made creatures, angel and man, / of wit and wisdom to know God almighty, / and, through their knowledge, to love and serve Him; / and so come to that bliss for which they were created.]

Gaytryge's inclusion of such material does not in itself violate the parameters set by the archbishop; Thoresby expects Gaytryge to flesh out the material in the *Injunctions*. The passage functions, however, not just as an expansion, but also as a revision. By situating his translation within Lombard's assertion that humanity was made to "know, love, and serve" God, Gaytryge radically redefines the Christian precepts he will describe.[45] Instead of mere defenses against ignorance and error, the tenets of the faith emerge as aspects of a sacred birthright given to all people at the Creation.

Gaytryge's preoccupation with the first part of Lombard's triad is unmistakable, as he says a great deal more about knowing than about loving and serving. Adam and Eve, he writes, enjoyed perfect knowledge of God, "withouten travaile or trey or passyng of time" [without labor or the passage of time (26)]. Although people in the postlapsarian world cannot achieve this kind of effortless interaction with the divine, they should make the most of the knowledge made available to them through "heryng, and lernyng and techyng of othir" [hearing, and learning, and teaching of others (28)]. Believers who fulfill their duty "to knawe and to kun" [to know and to learn] Christian precepts will attain the reward of heavenly bliss (31–2).

Only when he has established the significance of knowledge and emphasized the potential for salvation does Gaytryge translate the material found at the beginning of the *Injunctions*. Before he ever addresses the problem of ignorance or outlines Thoresby's specific syllabus, Gaytryge underscores laypeople's inherent ability to know God. From the outset, then, the *Catechism* offers laypeople a more substantial reward than does the *Injunctions;* instead of merely learning material in order to avoid punishment, Gaytryge's audience can work toward reclaiming the closeness with God lost at the Fall. By associating intellectual accomplishments with spiritual well-being, the *Catechism* implies that participation in ritual is not the only way for its audience to manifest their beliefs: Learning, thinking, and interpreting constitute crucial aspects of the Christian life as well.

To be sure, Gaytryge does not neglect the nuts-and-bolts aspects of instructing the laity. His introduction makes clear that he will cover all the major areas covered by Thoresby's syllabus, and he includes the archbishop's directives regarding parents' instructing their children and priests' examining (and, in some cases, punishing) their parishioners. Interestingly, however, Gaytryge almost always uses the word *kun* (a variation on the Middle English verb *connen*) when describing the archbishop's specific policies regarding Christian precepts. Laypeople should "oft sithes reherce [precepts] til that thai kun thaime [oftentimes rehearse precepts until they learn them (63)], priests should ask penitents "whethir thai kun this sex things" [whether they know these six things (68)], and "if it be funden it thai kun thaim noght" [if it be found that they do not know them (69)], they should be enjoined "of payne of penaunce for to kun tham" [under pain of penance to learn them (71)]. Gaytryge also employs this verb when translating the archbishop's rejection of the ignorance excuse: Thoresby has commissioned the text, Gaytryge writes, so that "nane sal excuse tham/ Thurgh unknalechyng for to kun tham [i.e., the precepts]" [none shall be excused through ignorance from learning them (72–73)]. Gaytryge does occasionally use *knawe* when referring to the basic assimilation of information: He writes, for example, that people must "knaw the articles that falles to the trouth" [know the articles that fall within the truth (78)]. But Gaytryge's prevailing practice within his introduction is to use *kun* when referring to rote learning, and *knawe* when he raises the possibility of interaction with God.

In making this distinction, Gaytryge draws upon well-established usages of these verbs in Middle English. Although the definitions of *connen* and *knouen* overlap in many respects—both denote mastery or familiarity with a language or skill, for example, or indicate one's knowing something by heart—the latter verb includes processes of mental and spiritual perception not encompassed by the former.[46] Another layer of *knouen*'s meaning that seems particularly relevant to Gaytryge's writing is its use to signify the acceptance or acknowledgment of God's power.[47] But while Gaytryge has ample precedent for the specific definitions he chooses, he stands apart from other pastoral writers in his highlighting of the potential differences between *connen* and *knouen,* and in the frequency with which he returns to these terms. Far more typical are the kinds of constructions found in Robert Mannyng of Brunne's *Handlyng Synne* (1303) and the anonymous *Jacob's Well,* an early-fifteenth-century text, which use *cunnen* as a helping verb to *knouen:* Mannyng claims that he writes so the unlearned "kun knowe" [can know] wherein sin might be found, while *Jacob's Well* states that the Holy Spirit gives the gift of knowledge so that people "kun knowe" [can know] themselves and their sins.[48] Even in cases in which a form of *connen* appears more independently, it rarely receives the specific meaning attached to it by Gaytryge. The anonymous writer of *Dives and Pauper,* for example, mentions several times that laypeople have a natural desire "to knowyn and to connyn" the attributes of the afterworld; he does not, however, indicate that he sees any differences between the two modes of knowledge.[49] By contrast, Gaytryge's frequent use of these terms does allow him to elucidate a key aspect of his pastoral objective. Even as he upholds the need to commit Christian precepts to memory, he insists that this learning is not an end in itself, but a means toward the more significant relationship with God entailed in "knowing."

The possibility of knowing God emerges repeatedly in the *Catechism*'s presentation of doctrinal material. Gaytryge introduces the Decalogue, for

example, by writing: "The secund thyng of the sex to knaw god almighten / Is the ten comandements" [The second thing of the six to know God almighty is the Ten Commandments (168–69)]. By contrast, the *Injunctions* describes the commandments in terms of obedience: "Second are the ten commandments observed inviolably by all the faithful" (68–69).[50] Gaytryge also departs from his source in his preliminary discussion of the seven deeds of mercy. The *Injunctions* reminds its audience that these works have their source in Scripture: "Similarly there are six works of mercy which are recounted in the gospel" (200–201).[51] For its part, Gaytryge focuses less on authorizing the works than on explaining their benefits, which include knowledge of God: "The ferthe thing of the sex to knaw God almighten / That us behoues to fulfill in al that we mai, / Is the seuen dedis of merci . . ." [The fourth thing of the six to know God almighty, that behooves us to fulfill in every way that we may, is the seven deeds of mercy (348–50)]. In another instance, Gaytryge seems to follow his source more closely. He introduces the seven virtues as "the fifte thing of the sex to knaw god almighten" [the fifth thing of the six to know God almighty (380)], while the *Injunctions* calls them "the third thing for knowing" (124).[52] Here again, though, the *Injunctions* emphasizes the need to learn precepts, not the chance to know God.

This disparity emerges even more forcefully in the two works' respective conclusions. As he brings the *Injunctions* to a close, Thoresby reminds clerics that they are "firmly enjoined" (240–41) to educate and examine their parishioners. He also suggests that priests appeal to laypeople's desire "to avoid divine indignation and the guilt of disobedience" (251–52).[53] Then the *Injunctions* sets forth a more positive incentive: "So that we could excite the minds of the faithful to this more willingly, from the mercy of the omnipotent God, his glorious mother the Virgin Mary, the blessed apostles Peter and Paul, the most glorious deserving Confessor William and from bold prayers . . . to those who observe and fulfill these aforesaid ideas in preaching, teaching, hearing and learning, we mercifully bring by concession forty days of indulgence" (252–61).[54] Tacitly acknowledging that the success of his plan depends at least partially upon the mindset of his audience, Thoresby promises that efforts to learn precepts will pay off in the afterlife. Through this concession, the Church emerges as an essential intermediary between the laity and God. The benevolence—and the power—of heaven's holiest denizens reach laypeople by means of episcopal magnanimity. Mercy is meted out by the Church, in carefully defined amounts.

The *Catechism* offers an additional reward. As he does elsewhere, Gaytryge places laypeople's need to know Christian beliefs in the larger context of their personal comprehension of God:

This er the sex thinges that I have spoken of,
That the lawe of halikirk lies mast in
That ye er al halden to knawe, and to kun,
If ye sal knawe god almighten, and cum un-to his
blisse. . . . (561–64)

[These are the six things that I have spoken of, / in which lies to the greatest extent the law of Holy Church, / that you are required to know, and to
learn, / if you shall know God almighty, and come unto his bliss.]

Knowledge represents both an obligation and an opportunity. Gaytryge
goes on to inform his audience about the archbishop's promise of an indulgence. Unlike his source, however, Gaytryge does not put this induce-
ment in the privileged place of the last word. He looks to the Gospel for
his *pièce de résistance:*

For if ye kunnandly knaw this ilk sex thinges
Thurgh thaim sal ye kun knawe god almighten,
Wham, als saint Iohn saies in his godspel,
Conandly for to knawe swilk as he is,
It is endeles life and lastand blisse,
To whilk blisse he bring us, amen. (571–76)

[For if you truly know these same six things, / through them you will be
able to know God almighty, / whom, as Saint John says in his gospel, / it is
endless life and lasting bliss / to know entirely such as he is, / to which bliss
may he bring us, amen.]

Leaving behind institutional indulgences in favor of an individual form of
fulfillment, Gaytryge resoundingly reaffirms the possibility of knowing
God, and illumines his conception of this knowledge by alluding to John
17:3.[55] The passage—"And this is life eternal, that they might know thee
the only true God, and Jesus Christ whom thou hast sent"—links salvation
to a full recognition of God's preeminence and Christ's divinity. If people
truly accept God, the passage suggests, God will accept them into heaven.
As depicted by Gaytryge, eternal bliss is achieved not solely through the
Church's largesse, but also through active, personal efforts to know God.

   The sheer frequency with which the words *kun* and *knawe* recur in this
passage lend a percussive force to the *Catechism's* conclusion, and allow
Gaytryge to underscore one final time the centrality of knowledge to salvation. In using phrases like "kunnandly knaw," "kun knawe," and "conandly for to knawe," however, Gaytryge departs from his practices earlier
in the work: As we have seen, he largely keeps these two verbs separate in

the *Catechism's* introduction, suggesting a distinction between rote learning and deeper spiritual knowledge. By juxtaposing these two words in his
conclusion, Gaytryge implicitly advocates a synthesis between the learning
sought by Thoresby and the broader form of knowledge he envisions. This
fusion seems true to the spirit of the *Catechism* as a whole: Gaytryge revises, not rejects, the *Injunctions'* ideas.

The presence of the *Catechism* within the York register indicates that the
work passed muster with the archbishop. Should we therefore assume that
Thoresby wholeheartedly approved of the broader form of knowledge
opened up to the laity by Gaytryge? Given his statements within the *Injunctions,* I think it is likely that the archbishop approved the translation for
the following reasons: It thoroughly renders the basic precepts set forth in
the *Injunctions;* it adheres to his directives regarding conciseness and a
straightforward style; and it does not say anything that directly encourages
questioning and/or dissent on the part of the laity. If Thoresby noticed
Gaytryge's frequent references to knowing God, he may have assumed that
no one would attempt this feat without the benefit of clerical mediation;
perhaps he anticipated that this goal would lead laypeople to submit all the
more enthusiastically to priestly authority.

In the space of a few decades, of course, the emergence of Lollardy—
and, as Watson has suggested, the profusion of "orthodox" but theologically
ambitious vernacular texts—would lead ecclesiastical leaders to repudiate
the idea that a well-informed congregation is a more obedient one.[56]
Gaytryge's translation does share some common ground with the vernacular texts produced by the Lollards, who also privileged the average Christian's individual relationship with God over the mediation provided by the
Church. In fact, as Powell notes, the translation "appears fairly frequently
in Lollard contexts." Several of the manuscript collections containing portions of the translation also include texts with Lollard ideas (there are
twelve manuscripts of the *Catechism* in its entirety, as well as numerous
fragments and reworked versions).[57] The *Catechism* also played a part in debates regarding appropriate material for lay consumption; for instance, the
English translation of Richard Ullerston's defense of vernacular scripture
notes that "Sire Wiliam [*sic*] Thorisby, Erchebiscop of 3ork did do drawe a
tretys in Englisce be a worschipful clerk wos name was Gaytrik" [Sir
William Thoresby, archbishop of York, had a worshipful clerk named
Gaytrik translate a treatise into English].[58] Fifteenth-century ecclesiastical
leaders were unmoved by these claims, and in 1410 Archbishop Thomas
Arundel passed a series of decrees severely curtailing the production of English instructional works.[59] When writers of this later period do address religious matters in the vernacular, they often urge lay audiences to focus
exclusively on cataloguing their own spiritual limitations; for example,

John Mirk writes in his influential *Festial* that each Christian should "know hymselfe that he ys not but a wryche and slyme of erth . . ." [know himself to be nothing but a wretch and slime of the earth].[60] Nowhere does the *Festial* raise the possibility of knowing God; indeed, it highlights the laity's shortcomings even more insistently than does the *Injunctions*. Despite Thoresby's overriding emphasis on obedience, by fifteenth-century standards his own text might be seen as dangerously "open" to strategic interpretation and appropriation.

Notes

1. Numerous examples of this practice can be found in *The Idea of the Vernacular: An Anthology of Middle English Literary Theory, 1280–1520*, ed. Jocelyn Wogan-Browne, Nicholas Watson, Andrew Taylor, and Ruth Evans (University Park: Pennsylvania State University Press, 1999). *Pastors and the Care of Souls in Medieval England*, ed. John Shinners and William J. Dohar (Notre Dame: University of Notre Dame Press, 1998), is another helpful compilation. See also Judith Shaw, "The Influence of Canonical and Episcopal Reform on Popular Books of Instruction," in *The Popular Literature of Medieval England*, ed. Thomas J. Heffernan (Knoxville: University of Tennessee Press, 1985), pp. 44–60.

2. Robert Mannyng, *Handlyng Synne*, ed. Frederick J. Furnivall (London: Early English Text Society, 1901); for the prologue to *Cursor Mundi*, see Wogan-Browne et al, *Idea of the Vernacular*, pp. 267–71.

3. All citations from the *Injunctions* and *The Lay Folks' Catechism* are taken from Thomas Simmons and Henry Nolloth, eds., *The Lay Folks' Catechism, or the English and Latin Versions of Archbishop Thoresby's Instruction for the People*, EETS o.s. 118 (London: Early English Text Society, 1901). I have used line numbers when citing both works within the text of my essay; when providing the Latin of the *Injunctions* in endnotes, I have given the relevant page number in Simmons and Nolloth.

4. For discussions of the translator's identity, see Simmons and Nolloth, p. xvii; R.N. Swanson, "The Origins of *The Lay Folks' Catechism*," *Medium Aevum* 60 (1991): 92–100; Sue Powell, "The Transmission and Circulation of *The Lay Folks' Catechism*," in *Late-Medieval Texts and Their Transmission*, ed. A. J. Minnis (Cambridge: D. S. Brewer, 1994), pp. 75–84; and Jonathan Hughes, *Pastors and Visionaries: Religion and Secular Life in Late Medieval Yorkshire* (Suffolk: Boydell, 1988), pp. 149–56.

5. Nicholas Watson, "Censorship and Cultural Change in Late-Medieval England: Vernacular Theology, the Oxford Translation Debate, and Arundel's Constitutions of 1409," *Speculum* 70 (1995): 822–64.

6. For discussions of this possible meeting, see Powell, "Transmission," pp. 70–71, and Swanson, "Origins," 94–96. For a description of the surviving manuscripts of the *Catechism*, see Anne Hudson, "A New Look at *The Lay Folks' Catechism*," *Viator* 16 (1985): 243–58.

7. G. R. Owst, *Preaching in Medieval England* (Cambridge: Cambridge University Press, 1926), p. 289; Simmons and Nolloth, p. xvii.

8. Hudson, "New Look," 245.

9. Hughes, *Pastors and Visionaries*, p. 151.

10. N. F. Blake, *Middle English Religious Prose* (Evanston: Northwestern University Press, 1972), p. 9.

11. See Powell, "Transmission," p. 69; and Blake, *Religious Prose,* p. 9. I call the translation *The Lay Folks' Catechism* in the spirit of Swanson and Hudson, who refer to the text "known as" *The Lay Folks' Catechism* (Swanson, "Origins," 92; Hudson, "New Look," 243).

12. David Lawton, "Gaytryge's Sermon, *Dictamen,* and Middle English Alliterative Verse," *Modern Philology* 76 (1979): 329–43.

13. Powell, "Transmission," pp. 73–77.

14. Nicholas Watson, "The Politics of Middle English Writing," in Wogan-Browne et al., *Idea of the Vernacular,* p. 336.

15. William Pantin, *The English Church in the Fourteenth Century* (Cambridge: Cambridge University Press, 1955), p. 211.

16. For a detailed study of Thoresby's tenure as archbishop, see Hughes, *Pastors and Visionaries,* pp. 127–73.

17. Shaw, "Influence of Canonical," p. 49.

18. D. W. Robertson, "Frequency of Preaching in Thirteenth-Century England," *Speculum* 24 (1949): 387.

19. Andrew Taylor, "Authors, Scribes, Patrons, and Books," in Wogan-Browne et al., *Idea of the Vernacular,* p. 360.

20. Hughes, *Pastors and Visionaries,* pp. 136–43.

21. Taylor, "Authors," p. 360.

22. "Ne quis super hiis per ignorantium se valeat excusare" (Simmons and Nolloth, p. 22). Except where otherwise noted, translations from the *Injunctions* are my own.

23. See Shinners and Dohar, *Care of Souls,* p. 128, for the analogous passage from *Ignorancia sacerdotum.* For the twenty-first Lateran decree, see *Decrees of the Ecumenical Councils,* ed. Norman P. Tanner, S.J. (Washington, D.C.: Georgetown University Press, 1990), p. 245.

24. Translated by Swanson in "Origins," 99–100.

25. E. J. Arnould, *Le manuel des péchés* (Paris: Droz, 1940), p. 37; see also Pantin, *English Church,* p. 234, and Hughes, *Pastors and Visionaries,* p. 151.

26. ". . . incuria, ne dicamus ignorantia, dicitur evenire" (Simmons and Nolloth, p. 4).

27. Hughes, *Pastors and Visionaries,* pp. 136–38.

28. Translated by Powell in "Transmission," 67.

29. Lawton, "Gaytryge's Sermon," 331.

30. ". . . sine exquisita verborum subtilitate . . ." (Simmons and Nolloth, p. 6).

31. Shinners and Dohar, *Care of Souls,* p. 128.

32. ". . . sub verbis planis et incultis, ut sic levius in publicam deducantur notitiam" (Simmons and Nolloth, p. 22).

33. Swanson, "Origins," 99–100.

34. Translated by Swanson in "Origins," 100.

35. Ibid.

36. Tejaswini Niranjana, *Siting Translation: History, Post-Structuralism and the Colonial Context* (Berkeley and Los Angeles: University of California Press, 1992), p. 3.

37. Ibid., p. 186.

38. Ruth Evans, "Translating Past Cultures?" *The Medieval Translator 4*, ed. Roger Ellis and Ruth Evans (Binghamton, N. Y.: Medieval and Renaissance Texts and Studies, 1994), p. 36.

39. See *The Middle English Dictionary*, eds. Hans Kurath and Sherman M. Kuhn (Ann Arbor: University of Michigan Press, 1952), 7:230.

40. Ibid., 7:231.

41. See volume 1 of *The Southern Version of Cursor Mundi*, ed. Sarah M. Horrall (Ottawa: University of Ottawa Press, 1978), p. 38; and volume 3 of the same work, ed. Henry J. Stauffenberg (Ottawa: University of Ottawa Press, 1985), p.20.

42. For a useful analogue, see the discussion of confession in Mannyng, *Handlyng Synne*, pp. 366–67.

43. Some scholars have suggested that medieval writers used "open" to refer to a particular kind of Latin-to-English translation, in which translators closely rendered the original language, but made changes when the following of Latin syntax would have produced noticeably stilted English. See, for example, Tim William Machan, *Techniques of Translation: Chaucer's 'Boece'* (Norman, Okla.: Pilgrim Books, 1985), pp. 63–68. Others have disagreed: see J. D. Burnley, "Late Medieval English Translation: Types and Reflections," *The Medieval Translator*, ed. Roger Ellis (Cambridge: D. S. Brewer, 1989), pp. 50–53. I do not think that Gaytryge is talking about a syntactic practice in this passage; at the same time, however, I disagree with Burnley's blanket statement that "medieval translators using the word 'open' use it of discourse and not of translation: the goal and not the process" (p. 52).

44. Lawton ("Gaytryge's Sermon," 330) points out that Lombard's *Libri quatuor sententiarum* also served as a source for Thoresby's *Injunctions*.

45. *Sentences* 2.1.4, in *Patrologiae cursus completes*, Series Latina, ed. Jacques-Paul Migne, volume 192 (Paris: Apud Garnieri Fratres, 1855), 653–54.

46. For *connen*, see *Middle English Dictionary*, 2:518–23; for *knouen*, see 5:579–90.

47. *Middle English Dictionary*, 5:586–87.

48. *Handlyng Synne*, p. 3; *Jacob's Well*, ed. Arthur Brandeis, EETS o.s. 115 (London: Early English Text Society, 1900), p. 276.

49. *Dives and Pauper*, ed. Priscilla Heath Barnum, volume 1 (New York: Oxford University Press, 1976), p. 171.

50. "Secundo decem sunt mandata a cunctis fidelibus inviolabiliter observanda . . ." (Simmons and Nolloth, p. 30).

51. "Item sex sunt opera misericordiae quae in evangelio recitantur . . ." (Simmons and Nolloth, p. 70).

52. "Tertio sciendum" (Simmons and Nolloth, p. 60).
53. "Firmiter injungentes . . . sicut indignationem divinam et inobedientiae reatum voluerint evitare" (Simmons and Nolloth, p. 96).
54. "Et ut mentes fidelium ad id propensius excitemus, nos de omnipotentis Dei misericordia, gloriosae Virginis Mariae matris ejus, beatorum Apostolorum Petri et Pauli, gloriosissimi Confessoris Willelmi meritis et precibus confidentes . . . qui praemissa in praedicando, docendo, audiendo et erudiendo devote servaverint et adimpleverint, quadraginta dies indulgentiae misericorditer duximus concedendos" (Simmons and Nolloth, pp. 96–98).
55. Blake, *Religious Prose*, p. 87.
56. See Watson, "Censorship," especially 822–30. One might, for example, perceive several points of connection between Gaytryge's ideas regarding the laity's ability to achieve (or at least pursue) wide-ranging kinds of knowledge and those expressed a few decades later in *Piers Plowman*. As Fiona Somerest has demonstrated, the various versions of *Piers* repeatedly disrupt conventional medieval conceptualizations of laypeople as inherently ignorant or intellectually limited and of clerics as masters of higher learning. See Somerset's "Vernacular Authorization in Piers Plowman," in her *Clerical Discourse and Lay Audience in Late Medieval England* (New York: Cambridge University Press, 1998), pp. 22–61. It is important to recognize, however, that the *Catechism* decidedly does not explore "tensions between learning and status," as does *Piers* (Somerset, *Clerical Discourse*, p. 23); it assumes without comment that the laity can and should attain transcendent forms of knowledge.
57. For a list of the manuscripts containing all or part of the *Catechism*, see Hudson, "New Look," 245–47. Powell ("Transmission," p. 73) revises some of Hudson's classification of the manuscripts.
58. Powell, "Transmission," pp. 75–77.
59. For discussions of the Constitutions and their impact, see: Watson, "Censorship," 825–40; Anne Hudson, *The Premature Reformation: Wycliffite Texts and Lollard History* (Oxford: Clarendon Press, 1988), pp. 82–86; and H. Leith Spencer, *English Preaching in the Late Middle Ages* (Oxford: Clarendon Press, 1993), pp. 163–88.
60. John Mirk, *Festial,* ed. Theodor Erbe, EETS e.s. 96 (London: Early English Text Society, 1905), p. 2.

CHAPTER 3

EXCITATIVE SPEECH: THEORIES OF
EMOTIVE RESPONSE FROM RICHARD
FITZRALPH TO MARGERY KEMPE

Fiona Somerset

Judith Butler's recent book *Excitable Speech* examines our society's attitudes to how public utterances on the most sensitive of controversial topics may provoke intense emotion, or even incite violent reactions: What are the possible consequences of such speaking, and to what extent are the speakers responsible for them?[1] These kinds of concerns are, as it turns out, nothing new. In 1357, when required to defend himself at the papal court against accusations by friars provoked by his views on voluntary mendicancy—one of the hottest topics of the day, and the main bone of contention between friars and their rivals—Richard Fitzralph wrote the *Defensio curatorum,* which became one of the most widely disseminated polemical statements of the later medieval period on the church's contested role in lay education.[2] Frequently copied and disseminated with the *Defensio* was a further reply to the friars' questions on mendicancy that has previously been overlooked by scholars, in which Fitzralph develops a theory of "excitative speech," whose importance among late medieval views about the dangers and benefits of emotionally provocative language has never been recognized. Nor, at the other end of the line I want to spin, has Margery Kempe's interest, as a vernacular theorist, in using some of the same tools to assess the consequences of excitative expression. Tracing these developments can give us new insight into the perceived consequences, and responsibilities, associated with late medieval vernacular publication.

The short work in which Richard Fitzralph explains his theory of "excitative speech" is entitled from its *incipit* the *Quia in proposicione nuper facta:* It is a detailed, point-by-point reply to the list of objections the friars had registered against the *Defensio curatorum,* focused largely on the seemingly trivial question (yet explosive at the time) of whether, and how, Christ begged during his life on earth. The *Quia* enjoyed a wide dissemination in company with the *Defensio,* to which it was frequently appended in manuscripts; while there are over eighty known manuscripts of the *Defensio,* however, the total number of copies of the *Quia* remains uncertain, since manuscript catalogues often fail to distinguish it from the *Defensio* or even to give an *explicit* that would make it possible to determine whether all or part of it is included. I have so far examined the manuscripts extant in English libraries; of those fifteen copies, twelve include the *Quia.*[3] Among Continental manuscript catalogues that give an *explicit,* there are plenty that do not end with the *Defensio's explicit*—three of the four copies in Prague, for example—so it seems likely that when all extant copies of the *Defensio* have been examined, a similar proportion of copies including the *Quia* may be found.

Yet Trevisa's translation of the *Defensio* into Middle English did not include the *Quia*—a rather surprising omission given Trevisa's involvement throughout his career in translating unprecedented sorts of academic material into the vernacular, but one perhaps prompted by the *Quia's* apparently narrow and abstruse subject. And the *Quia* has only ever been included in one printed edition of the *Defensio;* that of Peter Billaine, produced in Paris in 1633.[4] No other early printed copy of the *Defensio* includes the *Quia;* nor does Melchior Goldast's collection the *Monarchia* include it along with the *Defensio,* nor does the collection *Fasciculus rerum.* Following on from this early postmedieval disregard, the *Quia* has also been largely ignored by modern scholars. It is mentioned in passing by scholars of antifraternalism such as A. Gwynn and A. Williams; P. R. Szittya details its inclusion in antifraternal collections; and K. Walsh of course does not omit it from her book on Fitzralph—although unfortunately the index to her book confuses it with another work produced by Fitzralph in the wake of his confrontation with the friars at the papal court, the articles on *Vas eleccionis* called *De audientia confessionum.*[5]

Despite its postmedieval neglect, it is nonetheless plain that the *Quia,* and in particular the theoretical excursus that is the focus here, provoked considerable interest in late medieval England—the *Quia* may have been influential elsewhere as well, since the *Defensio* appears to have been widely read across Europe, but these other possible influences will have to await investigation elsewhere. That many readers were interested in the *Quia* as much as, or more than, the *Defensio* is suggested by its inclusion together with substantial excerpts from the *Defensio curatorum* in two miscellaneous *summae* (to use Szittya's term for them) containing antifraternal material: Oxford, Bodleian Library Bodley 784, a miscellaneous collection of theological extracts loosely organized into five sections, of which the third contains antifraternal materials from Fitzralph and other sources; and London, British Library MS Royal 6 E VI and VII, the *Omne Bonum,* a vast, unfinished encyclopedic compendium in which antifraternal sentiment is a recurrent theme, where the *Quia* is included in the entry for "Xpc" or "Christus" and material from the *Defensio* mostly under "Fratres mendicants."[6] Extensive marginalia in most of the copies of the *Quia* I have examined, particularly beside the discussion we will focus on, labeled by one annotator "on the authority of the saints," also indicate readers' interest.[7] So, most especially, does direct use of the section of the *Quia* that we will be examining by a variety of Latin and vernacular writers, including Wyclif, Richard Maidstone and apparently his opponent John Ashwardby, William Woodford, and William Taylor. Provable direct influence aside, writers such as Richard Rolle, John Trevisa, Thomas Usk, John Lydgate, the writer "Jack Upland" of the *Upland Series,* and Margery Kempe also help to demonstrate the importance and influence of Fitzralph's theory through their contributions to a broader cultural conversation about the potential effects of excitative speech.

   As is standard practice, Fitzralph proceeds in the *Quia* by rehearsing the friars' objections before giving his replies to them. In his reply to the friars' tenth objection, Fitzralph rehearses and refutes a common fraternal argument based on a sermon commonly attributed to Bernard of Clairvaux, but actually written by Aelred of Rielvaux.[8] Here is the argument.[9] "Bernard" unequivocally refers to Christ as an impoverished beggar in this address: "Vt te, Domine nostre, per omnia paupertati conformares,[10] quasi vnus in turba pauperum stipem[11] per ostia mendicabas" [So that you, our lord, should in all things conform to poverty, you begged money from door to door as if one among the mass of the poor (fol. 276r)]. Therefore fraternal begging may be justified as a meritorious imitation of Christ. Particularly when this quotation is ascribed to such an authoritative speaker, its description of Christ's mendicant activity is difficult to circumvent or discount. Fitzralph's strategy is to provide an elaborate theoretical excursus that justifies disregarding Bernard's apparent meaning. In the course of showing how the pseudo-Bernard sermon should be understood, Fitzralph explains that the saints have four ways of speaking: "aliquando excitatiue, aliquando expositiue, aliquando assertiue sed transcursiue siue inaduertentis, et aliquando assertiue ac probatiue seu diffinitiue" [sometimes excitatively, sometimes expositively, sometimes assertively, but in passing over certain matters or along the way, and sometimes assertively and in a probative or definitive manner (fol. 276r)]. By the time Fitzralph returns to explaining the pseudo-Bernard passage, after he has treated all four of the saints' ways of speaking in considerable detail, he has produced a remarkably radical method for—with however much professed humility and respect—weighing lightly, or even discounting when convenient, even what seem the most forthrightly assertive statements of the saints.

To be sure, most of the categories Fitzralph discusses here are far from new, as Minnis' work on medieval theories of authorship has extensively investigated.[12] Although Fitzralph's discussions of expositive and assertive speech are largely derivative, what is remarkable about them—as space does not permit me to show at length—is their detailed, exhaustive treatment of the possible types of speech, their provision of precise criteria for deciding whether a given statement is expositive or in what way it is assertive, and, most especially, the end to which they are harnessed—which can be illustrated by quoting the conclusion to Fitzralph's discussion of assertive/definitive speech:

> et sic ex nullo dicto alicuius sancti doctoris aut glose dicentis Christum fuisse mendicum aut etiam mendicasse siue egenum fuisse aliquid amplius potest concludi quam quod Christus erat inops aut pauper aut indigens nisi fortassis ex eius racionibus et circumstanciis sui dicti expresse appareat quod voluerat affirmare Christum fuisse corporaliter vere mendicum aut corporaliter elemosinam petiuisse quod preterquam a sancto Bernardo non memini me legisse qui sic excitatiue non assertiue locutus fuisse videtur. In quo dicto si assertiue locutus fuisset iuxta dictum predictum sancti Augustini eo maioris non est sibi credendum nisi quatenus dictum suum aliquo documento autentico poterit confirmari quod posse fieri non mihi videtur. (fol. 277v)

> [and so from no statement of any holy doctor, or gloss, saying Christ was mendicant or even that he begged or was destitute, can anything more be concluded than that Christ was poor, or a pauper, or indigent; unless by chance from his arguments and the context of his statement it should be expressly clear that he wanted to affirm that Christ was corporeally and truly a beggar, or corporeally asked for alms, and other than in St. Bernard I do not remember having read that, and he seems to have been speaking excitatively rather than assertively. Furthermore [Bernard's] statement, if he was speaking assertively, according to the previously cited statement of St. Augustine, who was greater than him, should not be believed unless insofar as [Bernard's] statement can be confirmed by some authentic document, which does not seem possible to me.]

Fitzralph's account is notable for its emphasis (not surprising in the circumstances, but perhaps influential) not so much on the *authority* of writers or their quoted sources—this has been the main emphasis, too, in previous scholarship—but on writers' *accountability,* both for their statements and for their interpretation of the statements of others.[13] As

Fitzralph concludes his excursus and returns to the troublesome pseudo-Bernard passage with which he began, he is less concerned with discounting Bernard's authority than with reevaluating Bernard's, and his own, accountability to the statement's face value. The theory he develops justifies his own claim that no saint, not even Bernard, who seems to say exactly this, states that Christ begged or was poor in a way that must be accepted as literally true.

This emphasis on accountability is nowhere more pregnant with implications—though most of them remain unexplored by Fitzralph, awaiting the attention of his contemporaries and successors—than in the discussion of the category of excitative speech that provides the basis for the definitive resolution just quoted. This category is apparently original to Fitzralph: Certainly it is cited as his by near contemporaries; and it is intriguing, even if merely an accident of organization, that he explains it first, at the opposite end of his theoretical excursus from the conclusion in which he puts it to use. When a saint speaks *excitatiue,* Fitzralph says, as Bernard does in the sermon quoted, "Vt te, Domine," or in his meditation on the Virgin Mary's compassion (usually entitled the *Quis dabit,* this popular devotional work commonly attributed to Bernard is, like the Aelred sermon, by another author),[14] the saint's statement is meant to excite himself, and others, toward devotion. But at the same time the saint's statement is not, strictly speaking, true. Fitzralph's exposition is worth quoting in full:

> Cum vero quisque sanctus excitatiue loquitur, scilicet ad deuocionem seipsum aut alios excitando, non videtur in eius dicto veritas exigenda, sed tantum vtilitas—dum tamen loquatur sine fidei inpugnacione expressa—quia non intendit quod dicit discutere siue asserere, sed edificare. Quale fuit hoc dictum sancti Bernardi hoc loco, vt multis videtur. Sicut in meditacione de compassione beate virginis gloriose, dicit "Quis dabit capiti meo aquam et oculis meis ymbrem vt possem flere per diem et noctem donec seruo suo dominus Iesus Christus appareat," etc., non intendens verum esse quod tanta aqua egeret aut oculis suis ymbre sed vt in seipso lacrimas prouocaret et alii attendentes deuocionem ipsius pariter prouocarentur ad lacrimas. Sicut (276v) econtra sanctus Job aperuit os suum et maledixit diei suo et locutus est "Pereat dies in qua natus sum," ostendendo vehemenciam sui doloris—quoniam immediate ibi premittitur "Videbant enim dolorem esse vehementem" (Job iii c')—non aliquid affirmando. Vnde tale dictum sancti Bernardi aut sancti alterius auctoritatem non habet, quoniam neque asseritur neque affirmatur ab ipso, et ob hoc ad aliquid probandum frustra et inepte adducitur. (fols. 276r-v)

> [But when some saint speaks *excitatiue,* that is, so as to excite himself or others to devotion, it does not seem to be required that his statement should be

[strictly] true, but only that it should be useful (provided of course that he speaks without expressing impugning faith) because he does not intend to discuss or assert what he says, but to edify. St. Bernard's statement in this place was of this sort, as it seems to many; just as in the meditation about the compassion of the blessed glorious virgin he says, "Who will give to my head water and to my eyes a well that I may weep day and night until lord Jesus Christ should appear to his servant," not intending to say that it is true that he needs so much water or that his eyes need a well, but so that he should provoke tears in himself and so that others attending to his devotion should similarly be provoked to tears. Similarly, St. Job opened his mouth and cursed his day, and said "Perish the day on which I was born," showing the vehemence of his sorrow—right before that it says "for they saw his grief was vehement"—but not affirming anything. That is why such a statement by St. Bernard or another saint does not have authority, since it is neither asserted nor affirmed by him; and thus to adduce it in proving something is useless and inept.]

Fitzralph's category of excitative speech permits the analysis of what we might call exaggeration, or perhaps poetic license: "Bernard" is not asking his readers to give his eyes a well, but using excessive or even contrafactual speech to excite himself, and them, toward devotion. But despite Fitzralph's attempt to cloak this interpretation as accepted wisdom by claiming that "Bernard's" statement in the first passage on Christ's begging seems excitative to many, "ut multis videtur," no previous writer involved in the poverty controversy who cites pseudo-Bernard on this point makes any such claim, whereas all subsequent writers who say something like this clearly rely on Fitzralph. That the category is original to Fitzralph also seems to be attested by the need he seems to feel to provide an explanatory gloss for *excitatiue,* "scilicet ad deuocionem seipsum aut alios excitando."

Thus, Fitzralph inserts into a discussion that has the air of a disquisition on accepted method a term not previously used in evaluations of authority and veracity, systematic or otherwise. What is more, his usage of the term he introduces oddly limits the semantic field it usually has in other contexts. These limitations virtually remove any considerations of audience, let alone the concerns about the relationship between an audience's social status, educational level, ease of access to the information provided whether in Latin or the vernacular, and potential subsequent behavior, with which English writers became increasingly obsessed in the later medieval period in which Fitzralph's theory seems to have become influential.[15]

In devotional contexts, *excitatio/excitare* and the Middle English equivalents *excitacion/exiten* or *meuyng/meue* were used to describe how readers or listeners might be brought to devotion by an outside agent through some nonrational process. For example, Fitzralph's near-contemporary

Richard Rolle uses the verb *excito* in the prologue to his *Incendium amoris* to describe the hoped-for effect of his emotionally charged prose style on his preferred audience:

> Istum ergo librum offero intuendum, non philosophis, non mundi sapientibus, non magnis theologicis infinitis quescionibus implicatis, sed rudibus et indoctis, magis Deum diligere quam multa scire conantibus. Non enim disputando sed agendo scietur, et amando. Arbitror autem ea que hic continentur ab istis questionariis (et in omni sciencia summis, sed in amore Christi inferioribus) non posse intelligi. Unde nec eis scribere decrevi, nisi postpositis et oblitis cunctis que ad mundum pertinent, solis Conditoris desideriis inardescant mancipari. . . . Quo enim scienciores sunt, eo de iure apciores sint ad amandum, si se vere spernerent et ab aliis sperni gauderent. Proinde quia hic universos excito ad amorem, amorisque superfervidum ac supernaturalem affectum utrumque ostendere conabor, iscius libri titulus Incendium Amoris sorciatur.

> [So I offer this book for the consideration not of philosophers, not of the worldly-wise, not of the great theologians enwrapped in endless *quaestiones,* but of the simple and untaught who strive more to love God than to know many things. For he is not known through disputation but through doing and loving. But I reckon that what is discussed here could not be understood by those intellectuals, who are supreme in all sorts of learning, but inferior when it comes to loving Christ. So I have forborne to write for them unless, putting behind and forgetting everything related to the world, they burn to be subjected to nothing but longing for the Creator alone. For the more knowledgeable they are, the more apt they would be, in principle, for loving, if they readily despised themselves and rejoiced to be despised by others. Consequently, because I here inflame all people to love, and try to manifest both the super-fervent and the supernatural effect of love, the title chosen for this book is The Burning of Love.][16]

Rolle focuses on the reaction of the audience he hopes to excite toward love. He is attentive to the social status of that audience's members, even if not to their probable capacities: He claims that his emotionally charged style will be especially appropriate for anyone with sufficient humility, but in the most likely case, for an uneducated lay audience of "rudis et indoctis"—even though such an audience is unlikely to have an easy time reading his rather ornate Latin.[17]

Fitzralph, in contrast, in the first instance uses *excito* reflexively, as if he would rather ignore the whole question of audience: The speaker's words are designed in the first instance to affect *himself.* And when he does acknowledge what would seem the obvious primary consideration, the possible effect of excitative language on its readers or listeners, he does so only in order to admit the possible devotional effect of excitation. While Fitzralph's interpretation does to some extent suit his example from the pseudo-Bernard *Quis dabit* meditation, in which the narrative persona of the prologue seems at least as interested in inciting his own emotions toward devotion as those of his audience, it seems odd to present this example as typical.[18] For not only does excitation to devotion more usually lead writers to worry more about their audience's reaction than their own, as we saw was the case with Rolle, but in many late medieval English contexts the audience response most typically expected to result from *excitacion* or *meuyng* is not devotional at all, but something much more akin to the reactions to excitable speech that interest Judith Butler. In such writings as Wyclif's "Petition to the King and Parliament," Thomas Usk's "Appeal" and his "Testament of Love," John Trevisa's translation of Ranulph Higden's *Polychronicon,* and the Parliament Roll's account of the rebellion of Sir John Oldcastle, the consequence of "excitation" that writers anticipate, especially when excitative speech is directed at the laity, is insurgent (or at the very least disruptive) action. These writers refer to words that "do things" in even more drastic ways than devotional words: their excitation encourages sedition, foments rebellions, and even causes the laity to disendow the clergy.[19]

What is more, the semantic restrictions on *excitare* that Fitzralph tries to impose are not even upheld by his chosen examples. It is unsurprising that in this portion of his discussion he wants to divert attention from the main example at issue in his excursus. "Vt te, Domine" has obviously tendentious implications: Fitzralph, of course, hopes to avoid discussing the possible emotive effects, on an audience of this sort, of inequality of wealth. But the second biblical quotation he claims is used by Bernard, "Quis dabit capiti meo aquam et oculis meis ymbrem vt possem flere per diem et noctem" [Who will give to my head water and to my eyes a well that I may weep day and night] is no less potentially controversial. Before—and, I think, heightening the emotional effect of—its use in Marian devotion, the phrase appears at Jeremiah 9:1, where it opens a chapter in which the prophet laments the sins of his people and threatens God's vengeance. Further, the phrase is used as an opening not just in the Latin *Quis dabit* attributed to Bernard and in its Anglo-Norman and Middle English translations, and in another fifteenth-century Marian devotional poem by Lydgate,[20] but in a number of mid- to late medieval controversial writings, where its excitative purpose (drawing more directly on its jeremiadic origins) is typically to dignify, and evoke sympathy for, the complainant who is about to detail the wrongs done to him.

For example, the anti-Wycliffite persona Friar Daw begins his early-fifteenth-century reply to the Wycliffite Jack Upland with "Who shal graunten to myn eyen a strong streme of teres" [Who shall grant my eyes a strong stream of tears]—Friar Daw later also uses the pseudo-Bernard quotation that is the basis of Fitzralph's excursus.[21] A satirical poem in defense of friars written at Oxford somewhere in the second half of the fourteenth century, and strongly critical of Richard Fitzralph, also begins with these words—perhaps, in its opening, intending a direct reference to Fitzralph's discussion of excitable speech.[22] The same opening is used by John Pecham in his *De perfectione evangelica*, a late-thirteenth-century defense of Franciscan poverty and mendicancy, and by an anonymous poem protesting at the manner of Richard Scrope's execution for treason in 1405.[23] While direct exposure to Fitzralph's theory of excitative speech seems less likely in these latter cases than in the first two, it is clear that uses of and responses to this quotation from Jeremiah came to partake in a broader cultural conversation, in both Latin and the vernacular, about the effects of excitative speech. Despite the temptations toward a wider consideration of the potential effects of excitation upon an audience posed by this lineage of topical complaint, however, Fitzralph sidesteps any such discussion.

Yet as we will see, Fitzralph's theory came to participate in this conversation, whether he wanted it to or not. And consideration of the effects of excitative speech became important not only to educated writers who clearly draw upon Fitzralph, but to lay readers and writers in the vernacular who were thought of as having little access to educated knowledge, such as Margery Kempe—in whose *Book* this quotation from Jeremiah comes to function almost as a leitmotif, stitching together her self-justifications for her emotional outbursts.

To return first to cases in which Fitzralph's theory has demonstrably influenced clerical writers, it is perhaps indicative of the term *excitatiue*'s disquieting potential, as well as its unfamiliarity, that all but one of the writers I have found who make direct use of Fitzralph's explanation of Bernard skirt round the question of its public potential even more carefully than Fitzralph: The one exception is the writer who agrees with Fitzralph's conclusions on the subject of Christ's mendicancy but, unlike Fitzralph, wholeheartedly embraces the possible disruptive social effects of excitation. If the anti-Wycliffites Friar Daw and William Woodford knew of the *Quia*, as seems likely from their reliance on other arguments made there, they avoid discussing any part of Fitzralph's explanation of excitative speech in their treatments of the pseudo-Bernard passage.[24] When in *De civili dominio* Wyclif asserts that Christ did beg, his contention is that "Bernard" (or possibly Aelred, as he later concedes)[25] "simpliciter assereret" [unconditionally asserted] that Christ begged.[26] Wyclif omits any reference to the alternatives to unconditional assertion or any explicit reference to Fitzralph—although this is perhaps simply because, rather unusually, he disagrees with Fitzralph on this topic.

Richard Maidstone accurately summarizes and refutes Fitzralph's argument in the fifth of the seven conclusions of his *Protectorium pauperis*, a Latin defense of voluntary poverty and mendicancy written (probably in the late 1380s or early 1390s) to counter antifraternal vernacular sermons preached by Ashwardby in St. Mary's Church, Oxford:

Numquid ista auctoritas expresse sonat Christum mendicasse?[27] Sed hic dicit adversarius quod haec auctoritas non est Bernardi, sed discipuli sui Ailredi, nec hoc dixit assertive sed ex devotione et pietate opinative tantum. Sed rogo eum qui sic respondet: numquid aliqua pietas vel devotio moveret Bernardum, vel etiam discipulum suum Ailredum, ad opinandum vel etiam ad imaginandum de Christo quod esset haeresis vel blasphemia affirmare de eo? Qui talem devotionem imponit Bernardo, vel eius discipulis, non est devotus contemplator veritatis.[28]

[Does this authority not expressly state that Christ begged? But here my opponent says that this authoritative statement is not by Bernard but by his disciple Aelred, and that he did not say this assertively, but from devotion and piety and only as an opinion. But, I ask him who replies in this way, surely no piety or devotion would move Bernard, or even his disciple Aelred, to opine or even imagine about Christ what it would be heresy or blasphemy to affirm about him? Whoever imposes this sort of devotion on Bernard, or his disciple, is not a devout contemplator of truth.]

Either Ashwardby knew Fitzralph's argument well and quoted from it extensively, or Maidstone is here using Ashwardby as a pretext for a rather belated response to Fitzralph: Since Ashwardby's sermons do not survive, we cannot tell which. Whatever the case, some participant in the debate has substituted for *excitatiue* the phrase "ex devotione et pietate opinative tantum," a description that makes no reference to the intended effects of Bernard's statement on others or even on Bernard himself, but only to Bernard's own mental state.

William Taylor is the only writer I know of who takes what Fitzralph says as it appears to be meant—and further. In his sermon on John 6:5, "Unde ememus panes ut manducent hii," he gives a translation that has the same sort of semantic range as Fitzralph's: "And as to Bernard or Alrede his clerk, answeriþ Ardmakan and seiþ þat it is seid bi maner of meuyng and not bi maner of affermyng": It is said in a manner designed to excite emotion, that is, rather than in a manner that affirms what is said as truth.[29] Within the sermon, this counterargument forms part of a wide-ranging dismissal of clerical privileges of all kinds. Taylor is not disturbed by the possible excitative effect of preaching publicly in the vernacular about Christ's destitution and need for alms, because his controversial sermon, delivered in public in English at St. Paul's Cross on November 21, 1406, aims at the worst sorts of effect that a more conservative churchman could fear. His final exhortation excites his lay listeners to take over the sort of pastoral role clerics are failing to fulfill:

> Wiþdrawe þee þerfore from yuel and do good, brekynge þe breed of almes amonge þe nedy, as it is seid bifore. And, as þou releeuest a man wiþ þi worldly goodis, so do wiþ þi goodis of kynde and of grace, þat wiþ þi kunnyng and discrescioun þou gouerne hem and enfourme hem. And so in alle wise letiþ ȝoure plentee, as Poul biddiþ, fulfille oþere mennys defautis.[30]

> [Withdraw therefore from evil and do good, breaking the bread of alms among the needy, as it is said before. And, as you relieve a man with worldly goods, so do with the goods of nature and of grace, so that with knowledge and discretion you govern and inform them. And so in all ways let your plenty, as Paul bids, fulfill other men's lack.]

Taylor is encouraging his listeners to relieve the clergy of their endowments and take over the clerical task of almsgiving; what is more, he is encouraging them to give out "alms" of guidance and instruction along with monetary alms. The accusation recorded in Archbishop Arundel's register, that Taylor claimed in his sermon that the possessions of the church might be forcibly removed "quasi per violentam cedicionem populi" [by violent popular sedition], suggests Taylor was engaging in a rather less responsible sort of excitation than this pious encouragement. Nonetheless, in presenting to the judgment of laymen a sophisticated clerical explanation for why clerical authority may be dismissed and exhorting them to act upon that dismissal, Taylor is putting Fitzralph's theory to a use that might surprise him.

Of course one factor to consider is the difference in intended audience between Fitzralph's *Quia* and Taylor's sermon. Fitzralph's reply to the friars' objections is at least moderately conciliatory. With it he means to excuse himself before the papal court, even if without backing away from any central tenet of his position. The sort of appeal to lay judgment that Fitzralph does in fact use elsewhere—in his public London sermons, for example, or in the *Defensio curatorum*'s frequent recursions to the biblical verse "Nolite judicare secundum faciem" [Do not judge by appearances]— would not be prudent in these circumstances. Taylor's publicly delivered sermon has no such need for conciliation, although his long survival as a heretic would seem to indicate that he was capable of it when necessary.[31] Still, even in his London sermons Fitzralph does not match what we might describe as Taylor's political vernacularizing, in this sermon, of scripturally based excitative speech. Rather than carefully emptying his examples of any implied accountability for their significance, Taylor passes that accountability on to his vernacular audience: Once they have understood him, they are *bound* to act unless they wish to be complicit with the sins he describes.

The sorts of gesture toward lay participation in both topics of discussion and domains of feeling previously thought appropriate only to the clergy that we have seen from Rolle, Fitzralph, and Taylor were relatively common among educated writers in late medieval England, when vernacular audiences seem to have received more attention (if not in practice, then at the very least in the clerical imagination) than they had previously.[32] Yet it is rare that we have any direct evidence of how lay audiences responded to these excitations. Vernacular readers and listeners are of course far less likely to write replies in kind than are educated colleagues, and despite what several writers seemed to have hoped about how vernacular audiences might be exhorted to political action, little seems to have resulted. In Margery Kempe, however, we have something even more valuable than evidence of a direct response to the ideas of Fitzralph or Taylor. Rather than merely reacting along the lines they might have hoped, she *contributes,* as a laywoman (albeit of some education), to the broader cultural conversation on the effects of excitable speech that I have briefly sketched out.[33] She is a vernacular theorist of excitative speech and its effects; her experimental ground is not (or not only) a projected audience who may or may not respond as she hopes, but her own life, whose spiritual project her *Book* attempts to defend. In Margery's *Book* the verse from Jeremiah "grawnt me a welle of teerys" [grant me a well of tears] appears repeatedly on occasions when she attempts to justify her socially inassimilable (and indeed frequently censured) outbursts of wailing and crying.[34] Margery tries to show that her crying is provoked by verbal or other reminders of Christ's life and Passion; that it is a gift from God she has explicitly requested; and that it is not only an expression of introverted (yet uncontainable) devotional emotion at the thought of Christ's suffering and her own contrition, but a form of social action: These words make things happen, and benefit others as well as herself.

Margery's wish to present herself as a social activist under divine orders is clearest in book 1 chapter 20, where she witnesses her Eucharistic vision (58). After she has watched the Eucharist shaking and fluttering during the elevation, Margery is granted a social role, and a relationship with Christ, that will be similar to (but better than) the one St. Bridget had. Christ informs her that she will not see this vision again, but should be grateful for what she has seen, because this was more insight than was ever granted to St. Bridget. Margery's vision and Christ's interpretation of it authorize not only herself, but Bridget too: "rygth as I spak to Seynt Bryde ryte so I

speke to the, dowtyr, and I telle the trewly it is trewe every word that is
wretyn in Brides boke, and be the it schal be knowyn for very trewth" [I
speak to you just as I spoke to St. Bridget, daughter, and I tell you truly,
every word that is written in St. Bridget's book is true, and by you it shall
be known as the very truth (58)]. Christ confides to her as well that there
will be an earthquake, that she will do well despite all her enemies, and that
the sins of the people are a great trial on his patience. In response to these
revelations, Margery asks directly just what her role in society should be:
"Alas, derworthy Lord, what schal I do for the pepyl?" [Alas, dear Lord,
what shall I do for the people?]. Christ answers, "It is inow to the to don
as thow dost" [It is enough that you do what you do (58)].

Even attentive readers of Margery's often self-absorbed narrative may
find themselves wondering just what it is that Margery does for the people,
whether from this point forward or at any earlier stage, and whether Christ
may in fact be authorizing Margery to continue to do nothing. But
Margery does have a mission to the people: that of mitigating their sin, most
importantly through crying for them.[35] In the final pages of Margery's
Book, a series of prayers central to her spiritual project, repeated by her frequently over many years, are set out. One of these prayers underscores the
central importance of weeping to her social role, employing the "well of
tears" phrase from Jeremiah in the process: "hafe mercy of me therfor and
grawnte me in this lyfe a welle of teerys spryngyng plenteuowsly, with the
which I may waschyn awey my synnys thorw thi mercy and thi goodnes.
And, Lord, for thi hy mercy, alle the teerys that may encresyn my lofe to the
and moryn my meryte in hevyn, helpyn and profityn myn evyn cristen
sowlys, lyfys er dedys, visite me with her in erth" [therefore, have mercy on
me and grant me in this life a well of tears springing plenteously with
which I may wash away my sins through your mercy and goodness. And,
Lord, for your high mercy, visit me here on earth with all the tears that may
increase my love of you and increase my merit in heaven, and aid and profit
my fellow Christian souls, living or dead (231)]. This final reiteration recalls
a number of occasions throughout the narrative on which Margery has
stressed the efficacy of her tears by means of this same scriptural phrase.

During her extended pilgrimage, soon after the occasion on which she
explains she was granted tears for the first time while watching friars reen-
act the stations of the cross in Jerusalem, she takes confession in Rome in a
vision from John the Baptist, then prays repeatedly, "Lord, as wistly as thu art
not wroth wyth me, grawnt me a welle of teerys, wherthorw I may receyve
thi precyows body with al maner terys of devocyon to thi worshep and en-
cresyng of my meryte" [Lord, as surely you are not angry with me, grant me
a well of tears, through which I may receive your precious body with all
manner of tears of devotion to your worship and the increasing of my

merit . . . (87)]. Tears that recall Christ's Passion prepare Margery to receive his human body. Still in Rome, praying in the church where St. Jerome is buried, Margery sees Jerome himself appear to her, saying: "Blissed art thow, dowtyr, in the wepyng that thu wepyst for the peplys synnes, for many schal be savyd therby. And, dowtyr, drede the nowt, for it is a synguler and a specyal gyft that God hath govyn the, a welle of teerys the whech schal nevyr man take fro the" [Blessed are you, daughter, in the weeping that you weep for people's sins, for many shall be saved thereby. And, daughter, do not be at all afraid, for it is a singular and special gift that God has given you—a well of tears which no one shall ever take from you (103)]. Jerome confirms that Margery's tears are a bountiful resource granted by God so that she may fulfill her social role. Later Margery claims that back home, the crying lasted for ten years, and that every year, she wept for hours on Good Friday. She explains in detail how during this weeping she wept for the sins of the people:

> Sumtyme sche wept . . . on owr for the synne of the pepil. . . . Sumtyme sche wept an other owr for the sowlys in Purgatory; an other owr for hem that weryn in myschefe, in poverte, er in any dises; an other owr for Jewys, Sarasinys, and alle fals heretikys that God for hys great goodnes schulde puttyn awey her blyndnes. . . . Sche seyd, "I aske ryth nowt, Lord, but that thu mayst wel gevyn me, and that is mercy whech I aske for the pepil synnys. Thu seyst oftyntymes in the yer to me that thu hast forgovyn me my synnes. Therfor I aske now mercy for the synne of the pepil, as I wolde don for myn owyn, for, Lord, thu art alle charite. . . . Therfor, Lorde, I wolde I had a welle of teerys to constreyn the wyth that thu schuldist not takyn uttyr venjawns of mannys sowle for to partyn hym fro the wythowtyn ende. . . .

> [Sometimes she wept . . . an hour for the sins of the people. . . . Sometimes she wept another hour for the souls in Purgatory, another hour for those that were in mischief, in poverty, or in any disease, another hour for Jews, Muslims, and all false heretics so that God, for his great goodness, should put away their blindness. . . . She said, "I ask nothing, Lord, except that which you may give me, and that is the mercy that I ask for the people's sins. You say to me often during the year that you have forgiven my sins. Therefore, I ask now mercy for the sins of the people, as I would do for my own, for, Lord, you are all charity. . . . Therefore, Lord, I would that I had a well of tears with which to constrain you in order that you should not take utter vengeance on men's souls to part them from you without end . . . (139).]

Not only are the tears granted by God, but here Margery imagines (or at least hopes) that they *constrain* God to save the people for whom Margery so copiously weeps: efficacious tears indeed.[36]

Although these instances are far from exhausting the importance of crying to Margery's spiritual project, it is clear that her uses of the "well of tears" quotation appear at some of the most important moments of that project's description and validation. In each case it is these words that provoke the emotion that leads to Margery's copious crying, and Margery is at pains to show how her tears further the spiritual project God has assigned her. Devotional emotion is brought on by emotionally provocative language linked to Christ's Passion: On many other occasions, too, where her tears are not specifically associated with the verse from Jeremiah, we see that they are explicitly described as being brought on by cues that recall Christ's life. But in Margery's Book, unlike any of the writings by educated writers aimed at lay audiences that similarly link excitative speech with devotional fervor, feelings are not separate from actions "for the pepyl," but *produce* them. While educated writers describing lay excitation seem only to be able to associate it with social disruption and dissent of a sort they (nearly always) censure in the strongest terms, Margery envisages a way in which lay devotional emotion may be socially beneficial. Even for less charitable readers of Margery's *Book* who see this linkage between emotion and activism largely as a mode of self-justification, the contrast between Margery's integrative vernacular theory and the bifurcation everywhere present among educated attitudes to lay excitation should be deeply intriguing. But pursuing this point further will have to be the topic of another paper.

Notes

1. Judith Butler, *Excitable Speech: A Politics of the Performative* (New York: Routledge, 1997).
2. In defending the prerogatives of secular clerics against what he saw as the illegitimate and unjustified encroachments of the friars, Fitzralph asserts that the secular clergy are the most appropriate pastoral educators of the laity, and even suggests that the laity can judge this to be true for themselves. See Fiona Somerset, *Clerical Discourse and Lay Audience in Late Medieval England* (Cambridge: Cambridge University Press, 1998), pp. 96–99. There is no modern critical edition of the *Defensio,* although T. P. Dolan reports that he is preparing one; the most widely available premodern edition is in Melchior Goldast, ed., *Monarchia S Roman Imperii . . .* , 3 vols. (Frankfurt, 1621), 3:1391–1410.
3. The extant copies of the *Defensio* in England are as follows:
   Cambridge, Peterhouse College MS 223 *Quia*
   Cambridge, Sidney Sussex College MS 64) 4 2 *Quia*
   Durham Cathedral MS 32 B IV *Quia*
   Hereford Cathedral MS P 2 VI *Quia*
   London, British Library MS Lansdowne 393 *Quia*
   London, Lambeth Palace MS 121 *Quia*

London, Lambeth Palace MS 1208 *Quia*
Oxford, Bodleian Library MS Auct F inf 1.2
Oxford, Bodleian Library MS Bodley 144 *Quia*
Oxford, Bodleian Library MS Bodley 158 *Quia*
Oxford, Bodleian Library MS Bodley 865
Oxford, Bodleian Library MS Lat misc c 75 *Quia*
Oxford, Corpus Christi College MS 182
Oxford, Magdalen College MS 38 *Quia*
Oxford, St John's College MS 65 *Quia*

In addition, there are two copies of the *Quia* in compilations (discussed below): London, British Library MS Royal 6 E VII (*Omne bonum*) *Quia*, and Oxford, Bodleian Library MS Bodley 784 (*Summa*) *Quia*

4. For details of this edition see Katherine Walsh, *A Fourteenth-Century Scholar and Primate: Richard Fitzralph in Oxford, Avignon, and Armagh* (Oxford: Oxford University Press, 1981), p. 422 n. 54.

5. See Aubrey Gwynn, "The Sermon Diary of Richard Fitzralph, Archbishop of Armagh," *Proceedings of the Royal Irish Academy* 44 C (1937): 1–57, and Arnold Williams, "*Protectorium Pauperis*, A Defense of the Begging Friars by Richard of Maidstone, O. Carm. (d. 1396)," *Carmelus* 5 (1958): 132–80. For Penn R. Szittya's discussion, see his *The Antifraternal Tradition in Medieval Literature* (Princeton: Princeton University Press, 1986). Walsh distinguishes the *Quia* from *De audientia confessionum* in *A Fourteenth-Century Scholar and Primate*, p. 441, but the index confuses the two works, listing "Quia in proposicione nuper facta" as the *incipit* to *De audientia confessionum* (p. 509), and so does a reference in the appendix, on p. 474.

6. For discussion of both these collections, see Szittya, *The Antifraternal Tradition*, pp. 112–22 and 291–300. As Szittya explains, the use each collection makes of the *Quia* and *Defensio* is very similar, but each contains material not derived from the other; one possible explanation is that both draw on another previous collection. On the *Omne Bonum*, see also the very thorough recent study (superseding her previously published discussions of particular aspects of the work) by Lucy F. Sandler, *"Omne Bonum": A Fourteenth-Century Encyclopedia of Universal Knowledge*, 2 vols. (London: Harvey Miller, 1996); Sandler discusses the compiler's use of the *Quia* at 1:46–47 (where she suggests that the compiler may have had access to a copy of Fitzralph's sermon diary), 1:114–15, 123–24, and describes the article in which it appears at 2:244–45.

7. A contemporary annotator of Bodley 144 labels Fitzralph's explanation "Nota bene pro auctoritatibus sanctorum" (fol. 276). In St John's 65 the passage is labeled "nota racionem" [notice this argument], while in Bodley 158 it is labeled "nota quod sancti quadrupliciter loquuntur" [notice that the saints speak in four ways], and also, beside the discussion of the quotation from the Bernard sermon, "nota compassionem beate marie hic allegata" [notice the compassion of blessed Mary adduced here]. Lambeth Palace 1208 labels the discussion "nota dictum Bernardi" [notice Bernard's

statement], while Lambeth Palace 121 observes "quatuor modis sancti lo-
cuntur i ii iii iiii" [the saints speak in four ways, i ii iii iv], and Lansdowne
393 has a large pointer labeling the beginning of the discussion "nota bona
doctrina et vtilem" [notice this good and useful teaching], as well as the
annotation "Ad 9a de dicto Bernardi" [against the ninth point about
Bernard's statement]. Interest in distinguishing the four modes of saintly
speech of Fitzralph's explaination might also be deduced from the fact that
they are distinguished and numbered in the margins of Bodley 158,
Bodleian Lat misc c 75, and Sidney Sussex 64.

8. Here, in context, is the corresponding quotation from the modern edition
of Aelred's short treatise on Christ's childhood, together with a recent
translation: "Quid dicam, Deus meus? An ut te per omnia nostrae conformares paupertati, et omnes in te humanae miseriae calamitates susciperes,
quasi unus e turba pauperum, stipem per ostia mendicabas? Quis dabit me
bucellarum illarum mendicatarum participem fieri, uel saltem divini illius
edulii saginari" ("De Iesu puero," I.6, Aelfredi Rievallensis, *Opera Omnia,*
I. *Opera Ascetica,* ed. A. Hoste and C. H. Talbot [CCSL, CM 1, Turnhout:
Brepols, 1971], p. 254). [What shall I say, my God? Did you, in order to
conform yourself to our poverty in everything and take upon yourself all
the mysteries of our human lot, beg for alms from door to door as one of
the crowd of beggars? Who will grante me a share in those crusts you obtained by begging, or at least let me feed on the remains of that divine
food?" ("Jesus at the Age of Twelve," trans. Theodore Berkeley, Aelred of
Rievaulx, *Treatises and the Pastoral Prayer,* Cistercian Fathers Series 2
[Spencer, M. A.: Cistercian Publications, 1971], p.10). My thanks to
Suzanne Akbari, who discovered the correct source, for this reference.

9. All quotations from the *Quia* are from my provisional edition based on my
collation of the copies extant in English libraries. My base text is Bodley
144, Gwynn's basis for his work on Fitzralph's sermon diary (see Gwynn,
"Sermon Diary"); I have as yet no grounds for preferring another copy. I
emend only where the text is obviously wrong, and include variants only
when they help to show how scribes and readers may have understood the
text. Modern punctuation and capitalization are supplied. I cite parenthetically from this manuscript by folio within the text.

10. conformares] confirmares

11. *corr.* per omnia.

12. See "Chapter 3: Authorial Roles in the 'Literal Sense'" in Alastair J. Minnis,
Medieval Theory of Authorship: Scholastic Literary Attitudes in the Later Middle Ages,
2nd ed. (Philadelphia: University of Pennsylvania Press, 1988), pp. 73–117.

13. This emphasis on accountability is prominent in many later medieval English academic works that variously protest their willingness to submit to
correction and insist that they are not asserting what they say, but merely
proposing or explaining it. Thomas Arundel's 1409 *Constitutions* attempt—
unsuccessfully, surely—to abolish this widely used mode of speculative academic expression: "[N]e quis, vel qui, cujuscunque gradus, status, aut

conditionis existat, conclusiones aut propositiones in fide catholica sue bonis moribus adverse sonantes . . . in scholis, aut extra, disputando aut communicando, protestatione praemissa vel non praemissa, asserat vel proponat, etiamsi quadam verborum aut terminorum curiositate defendi possint[,]" [No person or persons of whatever status or rank may state conclusions or propositions that sound as if they are contrary to Catholic faith or good morals, whether they are in the schools or outside, disputing or communicating, whether or not a protestation prefaces their remarks, regardless of whether they are asserting or proposing what they say, and even if their words can be defended by ingenious explanation]. See David Wilkins, ed., *Concilia magnae Britanniae et Hiberniae*, 3 vols. (Oxford: Clarendon Press, 1964), 3:314–19; 317 col. b.

14. For a detailed description of the *Quis dabit* as well as its translations into Anglo-Norman and Middle English, see C. W. Marx, "The Middle English Verse 'Lamentation of Mary to Saint Bernard' and the 'Quis dabit,'" in Derek Pearsall, ed., *Studies in the Vernon Manuscript* (Woodbridge, Suffolk: D. S. Brewer, 1990), pp. 137–57. The *Quis dabit* is derived from a longer work by Oglerius de Tridino, but circulated extensively as an independent meditation ascribed sometimes to Bernard, sometimes to Augustine (pp. 137, 140).

15. For more detailed treatment of several clerical writers' concerns with the implications of vernacular audience, see Somerset, *Clerical Discourse*. Many examples of such concern may be found in the vernacular prologues printed in Jocelyn Wogan-Browne, Nicholas Watson, Andrew Taylor, and Ruth Evans, eds., *The Idea of the Vernacular: An Anthology of Middle English Literary Theory, 1280–1520* (University Park: Pennsylvania State University Press, 1999).

16. Richard Rolle, *Incendium amoris* 145.1–147.32, quoted in Nicholas Watson, *Richard Rolle and the Invention of Authority* (Cambridge: Cambridge University Press, 1991), pp. 114–15. The text and translation are Watson's; emphasis is mine. Watson conjectures that the work was written in the late 1330s to early 1340s; see his appendix on dating, "Excursus I: The Chronology of Rolle's Writings," pp. 273–94, and especially p. 278.

17. There is of course a mid-fifteenth-century translation of this work by Richard Misyn, printed in Ralph Harvey, ed., *The Fire of Love and The Mending of Life or The Rule of Living* (London, 1896), but the work was nonetheless certainly inaccessible to an audience of *indoctis* at the time at which it was written. For more examples of the conventional range of devotional uses for *excitacio/excitare,* the reader may consult the computer indices to the CSEL and PL.

18. For a description of the narrator's prologue, see Marx, "Lamentation of Mary," 141.

19. See Hans Kurath et al, eds., *Middle English Dictionary* (Ann Arbor, MI: University of Michigan Press, 1954-), s.v. "exciten."

20. "Quis Dabit Meo Capiti Fontem Lacrimarum," in H. N. MacCracken, ed., *The Minor Poems of John Lydgate* pt 1, Early English Text Society e.s. 107

(London: Oxford University Press, 1911), pp. 324–29, especially p. 324. Heyworth notices this example; see Peter L. Heyworth, ed., *Jack Upland, Friar Daw's Reply, and Upland's Rejoinder* (Oxford: Clarendon Press, 1968), pp. 137–38.

21. On the *Upland Series*, which consists of Jack Upland's antifraternal questions (extant in both Middle English and Latin versions), Friar Daw's reply to them in Middle English verse, one or two further rejoinders to Daw in Middle English by the Upland persona, and a Latin reply to Jack Upland's questions by William Woodford, see Somerset, *Clerical Discourse*, pp. 135–78; in an appendix, pp. 216–20, I argue that these works should be dated between the late fourteenth and early fifteenth centuries, not (as Heyworth argues) in the later part of the fifteenth century. For an edition of the English portions see Heyworth, ed., *Jack Upland*; for the Latin texts, see Eric Doyle, O.F.M., "William Woodford, O.F.M. (c. 1330–c. 1400): His Life and Works, Together with a Study and Edition of his 'Responsiones Contra Wiclevum et Lollardos,'" *Franciscan Studies* 43 (1983): 17–187. Daw's opening lamentation and quotation of pseudo-Bernard may be found in Heyworth's edition at lines 1–2 and 718–21.

22. On the satirical poem criticizing Fitzralph, "Quis dabit capiti pelagus aquarum," see most recently Wendy Scase, "'Heu! quanta desolatio Angliae praestatur': A Wycliffite Libel and the Naming of Heretics, Oxford 1382," forthcoming in Fiona Somerset, Jill Havens, and Derrick Pitard, eds., *New Directions in Wycliffite Studies: Heresy and Reform* (Boydell and Brewer); the poem is printed (with some errors) by Wilhelm Heuser, "With an O and an I," *Anglia* 27 (1904): 315–19. See also Penn R. Szittya, "'Sedens Super Flumina': A Fourteenth-Century Poem Against the Friars" *Mediaeval Studies* 41 (1979): 30–43, especially 34, and Arthur G. Rigg, *A History of Anglo-Latin Literature 1066–1422* (Cambridge: Cambridge University Press, 1992), p. 272.

23. Heyworth, ed., *Upland*, pp. 137–38, notes the source in Jeremiah as well as the opening's use by John Lydgate and in the poem "On The Execution of Richard Scrope, Archbishop of York," in Thomas Wright, ed., *Political Poems and Songs*, 2 vols. (London, 1859–1861), 2:114–18, especially 114. John Pecham's use of the quotation appears in Andrew G. Little, ed., "Selections from Pecham's *Tractatus Pauperis* or *De Perfectione Evangelica*," *Brit. Soc. Franc. Stud.* 2 (1910): 13–90, especially 21.

24. For Daw's and Woodford's responses to Jack Upland's question about mendicant poverty, see Heyworth, ed., *Jack Upland*, pp. 94–95, lines 698–726, and Doyle, "William Woodford," *40a Quaestio*, 150–51, as well as Somerset, *Clerical Discourse*, pp. 162–78, where the passages are quoted in full, explained, and placed in context.

25. " . . . beatus Bernhardus vel, ut alii dicunt, fuit abbas Alredus Bernhardi discipulus" (John Wyclif, *De civili dominio*, 4 vols, vol. 1 ed. Reginald L. Poole [London, 1885], vols 2, 3, and 4 ed. Johann Loserth [London, 1900–4], 3:102).

26. Wyclif, *De civili dominio* 3:8.

27. mendicasse] mendicassse *sic* Williams. Obviously a printing error, since Williams has imposed classical spelling throughout.

28. Williams, "*Protectorium Pauperis*," 132–80, 158, lines 1–25.

29. "The Sermon of William Taylor," in Anne Husdon, ed., *Two Wycliffite Texts* (Oxford: Oxford University Press, 1993), p. 21, lines 687–89. The comma I have added to remove ambiguity. On Taylor's career and the occasion of the sermon, see Hudson's introduction, pp. xiii–xxv.

30. "The Sermon of William, Taylor," p. 23, lines 748–53.

31. On Taylor's career see Hudson, ed., *Two Wycliffite Texts,* pp. xvii–xxv

32. See above, n. 15.

33. While much past scholarship on Margery Kempe has chosen to believe that she had little if any learning and that her *Book* presents naive, unmediated emotional reactions given what form they have by the scribes who copied them, some recent scholars have instead suggested that Margery had much greater influence over the composition of her book than previously thought, and have presented evidence that she knew much more than she has often been given credit for. Although studies that stress Margery's deliberate fashioning of her *Book* and attribute evidence of learning within it firmly to Margery herself rather than to her scribes can run the risk of assimilating her *Book* to genres to which it only partly belongs and thus failing to recognize its unique qualities, or of asserting (this time overlooking different parts of the evidence) that Margery is always in full control of what she produces, they have nonetheless produced fresh new insights: see, for example, Diana R. Uhlman, "The Comfort of Voice, the Solace of Script: Orality and Literacy in *The Book of Margery Kempe*," *Studies in Philology* 91 (1994): 50–69; Lynn Staley, *Margery Kempe's Dissenting Fictions* (University Park: Pennsylvania State University Press, 1994); Ruth Shklar, "Cobham's Daughter: The Book of Margery Kempe and the Power of Heterodox Thinking," *Modern Language Quarterly* 56 (1995): 277–304; Melissa Furrow, "Unscholarly Latinity and Margery Kempe," in M. Jane Toswell and Elizabeth M. Tyler, eds., *Doubt Wisely: Papers in Honour of E. G. Stanley* (London: Routledge, 1996), pp. 240–51.

34. All references to Kempe's *Book* will use the recent paperback edition, *The Book of Margery Kempe,* ed. Lynn Staley (Kalamazoo, Mich.: TEAMS Medieval Institute Publications, 1996); subsequent references will be parenthetical. The verse from Jeremiah appears at pp. 87, 103, 139, and 231, and is linked as well with a number of other moments at which crying is important to Margery's spiritual project. No previous commentator or critic has devoted much effort to explaining Margery's quotations from Jeremiah: Hope Emily Allen gives the reference in Jeremiah and suggests that Margery may have been influenced by references to rivers and fountains of tears in the Sarum Use; see *The Book of Margery Kempe,* ed. Sanford Brown Meech and Hope Emily Allen, EETS o.s. 212 (London: Oxford University Press, 1940 [1982]), p. 299 note on 81/19. Allen also suggests that

Margery's theories about what tears can do may have been influenced in part by the *Speculum Christiani* (Meech and Allen, eds., *Margery Kempe*, p. 43, note on 43/7). For occasions on which Margery's crying is censured, see, for example, Staley, ed., *Book of Margery Kempe*, pp. 75–78, 88–89, 145–48, 150–51, 159–60, 160–61.

35. For a useful survey of the doctrine of compunction (according to which one person's tears may be helpful in gaining God's mercy for the sin of many others) and some helpful remarks on Margery's apparent knowledge of this doctrine, see Sandra J. McEntire, *The Doctrine of Compunction in Medieval England: Holy Tears* (Lewiston, N.Y.: Mellen, 1990).

36. While she does not mention this passage in the context in which she raises this point, Hope Emily Allen suggests early on in the notes to her edition that Margery is influenced by this quotation from the *Speculum christiani:* "Ieronimus: Prayer queme3 god, bot the tere constreyne3; prayer softe3, the tere compelle3" [Prayer petitions God, but the tear constrains; prayer softens, the tear compels] (Meech and Allen, eds., *Margery Kempe*, p. 299, note on 81/19).

FRENCH

CHAPTER 4

TRANSLATING SCRIPTURE FOR
MA DAME DE CHAMPAGNE: THE OLD FRENCH
"PARAPHRASE" OF PSALM 44 *(ERUCTAVIT)*

Morgan Powell

B eginning around 1150, there appear a handful of Old French religious
texts intended for the audience of the secular courts, usually described
as vernacular paraphrase and exegesis of Scripture.[1] These texts make up
one of the most neglected aspects of the study of twelfth-century French
literature. The neglect is all the more surprising, as our phenomenological
understanding of the explosion of vernacular literature in this period is still
in its infancy: Why was there suddenly such avid interest in written versions of the stuff of vernacular poetry? Why does the vernacular transmission of religious doctrine establish itself at the same time, despite orthodox
resistance, as a new vehicle for a layman's access to Scripture? These developments occur in an environment in which the notion of literacy is all but
synonymous with the social distinction of clerical orders, in which textual
production is still the exclusive province and prerogative of monastic scrip-
toria, and the great majority of secular literary "classics" are thought to
have been composed by clerics.[2] It follows that the handful of texts that
themselves claim to "translate" Scripture for the use of the layman should
have much to reveal that bears upon these larger questions, and yet these
texts have seldom been studied in their own right.[3] I am not speaking here
of the corpus of *legenda,* lives of saints and other holy figures; these had a
longer tradition of serving jointly as laymen's entertainment and religious
edification. My concern is with texts that aspire to offer a lay public the
experience of the cleric's reading, that present the reading of Scripture—
in the many ways this could be understood—in the vernacular.

A growing scholarly consensus now recognizes that vernacular texts of the late twelfth century were generally intended for delivery in performance—that is, for recital either with or without music, and with or without the text.[4] But far less recognized is the importance such delivery plays in the conception of a layman's reading, and the extent to which the clerical community exploited vernacular writing as an opportunity to appropriate the entertainment space of vernacular poetry for their own works. As I will argue here, the study of works that "translate" Scripture for the layman can reveal much that is of central importance to a poetics of vernacular writing—and is thus indispensable to a phenomenology of early vernacular literature.

The Old French poem known as the *Eructavit* is a case in point of the neglect of such early "vernacular exegesis." The poem claims to be a translation—"word for word"—of the Forty-fourth Psalm.[5] It is anything but this, in our understanding, but it does offer a very revealing picture of what such "translation" could be understood to comprise. It was written—and makes pointed reference to this fact—for Marie de Champagne, daughter of Eleanor of Aquitaine, celebrated patroness of courtly vernacular literature, and sometime presider over one of the "courts of love." Her tastes, to quote John Benton, were "avant-garde," and her preferences, if we are to believe Chrétien de Troyes and Andreas Capellanus, decidedly licentious from an orthodox churchman's point of view: she openly championed adulterous love over the marriage bond.[6] And yet the poet of the *Eructavit* can praise her for avid and reliable interest in his religious instruction, and offers her in return (he does not say, "at her request") a poem whose subject is the most exalted image of marital love and fidelity: the heavenly *epithalamium,* or wedding song for Christ and his Bride, Holy Church. If there is truth to the argument that attributes the poem to Adam de Perseigne, Cistercian abbot and preferred spiritual counselor of more than one noble lady, then Marie's interest would appear to be more than mere invention. As is well known, on her deathbed the *dame* of French vernacular literature called Adam to her side.[7] But whether or not Adam wrote the *Eructavit,* its author is anything but an inept or irate churchman trying to call Marie to order. His poem displays a sensitive and adept understanding of the social role and poetic potential of secular literary entertainment, and is a masterful example of the recasting of exegesis as vernacular poetic performance.

The author of the *Eructavit* presents himself as the personal spiritual director of "ma dame de Champaigne," her "true friend" who "taught her all she knows."[8] That his *dame* is none other than the countess Marie emerges in the epilogue, where she is apostrophized as "la jantis suer le roi de France" [the noble sister of the king of France (line 2079)].[9] The lady has proven always eager to hear his instruction, and on the basis of this receptiveness and familiarity, he presents his "chançon de chambre" [bedroom song (line 2075)]. This title he attributes to David,[10] but it is intended just as much as a title to the poet's own work, for the entire poem is constructed so as to make its instruction to Marie an avatar, a sort of earthly reperformance, of David's, the psalmist's, performance at the wedding of the King and Queen of Heaven. The heavenly performance and the courtly performance are set up as equivalent in mode and audience. Accordingly the author can insert his liturgical text and its exegesis into the court literary context, not only as a change of venue, but as an assimilation of poetic modes. The translation of Scripture is here not primarily a verbal exercise, but rather a form of social and cultural adaptation.

The parallel between David's singing and the poet's instruction is used to position the poem from the outset:

Une chançon que David fist
Que nostre sire en cuer li mist
Dirai ma dame de Champaigne,
Celi cui Damedés ansaigne
Et espire de toz ses biens. (lines 1–4)

[A song that David composed, / that our Lord placed in his heart, / I will recite to my Lady of Champagne, / she whom God teaches, / and inspires in all her virtues.]

The announcement of the poet's project cites David's direct inspiration from God and places the poet in direct "descendance" from David. David's communication, a song, is reiterated by her spiritual director to the "sister of the King," a formulation that is doubtless chosen—as we shall see—to enhance the parallel with the sister, bride and queen of the heavenly King.[11] But the relationship is not a simple parallel. David's audience is not named in the opening lines. Instead, God's communication has two audiences: David's "heart" and the Lady of Champagne. David's *chançon* instructs the Lady via the intermediary of the poet's *dire,* and yet the lines also imply that God instructs the Lady as directly as David received his song.[12] God's communication to David is conflated with the poet's communication to his (female) audience. This chain of privileged communication, in which the listening woman takes a doubled position as audience of both a divinely and a humanly communicated message, is at the center of a carefully woven strategy by which the author accomplishes his translation, a recasting of the experience of Scripture for a courtly, lay audience. After examining this strategy in some detail, I will return to Marie's role and her pivotal position.

The poet twice makes explicit statements on his activity as translator. The first emphasizes his mediation between the audience's previous experience of the psalm text, as part of the Christmas liturgy, and a vernacular version that places it entirely at their disposal:

> Le jor de Nöel au matin
> Nos dist sainte eglise an latin
> Le saume que je vos comanz;
> Metre le vos vuel en romanz,
> S'i porroiz prandre que que soit
> Se folie ne vos deçoit. (lines 15–20)

[On Christmas Day in the morning, / holy Church recites in Latin / the psalm that I begin for you; / I will translate it for you into *romanz,* / so that you may take whatever is there, / unless imprudence deceive you.]

The second statement places the poet again in poetic descendance from David, and claims—calling all good clerics to witness—to add nothing to David's song, save what the art of rhyme requires:

> Quant David ot ceste novele
> Sa harpe prant et sa vïele
> Si comance sa chançonete
> Qui mout est bele et sainte et nete.
> De latin l'a en romanz traite
> Au miauz qu'il puet cil qui l'afaite.
> Oiant toz bons clers dist il bien
> Qu'il n'i a antrepris de rien
> Fors la androit ou rime faut:
> S'i met le mot qui autant vaut. (lines 135–144)

[When David hears this news / he takes his harp and his fiddle, / and begins his tune, / which is pretty, holy and pure. / From Latin to *romanz* he has translated it / as well as he can, the one who prepares it. / And before all good clerics he attests / that he has not altered a thing, / except where the rhyme requires / a different word with the same meaning.]

These statements reveal much about the poet's understanding of his mediating position, but they are of little value, at least for modern ears, as a description of his work. The *Eructavit* is not David's song, but rather the explication of each line of the psalm as embedded within a continuous narrative of which David is the poet-protagonist. David is cast as a *jongleur* who sets out to sing at the wedding of the King and Queen of Heaven. The doorman/gatekeeper will initially not allow him—or any other "man of the flesh" ("hon charnés," line 223)—to enter, but David surprisingly prevails and the gates open to allow him a miraculous vision of heaven. He then proceeds to perform his song, which divides the Latin text into twelve segments for the Bridegroom and nine for the Bride.[13] This presentation makes up the actual exegesis of the psalm and the body of the poem. Moreover, the one thing the poet does not do is translate directly the Latin text of Psalm 44 into Old French: In the manuscripts, the lines of the biblical text are included in Latin at the point where each is explicated or inspires a narrative moment. Where these are "translated," this most often occurs only as a loose paraphrase that is indistinguishable from the rest of the author's exposition. Within the experience of the Old French text, then, the letter is often indistinguishable from the gloss, and the audience cannot so much as identify what is translated and what is not. The poet's attitude of exaggerated scruple is not merely disingenuous, however: it serves as a signpost to the audience that the idea of translation is indeed at stake here; the content of this idea, how he fulfills his claim, is revealed only by the poem itself.[14]

The author's public apology, directed to the ears of "all good clerics" in the passage cited above (lines 135–44) is a rhetorical gesture, and does not apostrophize his audience as churchmen. It rather places these latter outside the performance: the point of this rhetoric is complicity with a lay audience. By pretending to defer to criteria that he obviously flouts, the author delivers the message that "this is not Scripture as it is associated, in the lay mind, with the judgment of 'good clerics.'" The speaker defines the nature of his communication with an audience-in-the-text by highlighting what that communication is not. By the same token, this audience implicitly comprises the lay public generally, and not Marie alone.

An implicit dimension of public performance is characteristic of the text as a whole, but it is also enhanced through the device of narrative exposition. The author's narrative frame brings two aspects to the fore that are key to the construction of the work and its poetics, which I wish to examine in detail here: First, through the staging of David's performance within the poem, his song functions as a play-within-the-play, and forces the recognition that what happens in it is also happening here, now, in the performance as received. Second, the device of David's vision, which alone gives the poem its narrative character, associates the delivery of his "song" with visionary experience; the same aspiration thereby accrues to the author's song as the reduplication of David's performance.

The reduplication of performance will have presented itself almost inescapably to the contemporary audience: From the outset, the poem has two (human) authors, David and the authorial voice of the text, Marie's instructor; and—from the point David is actually introduced as a character—two performers, David and the singer/*jongleur* whom the audience actually saw and heard. There are three audiences: the King and Queen of Heaven, Marie, and the present audience. There are, in fact, four different levels of communication in play: God's communication to David, which first inspired his song; David's communication to the King and Queen of Heaven; the instructor/poet's communication to Marie; and the performer's communication with a wider lay audience.

The four levels of communication are united not only in content, but also in mode, and their interrelationship is worth examining in detail. The author refers to each with some variation of the formula *oïr et veoir,* see and hear, look and listen. This verbal pair has special significance *a priori* for the poet's subject, as one of the best-known verses of the Forty-fourth Psalm is the eleventh, understood to signal the psalmist's address to the Bride, or Church, with the words *Audi filia et vide et inclina aurem tuam* [Listen, daughter, and see, and bend your ear]. When the verbal pair first occurs in the poem, then—in connection with David's request to perform at the wedding (and address the *filia*)—it can be taken as an echo of the later verse. The heavenly gatekeeper seems to mock David's singing by referring to it as vain hue and cry that "no one will hear or see":

> Li rois se desduit et repose;
> Ne seroit pas sëure chose
> A ton hues öir ne veoir. (lines 220–22)

> [The King is taking his pleasure at rest; / there would be little chance indeed / that he see or hear your hue and cry.][15]

I will examine David's dispute with the gatekeeper in more detail below. For the moment, it should be noted that the debate focuses immediately on the mode of delivery, with David stridently defending himself and his art:

> Juglerre sui, sages et duiz;
> Se le roi plaisoit mes desduiz
> Ce sai je bien que les sodees
> Me seroient mout granz donees. (lines 235–38)

> [I am a *jongleur,* skilled and adept; / if my entertainment pleases the King / I know well that / there will be plenty of coins coming my way.]

David emphatically identifies himself as an oral performer, that is, as the double of the performer who is delivering the poet's text. Somewhat later, after the gates of heaven open and David is granted his vision of the wedding, the poet uses the verbs *veoir* and *escouter* to designate David's receptive experience:"Et David les voit et escoute; / Mout par i avoit bele rote" [And David sees them (the blessed) and listens; it was truly a beautiful company (lines 331–2)]. The surrounding description seeks to relate the *joie de paradis;* we may assume it includes music, for, as the poet indicates, David responds "by doing as others do" (line 355) when he "makes joy" by taking up his vielle and singing.[16] Thus David receives the knowledge that he will relate as the instructive content, or exegesis, of the psalm in a manner analogous to his own performance. Later, as if to reassert the authority of this instruction within the address to the *filia,* or Bride, the poet recapitulates the account of David's visionary reception, with emphasis on both sides of an audio-visual communicative equation: "Bien l'aparçut et bien le vit / Et bien li fut mostré et dit" [Well he perceived it, and well he saw / And well he was shown and told (1695–96)]. The staging of God's communication to David and David's to the King and Queen are thus comprised in one mode—and overlap in the same way as do God's communication to David, and God's and the poet's to the "Lady" in the poem's opening lines.

The overlapping between these different levels of communication obscures any temporal distance between them. The point at which David "learns" his song is in fact ambiguous. In lines 135–38 he would seem to know it before setting out for the wedding; its content, on the other hand, is largely determined by his visionary experience. In a similar and more consistently applied strategy, when David reaches the exposition of the *audi filia et vide,* the psalm's eleventh verse, his words to the *filia,* or the Bride, are indistinguishable from the poet's, or instructor's, address to Marie. Passages such as the following, in which David promises the Queen her eternal reward, play intently on this identification:

Rëine estes de riche cort,
Veez la joie qui vos sort!
. . .
Ceste chançon que ge vos chant,
Par quoi je vos guarnis avant
Ainsi con Dex le me consoile,
Vos dirai je pres de l'oroile
Quant ceste joie iert avenue
Que j'ai en vision vëue. (lines 1951–60)

[You are the queen of a rich court, / see the joy that awaits you! . . . / This song that I sing to you / (with which I prepare you in advance, / as God advises me to do) / I will whisper in your ear / when this joy has come to pass / that I saw in a vision.]

It is easy, when reading the poem, to miss the conflation of the different
levels of communication that occurs here, even while one retains the overall impression that such has occurred. The Bride is part of David's vision,
he sings to her as the Queen of Heaven; there is no need, then, for him to
relate its contents to her now, or in the future. The intimate communication that is evoked has no place in the dramatic representation of David's
performance; it can emerge only as a reflex of the communication to his
"daughter," as he properly addresses the Church,[17] or, on the level of the
historically staged performance, as the communication between Marie and
her *verais amis,* the personal spiritual director. The entire nine-line sequence in which the psalmist addresses the *filia* is addressed in the vernacular adaptation to the entire Church, within a poem to Marie. David
recounts the contents of his vision to *this* audience, even as he "whispers
into the ear" of the Bride. By analogy, the intimate communication,
whether between David and the Bride or poet and Marie, is always simultaneously directed to a larger audience. As the poet says to his *dame* within
the elaboration of the eleventh verse, the *audi filia et vide:*

> Por ce que doivent bien tuit savoir
> Cil qui tandent a Deu avoir
> Que chascune ame baptisiee
> Est a son criator loiee;
> Par la batesme et par la foi
> Est ele esposee le roi,
> Se doit öir que dist Daviz,
> Ses anseignemanz et ses diz.
> Ce qu'il dist et ansaigne a l'une
> Doit a son oés oïr chascune. (lines 1375–84)

[Because all those must know well / who strive to reach God, / that every bap-
tized soul is promised to its creator; / by baptism and faith it is wedded to the
King, / and should hear what David says, / his teaching and his words. / What
he tells and teaches to the one, / everyone should hear for his own good.]

The *audi filia et vide* of the psalm, then, applies to the Bride, Marie, and the
wider audience, but it is also identified with the *jongleur's* art of performance, and with David's reception of his vision.

   The verbs *oïr, conter,* and *dire* abound in the narratorial address of the
poem; use of verbs for vision occur far less frequently, but with special
force. The central locus for their combination must be the exegesis of the
eleventh verse. David does indeed call repeatedly on the *filia* to see and to
hear at this juncture, but he does not initially pair the two verbs. "File . . .
escoute" [Daughter . . . hear (line 1387)], he begins, and later, "Vien avant,

file, oevre les yauz" [Come forward, daughter, open your eyes (line 1413)].
In between, the verbs recur as well, but never paired and not in the imperative. The poet would sooner avoid the obvious opportunity to emphasize them. The reason for this emerges at the point when he finally
paraphrases the verse. The verbs occur there in the perfect tense:

> File, or as öi et vëu;
> Trop auras le cuer decëu
> Se tu n'i mez si t'antandue
> Que ta biautez li soit randue.
> Se li biaus rois au cuer te toche,
> Lieve sus, file, si t'aproche. (lines 1423–7)

[Daughter, now that you have heard and seen, / your heart will be much deceived / if you do not make it your sole intention / that your beauty be rendered unto him. / If the beautiful King touches your heart, / rise, daughter,
and approach.]

The poet reserves his paraphrase of the *audi filia et vide* to express the overall effect of the entire address to the Bride: Now that she has seen and
heard of the Bridegroom and all he offers, she is to surrender her beauty
to him. The seduction is here seen as accomplished, but it refers, in that
case, not only to the exposition immediately preceding (line 1387 ff.)—
which in fact delivers little of its content—but also to the entire poem.
This idea follows again from the allegorical understanding of the psalm:
David properly addresses no instruction to the King, the Bridegroom; and
his (or the poet's) elaboration of the "King's verses" is praise of the King
meant for the ears and eyes of the Bride, Marie, and the wider audience.
The content of the section is something of a haphazardly organized introduction to Church dogma by way of description of the Bridegroom. In
keeping with this, the poet leaves less than a quarter of the address to
David's voice, while David actually speaks nearly half the address to the
Bride.[18] When the verses to the King have been concluded and attention
turns explicitly to the Bride, what the poet evokes is the anticipated effect
on her as audience of the entire presentation.

The passage devoted to the *audi filia et vide* thus closes a parenthesis
opened with the gatekeeper's designation of David's "audiovisual" art by
evoking the effect of David's art and the present performance within the
narrative frame. Within the experience of the poem in performance, this is
an obvious point: The performance of instruction for the *filia* is one and the
same as that of the *jongleur* the audience sees and hears before them. All levels of communication are comprised in one mode, for which the exemplar
is the mode the psalm announces specifically for its female addressee. This

same mode is the subject of David's dispute with the heavenly gatekeeper, and the dispute and its resolution serve to put forward the *jongleur's* art as the medium of an alternative apprehension of truth.

David's exchange with the gatekeeper emerges from the author's carefully constructed analogy between liturgical and courtly poetic performance, and needs to be placed in this context to be fully understood. The poet introduces his subject for the laywoman and lay audience by means of this analogy. He appeals to their experience of a royal wedding in the secular world, specifically to the summons of the king for all to attend (line 21 ff.). The list of those who respond evokes vernacular literary culture generally, and includes a pointed allusion to one of its most notable representatives:

> Jugleor font sonez noviaus,
> Chançons et notes et fabliaus,
> Que droiz est que chascuns s'atort
> Contre *la joie de la cort.* (lines 31–34, italics mine)

> [The *jongleurs* spread the news, / songs and melodies and tales, / that everyone should make haste / to attend the court celebration.]

At the court of Champagne where Chrétien de Troyes composed for the same patroness, these lines could hardly fail to remind the audience of the grand concluding *avanture* of his *Erec et Enide* (ca. 1170), in which the name of the exploit, *joie de la cort,* comes to comprise all that the hero, Erec, seeks and must deliver. There, and at the earlier wedding of the two protagonists of his romance, Chrétien himself gave two memorable accounts of the variety of entertainers and their arts present at great court feasts.[19] The echo in the *Eructavit* corresponds perfectly to the poet's attempt to embed his vernacular exegesis in the court literary milieu.[20] This includes the use of the terms of courtly love lyric (*douce amie, fin amors*) for the love of Bridegroom and Bride, and possibly the use of the word *avanture* for the story of Daniel and the lions.[21] The appropriation of the terms of the love lyric, addressed to Marie and her "court of love," conflates sacred and secular, and the poet uses his reference to Chrétien's romance to similar effect. The *joie de la cort* is evoked here in a clear parallel to the *joie de paradis* some thirty lines later. The analogy is used to support an understanding of God's prophets as the *jongleurs* of the heavenly wedding; their *douz chanz,* duly repeated by Holy Church, call all humankind to the incipient *joie de paradis,* thus performing the same function as the *jugleor* for the *joie de la cort.* David, who will later identify himself as a *jugleor,* is here introduced as "Un des prophetes" [One of the prophets (line 80)].[22] As we saw earlier, the poet reminded his audience of the liturgical context of David's "song" in the opening lines. The sum total of this positioning is to place the *Eructavit* and its performance in dual analogy to the catalogue of secular poetic entertainment on the one hand, and to the liturgy on the other. The poet/performer brings the liturgy into the court literary context—and David himself, as prophet and *jongleur,* stands for, or authorizes, the assimilation of poetic modes. The wedding and coronation recounted in the course of the *Eructavit* become a heavenly parallel to Chrétien's romance, but also an appropriation of its voice, the voice of vernacular poetry, to a more exalted end. This voice, assimilated to his identity as prophet, David then brings to the gates of heaven, begging admission.

David sets out with high hopes of performing at the wedding, having also heard that through his descendant, Mary, God will be born of a woman.[23] His humility and habit of a "true penitent," proof of "great devotion" (lines 149–59), merit him the aid of an angel, who brings him to the gates of heaven. When he finds the gates securely closed—with the sword of the angel who drove Adam and Eve from Paradise—not daring to knock or call, he strikes up a song with his vielle ("Por ce qu'il n'osa apeler / Si comança a vïeler" [lines 201–202]). The song corresponds to the elaboration of the psalm's first verse, *Eructavit cor meum.* There ensues his dispute with the doorman. The second verse of the psalm, *Lingua mea calamus scribae, velociter scribentis,* is integrated into this debate as a denial of writing and corresponding insistence on the privilege of performance. The doorman suggests David write down his song:

> Mais la chançon que tu viaus dire
> Escri la en chartre ou en cire,
> Et je ferai bien tant por toi
> Que je la mosterrai le roi. (lines 225–8)

[But this song you want to sing, / write it on parchment or in wax, / and I will do this for you: / I will show it to the King.]

This suggestion is met with David's indignant response:

> Merci, sire, ce dist Daviz,
> Se je laianz antrez estoie
> Avuec mes moz vïeleroie.
> Juglerre sui, sages et duiz;
> Se le roi plaisoit mes desduiz
> Ce sai je bien que les sodees
> Me seroient mout granz donees.
> Ne dites pas que je l'escrive;
> La langue cui li cuers avive

L'escrivra sanz doiz et sanz mains
Assez miauz que nus escrivains. (lines 232–42)

[Thanks, sire, says David, / if I could get inside there / I would accompany
my words with the fiddle. / I am a *jongleur,* skilled and adept. / If my entertainment pleases the King, / I know well that / there will be plenty of coins
coming my way. / Don't tell me to write it down; / the tongue that the
heart quickens, / will write it without fingers and without hands, / much
better than any scribe.]

Writing has no place in the art of performance. The spoken word delivered in physical presence allows a more immediate apprehension of
truth—writes faster than any writer, to use the formula of the biblical text.
The "tongue" that the heart quickens, is, in this poem, a mode—the spoken word, and a language: the vernacular. This speech is related as well to
the communication through which David, in the opening lines, is seen to
receive the instruction from God that the poet writes down.[24] The same
language or voice from the heart is to move the Bride to surrender herself
to the Bridegroom.[25] The poet uses the occasion of the verse *Diffusa est
gratia in labiis tuis* [Grace pours forth from your lips (Ps. 44:3)], 150 lines
later—and very nearly the beginning of David's actual performance—to
have David sing of this voice, beginning: "La vostre bele sainte boche /
Don la voiz ist qui les cuers toche" [Your beautiful, sacred mouth, from
which comes the voice that touches hearts (lines 375–76)]. The continuation of the passage makes clear that the Word of John 1:1–3 is rendered in
this poem as "voice."[26] David's prophetic apprehension of the Word is
transferred to the *jongleur*'s art, that is, the poet appropriates the entertainment mode of courtly vernacular literature as a site of liturgical performance, accomplishing a sacralization of the vernacular performance space.

But it is the outcome of David's dispute that most persuasively portrays the
privilege of his audiovisual performance. The doorman repeats at length that
no "man born of woman" (line 243; previously, "no man of flesh," line 223)
can ever enter the gates or see what lies beyond them until the sins of his ancestors are atoned for and God comes to earth in the Incarnation. David refuses to despair, and begins to implore the doorman to open the door just a
bit (*antrueve* [line 284]), so that he may see how God's son will be born of the
"holy virgin lady who will be my descendant" (lines 288–89). He then rests
his case in a humble attitude of prayer. At this point, the doorman's catechism
is tossed to the winds, and with a great thunderclap God opens the door. This
reversal enables David's performance, enables the composition of the psalm
and the poem. The device of David's vision and the narrative context it provides can be seen as the poet's primary, if not sole, invention in the *Eructavit.*

How does it come about? David insists on two things: the privilege of presence, the living voice, as necessary to the adequate delivery of his message, and
the agency of Mary in the Incarnation. If his art precludes the resort to writing, it is his affinity, in the literal sense, with Mary that finally forces the gates
of heaven and allows him to perform. This woman will bear a man who
opens the gates of heaven for all, at least inasmuch as the Word will be revealed in its full meaning. But the same woman is the Bride and the *filia*, as
audience in turn indistinguishable from the other Marie, countess of Champagne. The poem conflates liturgy and secular poetry, prophets and *jongleurs*,
the Bride and Marie, the Church and the court audience, and makes them all
simultaneously present elements of one privileged communication: David's
audiovisual, visionary apprehension of the *joie de paradis*.

David's rejection of writing, his mix of humility before God and pride
of position before the dismissive gatekeeper (is he a "good cleric"?), and
his appeal to the position of Mary in the Incarnation all have a part in the
recasting of a prophet's aural and visual experience of the divine as the experience of the layman before the audiovisual performance. David as the
humble *jongleur* stands in for a layman's alternative performance of Scripture, and thus for his own audience. As Horst Wenzel has argued, the distinct coupling of verbs of seeing and hearing is not culturally "neutral" in
this period, but rather can be thought of as particularly associated with
nonliterate, layman's education, and thus constitutive for lay identity.[27] The
indignation and pride in David's voice, the jibe in the mouth of the
"cleric" become all the more tangible from this perspective. When used to
designate the reception of poetic texts, according to Wenzel, the verbal pair
signals an insistence on presence, on communication occurring through
immediate and reciprocal apprehension.[28] Where the *Eructavit* poet applies
the verbs of seeing and hearing to his own performance they support a
claim to deliver David's visionary experience to the poem's audience, both
now, momentarily, and in the future (at the Last Judgment), eternally. One
instance occurs when the poet calls upon his audience to observe how the
King is carried by the prophets and the evangelists:

Or antandons et si veons
Por nos ames reconforter
Comant li rois se feit porter: (lines 1078–80)

[Now let's listen and we'll see, / for the comfort of our souls, / how the
King has himself carried:]

The audience is invited to entertain the illusion of presence at the wedding, seeing and hearing what David did. What they "see" in this case is an

allegorical image for the revelation of the meaning of Scripture. Ultimately, the poem seeks to guarantee its audience's inclusion among the
blessed, and thus promises they will encounter face-to-face what David
was granted as prophetic vision: "Si verrons la procession / Que David vit
en vision" (lines 1743–4). This is the same promise David "whispered in
the ear" of the Bride in the passage quoted earlier, here made by the poet
to the audience. In the experience of performance, all levels of communication merge and occur simultaneously.[29] The poet intently manipulates
this fact, and uses it to construct an implicit argument for his mode of
translation as one that offers a privileged, immediate apprehension of the
Word that is demonstrated, as it were, by David's vision. David's words to
the Bride, "Now you have seen and heard," confirm his layman's victory
over the clerical interdiction. Where, according to the doorman, none
would see or hear his song, no man of flesh might accede into the divine
presence, this presence has now been seen and heard by all—through
David's vision and the song that recommunicates his experience. Between
David as humble, "illiterate" layman, and David as God's anointed, the poet
accomplishes a fusion of the "laical" and the liturgical significance of the
audiovisual.[30]

The figure of Marie de Champagne is as much a necessary part of this
construction as she is the real patroness and intended audience of the
poem. There is no reason to doubt that the poem was actually written for
Marie; it may even have been commissioned by her, but even if this is the
case, it must be recognized that she is at best both a real and a representative audience, both a historical recipient of the text and part of the text itself, of the communication it represents and exploits. At the court of
Champagne, Marie will have presided over the performance of the poem
for a wider audience, and we have seen that the poem amply anticipates
this function. The manuscript transmission shows that the *Eructavit* spread
through several regions of France in the thirteenth century if not before.
None of the extant manuscripts come from Champagne, and none can be
dated to the twelfth century.[31] A recently edited Provençal version attests
to translation into another vernacular.[32] The staging of the poem as personal instruction to Marie from her spiritual advisor did not exclude other
audiences from avid interest in the text. The opposite is more likely the
case: *Ma dame de Champagne* stands in this text for rising vernacular literary self-awareness in the same way that the Bride stands for the entire
Church; Marie's privileged reception of the poet's message performs a role
for the lay public that is both analogous to and dependent upon the experience of the Bride—and the individual woman, Mary—as it applies to all
humanity. Marie is the Bride of the vernacular *Eructavit*. Her role displays
a coalescence between a tropological understanding of Scripture—its ap-

plication to our moral lives—and its grounding in a historical, or literal, meaning. She returns the allegorical interpretation of the Bride as Church to "the historical stage . . . where (the Bride's) life is lived, so to speak, by all of us in the world of human history, in the very specificity and reality of the . . . vernacular community."[33] That the process of vernacularization borrows from and exploits exegetical habits of thought, while nonetheless applying them to an independent mode of representation, is characteristic of an emerging vernacular literary consciousness.

The pivotal position of the woman implicit in the opening lines of the *Eructavit* as the audience of several different communications simultaneously—David's, the poet's, and God's—is a keystone of the construction of the poem as vernacular Scripture. This woman-as-audience is the fulcrum of a sacralization of the audiovisual performance space, and the author is well aware of the value of her role to his project.

The other texts mentioned at the outset of this essay offer another parallel to the dual function of the woman audience as both historical recipient of the text and part of its rhetorical design. Two of them name historically known women as patronesses and recipients.[34] Another, the Le Mans commentary on the Song of Songs, is thought to have been written for Count Baldwin II of Guines on the basis of the testimony of Lambert of Ardres in his *Historia Comitum Ghisnensium*. Count Baldwin's remarkable literary accomplishments, according to Lambert, were due entirely to listening to others recite texts for him; he commissioned an impressive library of texts translated into the vernacular for this purpose.[35] The commentary on the Song of Songs was thus clearly intended for oral delivery, doubtless to an audience of "seignors"—who are once addressed in the poem.[36] But the text also twice speaks of a *dame* for whom the poet composes,[37] and seems to accomplish thereby a fusion of secular love poetry with exegesis similar to that attempted in the *Eructavit*. This unnamed lady has often been taken as evidence against the otherwise convincing identification of the poem with the one mentioned by Lambert. But her presence in the text may well affirm rather than deny this identification: She is part of the author's packaging of exegesis for the court literary environment, and presides over the poem's composition and performance in the same way as does Marie in the *Eructavit*.[38] Four of these five early vernacular adaptations of Scripture, then, cite a woman as their addressee, in a range that extends from the historical individual to a poetic fiction and exploits a collusion between the two.

Further investigation of connections and affinities with other texts would readily affirm that the poet of the *Eructavit* does not stand at all alone, but rather squarely in the middle of a developing understanding of the vernacular performance space as the receptacle of a layman's audiovisual encounter with the Word.[39] He manipulates the idea of translation to offer a layman's alternative to the lettered cleric's *lectio,* and in order to do so builds on an idea of immediate, "sensory" access to the Word—a privilege that arises from the conflation of vernacular poetic performance with God's call to the Bride. This idea is not the object of an expository prologue or of other explicitly formulated remarks. True to the nature of the text in performance, the poet manipulates signal terms, embeds the rhetorical vehicles of the argument in the text itself, so that the model at once relies on certain assumed understandings and is demonstrated to the audience throughout the text as a communicative event. In so doing, the poet offers an adept presentation of the power and social significance of the performed text, as well as a snapshot of vernacular literary self-awareness in later twelfth-century France.

Notes

1. Beginning with the earliest, these are: *Les proverbes de Salemon,* by Samson de Nanteuil, ca. 1150, written for Aeliz de Condet, a noblewoman of Lincolnshire; *Eructavit,* attributed to Adam de Perseigne, ca. 1180, and a commentary on Genesis, by Evrat, ca. 1198, both written for Marie, countess of Champagne; a commentary on the Song of Songs attributed to Landri of Waben and possibly written for Count Baldwin II of Guines, ca. 1200; and *La delivrance du peuple d'Israël,* a paraphrase of the Book of Exodus, ca. 1200. All five are written in verse. For an overview, see the article "Bible française" in *Dictionnaire des lettres françaises: Le Moyen Age,* eds. Geneviève Hasenohr and Michel Zink (Paris, Fayard, 1992), pp. 180–81; J. R. Smeets, "Les traductions, adaptations et paraphrases de la Bible en vers," *Grundriss der romanischen Literaturen des Mittelalters* (hereafter *GRLMA*) 6.1, pp. 48–53; and Hans Robert Jauss, "Entstehung und Strukturwandel der allegorischen Dichtung," *GRLMA* 6.1, pp. 152–55; also *GRLMA* 6.2, nos. 1824, 3116, 4052, 4116.
2. This view has recently been challenged by Evelyn Birge Vitz in *Orality and Performance in Early French Romance* (Cambridge: D. S. Brewer, 1999). Vitz argues that Chrétien de Troyes, for example, was not a cleric, but a minstrel. More important for my argument is the emphasis she rightly places on the new vernacular literature as the product of a collaboration between clerics and minstrels or *jongleurs.* See esp. pp. 62–73.
3. There is as yet no edition of Evrat's commentary of Genesis. Tony Hunt, "The O. F. Commentary on the *Song of Songs* in MS Le Mans 173," *Zeitschrift für romanische Philologie* 96 (1980):267–97, is the only study exclusively devoted to Landri of Waben's commentary that is known to me, and its primary objective is to offer corrections sufficient to rescue some value from the highly unreliable sole edition, *The Song of Songs: A Twelfth-Century Version,* ed. Cedric E. Pickford (London: Oxford University Press, 1974). There is a valuable and extensive analysis of the poem in Friedrich

Ohly, *Hohelied-Studien* (Wiesbaden: Steiner, 1958), pp. 280–302. The *Eructavit* is available in *'Eructavit': An Old French Metrical Paraphrase of Psalm XLIV,* ed. T. Atkinson Jenkins (Dresden: Gesellschaft für romanische Literatur, 1909), but study of the text beyond the editor's own introduction is limited to Maria Sampoli Simonelli, "Sulla parafrasi francese antica del Salmo *Eructavit,* Adamo di Perseigne, Chrétien de Troyes e Dante," *Cultura neolatina* 24 (1964):5–38; and George F. McKibben, *The Eructavit, An Old French Poem: The Author's Environment, his Argument and Materials* (Baltimore: F. H. Furst, 1907). Recently, a Provençal version of the text has also been edited by Walter Meliga, *L' 'Eructavit' antico-francese secondo il ms. Paris BN fr. 1747,* Studi filologici 6 (Alessandria: Ed. dell'Orso, 1992). The *Delivrance du peuple d'Israël* and Samson de Nanteuil's *Proverbes* have found similarly limited attention. For more extensive bibliography, see the references in n. 1, above.

4. Vitz's recent book (see n. 2, above), while controversial and far from representing a consensus position, is indicative of a trend in this direction, following largely from the work of Paul Zumthor. See esp. *La lettre et la voix: De la "littérature" médiévale* (Paris: Seuil, 1987). For a provocative and wide-ranging study of the roles of the aural and visual, voice and text, in medieval culture, see Horst Wenzel, *Hören und Sehen, Schrift und Bild: Kultur und Gedächtnis im Mittelalter* (Munich: Beck, 1995).

5. See the author's statement, discussed below, p. 86.

6. John Benton, "The Court of Champagne as a Literary Center," *Speculum* 36 (1961): 587. Chrétien de Troyes attributes both *matiere et san* of his Lancelot romance, which highlights adulterous love, to Marie (*Le Chevalier de la Charrette [Lancelot],* eds. Alfred Foulet and Karl D. Uitti [Paris: Bordas, 1989], lines 26–27); Andreas Capellanus' *De amore,* which, whether ironically or not, presents itself as a handbook for adulterous, "courtly" love, treats Marie as the leading authority on the subject (*Andreae Capellani Regii Francorum De amore libri tres,* ed. E. Trojel [Copenhagen: Gad, 1892], repr. 1972).

7. T. Atkinson Jenkins, the editor of the text, attributes it to Adam de Perseigne. Benton finds the evidence insubstantial (Benton, "The Court of Champagne," 582–84); Simonelli reviewed and rebutted his objections (see n. 3, above); Jung concurred in the judgment that the poem can be attributed to Adam "with a very small margin of uncertainty" (Marc-René Jung, *Études sur le poème allégorique en France au moyen âge,* Romanica Helvetica 82 [Bern: Francke, 1971], n. 6). The question of Adam's authorship does not concern my argument directly, and I thus refer to the author anonymously. For Jenkins' argument and further background on Adam and Marie, see his introduction, pp. vii–xx.

8. "Li bons maistre don vos avez / Retenu quanque vos savez, / Si comme il est verais amis" [The good teacher from whom you have learned all you know, as he is a true friend (lines 2097–9)]. For the phrase "my lady of Champagne," see below, p.85. Further references to the text are parenthetical. All translations are my own.

9. Philip Augustus, who ascended the throne in 1180, was Marie's half-brother, son of her father, Louis VII of France.

10. As noted by the editor, T. Atkinson Jenkins, the Vulgate uses the title *canticum pro dilecto* [song for the beloved], and this apparently allows the author to attribute the phrase *chanson de chambre* to David while clearly translating Augustine's term, *epithalamium* (Jenkins, p. xix). The *thalamus* is a bedchamber; by extension, a wedding bed.

11. The identification of Mary as sister and bride of Christ comes from the tradition of the Song of Songs, in which the *sponsa* [bride] is repeatedly also called *soror* [sister].

12. It is worth noting that the verb *espirer*, which here designates God's instruction of Marie, corresponds in the text to inspiration through the Holy Spirit. In lines 1901–1902 it applies to David receiving his verse from God; see also lines 80–82. In the epilogue it applies once again to Marie (and all Christians).

13. These divisions do not entirely correspond to the verse divisions of the Gallican Psalter, nor to the poet's own statement that David sings nine verses each for King and Queen (line 363). The text does not reveal exactly how the poet sees the division into nine verses for the King.

14. McKibben started in his study, *The Eructavit*, from the assumption that the poem was a translation into Old French of a Latin commentary on the psalm, but came to the conclusion after reviewing the possible sources that "the poet's claim to be a mere translator into verse is a matter of literary convention" (p. 27).

15. The phrase "a ton hues" is ambiguous here: It could be taken as "to your good," with *hues* understood as *ues/oes* 'use, benefit.' The spellings *oés* and *hués* both occur elsewhere in the text in this sense (lines 1384, 1663). In this context, though, it seems to me that the reading of "hue and cry" or *huëiz* (Tobler/Lommatzsch gives "Geschrei, Kriegslärm") is equally plausible. The large number of variants in the manuscripts may indicate that this pun confused the copyists.

16. "David mëismes se semont / De chanter et feire joie; / Mout desirre que li rois l'oie. / La vïele afaite et ajance" [David himself is moved / to sing and celebrate; / he desires greatly that the King hear him. / He takes up his fiddle and positions it (lines 356–59)].

17. As the narrator explains of the eleventh verse: "David, qui sainte eglise apele / Sa fille comme une pucele / Qui de son paranté fu nee" [David, who calls Holy Church / his daughter, as he would a young girl / born of his line (lines 1343–45)].

18. I take the section devoted to the King as lines 365–1308, and that devoted to the Queen as lines 1309–2070. David speaks 22 percent of the former, and 40 percent of the latter.

19. In both cases the revelry of the entertainers is identified with the concept of *joie*, or explicitly, the *joie de la cort*. The second emphasizes only the variety of musical instruments played, while the description of the wedding

festivities includes all manner of entertainers. See *Erec et Enide,* ed. Jean-Marie Fritz, in *Chrétien de Troyes: Romans* (Paris: Livre de Poche, 1994), lines 2031–50 and 6371–79. Passages from contemporary literature that describe entertainment at court feasts are collected and discussed in Vitz, *Orality and Performance,* pp. 165–73.

20. McKibben, *The Eructavit,* drew attention to similarities between the *Eructavit* and Chrétien's work a century ago—but saw these as best reflected in *Cligès* rather than *Erec et Enide.* Simonelli, "Sulla parafrasi," attempted to demonstrate a direct dependence on *Erec et Enide* through a series of echoes in the *Eructavit;* she also saw similar echoes of the poetry of Bernard de Ventadorn (pp. 28–36, see also Jung, *Études,* pp. 230–31). One need not insist on this extreme to make the point at hand: The author of the *Eructavit* was well versed in courtly poetry, and imitates its masters intently and adeptly. An instructive example can be seen in his prologue: The ploy of praising Marie by citing an overly liberal disposition (in rewarding her poets?) as her sole flaw displays a playful attitude similar to that addressed to her in Chrétien's *Chevalier de la Charrette* (compare lines 1–14 of the *Eructavit* with *Charrette,* lines 1–23). Chrétien's prologue flatters under the pretense of shunning flattery. With the *Charrette* generally dated around 1177–1781, the question of who may echo whom is less in order than the observation that both prologues reflect familiarity with one and the same literary milieu.

21. For the relationship of Bridegroom and Bride, see lines 1264 ff. and 1439 ff. The term *avanture* occurs several times in the poem, but only once (line 981) with a meaning similar to its usage in romances.

22. I cannot find any support for Jung's judgment that the poem sets up an opposition between the court *jongleur* and David as *ioculator dei* (Jung, *Études,* pp. 230–31). There is apposition and analogy here; the effect is cumulative, not contrastive.

23. "Bien sot que de ses hoirs seroit / La virge ou Deus s'aomberroit; / De ce n'ot il nule dotance / Ainz i mist tote s'esperance, / Que puis que Deus naistroit de mere . . ." [Well he knew that among his heirs / would be the virgin, / in whom God would take human form; / of this he had no doubt / and therein placed all his hope, / that, because God would be born of a mother . . . (lines 87–91)]. As Jenkins notes, the poet took special care in his exact—but inaccurate—dating of David's vision to 714 B.C. (line 216), some three hundred years later than the standard account found in patristic sources, apparently in order to make David subsequent to Isaiah's prophecy on the *virga ex radice Iesse* (Is. 11:1–2). The *virga,* or branch, was Mary; the trunk, Jesse, was Mary's and David's common ancestor. Isaiah's prophecy could then be the "news" evoked in vv. 87 and 135 (Jenkins, *Eructavit,* pp. xxiii–xxiv).

24. See lines 1–3, and p. 85.

25. See lines 1399–1400 and 1423–8.

26. "Plaine de douçor et de grace / Qui tot le monde resolace, / Puisse si les noz cuers tochier / Que vers vos nos face aprochier. / Ce est la fontaine

et la doiz / De quoi sordra la sainte voiz / Dont sainte eglise iert replenie / Et confermee et establie" [Full of sweetness and grace / that consoles all the world, / may it touch our hearts / and make us draw nearer to you. / It is the fountain and the conduit / from which the Holy Word comes forth, / by which Holy Church was nourished, / and confirmed and established (lines 377–84)].

27. Wenzel, *Hören und Sehen,* pp. 51–56 and passim. Although Wenzel's study is based almost entirely on German sources, the point here proves highly appropriate to an Old French text. Wenzel's argumentation is comprehensive in scope, and not intended as limited to Germany.

28. Wenzel, *Hören und Sehen,* p. 53. Wenzel's phrase is "Kommunikation im Raum der wechselseitigen Wahrnehmung."

29. For Zumthor, the performer "signifies" in the same way as does an eyewitness; his voice and presence mediate the inaccessible (Zumthor, *La lettre et la voix,* p. 256).

30. The boldness of the author's gesture appears in even greater relief read against the contemporary invective of the Church condemning *jongleurs* and all manner of theatrical performers. See Carla Casagrande and Silvana Vecchio, "Clercs et *Jongleurs* dans la société médiévale (XIIe et XIIIe siècles)," *Annales ESC.* 34 (1979): 913–28.

31. Jenkins, *Eructavit,* pp. xxix–xxxi. The fourteen manuscripts listed by Jenkins represent, among them, the regions of Burgundy, Île-de-France, Picardie, central France, Artois, southern France, and England. A fifteenth manuscript, also from the thirteenth century, that preserves a good copy of the complete text and has as yet gone unnoticed in literature on the *Eructavit* is St Petersburg, Fr. f. v. XIV 9, fols. 264r–277v. The manuscript is possibly from the region around Soissons, which would place it on the northern reaches of Champagne.

32. See note 3, above.

33. Karl D. Uitti outlines in these words a similar function for female saints as represented in their vernacular *vitae* in "Women Saints, the Vernacular, and History in Early Medieval France," *Images of Sainthood in Medieval Europe,* ed. Renate Blumenfeld-Kosinski and Timea Szell (Ithaca: Cornell University Press, 1991), p. 259.

34. See note 1, above.

35. For an excellent analysis of Lambert's remarks on Count Baldwin, and their relationship to the Le Mans Song commentary, see Michael Curschmann, "Höfische Laienkultur zwischen Mündlichkeit und Schriftlichkeit. Das Zeugnis Lamberts von Ardres," in *Aufführung und Schrift in Mittelalter und Früher Neuzeit,* ed. Jan-Dirk Müller (Stuttgart: Metzler, 1996), esp. pp. 164–5. The relevant passages of Lambert's text are also printed there, pp. 167–9.

36. *The Song of Songs,* ed. Pickford, line 173.

37. Ibid. pp. xx-xxi, lines 2363–78 and 3497–3500.

38. "Eher ist diese ungenannte Dame wohl als 'Kunstfigur' zu verstehen, die dann ja sogar nach Bedarf oder Geschmack mit mehr als einer der in diesen Kreisen lebenden Damen identifiziert werden konnte" [This unnamed lady should rather be understood as an allegorical figure who could be identified as needed or desired with more than one of the ladies living in that circle (Curschmann, "Höfische Laienkultur," p. 165)].

39. I am currently preparing such a study, as part of a monograph forthcoming with Palgrave. Further observations also in Morgan Powell, *The Mirror and the Woman: Instruction for Religious Women and the Emergence of Vernacular Poetics,* diss., Princeton University 1997, pp. 55–58 and 489–91.

CHAPTER 5

THE MIRROR AND THE ROSE:
MARGUERITE PORETE'S ENCOUNTER
WITH THE *DIEU D'AMOURS*

Barbara Newman

Several years ago I proposed the new term *mystique courtoise* to categorize an array of vernacular mystical texts from the thirteenth and fourteenth centuries, especially but not solely those written by beguines.[1] The
concept of *mystique courtoise* is meant to distinguish traditional forms of
spiritual writing that drew on the lush imagery of the Song of Songs to
characterize divine love, as Christian mystics had done ever since Origen,
from a newer literary/religious mode that self-consciously inflected this
tradition with the vernacular language of *fine amour,* adapted from secular
lyrics and romances.

While the connection between courtly literature and this new mode of
mystical writing has long been recognized, most studies to date have confined themselves to the borrowing of widespread motifs, such as boundless
longing, *amor de lonh,* or love from afar, prolonged and humiliating love-
service, and certain stock characters (Frau Minne, the Christ-knight, the
soul as princess-bride). Few scholars have set out to illustrate the debts of
specific mystical writers to specific courtly texts, and generally with good
reason. In the case of lyric, the repertoire of themes, tropes, and even
rhyme schemes was so universally shared by poets within the tradition that
it would be nearly impossible to prove a mystic's literary debt to one trou-
vère or minnesinger rather than another. But with longer and more distinctive texts, such as romances, a closer reading of secular and mystical
intertextuality may be possible. In this essay I will posit a literary relationship between Marguerite Porete's *Mirouer des simples ames*[2] and its unlikely
intertext, the *Roman de la rose.*

Now the linkage of a cynical, insistently secular love allegory with the most esoteric of mystical texts may seem arbitrary, even whimsical. But it becomes much less so when we recognize that in the Middle Ages, textual communities were not yet rigorously divided along the sacred/secular divide that operates today in our classrooms. The crusading Bishop Fulk of Toulouse and the missionary theologian Ramon Llull, not to mention Dante, all began their careers as poets of *fine amour*. Manuscript miscellanies commonly included romance literature and other secular texts side by side with devotional works, and even vowed religious were keenly aware of the popular literary currents of the day. In the seventy years that separate Guillaume de Lorris's *Rose* from Marguerite's *Mirror*, a culture of *mystique courtoise* developed quite rapidly in the francophone world, with the already celebrated *Rose* among its key points of reference. To indicate the course of this development, I will begin with a brief look at two works, now little known, that Marguerite might easily have read.

It was around 1250—a generation after Guillaume's *Rose*, but before Jean de Meun's—that Gérard of Liège wrote his *Quinque incitamenta ad deum amandum ardenter*, or *Five Incitements to the Ardent Love of God*.[3] Gérard was the Cistercian abbot of Val Saint-Lambert, in the heart of beguine country, and may have composed this extraordinary treatise for an audience of beguines and their confessors as well as monks. But he plainly assumed that his readers, male or female, would be as steeped as he was in the literature of *fine amour*. The treatise is part of a diptych: Its companion tract, *Seven Useful Remedies against Illicit Love*, is a wholly predictable text teaching contempt of the world and its corollary, contempt of women.[4] In *Five Incitements*, however, Gérard takes a different tack. Following the lead of Richard of St. Victor, he shows that divine and carnal love, though opposed in morality, are exactly the same in psychology.[5] But Gérard goes further than Richard, for along with citations from Augustine, pseudo-Augustine, and Bernard, he includes a generous sprinkling of French love songs among his *auctores*. For instance, to reinforce his point that God asks nothing but our love in return for all his gifts to us, he quotes this lyric:

Quankes il fist entiere
il le fist pour mamour auoir,
et quankes ie ferai dorenavant
ie le ferai pour plaire a lui seulement
et pour samour auoir.[6]

[Whatever he has done till now / he has done to win my love, / and whatever I do henceforth / I will do to please him alone / and to win his love.]

Anticipating Marguerite, Gérard also cites the maxim that "God is love" (1 John 4:8) in order to identify the creator of the world with the *fine amour* sung by poets, and even the *dieu d'amours* so memorably portrayed by Guillaume de Lorris: "Deus enim caritas est, dicit Iohannes, idest *amours.*" [God is love, says John, that is, *amours*].[7] But if *caritas* and *amours* could have the same denotation, their connotations differed radically, so in equating them Gérard is performing a remarkable sleight-of-heart trick. To love God, he wants to say, is to practice *fine amour,* and he can even take St. Paul to witness (1 Cor. 13:1): If I speak in the tongues of men and of angels, but have not charity—"idest, *se ie naime par amours*"—it profits me nothing.[8] A lover aspiring to please the God who is Love, like one who wishes to please the old pagan god of love, must be gracious in heart and body: "Oportet esse gratiosum exterius et deuotum interius eum qui uult amare et *au diu damours* placere" [One who wishes to love and to please the God of Love ought to be outwardly gracious and inwardly devoted].[9] Here, with surprisingly little ado, Gérard has transmogrified the capricious winged archer of Ovid and Guillaume into Jesus Christ. We must recall that the abbot wrote this tract before Jean de Meun completed the *Rose,* so he probably envisioned the *diu damours* as a genteel and idealized figure, rather than the opportunistic, heavily ironized deity who finally secures the lover's Rose.

Like a lyric husband, says Gérard, the biblical God is jealous, so his lovers may share the sentiments of the *mal-mariée* in the song:

> Quant plus me bat et destraint li ialous,
> tant ai ie mius en amours ma pensee.
> Deus enim, ut dixit Moyses, est fortis zelotes (Exod. 20.5), idest *ialous.*[10]

[The more the jealous one beats and confines me, / the more I think of love. / For God, as Moses said, is very jealous.]

But Gérard is willfully distorting the lyric situation, for the female speaker in the song intends to *contrast* her jealous, violent husband with the lover she refuses to abandon. Gérard, on the contrary, conflates the jealous husband with the desired lover: The female speaker in his scenario loves God all the more in spite of, or rather because of, his violence. This interpretation is confirmed by another passage in which Gérard presents God as the most desirable lover because he is not only the most beautiful and devoted, but also the most aggressive and threatening:

> If our love requires violence, *cest con li face force,* no one will do greater violence to attain it than he. For he seeks it as if with an unsheathed sword: either you will love him or you will die an eternal death. Hence David says, "unless you are converted" from love of the world to the love of God, "he

will brandish his sword" (Ps. 7:13). So here a certain popular song can be applied: *Tout a force maugre uostre uorsai uostre amour auoir* [By main force, in spite of you I will have your love.][11]

Some such formulation may underlie Marguerite's startling reference to God as "le treshault Jaloux" whose love robs the soul of her very self: "He is jealous indeed! This is apparent from his works, which have despoiled me of my whole self and set me in divine pleasure without myself."[12] The Free Soul rejoices in this high estate, just as Gérard presumes the beloved will do when God ravishes her at sword point, "tout a force."

In his discussion of "insuperable love" (one of Richard of St. Victor's "four degrees of violent charity"), Gérard again anticipates Marguerite. Love is rightly compared to death, he writes, because both are invincible: No one can taste either love or death without losing all the powers of his body and soul. "Thus love or charity is undoubtedly the strongest passion, which no one can feel or experience without necessarily losing all his senses and bodily movements; and even the movements of the soul, i.e., his knowledge, his power, and his will, are taken captive in love's service. Augustine, *li anguisseus damours,* was keenly aware of this when he said, "Mighty and almighty is the passion of love! It is indeed powerful, because it renders the spirit possessed by it powerless over itself."[13] Marguerite's Free Soul likewise has "lost the use of her senses":[14] She knows nothing, wills nothing, and can do nothing, being completely powerless and wholly possessed by Love.

Gérard's editor in the early 1930s, the distinguished Benedictine André Wilmart, was annoyed by his author's frequent resorts to the vernacular. Wilmart wondered if Gérard's fondness for French tags might be due to "an odd sort of quirk . . .an instinctive and bizarre desire to distinguish himself . . . by means of this somewhat childish artifice."[15] But from a contemporary critical perspective, Gérard's "quirk" makes more sense, for his unusual macaronic style marks him as one of the forgers of *la mystique courtoise.* This new idiom of divine love blended not only two languages, but the diverse thought-worlds they represented: the Latinate realm of monastic bridal mysticism, known to Gérard primarily through Augustine and Bernard, and the vernacular realm of *courtoisie* represented by his French lyrics. Peter Dronke was closer to the mark when he observed that "if sacred and profane love are wholly divorced, as by Gérard, then, as nothing is found in the intellect which was not first found in the senses, their metaphorics will be identical, as much as if they were wholly united." Further, "the more deeply religious the language, the closer it is to the language of *courtoisie.*"[16] The two languages—the Song of Songs and the tongue of the trouvères—have fused completely by the last page of

Gérard's treatise, when the "holy soul" cries out, "*Oi,* osculetur me, *mes tres dous amis,* osculo oris sui!" [Ah, let him kiss me, my sweetest love, with the kiss of his mouth!][17]

About fifty years later, an anonymous French cleric would advance the tradition of Gérard's *mystique courtoise,* placing vernacular thought and language at the service of that most Latinate of genres, the religious rule. *La Règle des fins amans,* a sprightly beguine rule contemporary with Marguerite's *Mirror,* systematically characterizes beguines as courtly lovers and represents their religious life as "li ordres des fins amans" [the order of true lovers].[18] Among the many romance conceits adopted by its author is a miniature allegory, transparently borrowed from the *Rose,* that concludes the rule. In this fable Conscïence, or Desire, the heroine, is yearning after her beloved Jesus when Jealousy appears with news that monastics—*li cloistriés*—have imprisoned him. So Conscïence breaks into the monastery garden, assisted by several Virtues, including Charité *and* Fine Amours, and is soon reunited with her love. This truncated plot pays homage to the central action of the *Rose,* in which Jealousy builds a castle to imprison Fair Welcome and keep the Lover from his goal. Thus the *Règle des fins amans* tells us something of the jealousy beguines must have felt toward cloistered nuns. But it also tells of their immersion in the culture of *fine amour,* for its author was able to assume that his readers would recognize the *Rose* allegory and doubtless smile at its transmutation. Marguerite Porete, a more than usually sophisticated member of the target audience, may or may not have known the *Règle* (it is not impossible that she even knew its author),[19] but it is certain that she knew the *Rose.*

Let us turn to that formidable poem itself. Halfway through the *Roman de la rose,* the God of Love makes a "prophetic" speech foretelling the career of Jean de Meun, who is to become Love's protégé by completing Guillaume de Lorris's unfinished poem and disseminating it in "crossroads and schools" all over France. In the act of appropriating Guillaume's romance, Jean and the God of Love give it a new name: The poem will no longer be called *Le Roman de la rose* but *Le Miroër as amoreus,* [The Mirror for Lovers]. All who read this book "properly" will find great good in it, says Love, provided they are not led astray by his adversary, Lady Reason. Thus the book's authorship and its revised title are closely linked with its ostensible purpose, which is to promote Love by discrediting Reason:

> . . . tretuit cil qui ont a vivre
> Devroient appeler ce livre
> Le *Miroër as amoreus,*
> Tant i verront de bienz por eus,

Mes que Raison n'i soit creüe,
La chetive, la recreüe. (lines 10649–54)[20]

[All who are living / ought to give this book / the title *The Mirror for Lovers.*
/ They will see so much good in it, / if they do not believe Reason, / that
miserable coward.]

Marguerite too wrote a mirror for lovers: The full title of her book may
be rendered as *The Mirror of Simple, Annihilated Souls Who Live Only in the
Will and Desire of Love.* And she too aimed to discredit Reason, who is
the chief antagonist of Lady Love and her protégée, the Free Soul. The
very form of Marguerite's text—a sprawling and, at first blush, shapeless
allegorical dialogue—seems to be self-consciously modeled on the *Rose.*
In fact, it would be difficult to think of any other generic model for the
Mirror, which bears little or no formal resemblance to any religious literature Marguerite could have known, whether we think of homilies, vision narratives, spiritual autobiography, saints' lives, exegesis, or systematic
treatises like those of Richard of St. Victor and Gérard of Liège.[21] Her
most recent translators, the late Edmund Colledge in collaboration with
Jack C. Marler and Judith Grant, have likewise acknowledged Marguerite's formal and rhetorical debt to the *Rose,* although their analysis
is hampered by an overly simplistic interpretation of what they call "Perfect Love."[22]

In naming her book a *Mirror,* Marguerite was following a thirteenth-
century fashion, so there would be little point in positing a specific source
for the title. Nevertheless, if we think of the *Rose* by the alternative title
Jean de Meun gave it, *The Mirror for Lovers,* we may pay more attention to
two key passages on mirroring that did, I believe, influence our beguine.
The first, by Guillaume de Lorris, is the famous "Mirror of Narcissus"
episode near the beginning of the romance; the second, by Jean de Meun,
occurs in Nature's speech near the end.

The Narcissus episode occurs when the Lover, already stalked by the
God of Love but not yet smitten, discovers the celebrated Fountain of
Love, with its two reflecting crystals and its memorial inscription. After de-
scribing the fountain at some length, Guillaume compares it to a mirror:

C'est li mirëors perilleus,
Ou Narcisus li orguilleus
Mira sa face et ses yex vers,
Dont il jut puis mors touz envers.
Qui en cest mirëor se mire
Ne puet avoir garant ne mire:
Que tel chose a ses yex ne voie

Qui d'amer l'a tost mis en voie.

. . .

Ici se changent li corage,
Ci n'a mestier, sens ne mesure,
Ci est d'amer volenté pure,
Ci ne se set consillier nus. (lines 1571–87)

[This is the Mirror Perilous / in which Narcissus, that proud man, / gazed on his face and his grey eyes, / and afterward lay stark dead. / Whoever looks in this mirror / can have no help, no physician: / whatever he lays eyes upon, / he is instantly bound to love . . . / Here is where hearts are changed: / here sense and measure have no place; / here is just the pure will to love; / here no one can take counsel.]

The dreamer of Guillaume's poem both repeats and avoids the mistake of Narcissus. Although he does gaze into the Mirror Perilous and falls hopelessly in love, it is not himself that he sees there, but the Rose.[23] That, however, may be a moot point. What Marguerite would have found most compelling in this description is not so much Narcissus' fate as the absoluteness of love, that immoderate and irresistible changer of hearts. To peer into the Mirror Perilous is to abandon Reason—*sens ne mesure*—for the relentless imperative of Love's pure will. Of course this view of love is not novel or unique to the *Rose*, but Guillaume's scene gives it a kind of iconicity, compressing into a single densely packed image the magical fountains so ubiquitous in romance plots, the exemplum of Narcissus, the ambiguity of the mirror in which he both discovers and loses himself, and the era's fascination with fatal, incorrigible love.

Almost sixteen thousand lines later, Jean de Meun revisits the subject of mirrors. In a long discourse on free will and providence, Nature introduces the metaphor of divinity itself as a mirror. Whatever has been, is, or shall be, God sees from eternity:

. . . A son mirooir pardurable,
Que nulz fors li ne set polir,
Sanz rienz a franc voloir tolir.
Cis mirooirs est il meïmes,
De qui commencement preïmes.
En ce biau mirooir poli,
Qu'il tient et tint touz jors o li,
Ou tout voit quanqu'il avendra
Et touz jors present li rendra
Voit il ou les ames iront
Qui loiaument le serviront . . .
C'est la predestinacion,

C'est la prescience devine,
Qui tout set et rienz ne devine. (lines 17468–86)

[. . . in his everlasting mirror, / that no one but he can polish / without detracting from free will. / This mirror is God's own self, / from whom we
took our beginning. / In this lovely, polished mirror / which he holds and
has always held, / where he sees all that will happen, / and renders it always
present / he sees where the souls of those go / who will loyally serve him.
/ . . . This is the predestination, / this is the divine foreknowledge, / which
knows all and guesses nothing.]

In this passage, indebted to Boethius and Alan of Lille, Jean equates the mirror of providence or divine foreknowledge with "God's own self" (*il
meïmes*).[24] Like Guillaume de Lorris, though less programmatically, he imagines a mirror that is also a fountain, in the dual sense of "reflecting surface"
and "source of life." Thus, from the "mirror" that is God or God's eternal
mind, all creatures "took [their] beginning." Yet only God can "polish" this
mirror without detracting from free will; in other words, if any creature could
see past, present, and future as God does, its freedom would be compromised.
So just as one who gazes into Guillaume's Mirror of Love (*miröor perilleus*) is
in danger of losing his reason, one who gazes into Jean's Mirror of Providence
(*mirooir pardurable*) would be in danger of losing free will. For Marguerite
Porete, the lover of God's infinity, these two mirrors are one and the same.

Unlike the *Rose* poets, Marguerite does not use explicit mirror images
in her text. But her title is most apt, for the concept of mirroring or spec-
ularity pervades the entire dialogue.[25] In fact, Marguerite's opening parable of the maiden and King Alexander distantly echoes the Mirror of
Narcissus episode. This classic exemplum of *amour loingtaigne,* borrowed
from the *Roman d'Alexandre,* is told by Amour. In it, the maiden who has
fallen in love with the faraway king has his portrait painted ("fist paindre
ung ymage qui representoit la semblance du roy"), and through her devotion to the image, "songa le roy mesmes" [she dreamed the king himself].[26]
The Soul responds by telling Amour of her own "similar" experience: She
too has come to love "a noble Alexander," but the picture she has of him
is "this book," which is his gift to her: "Il me donna ce livre qui represente
en aucuns usages l'amour de lui mesmes" [He gave me this book, which
shows in some usages the love of himself]. The hidden third term mediating between "image" and "book" is "mirror," the book's title. With pointed
ambiguity, Marguerite represents her book or *Mirror,* which reflects the
king's image, as at the same time his gift and her creation.[27] Like Guillaume's Lover, the Soul only dreams of her Beloved whom she does not
yet possess, yet her dream is his true reflection. He underwrites what she
writes, just as the Soul's opening speech deliberately mirrors Love's speech.

While the Soul's relation to Love is not precisely narcissism, it is an intense and mutual mirroring that begins with their very names, *Ame* and *Amour,* and continues throughout their dialogue: Love describes and praises the Soul, while the Soul explains and celebrates Love. Ultimately, the Free Soul becomes the Love that she beholds, or in a more precise formulation, she becomes an unclouded mirror in which Love beholds only itself.[28] The title *Mirouer des simples ames* has therefore a double reference. Marguerite's book is itself a Mirror of Narcissus into which souls, gazing intently, may lose themselves and find God in the *volenté pure d'amer:* "And so this beggarly creature wrote what you hear; and she wanted her neighbors to find God in her, through writings and through words."[29] Yet this divine mirror, which proved so perilous to its author, is in the end a mere painted image. For the Soul must acknowledge, in taking leave of it, that her book "has been made by human knowledge and human sense," and "all that one can say or write of God . . . is to lie far more than it is to tell the truth."[30] The only true *miroir pardurable* is the divine mind itself. No one can gaze in *this* mirror, as Nature warned in the *Roman de la rose,* without sacrificing *franc voloir,* which is presumably Marguerite's final wish for herself and her audience. In her leave-taking, the Soul suggests that the act of will involved in writing the book—or polishing the mirror—has been the final thread, now severed, that kept her from her goal of annihilation.[31]

After Guillaume's Lover gazes into the fountain of Narcissus and sees the Rose, he is promptly wounded by the God of Love and compelled to do homage. Love then presents him with the "commandments" that the Lover has already promised to obey. In Marguerite's *Mirror,* too, the parable of the maiden with the king's image immediately precedes the giving of Love's commandments. Presented as the commands of Holy Church, these are actually the Gospel imperatives to love God with all one's heart and soul and strength, and one's neighbor as oneself.[32] The speaker who expounds these commandments is neither Christ nor Holy Church, but once again Amour, a female figure who is sometimes called Dame Amour.[33]

Love's gender is a complex and curious signifier in Marguerite's dialogue. In the *Rose* and other texts influenced by Ovid, the *dieu d'amours* is a male deity identified with Cupid. *Amor* is a masculine noun in Latin, and in all medieval translations of the *Mirror* (Latin, Italian, and English), grammar dictates a reinscription of Love's male gender: Thus Dame Amour becomes Domine Amor.[34] Marguerite's French text, however, intensifies the specular relationship between Love and the Soul by keeping them both feminine. As a kind of goddess-figure, her Dame Amour seems to echo not so much the *Rose* as the troubadours, who cultivated a deliberate confusion between their personified feminine Love and the beloved lady, just as Dame Amour reflects and coalesces with Dame Ame.[35]

On a different level, however, the strategy of the *Mirror* is indebted here as well to the *Rose*, especially to Guillaume's portion of it. One of the *Rose*'s most original features is its fragmented representation of the Beloved. The Rose itself represents her body, and in the end her genitals, but it cannot represent her subjectivity. Unlike the Lover, the beloved lady is never portrayed as a unified subject, but her aspects are parceled out among personifications of both genders who side with and against the Lover: Franchise, Pitié, Honte, Poor, Dangier, and of course, Bel Acuel or "Fair Welcome." The last-named personage is the Lover's chief goal and ally until he can gain access to the Rose itself. Now Guillaume could easily have chosen a feminine persona—Courtoisie, for example, or Franchise or Amitié—to represent the lady's friendly, welcoming demeanor. But in fact he chose the cross-gendered figure of Bel Acuel, whose name will chime later on with *coilles* [testicles] and *cuellir* [to pluck/deflower], much to Jean de Meun's pleasure.[36] Bel Acuel's maleness seems to come and go in the text: la Vieille calls him "son" but gives "him" some intense girl-to-girl mentoring, and in illuminated manuscripts, he appears usually as a young man but occasionally as a woman.[37] If we take the putative maleness of Fair Welcome as a significant trait, it can be read in a variety of ways—as "queering" the Lover's affair, or as ennobling it with a patina of courtly friendship,[38] or as ensuring a measure of equality between the prospective partners.[39] But however we interpret Bel Acuel, his prominence alongside the Rose and her more "female" aspects assures that the Beloved will be a complex and enigmatic being whom her Lover may impregnate, but never fully fathom.

With this fragmentation of the Beloved in mind, let us return to Marguerite. We have considered Dame Amour as the mirror image and alter ego of the Soul, but she is more: She is also, quite explicitly, the chief mouthpiece of God in the dialogue. "I am God," she tells the scandalized Reason, " because Love is God and God is Love—and this Soul is God by the condition of love."[40] But Amour is not the only divine speaker in the text, which also features cameo appearances by God the Father, the Holy Spirit, the Bridegroom of the Soul, and the Trinity. Marguerite's God may be metaphysically simple, but s/he is relationally complex, multifaceted, and, like the Rose, androgynous. In one sense, the femininity of Amour functions, like the masculinity of Bel Acuel, to denaturalize gender. When a "Lady" speaks for God or a "man" for a lady, the unexpected cross-gendering compels us to question both erotic and theological conventions. Thus the Free Soul's love of God, like the Lover's passion for his Rose, reveals what could be called a homoerotic dimension beneath its surface. But however titillating this may be for modern readers, I do not believe medieval audiences would have found it so. For, in a different sense, the androgyny of the Beloved actually makes gender *less* relevant to the Lover's quest, since the blurring or effacing of sexual difference places the emphasis on sameness, the prospect of identity between Lover and Beloved. We will never know what Guillaume de Lorris may have intended in this regard: His poem breaks off with Fair Welcome in prison and the Lover in despair. Marguerite, however, decidedly preferred identity or "union without difference" to the tempestuous drama of the love-quest. Insofar as she identified with the position of the Free Soul, she was openly critical of the erotic mysticism cultivated by many nuns and beguines, which she regarded as an inferior brand of love and wished to transcend in a serene unity beyond the intoxicating sweetness of romance.[41]

Nevertheless, the *Mirror* does introduce an avatar of the divine Bridegroom: the mysterious male figure Marguerite calls *Loingpres* or "Farnear," recalling her parable of King Alexander and the maiden. In keeping with her suspicion of *Brautmystik*, Marguerite never describes union with this lover in the sexualized language characteristic of other beguine mystics, but she does end her dialogue with a song of fulfillment that may, in a supremely paradoxical sense, pay one last homage to the *Rose*. Jean de Meun's romance notoriously ends with the pregnancy of the newly plucked rose, a datum conveyed through horticultural metaphors so gleeful and transparent that Christine de Pizan would accuse the poet of obscenity.[42] Oddly enough, while pregnancy is not the consummation one would predict for a soul "annihilated in the will and desire of love," Marguerite's Free Soul concludes her song with these lines:

J'ay dit que je l'aymeray.
Je mens, ce ne suis je mie.
C'est il seul qui ayme moy:
Il est, et je ne suis mie:
Et plus ne me fault,
Que ce qu'il veult,
Et qu'il vault.
Il est plain,
Et de ce suis plaine
C'est le divin noyaulx
Et amour loyaulx.[43]

[I have said that I will love him. / I lie, for it is not "I" at all. / It is he alone who loves me: / He is, and I am not: / and I have no need / of more than what he wishes / and what he is worth. / He is full, / and from this I am filled: / this is the seed divine / and loyal love.]

The mischief in these lines turns on a characteristic double entendre: *de ce suis plaine* can mean something like "he is my fulfillment," but it can also mean "I am pregnant by his fullness."[44] Similarly, the *noyaulx* suggests the heart or core of divine love, as in the familiar exegetical metaphor of chaff and kernel; but it can also mean "seed," as in the *grenes* that Jean's Lover spills to fertilize his rosebud. Now pregnancy is hardly an integral theme in the *Mirror*, but the sudden appearance of this new subtext in the very last lines of her book suggests that Marguerite had, consciously or not, a reminiscence of that older *Mirror for Lovers* in the back of her mind. Like the Rose, the Free Soul becomes "pregnant" at the moment that her subjectivity is most fully annihilated by the overpowering love of her *ami*.

One of the most scandalous teachings of the *Mirror* was Marguerite's claim that the Free Soul, perfected in love, "takes leave of the virtues" and owes no more service to them or their ally, Reason.[45] The imperfect soul, Love proclaims, remains in bondage to Reason and the Virtues, who "demand honor and possessions, heart and body and life." But once the souls who dwell in Love are emancipated from this serfdom, they become ladies and "the Virtues do all that such souls wish, without pride or rebellion, for such souls are their mistresses."[46] All this may seem a far cry from the *Rose*. But here again, I believe, Marguerite presupposes the familiar plot of the romance, with its central conflict between Love and Reason, and adapts it for her purposes. In the *Rose,* the Lover twice rejects the counsel of Reason—briefly in Guillaume's text, then definitively in Jean's. Lady Reason begins the long speech that Jean gives her by denouncing the God of Love as a cruel *seignor*; she ends by asking the Lover to forsake the god's service and accept her instead as his *amie*. But the Lover scorns her and insists that virtuous love, which she advocates, has been impossible ever since antiquity when the Virtues fled the earth, driven off by Fraud.[47] After he has sent Reason packing, the Lover seeks out the cynical and misogynistic Ami, and from this point onward, he truly takes leave of the Virtues. By the end of the romance, the naive but well-intentioned youth introduced by Guillaume will have become complicit in treachery, murder, bribery, and arguably rape.[48] This is not to say that Jean's intention is consistently or even primarily moralistic; but it is to say that in the universe he constructs, no man can serve two masters. The Dreamer must choose between Love and Reason, between the Rose and the Virtues—and choose he emphatically does.

Marguerite accepts this dichotomy and her Free Soul makes the same choice, but she views it from the other side of the fence. For the sake of argument, I will hold with the long line of critics (beginning circa 1400) who have maintained that, whatever else he may be doing, Jean de Meun is ironizing the Lover. On that reading, it is Reason who speaks for the poet, and once our protagonist has rejected her, the subsequent plot unmasks his pretensions to *fine amour* as no more than *fole amour*.[49] As he pursues his passion, he becomes progressively enmeshed in vice. In the *Mirror,* by contrast, the Free Soul does not dismiss the Virtues in order to revel in vices. She rises above their level rather than sinking beneath it, and if she is guilty of anything, it is quietism, rather than gross sin or crime. Yet Reason is alarmed all the same and staunchly resists the absolutism of Love and the Soul. Now the difference between the foolish Lover's quest and the mystic's may seem painfully obvious—so obvious as to render comparison otiose. Yet it was not at all obvious to Marguerite's inquisitors, who followed the script she had laid out for them by insisting that Holy Church must be governed by Reason. Thus nothing in the *Mirror* antagonized them more than Marguerite's assertion that the Free Soul takes leave of the Virtues. Despite her careful insistence that the Virtues continue to operate in such souls, she was taken to be preaching antinomianism, and this claim became central to the case against her.[50] A year after her execution, her statement about taking leave of the Virtues was condemned once again at the Council of Vienne, among other errors ascribed to beguines and beghards concerning the state of perfection.[51]

In a second condemned proposition from the *Mirror,* Love states that the Free Soul "gives to Nature all that it requires, with no qualm of conscience; but such a Nature is so well ordered by its transformation in unity with Love . . . that it never demands anything which is forbidden."[52] Evidently Marguerite's inquisitors did not believe such a transformation possible in this life. By 1312, the clerics at Vienne would amplify this condemned doctrine, adding a codicil that does not appear in Marguerite's book but may have been inspired by it. This is the interesting proposition "that a woman's kiss is a mortal sin when Nature does not incline to it; but the carnal act itself is no sin when Nature does incline to it, especially when the one performing the act is tempted."[53]

Was this sexual interpretation of "transformed Nature" in its "unity with Love" inevitable? Marguerite herself never pursued that possibility, and her devout readers took pains to keep it at bay. In fact, her Middle English translator, the Carthusian "M. N.," glossed the suspect passage as follows: "God forbid that anyone should be so carnal as to think that this could mean giving Nature any pleasure which leads to sins of the flesh. God knows well that that is not how it is meant. . . . For I say this with truth, that souls who are such as this book describes are so mortified and freed from such miseries, are so illumined with grace and so armed with the love of God, that it extinguishes all fleshly sin in them."[54] But the libertine view of Nature certainly *had* occurred to Jean de Meun. The last major speech in the *Rose* is delivered by Genius, an ally of Nature and the God of Love, who embodies male reproductive power. This character preaches a provocative "sermon" on the universal duty to procreate, culminating in the injunction to "plow, barons, plow—for God's sake—and renew your lineages!"[55] The god in question is of course ambiguous, and becomes still more so when Genius goes on to offer some explicitly religious teaching about Paradise.

Such ambiguities were not received kindly by those who viewed themselves as guardians of orthodoxy. In 1277, shortly after the *Rose* was completed, the faculty of the University of Paris, led by Bishop Etienne Tempier, condemned a long list of "manifest and execrable errors."[56] Most of the two hundred nineteen condemned propositions are philosophical doctrines of skeptical or astrological bent, derived from the teachings of Siger of Brabant and Boethius of Dacia. But several are ethical doctrines redolent of the naturalistic discourse Jean had ascribed to Genius: namely that continence is not a virtue, that sexual abstinence corrupts the species, and that simple fornication is not sin.[57] Although the document does not mention Jean de Meun by name, it does cite and condemn one of his more notorious precursors—Andreas Capellanus and his *De amore*.[58] In short, the Paris theologians had already linked a series of disparate and, in their view, dangerous philosophical propositions with "doctrines" they derived from secular writings on love.

In such a context it stands to reason that Marguerite's *Mirror,* which uses the rhetoric of *fine amour* even though it has nothing to do with sexual behavior, should have been drawn into the vortex. At one time it was widely held that the Council of Vienne was reacting against the so-called "heresy of the Free Spirit," a movement that is supposed to have linked antinomian ethics (or lack of ethics) with mystical quietism of the sort that Marguerite taught. Robert Lerner's work has cast doubt on that hypothesis, showing that no identifiable heretic (let alone heretical movement) prior to 1311 can be found to have held such views.[59] But it remains the case that even if no actual heretics had thought to connect Marguerite's abstruse mysticism with Jean de Meun's sexual naturalism, the fathers at Vienne now did so. In their zeal to defend the faith, they made the *Mirror* reflect the *Rose* to a degree that would have astonished its hapless author.

Notes

1. Barbara Newman, "*La mystique courtoise:* Thirteenth-Century Beguines and the Art of Love," in *From Virile Woman to WomanChrist: Studies in Medieval Literature and Religion* (Philadelphia: University of Pennsylvania Press, 1995), pp. 137–67.

2. Its complete title is *Le mirouer des simples ames anienties et qui seulement demourent en vouloir et désir d'amour.* I have used the bilingual edition, *Le mirouer des simples ames,* ed. Romana Guarnieri, with its Latin translation, *Speculum simplicium animarum,* ed. Paul Verdeyen, CCCM 69 (Turnhout:

Brepols, 1986). Translations are my own, but I have consulted those of Edmund Colledge, Jack C. Marler, and Judith Grant, *The Mirror of Simple Souls* (Notre Dame, 1999), and Ellen Babinsky, *The Mirror of Simple Souls* (New York: Paulist Press, 1993).

3. "Les traités de Gérard de Liège sur l'amour illicite et sur l'amour de Dieu," ed. André Wilmart, *Analecta reginensia: Extraits des manuscrits latins de la reine Christine conservés au Vatican,* Studi e testi 59 (Rome: Vatican, 1933, repr. 1966): 181–247. The text of the *Incitamenta* appears on 205–47.

4. *Septem remedia contra amorem illicitum valde utilia,* in ibid., 183–205.

5. See Richard of St. Victor, *De quatuor gradibus violentae charitatis,* ed. Gervais Dumeige, in *Ives: Épître à Séverin sur la charité* (Paris: Vrin, 1955); trans. Clare Kirchberger, "Of the Four Degrees of Passionate Charity," in *Richard of Saint-Victor: Selected Writings on Contemplation* (New York: Harper & Brothers, 1957).

6. *Quinque incitamenta* 1.5, p. 209. I have printed Gérard's French quotations as verse, though they appear in the edition as prose. Orthography follows Wilmart's edition.

7. Ibid. 3.4, p. 228. Compare *Mirouer* ch. 21, p. 82: "Amour est Dieu, et Dieu est amour."

8. Ibid. 3.4.3, p. 232.

9. Ibid. 3.4.3, p. 233.

10. Ibid. 3.2.2, p. 219.

11. "Si autem uiolentiam requirit amor noster, *cest con li face force,* nullus maiorem uiolentiam pro eo faciet quam ipse. Petit enim eum quasi gladio euaginato. Aut enim eum amabis aut eterna morte morieris. Unde Dauid: Nisi conuersi fueritis, ab amore mundi scilicet ad amorem dei, gladium suum vibrabit. Unde hic potest dici quoddam carmen quod uulgo canitur: *Tout a force maugre uostre uorsai uostre amour auoir.*" *Quinque incitamenta* 2, p. 211.

12. "Jaloux voirement est il! A ses œuvres l'appert, qui m'ont desrobee de toute moy, et m'ont mise en divine plaisance, sans moy." *Mirouer* ch. 71, p. 198.

13. "Sic sine dubio amor siue caritas passio est fortissima, quam nullus sentire et degustare potest quin de necessitate oporteat eum omnes sensus et motus corporeos amittere et etiam motus anime, scilicet scire suum, posse suum et uelle suum, captiuare in obsequium amoris. Hoc enim bene senserat et cognouerat Augustinus, *li anguisseus damours,* qui dicebat: O potens et prepotens passio caritatis. Iure enim potens, quia animum quem possederit sui ipsius efficit impotentem." The "Augustine" quotation is actually from Gilbert of Hoyland. *Quinque incitamenta* 3.3.1, p.223.

14. "Elle a perdu l'usage de ses sens . . . car Amour l'a ravie du lieu ou elle estoit." *Mirouer* ch. 110, p. 300.

15. "On est tenté de croire que ce fut là plutôt chez Gérard une sorte de manie qui n'a fait que grandir, un désir instinctif et bizarre de se distinguer et, tout ensemble, de se distraire au moyen de cet artifice un peu puéril." André Wilmart, "Gérard de Liège: Un traité inédit de l'amour de Dieu," *Revue d'ascétique et de mystique* 12 (1931): 373.

16. Peter Dronke, *Medieval Latin and the Rise of European Love-Lyric* (Oxford: Clarendon, 1965), 1:62.

17. *Quinque incitamenta* 4.4, p. 246.

18. "La Règle des Fins Amans: Eine Beginenregel aus dem Ende des XIII. Jahrhunderts," ed. Karl Christ, in *Philologische Studien aus dem romanisch-germanischen Kulturkreise: Festschrift Karl Voretzsch,* ed. B. Schädel and W. Mulertt (Halle: Max Niemeyer, 1927): pp. 173–213. For a fuller analysis of the *Règle,* see Newman, *From Virile Woman to WomanChrist,* 139–43.

19. Marguerite apparently hailed from Valenciennes, a town on the present-day border between France and Belgium. Her book was burned there in 1306, and Jean Gerson, in an interestingly mixed assessment of the *Mirror,* named its author mistakenly as "Maria de Valenciennes." Gerson, "De distinctione verarum revelationum a falsis," in *Oeuvres complètes,* ed. Palémon Glorieux (Tournai, 1962), 3:51–52. Karl Christ, editor of the *Règle des fins amans,* assigned it on linguistic grounds to the neighboring province of Picardy.

20. *Le Roman de la rose,* ed. Daniel Poirion (Paris: Garnier-Flammarion, 1974). Translations are my own, but I have consulted the prose version by Charles Dahlberg, *The Romance of the Rose* (Princeton: Princeton University Press, 1971), and the verse translation of Harry Robbins, *The Romance of the Rose,* ed. Charles Dunn (New York: Dutton, 1962).

21. In the final chapters of her book (chs. 123–39), added as a kind of appendix after its initial condemnation in 1306, Marguerite does draw on some of these more traditional genres: exegesis of Gospel passages, hagiography (the legend of Mary Magdalene), and spiritual autobiography (how she herself entered the "Land of Freedom"). This appendix is the only part of the book where Marguerite speaks unambiguously in her own first-person voice.

22. Colledge, Marler, and Grant, "Introductory Interpretative Essay," *Mirror,* lxvi-lxix. Relying on the scholarship of past generations, these authors take Jean de Meun to be endorsing, rather than anatomizing or satirizing, the "enslavement by human passion" that typifies "Perfect Love" (lxvii).

23. As Karl D. Uitti points out, *se mirer* is often mistranslated: It means "to gaze intently," not necessarily at oneself. " 'Cele [qui] doit ester Rose clamee' (*Rose,* vv. 40–44): Guillaume's Intentionality," in *Rethinking the* Romance of the Rose: *Text, Image, Reception,* eds. Kevin Brownlee and Sylvia Huot (Philadelphia: University of Pennsylvania Press, 1992), p. 54.

24. Nature's reconciliation of free will with divine foreknowledge follows Boethius, *Consolation of Philosophy,* but Boethius does not use the mirror image. The *speculum providentiae,* symbolizing eternal mind, appears as an attribute of Urania in Bernard Silvestris' *Cosmographia.* In his *Anticlaudianus,* Alan of Lille gives Reason a triple mirror.

25. On this theme in Marguerite and other beguine mystics, see Newman, *From Virile Woman to WomanChrist,* pp. 153–58.

26. *Mirouer* ch. 1, p. 12. The last phrase is difficult to translate: Babinsky has "she dreamed of the king," and Colledge, Marler, and Grant render, "she could

imagine that the king himself was present." The medieval Latin translator evades the problem: "Et mediante tali imagine . . . semetipsam aliqualiter quietabat." I follow the literal version of Peter Dronke in *Women Writers of the Middle Ages* (Cambridge, Cambridge University Press, 1984), p. 219. *Songa* recalls the famous play on *songes/mençonges* in the opening couplet of the *Rose*.

27. Bernard McGinn, *The Flowering of Mysticism: Men and Women in the New Mysticism (1200–1350)* (New York: Crossroad, 1998), p. 247.

28. See ch. 118, describing the sixth and penultimate state of the Free Soul: "Mais ceste Ame, ainsi pure et clariffiee, ne voit ne Dieu ne elle, mais Dieu se voit de luy en elle, pour elle, sans elle." *Mirouer,* p. 330.

29. "Et ainsi escripsit ceste mendiant creature ce que vous oez; et voult que ses proesmes trouvassent Dieu en elle, par escrips et par paroles." *Mirouer* ch. 96, p. 268.

30. "Si a esté fait par humaine science et humain sens; et humaine raison et humain sens ne scevent rien d'amour denetraine . . . car tout ce que l'en peut de Dieu dire ne escrire, ne que l'en en peut penser, qui plus est que n'est dire, est assez mieulx mentir que ce n'est vray dire." *Mirouer* ch. 119, p. 334.

31. "J'ay dit, dit ceste Ame, que Amour l'a fait escrire par humaine science, et par le *vouloir* de la mutacion de mon entendement, dont j'estoie *encombree,* comme il appert par ce livre; car Amour l'a fait, en *descombrant* mon esperit parmy ces trois dons." Ibid., emphasis added.

32. *Mirouer* ch. 3, p. 16.

33. Raison, also grammatically feminine, is never called *Dame*—presumably because Marguerite regards her as a servant rather than a lady or mistress.

34. See for example ch. 31, pp. 102–3.

35. The same dynamic is at work in German and Dutch lyrics featuring Frau Minne, while the Italian *stilnovisti* developed alternative tropes to represent the masculine *Amore*. The French noun *amour* became masculine only in the sixteenth and seventeenth centuries under the influence of humanistic Latin, but its plural *les amours* remains feminine. Walther von Wartburg, *Französisches Etymologisches Wörterbuch* 24:469.

36. David Hult, "Language and Dismemberment: Abelard, Origen, and the *Romance of the Rose,*" in Brownlee and Huot, eds., *Rethinking,* p. 120.

37. Kevin Brownlee and Sylvia Huot, "Introduction: Rethinking the *Rose,*" in *Rethinking,* p. 15; Lori Walters, "Illuminating the *Rose:* Gui de Mori and the Illustrations of MS 101 of the Municipal Library, Tournai," in *Rethinking,* pp. 178–79.

38. C. Stephen Jaeger illumines the dependence of *fine amour* upon an older practice of passionate male friendship, understood as morally and socially ennobling rather than erotic. *Ennobling Love: In Search of a Lost Sensibility* (Philadelphia: University of Pennsylvania Press, 1999).

39. Joan Ferrante argues that Bel Acuel has to be male because he "plays the courtly game on the man's terms": *Woman as Image in Medieval Literature*

from the Twelfth Century to Dante (New York: Columbia University Press, 1975), p. 110.

40. "Je suis Dieu, dit Amour, car Amour est Dieu, et Dieu est amour, est ceste Ame est Dieu par condicion d'amour." *Mirouer* ch. 21, p. 82.

41. See especially ch. 118, pp. 322–24 (the fourth stage of the Soul), and ch. 133, p. 392. In these two passages Marguerite says that the Soul intoxicated by the sweetness of divine Love is often deceived, imagining wrongly that there is no higher stage of love than hers, and not realizing that it is herself rather than God that she truly loves. See also Amy Hollywood, *The Soul as Virgin Wife: Mechthild of Magdeburg, Marguerite Porete, and Meister Eckhart* (Notre Dame: University of Notre Dame Press, 1995), ch. 4.

42. "Et fis lors si meller les grenes / Que se desmellassent a penes, / Si que tout le boutonnet tendre / En fis eslargir et estendre." *Roman de la rose,* lines 21727–30. Christine calls the conclusion of the *Rose* "shameful and so very dishonorable . . . that nobody who loves virtue and honor will hear it without being totally confounded by shame and abomination at hearing described, expressed, and distorted in dishonorable fictions what modesty and reason should restrain well-bred folk from even thinking about." Letter to Jean de Montreuil, in *La Querelle de la Rose: Letters and Documents,* ed. and trans. Joseph Baird and John Kane (Chapel Hill: University of North Carolina Press, 1978), p. 53.

43. *Mirouer* ch. 122, p. 346.

44. Thus Colledge, Marler, and Grant render the lines unexceptionally: " He is complete, / And from this so am I" (pp. 153–54). But Ellen Babinsky reads, just as plausibly, "He is fullness, / And by this am I impregnated" (p. 201).

45. *Mirouer* ch. 6, p. 24.

46. "Mais ainçoys les Vertuz font tout ce que telles Ames veullent, sans danger et sans contredit, car telles Ames sont leurs maistresses." *Mirouer* ch. 8, p. 30.

47. *Roman de la rose,* lines 5388–404. Among the departed Virtues are Right, Chastity, Faith, and Justice.

48. The plucking of the Rose is not technically rape, since Bel Acuel has freely granted it to the Lover (lines 21340–5). But the sex scene that follows emphasizes the Lover's violent and selfish pleasure, while Bel Acuel protests that he is "trop outrageus" (21739). See Kathryn Gravdal, *Ravishing Maidens: Writing Rape in Medieval French Literature and Law* (Philadelphia: University of Pennsylvania Press, 1991), pp. 68–71; Leslie Cahoon, "Raping the Rose: Jean de Meun's Reading of Ovid's *Amores,*" *Classical and Modern Literature* 6 (1986): 261–85.

49. This was the stance of Christine de Pizan's adversaries (Jean de Montreuil, Pierre and Gontier Col) in the *querelle de la Rose.* More recently it has been argued by Joan Ferrante, *Woman as Image,* pp. 111–17, and John Fleming, *Reason and the Lover* (Princeton: Princeton University Press, 1984), among many others.

50. Colledge, Marler, and Grant, *Mirror,* pp. xliv–xlv; McGinn, *Flowering,* p. 245; Robert Lerner, *The Heresy of the Free Spirit in the Later Middle Ages* (Berke-

ley and Los Angeles: University of California Press, 1972), pp. 75–76. For the complete trial records, see Paul Verdeyen, "Le procès d'inquisition contre Marguerite Porete et Guiard de Cressonessart (1309–1310)," *Revue d'histoire ecclésiastique* 81 (1986): 48–94.

51. "Quod se in actibus exercere virtutum est hominis imperfecti, et perfecta anima licentiat a se virtutes." *Errores Beguardorum et Beguinarum de statu perfectionis, Constitutio* "Ad nostrum" (May 6, 1312), article 6. Henricus Denzinger, *Enchiridion symbolorum, definitionum et declarationum de rebus fidei et morum,* 33rd ed. (Freiburg: Herder, 1965), p. 282.

52. "[Laquelle Ame] donne a Nature tout ce qu'il luy fault, sans remors de conscience; mais telle nature est si bien ordonnee par transformacion de unité d'Amour . . . que la nature ne demande chose qui soit deffendue." *Mirouer* ch. 9, p. 32. Cf. Colledge, Marler and Grant, *Mirror,* p. xlv.

53. "Quod mulieris osculum, cum ad hoc natura non inclinet, est mortale peccatum; actus autem carnalis, cum ad hoc natura inclinet, peccatum non est, maxime cum tentatur exercens." "Ad nostrum," article 7; Denzinger, *Enchiridion,* p. 282.

54. Appendix 2 in Colledge, Marler, and Grant, *Mirror,* p. 187. On this translation, see Nicholas Watson, "Melting into God the English Way: Deification in the Middle English Version of Marguerite Porete's *Mirouer des simples âmes anienties,*" in Rosalynn Voaden, ed., *Prophets Abroad: The Reception of Continental Holy Women in Late-Medieval England* (Cambridge: D. S. Brewer, 1996), pp. 19–49.

55. "Arés, por Dieu, baron, arés, / Et vos linages reparés." *Roman de la rose,* lines 19701–2.

56. *Chartularium Universitatis Parisiensis,* vol. 1, no. 473, ad 1277, ed. Henri Denifle (Paris: Delalain, 1889), pp. 543–55.

57. These are propositions no. 168 ("Quod continentia non est essentialiter virtus"), 169 ("Quod perfecta abstinentia ab actu carnis corrumpit virtutem et speciem"), and 183 ("Quod simplex fornicatio, utpote soluti cum soluta, non est peccatum"). Ibid., p. 553.

58. "Librum etiam 'De amore,' sive 'De Deo amoris,' qui sic incipit: *Cogit me multum,* etc. et sic terminatur: *Cave igitur, Galtere* . . . per eandem sententiam nostram condempnamus." Ibid., p. 543.

59. Lerner, *Heresy of the Free Spirit,* especially pp. 78–84.

CHAPTER 6

DIGULLEVILLE'S *PÈLERINAGE DE JÉSUS CHRIST*: A POEM OF COURTLY DEVOTION

Maureen Boulton

At two periods separated by a quarter of a century, the monk Guillaume de Digulleville, attached to the Cistercian abbey of Chaalis, north of Paris, composed a series of three allegorical poems devoted to aspects of the Christian life.[1] In 1330–1332, Guillaume presented his first vision of the journey of the Christian in this world in the *Pèlerinage de vie humaine,* a work written in response to the *Roman de la rose* intended to create an art not of love, but of spiritual pilgrimage. The poem, originally aimed at a lay audience, circulated widely; it survives in fifty-three manuscripts (twenty-three of them cyclic), was adapted into prose in the fifteenth century, and was finally provided with a critical edition in 1893.[2] Claiming to be alarmed by its success, Digulleville subjected it to a thorough revision in 1355.[3] The second version of the poem was directed to a new (possibly monastic) audience, who were expected to read the work rather than hear it read.[4] Less popular than the original version (only nine manuscripts survive, including five of the complete cycle), the revised *Vie humaine* was the basis of Lydgate's *Pilgrimage of the Life of Man,* and made the transition to print in two separate editions.[5] Unfortunately, this version of the poem has not found a modern editor, and must be consulted in manuscript.

Immediately upon completing the revision of the first poem, Digulleville set to work composing two sequels. The first, which he called the *Pèlerinage de l'âme,* is preserved in forty-four copies, including those in the twenty-three cyclic manuscripts. It recounts the soul's adventures in the next world, and like Dante's *Commedia,* explores the regions of hell before providing a vision of Paradise.[6] Digulleville concluded his trilogy in

1358 with the *Pèlerinage de Jésus Christ,* which relates the salvation of
mankind by concentrating on the son of God made man. This work is preserved in three copies in addition to the cyclic manuscripts. The great
number of manuscripts of Digulleville's works reflect their popularity, and
many copies are lavishly illustrated, suggesting that they were held in high
esteem by people of substance.[7] The whole cycle made the transition to
print in the early sixteenth century, while the first two poems were not
only printed separately but also reworked into prose. The first poem was
also successful in translation: There are versions in English, Dutch, German,
Spanish, and Italian.[8]

By producing versions of the *Vie humaine* tailored for audiences both
lay and clerical, Digulleville cast his net very wide indeed, and the cycle
was undeniably successful, but not always as he intended. The second and
presumably definitive version of the *PVH* provided the impetus for the
cycle as a whole, but occurs in only five of the cyclic manuscripts. The
eighteen other cyclic manuscripts incorporate the first version, which was
more obviously influenced by the *Roman de la rose.* Where the provenance
of the surviving manuscripts can be determined, it tends to confirm the
success of the first version with lay audiences. Six of the cyclic manuscripts
appear in the possession of prominent laymen, including Philippe the
Bold, duke of Burgundy (Brussels, Bibliothèque royale, 10197–98); Jean
Bourré, the treasurer of France under Louis XI (Paris, Bibliothèque nationale, fr. 823); Claude Montaige, lord of Couche and knight of the
Golden Fleece (died 1470; London, British Library, Add. 22927), and
Charles VIII of France (Paris, Bibliothèque nationale, fr. 376). Similarly one
of the cyclic manuscripts based on the clerical revision was written in the
monastery of "Mortuimaris" or Mortemer (Paris, Bibliothèque de l'Arsenal, 3646). On the other hand, a Benedictine monk of the Guisnes family
commissioned a cycle incorporating the first version (Brussels, Bibliothèque royale, 10176–77). The Middle English translation presents a con-
verse situation: The cleric John Lydgate, writing at the request of the earl
of Salisbury, translated the second, clerical version for his patron. The second recension also served as the basis of the printed edition of the cycle
produced in Paris by Barthole and Jean Petit, ca. 1500.[9]

The messages of all three of the poems are religious, but only the third relates the life of Christ, and thus forms part of the corpus of New Testament
apocrypha in medieval French that has been the object of much of my scholarly attention for some years. I shall attempt in this article first to establish the
unity of the cycle as a whole. Since the *Pèlerinage de Jésus Christ* has been the
least studied of the three poems in the trilogy, I shall then situate it within the
context of the cycle, before concentrating on the innovations in literary technique that characterize it, particularly the dream vision, allegorical personifi-

cations, lyric insertions and direct discourse. In the last part of the essay, I will discuss how Digulleville adapted the devices of the courtly *dit* in order to enhance the affective quality of his account of the life of Christ.

In his second campaign of composition, Digulleville clearly conceived of the *Pèlerinage de vie humaine* as the first segment of a projected trilogy.[10] In revising the poem, for instance, he suppressed details of the death of Judas (*PVH* 9421–26, 9539–66), but gave a fuller account in the final poem of the series (*PJC* 8261–70, 8507–18), including references to the crimes of Judas' youth: like Oedipus, Judas was reported to have killed his father (during a theft), and later to have married his mother. The uniformity of their titles also suggests that Digulleville intended the poems to form a cycle, and they are presented as such in at least a third of the surviving copies.

The printed edition and most of the cyclic manuscripts follow the order of composition of the poems, beginning with a version of the *Vie humaine,* followed by the *Pèlerinage de l'âme,* and ending with the *Pèlerinage de Jésus Christ.* This order also reflects the narrator's experience: the first poem is autobiographical, and ends with the pilgrim's provisional failure. The sequel reports the pilgrim's prophetic vision of his own punishment. His failure illustrates the human need for salvation by Jesus Christ, and this in turn is dramatized in the final segment. In three manuscripts, however, the scribes have altered the conventional order: Arras, Bibliothèque municipale 845; Paris, Bibliothèque nationale, fr. 12464; and St Petersburg, National Library, Fr. f. v. XIV. 4—all begin with the *Pèlerinage de Jésus Christ* before continuing with the *Vie* and *Ame.*[11] This reordering provides a historical chronology: After Christ's salvific work, the pilgrim makes his inevitably flawed attempt to follow His teachings, and is punished for his failings before entering into Paradise. Although the change in order seems deliberate, it nevertheless reflects a literal misreading of Digulleville's project: By placing the life of Christ at the end of his cycle, the poet-monk intended to demonstrate to his readers their inability to reach their goal unaided, and hence their dependence on the savior.

Later scribes, adapters, and translators felt free to ignore the intended unity and produced copies of single poems or partial cycles. There are eleven manuscripts of the first version followed by the second poem, and three others with the second redaction and the sequel alone. The prose versions of the first two poems always circulated independently, both in manuscript and in printed editions.[12] Two fifteenth-century manuscripts (Paris, Bibliothèque de l'Arsenal 3169, Bibliothèque nationale, fr. 14976), which contain only the *Pèlerinage de Jésus Christ,* function as single-text volumes of the life of Christ, and resemble the verse compilation in Grenoble, Bibliothèque municipale 51 (1137), a fourteenth-century volume containing a series of older poems on the genealogy, infancy, life, and Passion of Christ.[13]

The *Pèlerinage de vie humaine* belongs to (and indeed is the defining work of) the genre described by Siegfried Wenzel as the Pilgrimage of Life. It is characteristic of the genre to be concerned with "man's entire spiritual way through life from the cradle to the grave."[14] In Digulleville's conception, however, the grave was not the end but a new beginning. The *Pèlerinage de l'âme,* continuing the pilgrim's journey to his true home in the next life, was thus a necessary conclusion to the quest. Since his aim in writing was to instruct, the third poem, presenting the model journey of the ideal pilgrim, Jesus Christ, was a logical conclusion to the series.

Beyond genre and title, the three poems are further unified by a common set of literary devices—the dream structure, allegorical personages (either borrowed from or modeled on those of the *Roman de la rose*), and forms of lyric insertions—and by motifs that recur to link one poem to the next. As he stated in an often-quoted passage in the prologue to the *Pèlerinage de vie humaine* (vv. 7–14), Digulleville fell asleep after reading the *Roman de la rose* and responded to it with a dream of his own. The dependence of the *Vie humaine* upon the *Rose* has been thoroughly explored. Badel has indicated how Digulleville appropriated the metaphor of the pilgrim, the figure of Reason from the earlier poem, in an attempt to correct it by providing for it a "contrepartie religieuse, édifiante."[15] Steven Wright has explored this relationship in more detail, while Sylvia Huot has examined Digulleville's poem as a rethinking of the *Rose.*[16]

In addition to the direct borrowing from the *Rose,* Digulleville's poem is related to it in its style, particularly in its use of direct discourse. In studying the proportion of narrative to direct discourse in the two parts of the *Rose,* Anouk de Wolf has remarked "une véritable inflation du discours direct au point que le rôle du narrateur semble se réduire à celui d'un metteur en scène."[17] Whereas 65 percent of Guillaume de Lorris's *Rose* is narrative, the proportion is reduced to 16 percent in Jean de Meun's section. In this respect, Digulleville's *Pèlerinage de vie humaine* resembles the continuation of the *Rose* very closely, for the narrative accounts for only 18 percent of the text. Digulleville may be seen quite literally as a "metteur en scène," for a version of the *Vie humaine* is included as a "moralité" in the dramatic MS 617 of the Musée Condé in Chantilly.[18]

Although the original version of the *Pèlerinage de vie humaine* was inspired by reading the *Roman de la rose,* Digulleville suppressed this reference in his revised version, replacing it with a passage condemning the moral failings of the *Rose.*[19] In keeping with his changed attitude toward the *Rose,* its influence on the sequels is less obvious. The second poem, which arose out of the poet's reflection on the (revised) version of the first, is distanced from the *Rose.* On the other hand, turning away from the *Rose* did not signal a rejection of the techniques of courtly poetry. On the contrary, in his *Pèlerinage de l'âme,* Digulleville resorted to the lyric insertion device common in secular works from the early thirteenth century.[20] Thirteenth-century writers usually borrowed extant songs and quoted them either partially or completely in the narrative context of a romance or a *dit.* In the next century, however, Digulleville's contemporaries, including Jean Acart and Guillaume de Machaut composed new lyric poems (with or without music) for inclusion in their *dits.* Digulleville adopted neither approach, but approximated the latter. His poem is studded with twelve "lyric" passages, described as sung in the text, but most are not cast in lyric form. Only the "Complainte de l'âme," the "Lettre de Grace Dieu," and the "Chanson piteuse" of the souls in hell are composed in the form standardized by Machaut in his *Remede de fortune,* in stanzas with the same meter and rhyme.[21] In contrast, the "Complainte de la Vierge" is composed in irregular laisses, distinguished only by the opening exclamatory syllable, while the "Complainte des enfans mors et non baptisés" interrupts neither the meter nor the rhyme of the surrounding narrative verse.[22] Similarly, the seven so-called chansons are all composed in octosyllabic couplets that are metrically indistinguishable from the narrative verse.[23] Lacking the metrical form of fourteenth-century lyric genres, and without musical notation, the status of these pieces as "songs" is established only by the narrative context, which presents them all as sung, and usually mentions instrumental accompaniment. Digulleville thus alluded to the lyric insertion technique that would have been familiar to his audience, but in failing to use courtly lyric forms, he signaled his distance from courtly poetry.

If Digulleville seemed to turn away from the *Roman de la rose* in his *Pèlerinage de l'âme,* the beginning of the third poem shows the poet-narrator succumbing once more to the spell of courtly poetry. The opening scene of the *Pèlerinage de Jésus Christ* takes place in a garden—of fruit trees rather than flowers—filled with singing birds. Enchanted by their song, he stops to listen and falls asleep once more: "Ainsi escoutai longuement / Ce douz chant tout a mon talent, . . . si m'endormi / Et en dormant mervelles vi / En songant songe mervelleus . . ." [So I listened as long as I wished to the sweet song . . . ; then I fell asleep and in sleeping saw marvels, dreaming a marvelous dream (*PJC* 49–50, 53–55)]. This courtly garden, reminiscent of the *Rose,* provides a frame for the poem, for when the narrator wakes at the end, the birds are still singing. The garden is not simply the place where the dreamer falls asleep, but it is also part of his dream, for it gradually reveals itself as the Garden of Eden. The *locus amoenus* of the *Rose* dissolves into the garden of original sin. The description of the garden illustrates both the continuing inspiring power of the *Roman de la rose* as well as Digulleville's adaptation of it. The garden here is both real and dreamed, but in the dream it becomes the locus of religious meaning.

The unity of the three poems is established not only by the influence of the *Rose* but also by a series of *reprises* that link them in sequence. The first two poems are linked by the repetition of the deadly sins, who appear as temptations in the *Vie humaine* and as vices punished in its sequel. The second poem opens with the death of the pilgrim and the judgment of his soul. Accused by Reason, Justice, and Truth, the pilgrim's soul is saved from hell by the intercession of Mercy. The debate of these four figures recurs in the context of the punishment of Adam at the beginning of the third poem.[24] At the end of the second poem, after the soul of the pilgrim has been escorted into heaven, he sees a magical circle that represents the celestial calendar and is made up of the principal feasts of the Church. The list of these feasts—from the Immaculate Conception to the Assumption— evokes the episodes of the life of Christ and provides a synopsis of the third poem. These repeated themes and motifs are not (as is sometimes alleged) signs of waning poetic inspiration, but are deliberate connecting devices that reinforce the coherence of the cycle.

The dream-vision—the most obvious of Digulleville's borrowings from the *Roman de la rose*—supplies the framing structure in all three poems. In the first two poems, the dream allows the narrator great temporal and spatial liberty: These works embrace the narrator's life from before birth to long after his imagined death. By means of the dream, he is able to explore not only the entire span of human life, but also the realms of the afterlife. These two poems are the most admired of Digulleville's work; Badel, for instance, describes them as "grandes réussites de la poésie allégorique."[25] Critical reaction to the use of the dream-vision in the third poem, however, has been unenthusiastic: Faral considered it a useless complication, required to conform to the series; Badel called it "une sorte de perversion du poème allégorique."[26] What these critics have failed to realize is that Digulleville needed the enormous freedom of movement afforded by the dream. It enabled him to observe the remote past (the fall of Adam) and also to enter the mind of God (as He considered how and whether to save mankind from the consequences of Adam's sin). The dreamer of the final poem is displaced as protagonist by the ideal pilgrim who is Christ; the dreamer is reduced to an observer of the journey. When Langlois dismissed the *Pèlerinage de Jésus Christ* as "une Vie de Jésus comme il y en a eu tant à l'époque,"[27] he neither characterized what it has in common with other lives of Christ, nor signaled how it differs from them. In fact, Digulleville's use of the dream-vision in the third poem allows his narrator to participate in the events of Christ's life, to respond to them, and to provoke reactions from his audience. Through the allegorical dream-vision, the poet is able to move from the realm of didactic exposition to that of affective devotion, and it is from this perspective that I propose to evaluate his adaptation of courtly techniques.

As the conclusion of the trilogy, the *Pèlerinage de Jésus Christ* is tied to the earlier poems by its title, the convention of the dream-vision, and the continuation of the allegorical interventions. Nevertheless, Digulleville also modified his techniques in this poem, as he did in the second poem. The dreamer here is no longer the protagonist of his dream, but the witness and interpreter of the actions he narrates. The other techniques employed in the first two poems, particularly lyric insertions, allegorical personifications, and direct discourse, are adapted in similar ways.

Digulleville did not abandon lyric insertions in the *Pèlerinage de Jésus Christ* but did reduce their number, including only five "chansons" and two "complaintes."[28] In contrast to his practice in the *Pèlerinage de l'âme,* Digulleville is less insistent on the instrumental accompaniment of the inserted "songs" in the third poem. Instead, he discusses the songs in a rather more theoretical way. Near the beginning of the work, in the context of commenting on the *Magnificat* (which he neither quotes nor translates,)[29] Digulleville indicates the qualities he believes necessary for a good song:

C'est qu'il y appartient biau dit,
Et qu'il y ait chant bien ellit,
Et que cil qui chanteur s'en fait
Ellite et bonne voiz il ait.

[These are that it must possess beautiful words / and excellent music, / and the one who sings / must have an excellent voice.] (*PJC* 1607–10)

For Digulleville, the art of the song required not only the highest quality of both words and music but also of performance. In articulating his lyric ideal, Digulleville suggested why he did not attempt to make his "lyric insertions" conform to the genres practiced by contemporary poets. Since he was clearly no musician, he may have felt it pointless to imitate the forms of lyric poetry. He relied instead on discursive description to convey the impression he wished to suggest. The *Magnificat* meets each of his criteria for a good song. Its words in praise of God are beautiful, and the voice of the performer (Mary) is sweet. The "biau chant," or music of the canticle, he found in its content, which he analyzed using the polyphonic motet as a metaphor.[30] Alluding to the three voices in a triple motet, the "teneure" or base line (1628) of Mary's canticle is her description of herself as the handmaiden ("chambriere" [1629]) of God; the middle voice (1631) is the delight she takes in her son (1632–33); the upper voice or triplum (1635) is her declaration that everyone will call her blessed ("chascun la dira / Benoite" [1636–37]). The metaphor continues, for the song is sung in B flat when it speaks of God's mercy to the humble, but changes to B natural when it states that the proud will be brought low (1645–54).[31] Although not a musician, Digulleville revealed himself in this passage to be familiar with musical terminology, which he used skillfully to illustrate how the interweaving of themes, like the counterpoint of voices, embellishes the poetic text.

Near the end of the work, the poet evokes the joy of the firmament at the Assumption of the Virgin by means of a technical description of polyphonic song:

> Longuement la feste dura
> Et grant joie avoit ca et la
> De sons, chans et melodies
> Par acors et armonies,
> Si entremellés doucement
> Qu'il sembloit que le firmament
> En fourmiast et en risist
> Ausi com se chanter vousist.
> Et telle l'ordenance estoit
> Selonc qu'à semblant me venoit,
> Quar Adam et ceuz qui la sus
> Estoient de nouvel venus
> Tenoient le pié de dessouz
> De quanque sus chantoient touz
> Les angres, la feste menans
> Sus les cercles et festoians.

[The feast lasted long, / and there was great joy here and there, / with music and songs and melodies / with chords and harmonies / so sweetly intermixed / that it seemed that the firmament / was moved by it and laughed at it / as if it wished to sing. / And such was the arrangement, / as it seemed to me, / for Adam and those who / had newly come up there / held the lower voice / of whatever all the angels / sang above, leading the feast / above the circles and celebrating.] (*PJC* 10607–22)

In a ranking of singers that reflects the celestial hierarchy, Adam and the other new arrivals from purgatory sing the tenor or bass line of the music, while the angels sing the upper voice. The words that follow this passage are those of the tenor. The text sung by the angels is not quoted, perhaps because heavenly voices are not comprehensible to mortal ears. The singers are grouped in a hierarchical order but sing together to produce a beautiful sound to illustrate the harmony of heaven. This passage recalls another in the final section of the *Ame* on the heavenly celebration of the feasts of the Virgin. The angels discuss at some length (*PA* 9855–9938) the role of music in the celebration, and stress the necessity of learning music, particularly harmony and "l'art organique," or *organum:*[32]

> Ordenons nous et aprestons
> A faire feste com devons!
> Aus escoles de musique
> Alons tous pour l'armonique
> Et pour la rethmique aprendre,
> Et pour aussi bien entendre
> A l'art organique savoir!

> [Let us arrange and prepare / to make a feast as we ought! / To the schools of music / let us go to learn harmony / and arithmetic, / and also to listen well to know / the art of *organum.*] (*PA* 9865–71)

Despite the use of the technical term here, Digulleville does not describe a particular type of musical composition, but only evokes a branch of musical study. The relationship of these passages is consistent with Digulleville's practice of repetition with development. In the second poem, he stresses the role of music, and particularly polyphonic music in the celestial harmony, while in the final poem, he develops his perception of the order of musical harmony and illustrates it, not through sound, but through the analysis of words.

The first two poems are similarly linked by a continuing cast of allegorical figures—some (like Raison and Oiseuse) borrowed from the *Rose,* others (particularly Grace-Dieu and the seven deadly sins) taken from religious allegory. In contrast, the role of allegorical personifications is altered in the final poem, where figures from the *Rose* are rare. Nature, for instance, appears only briefly, to debate with Joseph at the Nativity of Christ (*PJC* 1995–2145). The role of Poverty, on the other hand, who appeared only briefly near the end of the first poem, is significantly expanded in the third. It is Poverty who presides at the Nativity, serving as midwife to the Virgin (*PJC* 1811–46). Reason, Truth, Justice, and Mercy, who argued over the fate of the pilgrim's soul at the beginning of the *Pèlerinage de l'âme,* frame the long account of the life of Christ. It is their debate at the beginning of the final poem that dramatizes man's plight after Adam's fall. At the end of the poem, when Jesus has returned to heaven with his pilgrim's staff, God the Father addresses three of the ladies (Truth, Justice, and Mercy) to remind them of their dispute about the fate of Adam, and to ask if they are now satisfied with the result (*PJC* 10421–62). They are pleased to approve and to join in the songs of the angels celebrating Christ's return to heaven (*PJC* 10471–10594). Other characters, such as Ignorance and Old Law (Vieille Loi) appear to be new introductions in the final poem. Old Law debates with Mary over the Circumcision (*PJC* 2410–2494) and with Joseph on the occasion of the Purification (*PJC* 2800–2934). Although Jesus in his youth conformed to the requirements of Old Law so as to serve as an example of humility (*PJC* 2770–74), he informs her of the end of her rule when he begins his public life (*PJC* 4747–63). Nevertheless, allegorical characters appear only intermittently in the third poem, and are much less important to the plot than they or their analogues were in the first two.

Corresponding to the decline in allegorical personifications is the greatly increased role of the narrator in the third poem. In contrast to the first poem, where narration accounted for less than a fifth of its total length, nearly half (48 percent) of the *Pèlerinage de Jésus Christ* is narrative, or at least attributable to the narrator. These interventions serve a variety of purposes. Part of the increase is certainly due to the fact that the third poem is not autobiographical. In the middle section of the poem (*PJC* 5177–7562), Digulleville summarizes the events and sermons of the public life of Christ:

> Or est m'entente de dire
> Puis ci avant et escrire
> Mainz faiz et mainz dis qu'en chemin
> Fist puis et dist ce pelerin,
> Des plus notables mesmement
> Selonc que pourrai plus briément.

[Now I intend to say, / and then to write / many of the most notable deeds and sayings / that were performed by this pilgrim, / as briefly as I can.] (*PJC* 5177–82)

Unlike most similar works, which concentrate on the Infancy and the Passion, Digulleville highlights Christ's teachings. But his attempt to collect the sayings of Jesus from the Gospels leads to a succession of narrative sentences in the third person broken only by scriptural quotations and occasional authorial comments.

Although the convention of the dream-vision served Digulleville well in allowing him to cover immense stretches of time and space, there are moments when he modifies his technique. In the opening section of the work, for instance, there is an interesting example of *mise-en-abyme* narration. After reporting the dispute among the "Daughters of God" (Reason, Truth, Justice, and Mercy), there is a brief passage (*PJC* 643–72) in which the narrator disappears behind the character of Truth.[33] In order to resolve the dispute, Truth calls on God to decide the fate of mankind, and she reports the debate among the persons of the Trinity:

Lors monta haut et demoura
Par longue espace et sejourna,
Et puis revint où elle estoit
Par devant où en l'atendoit,
Et dist ainsi: "Jë ay parlé
Au roy, un Dieu en trinité,
Si com assez tost le verres
Par effet et bien le sares."

[Then she rose on high and remained / and stayed a long time, / and then came back where she had been before, / where she was awaited, / and said: "I have spoken / to the king, a God in trinity, / and as you will see it soon enough / by its effect and you will know it well."] (*PJC* 639–46)

On her return, Truth reports the debate of the separate persons of God:

Quant devant le roy o conté
Ce de quoi avïons parlé
Et quelles les opinions
Ëu ensemble en avïons,
Le pere le fil regarda
Et a dire ainsi commenca . . .

[When I had recounted before the king / what we had discussed, / and what opinions / we had about it, / the Father looked at the Son / and began to speak. . . .](*PJC* 667–72)

This introduction has the effect of displacing the narrative to one of his allegorical personifications. In this way, Digulleville distances himself from his narrative, and makes his imaginative representation of the mind of God seem less presumptuous.

In the Infancy and the Passion sections, the action advances through dialogue, and the narrative technique more closely resembles that of the first two poems. But even here, the proportion of narration is significantly greater. As in the first two poems, the narrator recounts by presenting a cast of characters who enact a drama before the eyes of his reader. Here, however, the chief actors in these parts are historical figures, rather than allegorical personifications. Since in this poem the narrator is no longer the protagonist, he can participate in the narrative only by exploiting the possibilities of the dream-vision, which allows him to enter the action by reacting to the story he tells. The narrator's interventions are consequently more frequent in the third poem than in the first two. Near the end of the passage on the Nativity, for instance, the narrator explains to the Virgin the reason for the poverty of her surroundings:

He tres douce chamberiere,
La chambre où tu sers mont chiere
Ne te doit estre ne plaisant
Se n'est pour cause de l'enfant
Qui y est venu reprimer
L'orguel du monde et supplanter.
Petit s'est fait qui estoit grant,
Povre qui estoit habundant.

[Ah! Sweetest handmaid, / the chamber where you serve most dearly /
would not be pleasing to you, / if it were not for the child / who came to
repress / and supplant the pride of the world. / He has made himself small
who was great, / poor who was rich.] (*PJC* 2267–74)

By addressing the Virgin, the narrator inserts himself into the scene and
also explains it to his audience. On other occasions, the narrator's excla-
mations express an emotional reaction to the events he recounts. As Joseph
flees Herod's menace and leads his family to Egypt, the narrator exclaims
in a passage beginning:

He Egypte, apparelle toi!
Voiz ci ton sauveur et ton roy
Qui toi vëoir et visiter
Vient pour tes erreurs dissiper!
Va, si abat tes ydoles, . . .
Voiz ci le sauveur d'Israel.

[Ah! Egypt, prepare yourself! / Behold your savior and your king / who
comes to see and visit you / to dispel your errors! Go, strike down your
idols. . . . Behold the savior of Israel.] (*PJC* 3643–47, 3651)

Such interjections draw attention to remarkable aspects of a very familiar
story; they both provoke and guide the readers' response to the story. In
personalizing his narrative with his own emotional response, Digulleville
participated in the tradition of affective devotion that became increasingly
important throughout the fourteenth and fifteenth centuries.

In the section dealing with the Passion, the narrator's interventions are
more frequent and more intense. By exclaiming on the events he reports,
he enters the action and becomes a participant. After the arrest of Christ,
for instance, the narrator addresses Peter:

He, Pierre, comment as tu non?
De pierre la condicion
N'as mie, se mont mole n'est. . . .

En peril es, se ne reprens
En toi vigueur tant com as tempz.
Bien as trouve ce que te dist
Jhesus, que prest est l'esperit
De prametre et de soi vanter,
Mez la char de l'executer
Est enferme et pereceuse. . . .

[Ah! Peter, what is your name? / You have not the condition / of rock unless it is soft. . . .You are in danger, if you do not regain / your strength while
you have time. / You have indeed discovered / what Jesus told you, that the
spirit is ready / to promise and to boast, / but the flesh is infirm / and lazy
in execution. . . .] (*PJC* 8335–37, 8355–61)

The spectacle of Christ alone among his tormentors, abandoned by his
disciples, elicits a similar reproach (*PJC,* 8453–72), but Pilate's judgment
provokes a different outburst:

O mauvaiz juge, que feras?
Nulle cause trouvee n'as
Pour quoi doie painne soufrir,
Tu ne m'en pues jamaiz mentir,
Quar tesmoingnié publiquement
L'as maintenant devant la gent. . . .

[O wicked judge, what will you do? / You have found no cause / why I
should suffer a penalty; / you can never lie to me / about it for you testi-
fied publicly / before the people. . . . (*PJC* 8783–88)

As he draws his reader's attention to Pilate's injustice, the narrator's own
emotional involvement in the scene leads him to imagine himself in the
place of Christ. He seeks to provoke an emotional response from his readers
as he guides their reactions to his narrative. Such techniques—characteristic
of Latin devotional texts from the later thirteenth century—become common in the vernacular in the fifteenth century.[34]

After recounting the jibe of the bad thief, the narrator addresses the
crucified Christ:

He Jhesu, ne me puis taire,
Comme en ce fait debonnaire
As este et tres patient!
Se n'avoies autre tourment
Que ces dis tres envenimés,
Si es tu mont au cuer navrés.

[Ah, Jesus, I cannot be silent: / how you have been / most patient in this fair deed! / If you had no other torment / than these poisonous words, / you are still wounded to the heart.] (*PJC* 8973–78)

When he goes on to compare Jesus to the pelican that pours out its blood for its young, he demonstrates that his narrative is moving, and also seeks to provoke a similar reaction from his readers.

Emile Mâle stated that the *Pèlerinage de Jésus Christ* was influenced by, and is indeed often a paraphrase of, the *Meditationes vitae Christi,* composed in Italy for a Franciscan nun in the first part of the fourteenth century.[35] Since the only surviving French translations of *Meditationes* date from the fifteenth century, this influence would be significant if it could be substantiated. A comparison of the two works certainly reveals striking similarities of tone, theme, and technique. After the opening dream-vision, which is unique to the *Pèlerinage,* the two works also share the same general structure, and it is possible that Digulleville was familiar with the *Meditationes.* Nevertheless Digulleville's work is also markedly different from the *Meditationes* in a number of important ways. A particularly striking parallel between them, for example, is the debate among the daughters of God over the redemption of mankind. Even here, however, Digulleville's version of this scene differs significantly from that in the *Meditationes,* and appears to be an independent treatment.[36] Both narratives are punctuated by narratorial comments that are emotional responses to the events related, but here again there are marked differences. When Judas kisses Jesus in the garden, the narrator of the *Meditationes* exclaims:

> Or du faulx traitre Judas que a il fait, regarde, beau filz, le bon seigneur Jhesucrist comme paciamment et benignement il reçoit les enforcemens et le traictreux baiser de ce maudit homme a qui ung pou paravant il avoit lavé les piez et l'avoit aviandé de la tres souveraine viande de son tres precieux corps. . . ."[37]

> [Now, regarding the false traitor Judas, and what he did; look, fair son, at the good Lord, how patiently and benignly he receives the forcing and the treacherous kiss of that accursed man, whose feet he had washed a little while ago, and whom he had fed with the most sovereign meat of his precious body. . . .]

The point of the exclamation is to draw the attention of his reader (consistently addressed in this translation as "beau filz") to the spectacle that the narrative creates before his eyes.[38] The same moment provokes a different response from Guillaume, who addresses first the Virgin, and then Judas:

Douce Virge, que feroies,
Se ce baisier tu vëoies,
Que ce trahitre ainsi baisast
Ton fil, et touchier y ousast?
C'est ausi com acolement
De faucille qui asprement
Soie le ble a l'acoler
Pour li du tout jus aterrer.
Et tu Judas, comment ousé
De li aprochier as esté?
Ne scez tu pas quë il scet bien
Que n'en aproches pas pour bien. . . .

[Sweet Virgin, what would you do, / if you saw this kiss, / that the traitor gave / your son and dared to touch him? / It is like the embrace / of the scythe that saws the wheat / to cut it to earth. / And you Judas, how did you dare / to approach him? / Don't you know that he knows well / that you do not approach for good. . . .](*PJC* 8223–34)

Unlike the author of the *Meditationes,* who addresses his reader, the narrator of the *Pèlerinage* usually addresses the characters in his narrative. He thus inserts himself into the action. The purpose of these interventions is to guide the reactions of this audience, but they do not address the latter directly. In shaping the reactions of his readers, Digulleville invites their participation through emotional response to the narrative.

The most important difference between the works, however, is the framing technique of the dream-vision, employed by Digulleville, as we have seen, on the model of the *Roman de la rose.* Despite Faral's strictures, the dream-vision adopted by Digulleville is well suited to the mode of affective devotion of his source. The form enables the dreamer-narrator to place the life of Christ within a cosmological framework, and to present it as a drama that unfolds before his (and therefore the reader's) eyes.

In conclusion, it may be said that Guillaume de Digulleville's *Pèlerinage de Jésus Christ* is an important example of the appropriation of the techniques of secular literature by authors of religious texts. Digulleville's introduction of allegorical figures, like "Poverty," distinguishes his account from earlier French versions of the life of Christ. The *Pèlerinage* was written at a turning point in religious literature in the vernacular, and participates in two separate traditions. On the one hand, as the last "life of Christ" written in French verse in the Middle Ages, the *Pèlerinage* is a worthy contribution to the body of such narratives that were produced from the twelfth century onward.[39] These works, most of them written in verse, include more or less fictional as well as canonical lives of Christ and his ancestors, and belong to the broader category of "New Testament apocrypha." With its strategies to engage the reader's emotions, on the other hand, the poem reveals a markedly affective approach to its subject, and anticipates the French translations of Latin works of affective devotion that proliferate in the fifteenth century.[40]

Notes

1. The author's name occurs in various spellings, some based on the acrostics that read "Guillermus de Deguilevilla" found in his poems: *Le Pèlerinage de l'âme,* ed. J. J. Stürzinger, Roxburghe Club 127 (London: Nichols, 1895), lines 10751–10980 (hereafter cited parenthetically by line number as *PA*); and *Le Pèlerinage de Jésus-Christ,* ed. J. J. Stürzinger, Roxburghe Club 133 (London: Nichols, 1897), lines 3679–3966 (hereafter cited parenthetically by line number as *PJC*). Paul Meyer ("Notices sur quelques manuscrits français de la bibliothèque Phillipps à Cheltenham" in *Notices et extraits* 34.1 [1891]: 172) notes that the name is based on the village of Digulleville in the arrondissement of Cherbourg, in the canton of Beaumont-Hague. Since then French critics have used the form "Guillaume de Digulleville," which I have adopted here.

2. J. J. Stürzinger, ed., *Le Pèlerinage de vie humaine, de Guillaume de Deguileville,* Roxburghe Club 124 (London: Nichols, 1893); the introduction lists the manuscripts for all three poems. For a translation into modern English, see Eugene Clasby, trans., *Guillaume de Deguileville: The Pilgrimage of Human Life (Le pèlerinage de la vie humaine)* (New York & London: Garland, 1992). See also Marion Lofthouse, "'Le pèlerinage de vie humaine' by Guillaume de Deguileville with Special Reference to the French MS. 2 of the John Rylands Library," *Bulletin of the John Rylands Library* 19 (1935): 170–215. This manuscript figures in Stürzinger's list as the manuscript of the earl of Crawford; by his count there are fifty-three manuscripts of the verse original and four manuscripts and three printed editions of the prose version (pp. 178–79). Rosemund Tuve (*Allegorical Imagery: Some Mediaeval Books and Their Posterity* [Princeton: Princeton University Press, 1966]) identifies the Huth manuscript as London, British Library Add. 38120 and adds Oxford, Bodleian Library Add. C.29 (p. 147, n.1). On the editions of the French prose version, see also Edmond Faral, "Guillaume de Digulleville, Jean Gallopes et Pierre Virgin," in *Etudes romanes dédiées à Mario Roques* (Paris: Droz, 1946), pp. 89–102.

3. On the second version, see Edmond Faral, "Guillaume de Digulleville: moine de Chaalis," *Histoire littéraire de la France,* 39 (Paris: Imprimerie Nationale, 1952), pp. 29–47; Lofthouse, "Le pèlerinage," pp. 184–88; and Sylvia Huot, *The Romance of the Rose and its Medieval Readers* (Cambridge: Cambridge University Press, 1993), pp. 225–30.

4. Geneviève Hasenohr, "Guillaume de Digulleville," in *Dictionnaire des lettres françaises,* 2nd ed. (Paris: Fayard, 1992), p. 615.

5. Lofthouse, "Le Pèlerinage," pp. 180–81. John Lydgate, *Pilgrimage of the Life of Man,* ed. F. J. Furnivall, EETS e. s. 77, 83, 92 (London: Early English Text Society, 1899–1904).

6. In Stürzinger, ed., *Pèlerinage de l'âme,* Paris, Bibliothèque nationale, fr. 12466 is the base manuscript. S. L. Galpin, "On the Sources of G. De Diguleville's *Pèlerinage de l'âme,*" *PMLA* 25 (1910): 275–308; and *Modern Language Notes* 28 (1913): 8–10. On the first two pilgrimages, see Ch.-V. Langlois, *La vie en France au Moyen Âge . . . IV. La vie Spirituelle . . .* (Paris: Hachette, 1928), pp. 99–268.

7. On the illustrated manuscripts see L. M. J. Delaissé, "Les miniatures du 'Pèlerinage de la vie humaine' de Bruxelles et l'archéologie du livre," *Scriptorium* 10 (1956): 233–50 and plates 16–25; Michael Camille, "The Illustrated Manuscripts of Guillaume de Deguileville's *Pèlerinages* 1330–1426" (Ph. D. thesis, Cambridge University, 1985) and "Reading the Printed Image: Illuminations and Woodcuts of the *Pèlerinage de la vie humaine* in the Fifteenth Century," in Sandra Hindman, ed., *Printing the Written Word: The Social History of Books, circa 1450–1520* (Ithaca: Cornell University Press, 1991), pp. 259–91; Rosemarie Bergmann, *Die Pilgerfahrt zum himmlischen Jerusalem. Ein allegorisches Gedicht des Spätmittelalters aus der Heidelberger Bilderhandschrift Cod. Pal. Lat. 1969 . . .* (Wiesbaden: Verlag, 1983).

8. Tuve, *Allegorical Imagery,* pp. 146–50. On the Spanish translation, see Langlois, *La vie en France,* p. 207 n.1; and Maryjane Dunn-Wood, "El pelerinage de la vida humana: A Study and Edition" (Ph. D. dissertation, University of Pennsylvania, 1985).

9. J. C. Brunet, *Manuel du libraire,* 2 (Paris: Firmin Didot, 1861), col. 1822–23; L. Hain, *Repertorium bibliographicum,* 1.2 (Stuttgart, Paris, 1827) No. 8327; W. A. Copinger, *Supplement to Hain's 'Repertorium bibliographicum,'* (London: Sotheran, 1895–1902) no. 8326 lists two copies in Paris; see Lofthouse, "Le pèlerinage," 181, for shelfmarks of copies in London and Oxford.

10. I differ here from Faral, who dismisses the unity of the trilogy as "bien discutable" ("Digulleville, Moine," 79).

11. In addition, Brussels, Bibliothèque royale 18066–67 and Paris, Bibliothèque de l'Institut 20 contain the *Pèlerinages de Jésus Christ* and *de l'âme;* the Paris manuscript has the second redaction of the *Vie humaine* in final place. On the Arras manuscript, see Huot, *Rose,* pp. 231–38; and Ernest Langlois, *Les manuscrits du 'Roman de la rose': Description et classement* (Lille: Tallandier; Paris: Champion, 1910), pp. 98–110.

12. Faral, "Digulleville, Moine," p. 11 n. 1; Lofthouse, "Le Pèlerinage," pp. 179, 181; Tuve, *Allegorical Imagery,* p. 148.

13. On this manuscript see Paul Meyer, "Notice du MS. 1137 de Grenoble," *Romania* 16 (1887): 214–31. Montpellier, Bibliothèque Interuniversitaire 350 is a similar volume.

14. Siegfried Wenzel, "The Pilgrimage of Life as a Late Medieval Genre," *Mediaeval Studies* 35 (1973): 371.

15. Pierre-Yves Badel, *"Le Roman de la rose" au XIVe siècle: Etude de la réception de l'oeuvre,* Publications romanes et françaises 153 (Geneva: Droz, 1980), p. 363.

16. Stephen Wright, "Deguileville's *Pèlerinage de vie humaine* as 'Contrepartie Edifiante' of the *Roman de la rose,*" *Philological Quarterly* 89 (1989): 399–422; and Huot, *Rose,* pp. 208–25; this chapter also examines how the scribe of Arras, Bibliothèque municipale 845 adapted the *Roman de la rose* to the theological context of the *Pèlerinage* through a judicious choice of extracts.

17. Anouk de Wolf, "Pratique de la personnification chez Guillaume de Digulleville et Philippe de Mézières" in *Ecriture et modes de pensée au Moyen Age (VIIIe-XVe siècles),* ed. Dominique Boutet and Laurence Harf-Lancner (Paris: Presses de l'Ecole Normale Supérieure, 1993), p. 126.

18. Gustave Cohen, ed., *Mystères et moralités du ms. 617 de Chantilly* (Paris, 1920; repr. Geneva: Slatkine, 1975), pp. 93–134.

19. This passage from the unedited version has been printed by Badel, *"Roman de la rose" au XIVe siècle,* pp. 368–69, from Paris, Bibliothèque nationale, fr. 12466; by Lofthouse, "Le pèlerinage," 188–89, from Manchester, John Rylands University Library MS. Fr. 2; cf. Huot, *Rose,* pp. 226–27.

20. See my *The Song in the Story: Lyric Insertions in French Narratives, 1200–1400* (Philadelphia: University of Pennsylvania Press, 1993).

21. *PA* 739–1074: "Oraison ou complainte de l'ame" (28 douzains rhyming aabaab bbabba); *PA* 1593–1784: "Lettre de Grace Dieu" (24 monorhymed huitains); *PA* 4703–4836: "Complaincte ou chanson piteuse et lugubreuse faicte en enfer par traistres et detracteurs" (one 6-line stanza [abccab] plus 32 quatrains, rhyming ddab, eeab, etc).

22. "Complainte piteuse de la Vierge" (*PA* 6353–6644: 292 lines in couplets: 19 laisses beginning "Hé!"); "Complainte des enfans mors et non baptisés" (*PA* 4397–4406: 5 couplets).

23. "Chançons": *PA* 2653–74; 2678–98; 2711–54 ; 2769–2804; 9681–84; 9996–10016; 10147–52.

24. On the allegory of these allegorical figures, see Hope Traver, *The Four Daughters of God: A Study of the Versions of this Allegory* (Bryn Mawr, Pa.: Bryn Mawr College, 1907), especially pp. 70–78 for Digulleville's treatment of it.

25. Pierre-Yves Badel, "Le poème allégorique," in *La littérature française aux XIVe et XVe siècles* (*GRLMA* 8.1; Heidelberg: Winter, 1988), p.151.

26. Faral, "Guillaume de Digulleville," p. 79; Badel, "Le poème allégorique," p. 151.

27. Ch.-V. Langlois, *La vie en France au moyen âge. IV, La vie spirituelle. Enseignements, méditations, et controverses* (Paris: Hachette, 1928), p. 202.

28. *PHC* vv. 10551–52 (2 lines); 10599–606 (8 lines); 10625–44 (20 lines); 10978–86 (8 lines); 11146–69 (24 lines). There are also two complaintes,

vv. 3697–3966 (24 12-line stanzas); 9151–9399 (18 laisses beginning "Hé!"; virtually identical to *PA* 6353–6644).

29. The canticle is named in v. 1613, and parts of it are paraphrased in the commentary.

30. On the motet, see the entry in *Dictionnaire des lettres françaises,* pp. 1030–31; Sylvia Huot, *Allegorical Play in the Old French Motet: The Sacred and the Profane in Thirteenth-Century Polyphony* (Stanford: Stanford University Press, 1997); Mark Everist, *French Motets in the Thirteenth Century: Music, Poetry and Genre* (Cambridge: Cambridge University Press, 1994).

31. This shift reflects the presence of the different notes in different hexachords: B flat occurs in the *hexachordum molle* (F-G-A-B flat-C-D), which is lower than the *hexachordum durum* (G-A-B natural-C-D-E) where B natural occurs. See David Hiley, "Accidental," Stanley Sadie and John Tyrrell, eds., *New Grove Dictionary of Music and Musicians,* 2nd ed. (New York: Grove's Dictionaries, 2001), 1:51–52.

32. On *organum,* see *New Grove Dictionary of Music and Musicians,* 18:671–95.

33. Judging from the variant verbal forms that Stürzinger recorded for this passage, the scribes had some difficulty following the shift in narrative voice.

34. On Latin texts, see Thomas H. Bestul, *Texts of the Passion: Latin Devotional Literature and Medieval Society* (Philadelphia: University of Pennsylvania Press, 1996). On French texts, see Maureen Boulton, "La passion pour la Passion: Les textes en moyen français," *Le moyen français* 44–45 (2000): 45–62. For examples of French texts, see Jean Gerson's sermon on the Passion "Ad Deum vadit" (P. Glorieux, ed., *Oeuvres complètes,* 7.2 [Paris: Desclée, 1968]); Christine de Pizan's *Heures de contemplation de la Passion* (edition forthcoming by Liliane Dulac); and Jehan Miélot's *Tresdevotes contemplations sur les.vii. heures de la Passion* (Paris, Bibliothèque nationale, fr. 12441, fols. 44r–65r).

35. Emile Mâle, *Religious Art in France: The Late Middle Ages* (Princeton: Princeton University Press, 1986). He states, "The celebrated poem by Guillaume de Deguileville, *Le Pèlerinage de Jésus-Christ* (Paris, Bibl. Nat., MS. fr. 14976), fourteenth century, is often only a paraphrase of the *Meditations*" (p. 459, n.25). On the *Meditationes,* see Columban Fisher, "Die 'Meditationes Vitae christi'. Ihre Handschriftliche Überlieferung und die Verfasserfrage," *Archivum franciscanum historicum* 25 (1932): 3–35; 175–209; 305–48; 449–83. The text was edited by A. C. Peltier, *Bonaventurae Opera omnia* 12 (Paris: Vives, 1968). For an English translation, see Isa Ragusa and Rosalie B. Green, *Meditations on the Life of Christ: An Illustrated Manuscript of the Fourteenth Century, Paris: Bibliothèque nationale, MS. Ital. 115* (Princeton: Princeton University Press, 1961).

36. Traver, *The Four Daughters,* p. 78.

37. Brussels, Bibliothèque royale, II. 2547, fol. 124r.

38. This translation was commissioned by Henry V of England, and his translator consistently replaced the feminine address of the Latin with the masculine phrase "beau filz." See my "Jean Galopes, traducteur des *Meditationes vitae Christi*" forthcoming in *Le moyen français.*

39. Jehan de Venette's *Les trois Maries,* much more comprehensive than its title suggests, was composed in 1357. This still unedited work of some 35,000 lines survives in only four manuscripts. For the earlier texts—for example, Herman de Valenciennes' *Roman de Dieu et de sa mère* and the anonymous poems entitled "Histoire de Marie et de Jésus," "Histoire de Jésus jusqu'à la passion," "Histoire de Jésus après son enfance"—see "Les traductions, adaptations et paraphrases de la Bible en vers" in *Grundriss der romanischen Literaturen des Mittelalters* 6.1 (Heidelberg: Winter, 1968), pp. 48–57; 6.2 (1970), pp. 81–96. For editions, see Ina Spiele *Li Romanz de Dieu et de sa mere d'Herman de Valenciennes,* Publications romanes de l'Université de Leyde 21 (Leiden: Presse Universitaire de Leyde, 1975); for the "Histoire de Marie et de Jésus," C. Chabaneau, "Le Romanz de Saint Fanuel," *Revue des Langues romanes* 28 (1884): 118–23, 157–258; 32 (1888): 360–409. See also Maureen Boulton "Transmission or Transformation: Scribal Intervention in French Apocryphal Texts (13–15th Centuries)," *Romance Languages Annual* 5 (1993): 14–18; and "The Manuscript Tradition of the *Histoire de Marie et de Jésus:* Medieval Modes of Reading and Modern Methods of Editing," *Romance Languages Annual* 2 (1990): 63–69.

40. On these texts, see Bestul, *Texts of the Passion;* Geneviève Hasenohr, "La littérature religieuse," in *La littérature française aux XIVe et XVe siècles. GRLMA* 8.1 (Heidelberg: Winter, 1988), pp. 266–305; and Maureen Boulton, "Le langage de la dévotion affective en moyen français," *Le moyen francais* 39–41 (1996–1997): 53–63.

CHAPTER 7

THE ROYAL VERNACULAR: POET AND PATRON
IN CHRISTINE DE PIZAN'S *CHARLES V*
AND THE *SEPT PSAUMES ALLÉGORISÉS*

Lori J. Walters

Introduction

Christine de Pizan's *Sept psaumes allégorisés* of 1409 (henceforth *SPA*) is a work whose intellectual import and verbal artistry have up to now gone unnoticed.[1] Her commentary on the seven penitential psalms proves to be a carefully executed and commanding ventriloquist performance that was calculated to elicit a powerful moral response in a medieval audience. Christine in effect has the Old Testament patriarch David, the purported author of the psalms, speak French to teach a lesson to her patron, Charles the Noble, and to the entire country. In the *SPA,* Christine "allegorizes" the seven penitential psalms in conformity with the "translation" campaign launched by King Charles V. As she explains in her *Livre des faits et bonnes meurs du sage roi Charles V* of 1404 (henceforth *Charles V*),[2] Charles V had designated works that he deemed important to the proper function of the monarchy to be "translated" into the Middle French vernacular. Works like Augustine's *City of God* and Aristotle's *Ethics* and *Physics* were adapted, and in most cases substantially rewritten, by an impressive team of writers who included Raoul de Presles and Nicole Oresme.[3] One way to adapt a work in the vernacular was to "allegorize" it, which to Christine meant using each psalm as the basis for extended moral commentary on the speaker's vices and virtues (tropology). In "allegorizing" the psalms, Christine applies a lesson drawn from Scripture to her patron Charles the Noble. Charles, who ruled over the kingdom of Navarre from 1385 to 1425, occupied a vital position in the French royal dynasty, first as Charles the Bad's son, and even more portentously, as Saint Louis's descendant on both his mother's and his father's side. By virtue of his double lineage from Saint Louis, Charles the Noble was strategically placed to anchor Christine's implicit message to the French people concerning the country's dangerous political situation in 1409.

In choosing to speak "through" David, Christine capitalizes on the Old Testament king's representation as repentant sinner, figure of Christ, spokesman for the Church, and late medieval model of kingship.[4] By appropriating David's well-known prayers of forgiveness addressed to God the Father, Christine engages the French in a dialogue with the divinity. Through Christine's poetic intervention as transmitter of the divine logos and as spokesperson of *sainte Eglise,* she reveals God's intentions to the French people, much as they had been revealed to the people of Israel in Old Testament times. And God's message is clear: The future of Christendom, which in fifteenth-century terms meant the entire human race (since Jews and infidels were considered to be unconverted Christians) was being determined then and there, in 1409 on French soil. It is logical that since Christine wants to communicate an idea that has a certain urgency to the widest possible audience, she delivers it in the French vernacular, a language more easily understood by all than Latin, whether Ciceronian, vulgar, or Church Latin. But Christine's use of the vernacular has even more important implications.

My topic brings up the compelling, and still largely unexplained, question of Christine's adoption of the French vernacular as her own. Her relationship to Middle French was not a natural one: Her native tongue was Italian. Moreover, the formative influence on her intellectual development was an erudite Italian father versed in the Latin tradition. Christine's exclusive recourse to Middle French and its relation to her knowledge of Latin have been vexing topics in recent critical studies. Thelma Fenster phrases the question in the following way, "Did Christine know Latin, and if so, how well?" Fenster amasses evidence for concluding that Christine had a strong reading knowledge of Latin. Most persuasive in this regard is the demonstration made by Liliane Dulac and Christine Reno that Christine translated part of Thomas Aquinas' *Commentary on Aristotle's Metaphysics* in the *Advision Cristine* (henceforth *Advision*) of 1405.[5] Fenster goes on to suggest links between the author and Charles V's translation program, a contention that she supports in part by my observation that Christine had ideological reasons for supporting a vernacular tradition.[6] Christine not only documented Charles V's translation campaign, she imitated his translators' techniques in her works,[7] becoming in some sense of the word a translator herself.

My study explores these issues in the following interrelated ways. First, in writing in Middle French rather than in Latin, Christine was allying

herself with the ideological promotion of the vernacular by French rulers
through their sponsorship of the *Grandes chroniques de France* (henceforth
GCF), a major source for both *Charles V* and the *SPA*. Initiated by Louis
IX (who ruled from 1226 to 1270), the compilation of this vernacular
prose history of the French royal house had been extended by his descendant Charles V (who ruled from 1364 to 1380).[8] Second, several Latin
verses in the *SPA* appear to have been composed by Christine herself.
Based upon hints that she gives in her *Advision,* I am led to believe that
Christine usually wrote in the vernacular because her competency in Latin
was not as strong as her competency in French. This, however, by itself
would not rule out ideological reasons why she decided to compose in the
vernacular. These I believe to be paramount. Third, the *SPA* presents the
atypical example of a vernacular version of the penitential psalms meant
for oral delivery in a court setting as well as for private devotion. By connecting her own translation practices to official state policy, Christine gave
new life to the concept of the writer as translator of key classical texts to
the audience of a cosmopolitan court culture, a concept that she had inherited from writers such as Chrétien de Troyes and Jean de Meun.[9]

Christine's view of translation, indeed her idea of herself as one who
had been "translated" (her term in *Charles V* 1.15) from Italy to Paris
around the age of five, was tied up with the Latin theoretical concept of
the *translatio studii et imperii,* the transfer of the favored locus of culture and
political power from one country to another.[10] The most penetrating contemporary statement on vernacularity was the work of Christine's foremost literary model, Dante. In the *De vulgari eloquentia* [On Eloquence in
the Vernacular], circa 1300,[11] Dante employs the framework of the *translatio studii et imperii* to displace Latin in favor of the vernacular. At first equating the vernacular with the spoken, rather than the written, language and
with the loss of the unitary language spoken in the Garden of Eden, he
then moves to posit an ideal grammatical form of Italian:

> I proclaim an illustrious, cardinal, *royal* and courtly vernacular in Italy, which
> is of every Latin city and seems to be of none, and by which all the munic-
> ipal vernaculars of Latin are measured and weighed and compared.[12] (my
> emphasis)

With one stroke Dante replaces and parallels Latin as the linguistic ideal
with the vernacular. In the words of J. Wogan-Browne and others:

> Uniting all the scattered Italian dialects, as Latin unites the languages of
> Europe, Dante's "illustrious" Italian repositions the vernacular within the
> myth of unity and of unitary language, redefining it not as a mutating

reminder of the confusion of Babel but as a partial return to the harmony Babel destroyed.[13]

The strategies of "deferment and displacement" that according to these critics characterize the *translatio* can be found in Christine's view of Dante's conception of the vernacular. Following his lead in asserting the primacy of the vernacular, she displaces his Italian with her French. To Dante's written literary language—what Mark Fumaroli claims amounts to a "neo-Latin"[14]—Christine opposes a vernacular that is a living social and political bond. Her critical swerve from her esteemed forebear is all the more remarkable because she takes one of his own political notions to its logical conclusion. In *De vulgari eloquentia* 1.18, as well as in his *De monarchia* (*On Monarchy*), Dante laments the absence of a monarchy in Italy to confer political and linguistic unity on the country. It is precisely by connecting her work to the furthering of the French monarchy, and specifically to its promotion of the vernacular, that Christine implicitly posits the superiority of French over Italian. Christine at once captures all of the force of Dante's "royal vernacular" while showing why France's vernacular is even more suited to be deemed "royal" than Italy's.

The *Sept psaumes allégorisés* and *Charles V* as Related Works

In the *SPA*, Christine de Pizan develops a notion of the vernacular as a tool for the furthering of the divinely sanctioned mission of the monarchy, a notion that she had set forth several years earlier in *Charles V*.[15] Christine's *SPA* is a prayer based on the seven penitential psalms,[16] a subgroup of the one hundred-fifty psalms found in the Old Testament. The psalms[17] were often transmitted in their entirety in psalters[18] or incorporated into even more comprehensive Books of Hours, which typically consisted of a calendar, readings from the four Gospels, prayers for the Virgin, prayers for the dead, and short prayers for various saints. These standard prayers were customarily embellished with other illustrations and each book was personalized in some way. Christine "allegorizes" the penitential psalms; that is, she gives each psalm a figurative interpretation complete with prose meditation and petition.[19] The *SPA* thus comprises a translation into Middle French of each of the seven penitential psalms (preceded, at least in one case, by the beginning of the psalm in Latin).[20] We do not know if Christine did the translation of the psalms herself or borrowed an available one.[21] The translation was followed by Christine's interpretive reading of each psalm, done, like the translation of the seven psalms, in Middle French. The four manuscripts of the *SPA*[22] whose present location is known appear to be devoted

solely to Christine's psalms followed by litanies.[23] Christine renders her litanies principally in the vernacular, but nonetheless has introductory and
concluding verses in Latin.[24] I will leave the question of the authorship of
some of these Latin verses for later discussion.

In vernacularizing the psalms, Christine furthers the program of translation undertaken by Charles V that she describes in the king's biography.
St. Augustine's *Civitas,* in its adaptation by the unnamed Raoul de Presles,
heads the list of works that the king had translated, on the model of vernacular translations of the Bible:

> [Charles] fist par solempnelz maistres . . . souffisans en toutes les sciences et
> ars, translater de latin en françois tous les plus notables livres, si comme la
> Bible, en iii. manieres, c'est assavoir: le texte, et puis le texte et les gloses en-
> semble, et puis d'une autre maniere, *alegorisee.; item,* le grant livre de St. Au-
> gustine, *De la cité de Dieu* (3.12, p. 43).

> [(Charles) had worthy masters . . . expert in all the sciences and the arts,
> translate from Latin into French all the most important books, like the Bible,
> in three ways, that is: the text, and then the text together with glosses, and
> then in another way, *allegorized; item,* the great book of St. Augustine, *Of the
> City of God].* (Here I have added my italics to Solente's. In the quotations to
> follow, the emphasis is mine, unless otherwise noted.)

Christine's use of the term "alegorisee" in this passage and in the title of
the *SPA* indicates that the latter is an example of the allegorized commentary that she had discussed five years earlier in *Charles V.*

In composing her *SPA,* Christine continues the tradition of translating
the Bible into the vernacular begun by Charles V. Describing herself in the
final lines of the king's biography as one "nourrie de son pain" [nourished
by his bread], Christine expresses her gratitude to Charles in terms with a
wide range of meaning. On the literal level, she acknowledges that the
king, the person ultimately responsible for her move from Italy to France
when he appointed her father to be his physician and adviser, had for many
years provided generous economic sustenance to herself and her family.
On a higher level, she thanks the king for having served as a sort of father
figure inspiring the work of compilation[25] and "translation" involved in
composing his biography. On an even higher level, by playing on the imagery of the well-known prayer the *Pater noster,* and by evoking Eucharistic analogies, Christine emphasizes the sovereign's status as God's
representative on earth as well as the clerkly writer's duty to perpetuate the
divine will as manifested in the monarchy.

The *SPA,* as it were, organically grows out of *Charles V,* like a branch
from a tree trunk. If my prose here seems too flowery, let me point out that

I am prompted by Christine's own rhetorical flourishes. Her biography of the king, which emphasizes his place in the royal dynasty, abounds in arborial metaphors, the most frequent being that of the genealogical tree. It is in her prefatory gloss to the *Advision,* a mirror for princes[26] that is also indebted to the *GCF,*[27] that Christine waxes most poetic: Trees and other plants produce seed, send out shoots, and are grafted. The plant then materializes as "Libera," a figure of France; and, in a final incarnation, Libera mutates into Jesus Christ himself. A key to this imagery lies in Hugh of St. Victor's treatises on the processes of reading and writing, the *Didascalicon* and the *Chronica.*[28] We know that Christine was familiar with this well-known early twelfth-century Parisian monastic writer because in *Charles V* 2.22 she cites him by name.[29] In claiming that a piece of wisdom should be judged on its own terms, rather than on the value of the person emitting it, Christine bases herself on the *Didascalicon*'s authority in defending herself against accusations of presumption that she, a woman with no formal schooling,[30] should pronounce on military matters. In *Didascalicon* 4.16, "Some Etymologies of Things Pertaining to Reading," Hugh describes the relationship between codices and books using arborial metaphors.[31] Christine borrows Hugh's imagery to describe a concept encompassing the spread of knowledge and Christ as the divine logos, with the poet defined as interpreter of Christian wisdom as revealed in sacred scripture.

Another implication of the trunk-and-graft metaphor becomes clear when the short prayers with which Christine frames *Charles V* are compared with the *SPA,* which is a prayer or group of prayers uttered for forgiveness by a deeply contrite sinner, traditionally identified as David. The last section of *Charles V,* discussed above (3.72), takes the form of a prayer in which Christine thanks God for having given her "engin, santé, temps et lieu" [intelligence, health, time, and place] to bring her treatise to completion. This last section complements and completes the prayer uttered by Christine in the opening lines of the biography:

> Sire Dieux, *euvre mes levres,* enlumine ma pensee, mon entendement esclaires à celle fin que m'ignorance n'encombre mes sens à *expliquer les choses conceues en ma memoire,* et soit mon commencement, moyen et fin à la louenge de toy, souveraine poissance et digneté incirconscriptible, à sens humain non comprenable! (*Charles V* 1.1:4)

> [Lord God, open my lips, illuminate my thoughts, enlighten my understanding, so that my ignorance does not weigh on my understanding and prevent me from *explaining the things conceived in my memory,* and may my beginning, middle, and end be to your praise, oh you Sovereign Power, inexpressible Majesty, who goes beyond all human understanding!]

This passage from *Charles V* in fact corresponds to the opening verse of the Hours of the Virgin of a typical Book of Hours[32] as well as to *SPA* 50.16. In Christine's version of Psalm 50.16, one reads: "Sire, euvres mes levres, et ma bouche annoncera ta louange" [Lord, open my lips, and my mouth will announce your praise], to which she adds her meditation in the form of vernacular commentary. The arborial metaphor thus also applies to the *SPA* as a metaphorical "offshoot" of the verse from 50.16 with which Christine opens *Charles V.*

The allegorical commentary that follows the biblical verse in *SPA* 50.16 also relates to considerations found in *Charles V.* Christine's commentary on the verse in Psalm 50 reads:

> Jhesus, qui as souffert pour nostre salut et lequel descendi es enfers et ressuscita le tiers jour de mort a vie, par toy et de toy soit ma bouche ouverte, quant *elle* parlera en tel maniere que riens n'en puisse yssir contre ta reverence: ta louange soit continuellement en *elle,* et *me soit de toy ottroyé le don de sapience,* par quoy en parolle, en fait, ne en quelconques chose je ne puisse errer. (114)

> [Jesus, who suffered for our salvation and who descended into hell and was resurrected on the third day from death to life, by you and of you may my mouth be opened, when it [she] will speak in such a way that nothing can issue forth from there against your reverence: may your praise be continually in it [her], and *may the gift of wisdom be given to me by you,* by which in word, in deed, nor in anything can I err.]

Note here, for later development, that through her assimilation to the feminine *bouche,* Christine becomes a personified mouth that draws its authority from the Virgin's wisdom. Christine's request for the gift of *sapience* in her commentary included in *SPA* 50.16 is connected to the explanation that she gives of the meaning and significance of Charles's *sapience* in his biography. Mary Carruthers explains that in the Middle Ages *sapientia* meant wisdom or prudence and involved the suitable use of all knowledge, practical and speculative.[33] *Sapience* is likewise a key quality for the clerkly writer figure who wishes to disseminate knowledge of the ruler's wisdom, perpetuate his or her glory, and provide a model for other regents to emulate. How Christine wishes to communicate her *sapience* is revealed by reference to the political situation. Philip the Bold intended his brother's biography to function as a *miroir des princes* to guide the dauphin, Louis of Guyenne (who was twelve years old in 1409 when he became Philip's ward) in the ways of responsible leadership needed to stabilize the situation created by the intermittent bouts of madness of Louis's father, Charles VI.[34] *Charles V* legitimized Charles V and his descendant the young Louis as members of the Valois branch of the Capetian dynasty.

In sum, the relationship between the *SPA* and the *Charles V* is akin to
that of a branch or graft of an original tree trunk, since the *SPA* is an example of an allegorized commentary on the Bible authorized by Charles
V's translation project discussed by Christine in the king's biography. Although not a sacred work in the strict sense, *Charles V* has religious over-
tones, as shown by its likeness to biographies written about Charles V's
ancestor Saint Louis by Geoffroi de Beaulieu, Guillaume de Saint-Pathus,
and Jean de Joinville. Joinville stresses the holiness of the king's spoken
word in the vernacular biography that he undertook at the express command of Joan of Navarre, the wife of Philip IV the Fair (who reigned from
1285 to 1314), grandson of Saint Louis. Joan enjoined Joinville to "faire un
livre des saintes *paroles* et des bons faits de notre roi Saint Louis" [compose
a book of the holy words and good deeds of our king Saint Louis].[35] In
the vernacular prayer that concludes *Charles V,* Christine asks that God
admit the souls of Charles V the Wise, his brother Philip the Bold, duke of
Burgundy, and all their ancestors (who, I might add, include Saint Louis)
among the elect. Philip, who had commissioned the work from Christine
some twenty-four years after his brother's death, died unexpectedly on
April 27, 1404, a fact that Christine laments bitterly in *Charles V* 2.1. If
Charles V had not attained the status of Louis IX, who was canonized in
1297 (just twenty-seven years after his death in 1270), Christine may well
have been trying to have the king participate in the aura of sacredness surrounding his only canonized ancestor who could be unequivocally said to
be French.[36] To accomplish this goal, Christine develops the parallels that
had been made between Charles V and Saint Louis in the text and the illustrations of the *GCF.* In documenting how Charles strengthened relations between the monarch and the University of Paris, Christine shows
how Charles continued Saint Louis's achievement.[37] Christine, then, continues the effort, begun in the *GCF,* of strengthening the monarchy by
emphasizing its privileged association with Holy Church and the saints.

In becoming the "translator" of a biblical text in her *SPA* in conformity
to Charles's wishes, Christine again shows her indebtedness to *Didascalicon*
4, a chapter entitled "Concerning the Study of the Sacred Scriptures." As
in many medieval texts, the family tree has its justification and model in
St. Matthew's elaborate genealogy of Christ, which is secondarily a genealogy of the books of the Bible.[38] Basing myself on Alastair Minnis' observation of the widespread reliance of writers on scriptural models in the
Middle Ages,[39] I believe that in writing the prefatory gloss to the *Advision*
Christine may have also drawn inspiration from the "Deus erat Verbum" of
John's Gospel,[40] in which God is at once noun and verb, being and activity. As speech in action, John's "Verbum" figures the divinity as the ultimate
power to transform all things and the writer as imitator, facilitator, and dis-

seminator of the divine word. The frequent appearance of author portraits in illustrated manuscripts that are modeled on pictures of the four evangelists suggests that this conception of writerly activity was widespread throughout the Middle Ages.[41] Whether manuscript producers were invoking the Evangelists per se or merely copying an iconographic model remains an open question,[42] but it is undeniable that Christine allies herself with scriptural authority in representing herself as a translator of a biblical text. As a writer who belongs to a gender whose members are usually not literate enough to compose literature, let alone write with skill, Christine appeals to a sacred conception of the writer as servant of the divine logos in order to legitimize her stance as interpreter of the divine will for her noble patrons.

Christine and Her Patron,
Charles III the Noble, King of Navarre

The relationship between Christine and Charles III, also called Charles the Noble, king of Navarre, is crucial to understanding her *SPA*. In a verse that speaks of the duty of kings to serve God (*SPA* 50.23), Christine tells us that she undertook the commission "au prouffit de son ame et de moy" [for the benefit of his soul and mine]. Christine worked on the *SPA* during the second half of 1409,[43] which was the twenty-second year of Charles's thirty-eight-year reign as king of Navarre.[44] The first-person "I" that Christine assumes in the *SPA*, traditional to these psalms, is in this case a mixture of male and female voices for the simple reason that Christine is a woman, whereas her patron is a man. In writing her allegorized commentary to each of the seven psalms, Christine intersperses considerations applicable to Charles's situation as knightly ruler with others more particular to her own. Her widowhood is a recurrent theme. When she prays for the safety of pilgrims, she adds a parallel figurative petition for herself: "Que tu me vueilles conduire par le pelerinage de ce monde" [May you lead me through the pilgrimage of this world]. And when she precedes her prayer for "navigans par mer" [those traveling by sea] with the plea "je te prie que en la mer ce ce monde me vueilles garder de periller, Sire" [I implore you to protect me from perishing on the sea of this world],[45] she brings to mind her self-depiction as a passenger lost at sea whose ship captain has just drowned in *La Mutacion de Fortune* of 1403 (henceforth *Mutacion*).[46]

Christine's first-person paraphrase in Middle French of the penitential psalms conjoins Charles as *chevalier* and herself as female *clerc*. To borrow the term that she applies to the relationship between her character "Christine" and Libera in the *Advision,* Christine becomes Charles the Noble's *antigraphus*, a sovereign's clerkly scribe or secretary. As "antigraphe" of France's "aventures" in *Advision* 1.5 (16), Christine makes herself analogous to "Sainte Sapience divine" [Divine Holy Wisdom], the "antigraffe" of the world's "aventures" (6). Christine ingeniously establishes a parallel between her own work as France's secretary and the work of God and his Evangelists, who served as the world's secretaries in writing Holy Scripture.[47] As clerkly servant of the divine Word in the *SPA*, Christine voices what the knightly ruler Charles would be unable to put in his own words. The androgynous "I" also brings together reflections bearing on Charles's salvation and her own.[48] In reflecting on final ends, the ultimate destiny of the human being, Christine in the *SPA* is able to speak in her own voice, yet can participate fully in the spiritual meditations that she dedicates to her patron. Adopting an androgynous "I" in order to go "beyond gender," in Rosalind Brown-Grant's words, Christine expresses preoccupations crucial to sovereign and subject about the well-being of the Christian state.

The nature of Christine's androgynous and vernacular first person can be better understood by considering how the penitential psalms were traditionally read. The "I" of the psalms was assumed by the person praying as he or she looked at the devotional book—the Book of Hours, the psalter, or Christine's penitential psalms plus litanies. David—musician, poet, and king of Israel in the Old Testament—is traditionally seen as the first-person speaker and author of the psalms, including the ones referred to as the seven penitential psalms.[49] Christine's androgynous "I" concretizes two aspects of David's multifaceted persona: The female voice represents David as poet; the male voice, David as king and patron of the arts. The male voice recalls the traditional persona of David as the model penitent, the proud and powerful ruler who in the penitential psalms begs God's forgiveness for his sins of adultery and murder.[50] Christine prepares Charles to receive her message in the proper spirit by giving special emphasis to the psalms' treatment of the seven sins of pride. The female voice is doubly resonant: Besides evoking David as poet, it recalls David as ancestor not only of Christ, but also of Mary. The first verse of Psalm 50.16, as noted above, is the traditional opening of the Hours of the Virgin. Christine encourages Charles to accept her message with humility, by reminding him of the precedent set by Mary in accepting her role in the Incarnation. By conjoining David's male and Mary's female voices in her androgynous and vernacular first person, Christine gives a lesson to her patron on how to be a good ruler, but maintains all the while an especially modest and humble stance as royal servant and adviser, as suited her status as a woman who had not received a formal education.

After establishing herself as Charles's teacher by presenting herself as a personified tongue and mouth invested with sacred authority, Christine has Charles mouth the lesson that she wishes to teach him. The dialogue between poet and patron established by Christine is beautifully illustrated by the two verses that precede *SPA* 50.16, which, as I have shown above, relate to the prayerful invocation that opens *Charles V.* In the allegorized commentary accompanying *SPA* 50.14, the speaker expresses the desire to learn "ce qui m'enseigne le psalmiste" [what the psalmist teaches me]. Christine's translation of *SPA* 50.15 is "Delivre moy de mes crimes, Dieu, Dieu de mon salut, et ma lengue s'esjouira en ta justice" [Deliver me from my crimes, Lord, God of my salvation, and my tongue will rejoice in your justice]. It is evident that the *langue* in question, like the personified *bouche* in the quotation above from *Charles V,* belongs to Christine, the *porte-parole* of her less articulate patron.[51] Christine has the first voice, apparently Charles the Noble's, say that he will accept the teaching of the psalmist, that is, David.[52] Christine, as it were, ventriloquizes Charles to have him promise to take to heart the instruction, both explicit and implicit, that can be drawn from David's experience. The explicit lesson is given directly by Christine's voice, speaking as courtly adviser; the implicit lesson is given when Charles applies to himself the parallels between David's story and his own. Christine assumes the role of pedagogue who can understand what the psalmist says and teach it to others (and as a good Christian, she also applies his teaching to herself).

In representing herself as a personified tongue and mouth, Christine confers great importance on the vernacular status of her project. Drawing, it would seem, on the intimate nature of prayer in the vernacular (where the person praying traditionally addresses God with the *tu* form), Christine becomes the agent of God's word in a communication that takes place between God and human beings in Middle French. By echoing Mary's words, Christine subtly builds her own authority on the sacred role of mediator assigned to the Mother of God, and on Mary's role as teacher who instructed her son through her personal example and by means of the "mother tongue." It is left to the audience—and besides Charles of Navarre, Christine addresses Queen Isabeau, the French princes, the students of the University of Paris, the Church, and the Popes, as well as her own relatives, friends, and benefactors—to decipher the lesson encoded in the parallels between Charles's situation and the biblical King David's (*SPA* 101.23).

This passage, in which Christine mentions her patron and other nobles and clerics by name, hints at Christine's more public intentions, intentions connected to her practice of writing in the vernacular. The idea of paraphrasing the penitential psalms in *langue vulgaire* was not new; Dante had done it in *terza rima*,[53] and French versions of them circulated as early as the twelfth century.[54] Christine's compatriot Petrarch had paraphrased the psalms before her, but in Latin, and in an "intensely personal and introspective" manner.[55]

Christine's more public aims are related to her patron's place in history. In asking for help for all Christian princes in *SPA* 101.23, Christine specifies "et par especial ceulx du sanc royal de France" [and especially those of royal blood of France]. Her patron Charles the Noble was of *sang on ne peut plus royal:* He was the cousin of Charles VI, the reigning French sovereign in 1409; he was the nephew of his predecessor, Charles V; and he was related to Saint Louis through both his paternal and maternal lines! In "reading" Charles's experience through that of the Old Testament David in her *SPA,* Christine imitates earlier practice relating to Charles's illustrious ancestor Saint Louis. Contemporaries of Louis IX had associated the soon-to-be-canonized king with the biblical kings David and Solomon. Ordination and crowning ceremonies during Louis's reign had begun to include reference to these two Old Testament rulers as models of wisdom prefiguring the present monarchy.[56] Christine's conception of the vernacular is related to the one perpetuated by the monastic keepers of the *GCF.* They compared Louis IX to David and Solomon and further extended the line of wise kings to include Charles V and his successors. Christine participates in the *GCF's* promotion of wise leadership in France in undertaking her biography of Charles "le Sage" and in paraphrasing the Old Testament King David's penitential psalms in the vernacular for Charles V's nephew, Charles III the Noble.

A few basic facts about the historical background of the *SPA* bear repeating here. Charles III's father, Charles II the Bad, the earlier king of Navarre, was, despite his title, a French prince with claims to the French throne. On his father's side, the kingdom of Navarre became joined to France when Charles the Noble's great-great-grandmother, Joan, married Philip IV the Fair. Although Charles the Noble's great-great-grandfather had been king of France, the family's claim to the throne was put into jeopardy when the three sons of Joan and Philip all died without male issue following an adultery scandal implicating all their wives. In 1314, the last year of his reign, Philip the Fair had his three daughters-in-law arrested on charges of adultery. One of them, Marguerite of Burgundy, wife of Prince Louis, king of Navarre and the future Louis X, died in prison after having been charged with the crime. Louis X succeeded his father Philip the Fair on the throne in 1314. Two years later France proclaimed the so-called Salic law, which officially excluded women from royal succession. When it came time for someone to follow Louis X, his daughter by Marguerite of Burgundy, Joan, was passed over in favor of Philip of Poitiers (subsequently king Philip V), Louis X's brother. Charles T. Wood claims that "succession devolved on Philip V largely because, given Jeanne's [Joan's] possible illegitimacy, he was Louis X's closest blood heir."[57] Joan was crowned queen of Navarre in return for giving up all her claims to the French throne.

The conflict did not take long to flare up again. When John II the Good (king of France from 1350 to 1364) gave his elder daughter, yet another Joan, to the young king of Navarre, the latter, Charles II (Charles III the Noble's father) felt compelled to reassert his family claim to the French throne. Charles II fomented rebellions in Paris and Normandy and conspired with England's Edward III in vain attempts to displace Charles V, acts that earned him the moniker "Charles the Bad" (although he has gone down in history as a villain, his cause enjoyed a certain celebrity at the time). Charles III the Noble did not follow his father's lead in pursuing family claims to the throne. On the contrary, during several trips to Paris to reclaim hereditary holdings in Normandy that had been confiscated by Charles V after his father's rebellion, Charles often acted as peacemaker between Armagnac and Burgundian factions whose rivalries were exacerbated by the intermittent but frequent bouts of insanity of the French king, Charles VI.

Charity Cannon Willard surmises that Charles the Noble commissioned Christine to write the psalms during a moment of acute crisis in France in 1409. Antagonism between the Burgundians and the Armagnacs had been intensifying ever since the assassination of Duke Louis d'Orléans, brother of Charles VI, on November 23, 1407, on the orders of John the Fearless (who had become the second duke of Burgundy after Philip the Bold's death).[58] John earned a royal pardon for his crime by justifying his actions on the grounds that the duke of Orléans was a tyrant who had been contemplating regicide.[59] Despite his efforts to make peace, Charles the Noble found himself drawn into the conflict in 1409. Although Charles held the assassination of Louis against John,[60] his own role in engineering the Treaty of Chartres of March 9, 1409, helped prepare John's return to Paris, and on July 7 of that year Charles even entered into a treaty of mutual assistance with John,[61] an alliance that appears to have been motivated in part by a desire for financial gain.[62] This departure from neutrality was to compromise Charles the Noble's position as peacemaker, since John then turned on John of Montague, a member of the royal household highly esteemed by Charles and Christine.[63] Willard believes that Charles commissioned the *SPA* from Christine following John of Montague's arrest and summary execution, accomplished when Charles VI was temporarily insane. Shocked by this act of his supposed ally, John the Fearless, the king of Navarre left Paris soon afterward.[64] Like many others, Charles the Noble must have realized that this act signaled even worse things to come. Catastrophic events arrived in quick succession: Civil war broke out in 1409, which opened the way for an attack by the English. Charles left Paris in November 1410, never to return.[65] Events continued on their downward spiral, culminating in the disastrous defeat of the French at Agincourt in 1415.

Charles the Noble and King David:
Old Testament Echoes for a Christian Ruler

Christine's choice to compose "allegorized" psalms provides a clue to her intentions in the *SPA*. Again, it is Hugh of St. Victor who, in setting forth the three levels of interpretation of a sacred text in his introductory gloss to the *Chronica*, helps us interpret Christine's allegorized commentary on the Old Testament penitential psalms. Hugh's three levels are: history, the narrative of actions; allegory, an action in past or future time that is evoked by an event in the narrative; tropology, or the exemplary sense, when actions or events in the narrative provide a guide for the reader's own conduct.[66] In Hugh's theory of reading, allegory prepares the type of tropological interpretation called for by the didactic situation inscribed in *SPA* 50.14, 15, and 16, discussed above, which consists of a clerkly counselor and a ruler respectful of advice given concerning his responsibilities to God and his people. Charles the Noble is called upon, first, to grasp the analogy between scriptural narrative and current events (allegory), and second, to apply the lesson to his own experience (tropology). A text made up of biblical allusions like Christine's holds a mirror up to life in which her reader Charles sees himself compared to scriptural characters, with the mandate to act in accordance with the lesson inscribed in the biblical text.

Since the influence of the psalms on medieval social action was dependent on the strength of the analogy between David's history and the target audience,[67] it is helpful to recall that David was an Old Testament king brought down by adultery. Applying the example of how a king's illicit passion for another man's wife undermined his rule to the situation in France in 1409, Christine warns Charles against the dangers of adultery. In *SPA* 101.4 Christine applies the seventh commandment to Charles: "Tu ne feras point de adultere ne fornicacion" [you will not commit adultery or fornication], an injunction to which she returns in *SPA* 101.9, when she requests God: "le feu de fornication vueilles en moy esteindre" [please extinguish the fire of fornication in me]. That she applies this principally to Charles rather than to herself is shown by her petition that "entre les autres pechés me vueilles deffendre que je ne convoite la femme, fille, parente ou servante de mon prochain . . ." [among all the other sins please prevent me from coveting the wife, daughter, relative, or servant of my neighbor]. Little is known about Charles the Noble's personal life. Putting aside the question of this ruler's propensities for *luxure,* Christine's warning is one applicable to any regent, since adultery is considered more severe in a ruler than in a subject because of the possible repercussions for the stability and the purity of the realm. Christine chastises King Childeric for his "lustful ways" in the prologue-gloss to the *Advision*[68] and is careful to assure her readers that Charles

V, whom she also compares to David, was free of this vice.[69] Concupiscence was one of the royal sins *par excellence,* because it perverted lineage and confused succession, conditions that fostered civil dissent that left the country open to invasion by foreign powers. Charles the Noble would have been especially sensitive to this issue given the role that adultery had played in frustrating his family's claim to the French throne.

The major parallels between political circumstances in France in 1409 and David's story turn on the danger to a country of internal division. This fear is particularly applicable to Charles the Noble's circumstances, since 1378 was the year of both the rebellion organized by his father Charles the Bad against the king and the beginning of the Great Schism. In the commentary accompanying *SPA* 101.18, Christine says a prayer to help repair the "ruine passee" [former ruin] of "la sainte Eglise catholique" [the Holy Catholic Church] and expresses confidence in the new pope, Alexander V, elected in an effort to put an end to the Church schism. His election failed to resolve the issue, since instead of two popes, the Church thereby had three.[70] Navarre had first adopted a wait-and-see attitude that was much criticized by France, and later opted for the Avignon papacy. The division in France caused by Charles the Bad was reflected in, and had a pernicious effect on, the division in the Catholic Church. It was vitally important that Charles the Noble not follow the example set by his father and that he instead live up to the model of kingship set by his ancestor Saint Louis, whose achievements reflected his impeccable morals. In writing her *SPA* Christine tacitly encourages Charles the Noble to learn a lesson from the story of David's often roundabout efforts to find a successor who would establish a lasting peace, achieved only by his son Solomon. Christine in effect intimates that Charles the Noble should play Solomon to his father's David. She wants him to read the Old Testament father-and-son story typologically, and thus help institute a Christian realm of peace to replace the internecine battles that were currently tearing the country apart.

In writing the *SPA,* Christine was trying to influence Charles's conduct on earth as much as in his spiritual afterlife. For any medieval ruler, seen as God's representative on earth, the public and the private, the earthly kingdom and that kingdom's status as a stage on the way to the establishment of the heavenly Jerusalem, were inseparable. Although as part of Books of Hours the *SPA* is thought of as comprising objects of private devotion, Willard suggests that Christine's psalms may have shared the public function sometimes assumed by the penitential psalms. Willard contends that the penitential psalms were often recited in public during times of great misfortunes, like famines, plagues, and disasters. The *SPA* would seem to have had a public function different from the more private purposes envisaged for the "unallegorized" psalms that are present in an illustrated copy of a Book of Hours once owned by Charles the Noble.[71]

In the *SPA,* Christine tacitly encourages Charles the Noble to continue his political stance as neutral peacemaker, a stance that was supportive of the reign of Charles VI and of the stability of the realm. This position marked a radical change from the politics of his father, Charles II the Bad, who, because of his claims to the throne, had stirred up rebellion against the reigning monarchy of Charles V. Charles the Noble's one departure from neutrality had contributed to the crisis of 1409. Although, as Willard suggests, Charles may have engaged Christine in some sort of a contract to compose the *SPA* as early as 1405,[72] the powerful immediacy of her voice asking for contrition on the part of the erring ruler David in the *SPA* may express some of Charles's misgivings at having been drawn into the conflict that threatened to shatter the legitimacy and stability won by his relatives Louis IX and Charles V. The position of neutrality that I believe that Christine is promoting to Charles would in fact mirror her own position at the time. Christine rather miraculously managed to enjoy the substantial patronage of John the Fearless while producing works for other patrons with Armagnac sympathies.[73] The evidence that I will present below implies that Christine's stance of neutrality was motivated as much by personal conviction and heartfelt belief as by political expediency.

Christine's choice to render the penitential psalms in the vernacular was part of a well thought-out agenda that escapes narrow classification as being either religious or political in nature.[74] Christine played a role as adviser to Charles the Noble that she delineates in her *Advision* of 1405, the year after she had completed *Charles V.* In *Advision* 2.22 (89–90) Christine has Lady Opinion predict that after Christine's death a wise prince will come, who, because of her books, will wish that she had lived in his time so that he could have known her. May we not infer from Opinion's somewhat mysterious statement that Christine hopes that a future monarch will be able to establish a time of peace and prosperity in France thanks to her advice? By linking the *SPA* with *Charles V,* Christine expresses the desire that the example set by the wise king Charles V might set the stage for the time of peace and prosperity that she thought to be France's destiny. In her prefatory gloss to the *Advision,* Christine states her belief that the place where Christ will liberate humanity and create the City of God on earth is France, the country that serves the Church better than any other in Christendom (5). If, like David's land of Israel in the Old Testament, France is the promised land of the fifteenth century, Christine is one of its prophets.[75] In order to ensure the realization of her prophecy, Christine had to try to avert political disaster in 1409. In composing the *SPA* at

Charles the Noble's request, Christine implicitly encourages him to pursue a political course that will strengthen the monarchy during the troubled times of 1409–1415 and beyond.

The point does not seem to have been lost on Charles the Noble. Judging by his actions after the trying events of 1409, the king of Navarre appears to have taken to heart Christine's powerful but modestly offered advice. Whereas his father before him had courted favor with and betrayed both sides trying to claim the French throne as his own, Charles the Noble maintained an admirable neutrality in the French–English conflict. After returning to Navarre in 1410, he continued to keep peace in his own realm. His firm governance allowed him to institute judicial reforms, and gave him the economic resources to undertake an ambitious building program and to become an energetic promoter of the arts.[76] A sixteenth-century historian records how he was mourned at his death at age sixty-four: "Prince regreté des siens et des étrangers pour ses vertus et paisible nature" [A prince missed by his own people and by foreigners because of his virtues and his peaceful nature].[77] Besides continuing his efforts supportive of the crown, Charles the Noble achieved a state of peace in his own kingdom of Navarre, both desired results of his tropological reading of the "allegory" of David's story found in Christine's vernacularized version of the seven penitential psalms.

Christine's Vernacular and Latin "I": Performance and Persuasion

Christine conveys her message to Charles with great persuasiveness through a skillful telescoping of first-person voices. In private meditational practices, Charles, the primary intended reader, would identify with the first person "I," which, since Christine's psalms were in the vernacular, is at once more personal and easier to understand than Latin psalms would be. Charles would also identify himself with the persona of the Old Testament king David, whose situation was so similar to his own in 1409. Through those conjoined male voices could also be heard the strains of Christine's own voice, that of Charles's *antigraphus* and mouthpiece. But if this were not remarkable enough, in the final section of the *SPA*, Christine further nuances the four-part telescoping of the first-person voice heard up to that point (David/Charles–Mary/Christine). She begins *SPA* 142.14 with a translation of the Latin text: "Et perdras tous ceulx qui tribulent et troublent mon ame, pour ce que je suis ton servant" [And you will destroy all those who perturb and trouble my soul, because I am your servant]. She then conjoins Charles and herself as humble servants of God seeking forgiveness for their sins:

Avec ce vueilles, benoite Trinité, un seul Dieu, avoir agreable mon petit labour en ceste present oeuvre, laquelle soit accroiscement de merite et devocion au bon roy Charles de Navarre dessus dit, de par qui est faite a moy pecharresse qui l'ay compilee, soit prié pour l'ame apres mon trespas. Et a tous ceulx et celles qui par devotion *la diront ou orront,* puist estre meritoire et a salvacion des ames, ainsi soit-il.

[With this, blessed Trinity, one God, I beg you to find pleasing my small labor in this present work, which is directed toward increasing the merit and devotion of the good king Charles of Navarre mentioned above, and by which (work) my soul will be prayed for after my death, the soul of the (female) sinner who compiled it. And for all those men and women who in devotion *will say it* or *will hear it,* may it be helpful for them and for the salvation of their souls, please let it be.]

And in the invocation to God the Father in the final lines of the *SPA* (142.14), the male voice is enlarged to include "*les freres Crestiens* " [all Christian brothers] and Christ himself, while Christine's female voice melds with that of "*une Mere sainte Eglise catholique*" [one Mother Holy Catholic Church]. In line with the typological readings that she insists upon throughout the *SPA,* in the final lines of the work Christine and Charles, albeit lowly sinners, can nonetheless be seen as images of Christ and his Mother and Christ and his Church. In this Christine follows St. Augustine, author of the *Enarrationes in Psalmos,* one of the most influential of the psalm commentaries,[78] who had maintained that in the psalms David speaks both in his own person and in the person of *Ecclesia.*[79]

By means of her allegorized penitential psalms, collectively a prayer that was to be recited in the first person by Charles but that Christine also addresses to members of the royal court and its associates (e.g., members of the University of Paris and the papal curia) Christine has the entire nation express its dismay at the turn that recent events were taking.[80] St. Augustine had emphasized the psalms' dual status as private and public texts, as acts of devotion and as moral instruction for individuals and entire communities, true penitential performances enacted to purge congregations of their collective guilt.[81] Christine's *SPA* would gain added significance by being read publicly during the tumultuous years of 1409–1415, as Willard's comments suggest that it was. When Christine says "And to all those men and women who by means of devotion *will say* it or *will hear* it [the *SPA*]," she indeed does seem to imply that such a public reading of her *SPA* would take place. Her phrase *will say it* would appear to refer to private meditational practices by which the reader repeats to him- or herself the psalms, whereas her phrase *will hear it* would appear to describe public devotional practices in which the work is recited aloud to a group.[82] Christine's own words, then, seem to anticipate, even encourage, a public reading of her *SPA* in a secular setting, most probably at the royal court.

Several types of public readings are possible, all of which would bring about a melding of male and female voices, no matter if the work were recited by one man or by one woman, or by a man and a woman taking different parts. The reading closest to the text would of course have Charles the Noble in person reciting the original psalms, with Christine adding her commentary. Since, as Carruthers reminds us, "the book which Christians, both clergy and educated laity, were sure to know by heart was the psalms,"[83] the audience could follow along easily, given that few if any members would have had their own copy of the manuscript book. In any public reading, the voice of the primary speaker or speakers would be identified first of all with that of Charles assuming the persona of the Old Testament king David, although through that primary voice could also be heard the strains of a secondary voice, Christine's own, strengthened and legitimized by echoes of Mary's voice. Christine's vernacular and androgynous "I" could potentially be assumed by anyone and everyone, be they readers or listeners. Judging by her term "ceulx et celles," Christine conjoins David and Charles's version of everyman with her version of everywoman. By identifying her voice with that of Holy Mother Church, Christine enlarges the context of the reading even further to encompass all Christendom. Charles's prayer, the prayer of one individual, thus transforms itself into a communal lament for the country by members of the French nation that was in the process of being formed by just such performances. The conjoined voices of Christine and Charles would meld with the collective voice of the nation as it reflected the history of the human race as it had been recounted by an Israelite king in sacred scripture. The "body politic" would seemingly cry out with one voice, like David from the depths of his despair, to express the fervent hope that the reign of Solomon would succeed David's dark trials.[84]

Christine continues many of the major themes of the *SPA* in the litanies that follow it. Noteworthy in this regard is her request that God the Father "humiles les ennemis de sainte Eglise" [humiliate all the enemies of Holy Church]. The two lines in Latin, the ones that Christine may have composed herself, deserve special mention.[85] These lines, which are placed at the end of all the prayers, are different from the other short formulaic Latin phrases found in the litany, such as "Kyrieleyson / Xpisteleyson / Kyrieleyson / Xpiste audi nos," which occur at the beginning, and "Per Xpistum Dominum nostrum. Amen," which are found at the end of the litanies. These atypical lines are the following:

Fructibus eloquii prophete in nomine Xpisti
Nascitur istud opus quod corpore parva peregit.

[By the fruits of the utterance of the prophet (i.e., David), in the name of
Christ / is born this work which one small (feminine adjective) in body
completed].[86]

There are many reasons to believe that Christine wrote these lines herself.
They embody a variety of techniques and themes that she uses elsewhere
in her *oeuvre:* Christine plays on the name of Christ in the *Mutacion;* she
frequently represents herself as a prophet; she employs the image of giving
birth to her works in *Advision* 3; she has frequent recourse to a humility
topos, as when she refers to the insufficiency of her intellect. In more general terms, Christine makes implicit reference to the story of the diminutive David who slew the giant Goliath, which in *Charles V* 2.27 Christine
had evoked as a prophetic foretelling (an "allegory," to use Hugh of St. Victor's term) of the ultimate victory of the French over the English. The
Latin verses also anticipate imagery that Christine would employ in her
Ditié de Jehanne d'Arc of 1429. In stanzas 35–36 Christine describes Joan as
a diminutive maiden who is vested with a divine mission that fulfills
prophecies of Charles VII's eventual triumph.[87]

Even more significant is that these lines continue the major ideas and
imagery of the *SPA,* which she represents as the fruition of things begun
in *Charles V.* We note Christine's emphasis on the work itself, especially on
the insignificance of her labor involved in writing it, with her play on the
small size of the devotional book produced and the insignificance of the
writer who wrote it.[88] The Latin verses similarly continue her reference to
"la petite oeuvre de mon labour non souffisent" [the little work of my insufficient labor] in the prologue of the *Charles V,* and the allusion to her
"petit labour en cete present oeuvre" [little labor in this present work] at
the conclusion of her psalms (*SPA* 142.14).[89] Finally, the Latin verses develop the image of the devotional book as the concrete realization of
"things conceived in memory" that Christine employs at the very beginning of *Charles V.* In light of the Eucharistic imagery present in both passages, Christine's small devotional collection of psalms and litanies becomes
a metaphorical host to be consumed in a public or private *ruminatio.*

An examination of Christine's use of Latin quotations in her other
works can help determine whether the Latin verses at the end of the litanies are her own. In the section entitled "Allegory" that follows each of the
one hundred entries of one of her first works, *L'Epistre d'Othéa* (hereafter
Othéa) of 1399–1400, Christine alternates a Latin quotation, usually taken
from the Scriptures or the Church fathers, with another in Middle French.

In one of her last works, *Les heures de contemplation sur la passion de Nostre Seigneur* (ca. 1420–1424; henceforth *Heures*), which follows the form of a Book of Hours, Christine does something similar to what she had done in the *SPA:* She quotes a verse in Latin, translates it into Middle French, and then comments on it. Whereas Christine's use of Latin in the *Othéa* and the *Heures* is systematic—which it is likewise in the *SPA* if we discount the final two Latin verses that end the litanies—the Latin quotation in her *Cité* stands out as being the *one and only* one. When Christine has Lady Justice exclaim near the conclusion of her work: "Gloriosa dicta sunt de te, civitas Dei" [Glorious things are spoken of you, city of God (3.18.9)], she thus calls attention to her consistent play on the *Civitas* in her *Cité,* a reference that would not have been lost on a medieval reader. Christine once again uses a Latin quotation in Charles's death scene at the end of his biography (*Charles V* 3.71). Before bidding farewell in French to those kneeling around him, Charles pronounces a blessing in Latin over their bowed heads: "Benedicio [should read Benedictio][90] Dei, Patris et Filii et Sp[irit]us sancti, descendat super vos et maneat semper" [May the blessing of God the Father, and of the Son, and of the Holy Spirit, descend upon you and remain with you always]. In all of these examples, as opposed to the one at hand, it is clear that Christine is quoting prior sources.

In summary, several pieces of evidence lend support to the idea that Christine did indeed compose the Latin verses:

1. Christine does not indicate that she is quoting someone else as she does elsewhere.
2. The Latin verses express themes treated elsewhere by Christine.
3. The phrase *corpore parva* [one small (feminine) in body] would seem to refer to a female author, and the same female author who had composed the companion piece, the *SPA,* that is included in the same devotional book.

   To these internal pieces of evidence can be added an external one:

4. Roger S. Wieck, curator of Medieval and Renaissance Manuscripts at the Pierpont Morgan Library in New York, a major expert on the medieval Book of Hours, has not seen anything like these Latin verses in other manuscripts of the litanies.

In adding some original lines in Latin at the end of the *SPA,* Christine would be underscoring the continuity between the Latin rituals of Holy Church[91] and the popularizing intent of her vernacularization of the penitential psalms. Some of the earliest attempts to legitimize the vernacular grew out of the Church's desire to spread God's message to the laity. The

Fourth Lateran Council of 1215 increased the demand for works of religious instruction in Latin and in the vernacular. Since Christine had been born in Italy, a country whose vernacular was closer to Latin than was French, she provided the living link between the Latin of the Church and the Middle French vernacular.[92] If my theory of Christine's authorship of these two Latin verses is correct, the *SPA* would be bound up in a volume with litanies "signed" in the Latin of the Church by a speaker who transcends her female gender to exist in a desexualized, spiritualized universal first person.

Although the reasons listed above lead me to believe, and very strongly, that Christine did indeed compose the verses herself, the sheer number of copies of such litanies[93] does preclude drawing hard-and-fast conclusions. At the risk of weakening my painstakingly established hypothesis, I would add that the presence of these two Latin verses at the end of the litanies accompanying Christine's *SPA* is significant regardless of who composed them. Even if Christine were quoting someone else, that act would in itself be meaningful. Such a quotation would contribute to the universal quality of the first-person speaker of the *SPA,* one of the effects that Christine is striving for. The individual self is subsumed into Christine's universal "I," a vernacular first person that melds with the Latin of the Church, a language heard by, and thus known to, everyone who attended mass. If Christine were in fact playing upon some Latin verses composed by someone else (undoubtedly famous to medievals but out of favor with modern critics, like Gregory the Great or Jean Gerson, or someone known to us whose corpus of written works is of daunting proportions, like St. Augustine, with ninety-seven works to his credit!), this would serve to reinforce the importance of reported speech. In quoting the phrase "gloriosa dicta sunt de te, civitas Dei" [glorious things are spoken of you, city of God], Christine, St. Augustine, and the author of Psalm 86 are doing something similar.[94] In incorporating this phrase into the fabric of their written texts, these three authors all cleverly exploit the potential of reported speech to mimic the original speech acts that formed the basis for Holy Scripture. These speech acts were *re-membered* (given new life and integrity) each time that the psalms were recited, whether in the original Latin or in Middle French translation and/or commentary. The Scriptures, the ultimate repository of cultural memory for all Christians (with particular pertinence to one whose name was Christine), were kept alive through "liturgical memory,"[95] the rituals of Holy Church. As opposed to purely textual (i.e., written) transmission of the Scriptures that would reach only an educated minority who had access to books, the oral rituals of the Church disseminated God's word to all "who had ears to hear," to paraphrase biblical commentators from St. Paul to St. Augustine.

When St. Augustine links his City of God with Psalm 86,[96] he realizes several related objectives: He connects his *Civitas* with scriptural authority, he indicates that scriptural authority has its basis in a speech act, and he stresses the role of church rituals in maintaining the precarious relationship between the human and divine realms. St. Augustine's *City of God,* whose title Christine echoes in the *Cité* that she constructed almost a millennium later, is not only illustrative of the heavenly Jerusalem that will be realized at the end of time, but represents a group of people in the here-and-now, identified as the elect or Holy Church as an ideal entity (distinct from corrupt members of the Church at any historical moment).[97] The relationship between God and human beings is maintained by the rituals of Holy Church, whose Latin wisdom, albeit the surest form of Christian knowledge, is nonetheless only a distant echo of the original *Verbum* through which everything was created ("omnia per ipsum facta sunt," John 1:3). Since John's Gospel posits a speech act at the origins of all creation, the vernacular, the living language, is potentially endowed with the highest possible authority. I will return to this point in the conclusion to my study.

Christine's Royal Vernacular and
the *Grandes Chroniques de France*

Christine's conception of the vernacular reflected the political agenda of the *GCF,* in particular its support of the Valois dynasty. Commissioned during the reign of Louis IX (1226–1270) from the monks at Saint-Denis, who had traditionally compiled Latin royal chronicles, these prose chronicles in Middle French effectively supplanted the Latin originals. They assimilated elements of the newly emerging vernacular prose history rather than passively reproducing their Latin models. Surviving in approximately one hundred-thirty manuscripts, the *GCF* in its form describes a chain of royal lives from the fall of Troy to the reign of Charles VI in the 1380s. The *GCF* promoted what Anne D. Hedeman refers to as the "religion royale," an ideology that the monarchy intended to implement, perpetuate, and disseminate. Indeed, the French royal house adopted the vernacular as a primary vehicle for the consolidation of its power and legitimacy largely because it could reach a wider audience than Latin.[98]

The original author-translator, the monk Primat, makes a statement of royal political ideology that Charles V and his successors would continue to maintain and develop. In this scheme France had a distinctive role as defender of the church. One of the reasons that the country enjoyed this special status was because, as stated by Primat, "la fonteine de clergie, par cui sainte Eglise est soustenue et enluminée, florist a Paris" [the fountain of *clergie,* by which Holy Church is maintained and illuminated, flourishes in

Paris],[99] and this because, in a classic statement of the *translatio studii et imperii*, *clergie* and *chevalerie* had passed from Greece to Rome to settle definitively, if the country remained worthy of keeping it, in France. The histories of the kings of France contained in the *GCF* served as models for the behavior of present and future rulers as well as for their noble subjects. In the *SPA* and the litanies that follow it, which together make up a devotional book that contains numerous references to "sainte Eglise" and a two-verse Latin signature in which the author represents herself as continuing David's role as a Christian prophet, Christine implicitly places herself in the line of the monastic keepers of the *GCF*. As a clerkly supporter of the monarchy like Primat before her, Christine tries to help bring about his vision of France's manifest destiny by the stance that she, an established royal biographer, assumes toward her patron Charles the Noble, a man whose royal lineage gives him a pivotal position in French history. Charles was at once the son of a person who had tried to subvert God's intentions for the monarchy by disputing Charles V's claim to the throne and a descendant of Louis IX, the king and saint who had worked so hard to strengthen the monarchy.

In *The Royal Image,* Hedeman explores how Charles V had those whom he commissioned as translators and producers of illuminated manuscripts project an image of himself as continuator of Louis IX's campaign to enlist the vernacular in support of royal power. A cycle of miniatures in Charles V's *GCF* portrays the king's struggle with Charles the Bad as claimant to the French throne. The ceremonial images stress the idea of French supremacy over the English, and the continuity of the Valois line in Charles V's heir, Charles VI.[100] If, as I am arguing here, Christine implicitly gives advice to Charles the Noble in her *SPA,* she is continuing the work of strengthening the monarchy undertaken in Charles V's *GCF* at a time when Charles VI's madness threatened the stability of the realm. In the *SPA,* Christine also assumes a function that the *GCF* failed to fulfill during the first half of Charles VI's rule. Hedeman cites Christine along with Jean Gerson and Philippe de Mézières as royalists whose writings "exhorted the king to encourage good government and counseled the queen and princes of the fleur-de-lis to work for peace and for the good of France." But Hedeman singles out Christine's works in particular as focusing "on themes that became important in copies of the *Grandes Chroniques* during the second half of Charles VI's reign."[101] I second Hedeman's contention that Christine saw herself as a supporter of Louis IX's initial conception of the monarchy that the clerkly keepers of the *GCF* were called upon to maintain and continue.

Important as it is, the "royal image" projected in the illuminated copies of the *GCF* is founded on an even more fundamental conception, which I refer to as the "royal vernacular." Following in the wake of Louis IX, Charles V constructed a version of monarchy by means of the vernacular, a language understood by all. Power and language are intimately related in the history of a country. The French Middle Ages saw the progressive dominance of *francien* over other dialects because it was spoken in Île-de-France, the center of royal power. The royal vernacular was at once the creation and tool of a monarchy that was carving out its legitimacy in an era marked by the squabbles of rival princes and the encroachments of outside powers, notably England, with its claims to the French throne. It was only in the early fifteenth century, at the time when Christine was writing the *SPA,* that the French language attained a fairly stable *koiné*—an image and, in light of subsequent developments, a promise of the desired stability of the kingdom.

The term "royal vernacular" signifies the construction of the French nation through its language. In the words of Pierre Nora: "The thirteenth-century *Grandes Chroniques de France* condensed dynastic memory and established the model for several centuries of historiography."[102] I have begun to sketch here how in *Charles V* Christine has the vernacularization of the Bible form the basis for her own construction of dynastic memory. Christine presents language as personifying the history of the French nation; the French vernacular is the vehicle of France's *memoria,* its spoken and written history. *Memoria,* in *Charles V,* becomes institutionalized in written history in the same way that it does in the *GCF.*[103] In her initial prayer in *Charles V,* Christine asks to be able to explain "the things conceived in my memory" (full quotation above). The notion of *memoria* as Christine employs it here comprises both lived history and the intellectual operation that renders that lived history intelligible. As opposed to Latin in early fifteenth-century France, the vernacular was able to incarnate both lived history, as it was conserved in spoken memories, and the written version of that history—the two dimensions conveyed in the German language by the terms *Geschichte* and *Historie.* Following the lead of the monks of the royal abbey and necropolis of Saint-Denis, Christine did her part in helping construct the dynastic memory of her country in the French vernacular and in prose, which by the early fifteenth century was seen as more capable of conveying truth than verse.[104]

Conclusion: The Authority of the Royal Vernacular

Christine allies herself with Saint-Denis's project of creating an entity called France by referring to the country as "cele noble nacion françoise" (*Charles V* 11.5), which closely evokes the terminology of Primat's prologue. She continues the Dionysian chroniclers' attempt to unify the country under God's aegis and protection, by imitating their use of the royal

vernacular. The divine authority that Saint-Denis had claimed for the vernacular explains and justifies Christine's assumption of the role of translator who interprets the word of God to the French people in a language
that all can understand. The assertion that the vernacular is at least as close
to divine authority as Latin is related to the history of the Vulgate, whose
Latin is a translation from Greek, Hebrew, and Old Latin.[105] To explain
this in terms of the story of creation in the Book of Genesis: In consequence of the Fall, direct communication between God and his creatures
became exceedingly difficult. Even when God appeared to speak directly
to humans through miracles or by his sacrificial gesture of sending his
only-begotten son in order to redeem the world, these acts called for interpretation by commentators to reveal their full meaning. The interpretations of these events were never unambiguous, as shown by the differing
versions of Christ's life and words given by the four Evangelists. It is perhaps no exaggeration to say that after the breakup of the unitary language
used in Paradise, an event that was symbolized by the construction of the
Tower of Babel, all communication—whether between God and human
beings, between human beings speaking different languages, or even between human beings speaking the same language—became essentially an
act of translation.[106] These translation acts were mediated by various types
of interpreters—commentators, prophets, intercessors, messengers—
including, for our purposes here, the translator. The main way for human
beings to know God's word after the Fall was through Holy Scripture,
which in the Middle Ages meant the Vulgate. Its Latin was itself only a
translation from other languages, themselves a translation of the original
language used by God to communicate with Adam and Eve in Eden.[107]

Christine, like many others, believed this language to have been Hebrew.[108] Evoking a tradition that dates back to the fourth-century Eusebius of Caesarea, author of the first synopsis of the New Testament and of
the *Chronicles,* a universal history stretching from the Creation to 324 A.D.,
Christine in her own universal history in the *Mutacion* posits that prior to
the confusion of languages of Babel "estoit q'un lengage, / C'estoit he-
brieu" [there was only one language, Hebrew]. She then emphasizes Hebrew's status as a vernacular, a spoken language: "que par usage / Et par
nature Juïfs parlent" [which through custom and nature Jews speak (lines
8687–9)]. She insists on Hebrew's supreme place among human languages:
"Tous les autres cellui ne valent, / Si est tout le plus approuvé" [No other
language equals it, / It has the greatest approval (lines 8690–91)]. Hebrew
owes its transcendent status to God, who invented it himself ("Car de Dieu
mesmes fu trouvé," line 8692). Christine's use of the verb *trouver,* which
refers to literary composition, recalls once again the opening of John's
Gospel. Rather than translating the Latin Vulgate, in *SPA* Christine trans-

lates the speech act of which the Latin was only the translation,[109] a speech act that had been rendered in Hebrew.

In having David speak French in the *SPA*, Christine replaces the original Hebrew prayer that he made in the Old Testament with a prayer in her own national vernacular. In so doing, she simultaneously evokes the memory of a language that is closer to God's than the Latin of the Bible, and she associates that language with Middle French. With an adroit sleight-of-hand Christine presents the French vernacular, at least in the hands of those like herself and the Dionysian chroniclers, as having the potential to be the New Testament equivalent of Hebrew. As such, French is eminently worthy of conveying God's message to his present chosen people of France, modern Israelites lost in troubled times, eagerly awaiting entry to the New Jerusalem.

It is by assuming a prophetic voice, conveyed in the vernacular, that Christine attempts to attain an authority beyond reproach. Rita Copeland, in examining the patristic model of translation and its influence, discusses how Augustine sought to "recover a kinship or wholeness of meaning beyond the circumstances of individual languages."[110] For him, translation of Scripture performed "a teleological office of revelation and prophecy."[111] Once again Christine follows in the footsteps of Augustine, who is among her most often cited *auctoritates*. By ventriloquizing David in the *SPA,* she adopts a prophetic voice to try to harness for her own ends, which were also the ends of the French royal house, the authority of the divine *Verbum* that had originally authored the Scriptures.

My contention that Christine in the *SPA* speaks from the perspective of a *female* Evangelist who tries to influence the present by calling on lessons culled from the Old Testament calls for further clarification. Her self-presentation as female Evangelist is implicit in her representation of Christ's story from the Nativity to Pentecost in the *SPA*.[112] Christine's metaphorical self-presentation as a personified tongue predated the *SPA* (the most notable example appears in *Cité* 3.10),[113] and she had expressly led the readers of her *Mutacion* to see her name as a variant of Christ's. In the *SPA* she takes up the pentecostal injunction to spread God's message in all the languages of the world through her work as translator. The performance of the psalms and litanies that she orchestrates in the *SPA* is part of her authentic witness to the acting out of biblical tradition for contemporary purposes. Her femaleness is tied up with her substitution of Middle French for Hebrew. The tradition originating with Eusebius evoked by Christine viewed Hebrew as the mother tongue.[114] Obscured by Latin, the reigning "father language," Hebrew is a female progenitor, a vernacular whose former power as sacred language is now assumed by the French vernacular. Primat established French's stellar status in his confident (but not

self-confident) restatement of the *translatio studii et imperii* topic. In face of
the lingering doubt left by Chrétien de Troyes regarding whether or not
chevalerie had come to settle permanently in France along with *clergie*,[115]
Primat affirmed (and significantly in prose) that the French would remain
God's chosen people as long as *clergie* and *chevalerie* supported each other.
This symbiosis implied a set of reciprocal obligations for *clercs* and rulers:
The French nobility's obligation to preserve learning was balanced by the
duty of the educated to guide the nobility in bringing about the realiza-
tion of the City of God on earth—in France and in all of Christendom.

Christine inserts herself into this scheme as a female defender of *sainte
Eglise* (which explains the frequent appearance of the *chevalière* in her
works) who writes in the vernacular, the contemporary substitute for Hebrew, the mother tongue, that is, the original vernacular, coded by tradition as female. Just as in her *Cité* Christine had uncovered a heretofore
obscured female genealogy behind cultural achievement, so Holy Church
is supported by its Latin and vernacular rituals and its male and female
guarantors and defenders.[116] Primat casts France as the defender of Holy
Church using the metaphor of a daughter taking care of her mother:
"France comme loiaus fille secourt sa mere en touz besoinz" [as a loyal
daughter France comes to her mother's aid on every occasion], an image
that brings to mind Christine's support of her own mother and the story
that she recounts in *Cité* 2.11 of the woman who breast-fed her mother in
prison. Christine's evocation of liturgical *memoria* in *Charles V* and *SPA* is
yet another way in which she indissolubly joins her female *clergie* to that of
the monastic keepers of the *GCF*. As such, male and female clerks engage
in a discourse beyond gender in order to make God's will known to the
French people in a language endowed with the sanctity of Old Testament
prophecy. In expressing her fervent hopes for the future of the "noble nacion françoise,"[117] Christine situates herself as "translator" in a movement
begun over a century earlier by Louis IX, the saintly king who had chosen the vernacular, rather than Latin, as the language suited for expressing
the nascent linguistic and cultural entity of "France."

Notes

1. All quotations will be taken from the edition by Ruth Ringland Rains, *Les
   Sept psaumes allégorisés of Christine de Pisan: A Critical Edition from the
   Brussels and Paris Manuscripts* (Washington, D.C.: Catholic University of
   America, 1965), hereafter cited as *SPA*.
2. All quotations will be taken from Suzanne Solente's two-volume edition
   (Paris: Champion, 1936–1941), hereafter cited as *Charles V*. The translations
   into English are my own.

3. See Claire Richter Sherman, *Imaging Aristotle: Verbal and Visual Representation in Fourteenth-Century France* (Berkeley and Los Angeles: University of California Press, 1995).

4. Alastair J. Minnis, *Medieval Theory of Authorship: Scholastic Literary Attitudes in the Later Middle Ages* (Philadelphia: University of Pennsylvania Press, 1988), pp. 104–11.

5. "L'Humanisme vers 1400, essai d'exploration à partir d'un cas marginal: Christine de Pizan traductrice de Thomas d'Aquin," in *Pratiques de la culture écrite en France au XVe siècle,* ed. Monique Ornato and Nicole Pons (Louvain-la-Neuve: Turnhout, 1995), pp. 160–78, and "Traduction et adaptation dans l'*Advision Cristine* de Christine de Pizan," in *Traduction et adaptation en France à la fin du Moyen Age et à la Renaissance. Actes du colloque organisé par l'Université de Nancy II, 23–25 mars 1995,* ed. Charles Brucker (Paris: Champion, 1997), pp. 121–31.

6. Thelma Fenster, "'Perdre son latin': Christine de Pizan and Vernacular Humanism," in *Christine de Pizan and the Categories of Difference,* ed. Marilynn Desmond (Minneapolis: University of Minnesota Press, 1998), p. 105, n. 2. Fenster quotes from the text of comments that I had made during a session on Christine's use of the vernacular at the 1995 Christine de Pizan conference at Binghamton, New York. No supporting material is supplied in that article. I am providing references here along with the development of my argument.

7. For Christine's indebtedness to Raoul de Presles's adaptation/translation of St. Augustine's *De civitate Dei,* see Lori J. Walters, "La réécriture de saint Augustin par Christine de Pizan: De la *Cité de Dieu* à la *Cité des Dames,*" in *Au champ des escriptures,* ed. Eric Hicks (Paris: Champion, 2000), pp. 197–215. For her indebtedness to Jean Daudin's translation/adaptation of Petrarch's *De remediis,* see Lori J. Walters, "'Translating' Petrarch: *Cité* II.7.1, Jean Daudin, and Vernacular Authority," in *Christine 2000: Studies on Christine de Pizan in Honour of Angus J. Kennedy,* eds. John Campbell and Nadia Margolis (Amsterdam and Atlanta: Rodopi, 2000), pp. 283–97.

8. Anne D. Hedeman, *The Royal Image: Illustrations of the "Grandes Chroniques de France," 1274–1422* (Berkeley and Los Angeles: University of California Press, 1991). Hedeman, pp. 137–44, describes how the situation changed with the reign of Charles VI, who, unlike his father Charles V, was not interested in political theory.

9. Chrétien presents himself as translator of Ovid and of Tristan material in the prologue to his second extant romance, *Cligés* (ca. 1176). He identifies himself as a court poet when he dedicates his *Chevalier de la charrette* (1177) to Marie of Champagne and his *Conte du graal* (1181–1190) to Philip of Flanders. In the prologue to his prose adaptation of Boethius' *Consolatio,* known as the *Livres de confort de philosophie* (ca. 1300), Jean states that he had previously "translated" Vegetius' *On Warfare,* the *Marvels of Ireland,* the life of Peter Abelard and the letters of Abelard and Heloise, and Aelred's *On Spiritual Friendship.* Jean dedicates his work to Philip IV the Fair (reigned

1285–1314). See Rita Copeland, *Rhetoric, Hermeneutics and Translation in the Middle Ages: Academic Traditions and Vernacular Texts* (Cambridge: Cambridge University Press, 1991), pp. 132–50. In this essay only writers will retain their French names; the names of all other figures will be anglicized.

10. *Le livre de l'Advision Cristine,* eds. Christine Reno and Liliane Dulac (Paris: Champion, 2001), p. 12. See my "Christine de Pizan as Translator and Voice of the Body Politic," in *Christine de Pizan: A Casebook,* ed. Barbara K. Altmann and Deborah McGrady (New York: Routledge), forthcoming.

11. I realize that the *De vulgari eloquentia,* of which we have only three surviving manuscripts, was not widely disseminated. However, Dante had written it roughly a century before the height of Christine's career, and if anyone in France would have known the treatise on the vernacular, it would have been Christine. Second, even if she did not know the treatise itself, many of Dante's ideas on the vernacular are implicit in the *Commedia.* For example, Dante's treatment of Brunetto Latini and Orlando (Roland) reveals his belief in the superiority of Italian to French. Finally, Christine's echo of the notion of the "royal vernacular" provides another link between the two authors.

12. "Dicimus illustre, cardinale, aulicum et curiale vulgare in Latio, quod omnis latie civitatis est et nullius esse videtur, et quo municipalia vulgaria omnia Latinorum mensurantur et ponderantur et comparantur." Warman Welliver, *Dante in Hell: The 'De Vulgari Eloquentia': Introduction, Text, Translation, Commentary* (Ravenna: Longo Editore, 1981), p. 81.

13. Jocelyn Wogan-Browne et al., *The Idea of the Vernacular: An Anthology of Middle English Literary Theory, 1280–1520* (University Park: Pennsylvania State University Press, 1999), p. 319.

14. "The Genius of the French Language," in *Realms of Memory: Rethinking the French Past,* ed. Lawrence D. Kritzman, trans. Arthur Goldhammer, 3 vols. (New York: Columbia University Press, 1996), 3:568.

15. Christine in fact acknowledges that the *GCF* furnished background information for two of the episodes (1.32 and 3.52) of *Charles V,* composed between January 30 and November 30, 1404.

16. The psalms have different numbers in diverse biblical traditions. I will refer to the Vulgate numbering of the psalms.

17. On other French translations of the penitential psalms, see Jean Bonnard, *Les traductions de la Bible en vers français au Moyen Âge* (Paris: Imprimerie Nationale, 1884), p. 139, and Pierre-Maurice Bogaert, "Adaptations et versions de la Bible en prose (langue d'oïl)," in *Les genres littéraires dans les sources théologiques et philosophiques médiévales: Définition, critique et exploitation,* Actes du Colloque international de Louvain-la-Neuve 25–27 mai 1981 (Louvain-la-Neuve, 1982), pp. 259–77; J.-R. Smeets, "Les traductions-adaptations versifiées de la Bible en ancien français," in *Les genres littéraires,* pp. 249–58; C. A. Robson, "Vernacular Scripture in France," in *The Cambridge History of the Bible,* 2 vols. (Cambridge: Cambridge University Press, 1969), 2:436–51 and 529–31. I thank Maureen Boulton for supplying me with references on vernacular renditions of the psalms.

18. Stewart Gregory, ed. *The Twelfth-Century Psalter Commentary in French for Laurette d'Alsace,* 2 vols. (London: MHRC, 1990).

19. For earlier studies of Christine's psalms, see in particular Nadia Margolis, "La progression polémique, spirituelle et personnelle dans les écrits religieux de Christine de Pizan," in *Une femme de lettres,* pp. 297–316; Gérard Gros, "'Mon oroison entens . . . ': Etude sur les trois opuscules pieux de Christine de Pizan," *Bien dire et bien aprandre* 8 (1990): 99–112; and Willard, "Allegorized Psalms," pp. 317–26. Margolis gives a particularly helpful overview of the *SPA* on pp. 303–305.

20. In Paris, Bibliothèque nationale de France (BNF), nouv. acq. fr. 4792, Christine introduces her translation of each psalm by the first (two or three) words of the Latin Vulgate. For example, "Domine ne in furore" precedes "Sire, ne m'argues en ta fureur, et ne me corriges en ton yre." See Léopold Victor Delisle, "Notice sur *Les sept psaumes allégorisés* de Christine de Pisan," *Notices et extraits des manuscrits de la Bibliothèque Nationale et autres bibliothèques* 35 (1896): 552. Rains's lack of precision in matters relating to the manuscript tradition of the *SPA* is just one of the reasons that a new edition of the work is desirable.

21. Rains, *SPA,* p. 22, states that Christine's source was a Gallican text.

22. They are:
  1) Brussels, Bibliothèque royale 10987 (Rains's B). Brussels 10987 once belonged to the Dukes of Burgundy and dates from between 1409 and 1420 (Rains, p. 81).
  2) Paris, BNF, nouv. acq. fr. 4792 (Rains's P), formerly owned by the earl of Ashburnham. Delisle, "Notice," 551–9, believes that Christine presented this copy, decorated with historiated initials and miniatures, to the duke of Berry on January 1, 1410.
  3) Willard, "Allegorized Psalms," p. 322, mentions the existence of another manuscript, Brussels, Bibliothèque royale IV, 1093 (ancien Collection J. Dumont à Palaiseau), fols. 1–88, which dates from the mid-fifteenth century.
  4) Paris, BNF, fr. 15216, fols. 1–48.
  5) Ashburnham, ancien Barrois 203; England's earl of Ashburnham purchased this manuscript of the *SPA* in 1849; in 1967, it was for sale by a Parisian bookseller. The present location of this manuscript is unknown. Rains, p. 82, speculates that this manuscript was the copy that Christine presented to Charles of Navarre or her own copy.
      I have not had the opportunity to view any of these manuscripts myself. Sylvie Lefèvre provided me with the most up-to-date information on these manuscripts. I am most grateful for her help.

23. Litanies traditionally follow the penitential psalms when these are transmitted as part of a Book of Hours. Roger S. Wieck, curator of Medieval and Renaissance Manuscripts, the Pierpont Morgan Library, New York, gave me this information during a private consultation in February 2000. Wieck, with essays by Lawrence R. Poos, Virginia Reinburg, and John Plummer, is the author of *Time Sanctified: The Book of Hours in Medieval Art*

and *Life* (New York: George Braziller, 1988) and *Painted Prayers: The Book of Hours in Medieval and Renaissance Art* (New York: George Braziller, in association with the Pierpont Morgan Library, 1997).

24. See Rains, *SPA,* pp. 155–58, and Delisle, "Notice."

25. In *Charles V* 2.21, Christine explains and justifies her work as a compilation.

26. Rosalind Brown-Grant, "*L'Avision-Christine:* Autobiographical Narrative or Mirror for the Prince?" in *Politics, Gender, and Genre: The Political Thought of Christine de Pizan,* ed. Margaret Brabant (Boulder, CO: Westview Press, 1992), pp. 95–112. See also Brown-Grant's reworking of these arguments in *Christine de Pizan and the Moral Defence of Women: Reading Beyond Gender* (Cambridge: Cambridge University Press, 2000), pp. 89–127.

27. Christine Reno and Liliane Dulac, eds., *Le livre de l'advision Cristine,* pp. xxxvii–xxxviii. All references will be to this edition of the *Advision.*

28. The introductory gloss of the *Chronica,* "De Tribus Maximis Circumstantiis Gestorum," was translated and published by Mary Carruthers as an appendix to *The Book of Memory: A Study of Memory in Medieval Culture* (Cambridge: Cambridge University Press, 1990), pp. 261–66.

29. She also cites him by name in the one-hundredth and final section of her *Epistre d'Othéa.*

30. "moy non instruicte de science en aucun atouchement de degré" [I who was not instructed in learning at any level], *Charles V* 1.1.

31. "A codex is composed of many books, a book is composed of one volume. And a codex is so called, by transference, from the trunks (*codicibus*) of trees or vines, as if it were a trunk because it contains a multitude of books coming out of itself like so many branches[. . .] *Liber* is the inner rind of a tree, upon which the ancients used to write before the use of paper or parchment." Jerome Taylor, trans., *The 'Didascalicon' of Hugh of St. Victor: A Medieval Guide to the Arts* (New York: Columbia University Press, 1991), p. 118. A very popular work, the *Didascalicon* circulated in over one hundred manuscript copies between the twelfth and the fifteenth centuries.

32. Wieck, *Time Sanctified,* p. 41, and pp. 157–68, Appendix: Texts and Prayers of the Book of Hours.

33. Carruthers, *The Book of Memory,* p. 66.

34. Charity Cannon Willard, *Christine de Pizan: Her Life and Works* (New York: Persea Books, 1984), p. 17 and pp. 115–18.

35. Le Goff, *Saint Louis* (Paris: Gallimard, 1996), p. 598.

36. The case of Charlemagne is more complex. The Capetian projection of a French Charlemagne was countered by Frederick Barbarossa's canonization of Charlemagne in 1165. In his turn, Charles V tried to elevate the sacred character of the monarchy by associating his rule with Charlemagne, viewed as a French rather than as a Germanic saint. See Gabrielle M. Spiegel, *The Past as Text: The Theory and Practice of Medieval Historiography* (Baltimore: Johns Hopkins University Press, 1997), pp. 125, 131. In referring to Charlemagne as "saint charlemaine" in a speech delivered in 1378, and in having the feast day of Saint Charlemagne celebrated in his chapel

(Raymond Cazelles, *Société politique: Noblesse et couronne sous Jean le Bon et Charles V* [Geneva: Droz, 1982]), Charles V accorded the Carolingian ruler a status he had not ordinarily been given in France (Hedeman, *The Royal Image*, p. 98), as a response to the German reappropriation of the king of the Franks. Claire Richter Sherman, *Imaging Aristotle: Verbal and Visual Representation in Fourteenth-Century France* (Berkeley and Los Angeles: University of California Press, 1995, p. 10), discusses other strategies used by Charles to connect his rule with Charlemagne's.

37. In the words of Jacques Le Goff, *Saint Louis*, p. 355: "Saint Louis, en stabilisant l'université de Paris, a assuré au royaume de France sa prééminence."

38. R. Howard Bloch, *Etymologies and Genealogies: A Literary Anthropology of the French Middle Ages* (Chicago: University of Chicago Press, 1983).

39. Minnis, *Medieval Theory*.

40. All quotations from the Bible will be taken from the *Biblia Sacra iuxta Vulgatam Versionem*, ed. Bonifatius Fischer (1969; Stuttgart: Deutsche Bibelgesellschaft, 1983).

41. On author portraits in manuscripts of the *Romance of the Rose*, see Lori Walters, Appendix: "Author Portraits and Textual Demarcation in Manuscripts of the *Romance of the Rose*," in *Rethinking the* Romance of the Rose: *Text, Image, Reception*, eds. Kevin Brownlee and Sylvia Huot (Philadelphia: University of Pennsylvania Press, 1992), pp. 359–74.

42. In an essay entitled "Who Was Chrétien de Troyes?," *Arthurian Literature* 15 (1997): 1–35, Sarah Kay explores the Christian orientation of writers like Chrétien de Troyes during the Middle Ages.

43. Between June 26, 1409 and January 1, 1410. Willard, "Allegorized Psalms," p. 321.

44. Charles's family history helps explain why he would have wanted Christine to compose the *SPA*. Charles III was the great-great-grandson of the same Joan of Navarre who had commissioned Louis IX's biography from Joinville. Charles III was not only related to the Valois's saintly ancestor Louis IX through his father's line (which included Joan of Navarre), but also through his mother, another Joan, Charles V's sister. It would be normal for Charles of Navarre to commission a work from Christine, since she had already established her reputation as a writer who dealt with topics pertaining to the monarchy several years earlier in completing the biography of Charles V, Charles of Navarre's uncle.

45. Rains, *SPA*, p. 50.

46. Willard, "Allegorized Psalms," p. 319.

47. See Lori J. Walters, "Constructing Reputations: *Fama* and Memory in *Charles V* and *L'Avision Christine*," in *Fama: The Politics of Talk and Reputation in Medieval Europe*, eds. Thelma Fenster and Daniel L. Smail (Ithaca: Cornell University Press), forthcoming.

48. In so doing, Christine follows the lead of one of her major *auctoritates*, St. Augustine, who had posited the equivalence of the male and female soul. As human beings on earth, what Augustine termed the "order of creation,"

both men and women are alike in being sinners; as souls in the eternal "order of salvation," each has an equal opportunity to achieve heavenly glory.

49. In Psalm 50, the chief penitential psalm, David connects his personal penance for his crimes and his ability to serve as a moral counselor for others. Michael P. Kuczynski, "The Psalms and Social Action in Late Medieval England," in *The Place of the Psalms in the Intellectual Culture of the Late Middle Ages,* ed. Nancy van Deusen (Albany: State University of New York Press, 1999), p. 194.

50. See Minnis, *Medieval Theory,* pp. 103–106 for David as a prefiguration of Christ despite his sins.

51. The tongue of Saint Christine, with all its implications for the writer who shares her name, is the subject of a study by Kevin Brownlee, "Martyrdom and the Female Voice: Saint Christine in the *Cité des dames,*" in *Images of Sainthood in Medieval Europe,* eds. Renate Blumenfeld-Kosinski and Timea Szell (Ithaca and London: Cornell University Press, 1991), pp. 115–35. One could also speak of an androgynous narrative voice in François Villon's "Ballade pour prier Nostre Dame," where the poet composes a prayer to the Virgin to be recited by his devout but less articulate mother.

52. Minnis, *Medieval Theory,* p. 109.

53. Willard, "Allegorized Psalms," p. 319.

54. Jocelyn Wogan-Browne et al., *The Idea of the Vernacular,* p. 291.

55. Willard, "Allegorized Psalms," p. 319.

56. Le Goff, *Saint Louis,* pp. 394–96.

57. Charles T. Wood, "Queens, Queans, and Kingship: An Inquiry into Theories of Royal Legitimacy in Late Medieval England and France," in *Order and Innovation in the Middle Ages,* eds. William C. Jordan, Bruce McNab, and Teofilo F. Ruiz (Princeton: Princeton University Press, 1976), p. 387. Wood is quoted by Peggy McCracken, *The Romance of Adultery: Queenship and Sexual Transgression in Old French Literature* (Philadelphia: University of Pennsylvania Press, 1998), p. 174; see McCracken's analysis of the adultery issue, pp. 171–77, in particular p. 21.

58. John the Fearless would in his turn meet a similar violent death in 1419.

59. Jan R. Veenstra, *Magic and Divination at the Courts of Burgundy and France: Text and Context of Laurens Pignon's 'Contre les devineurs' (1411)* (Leiden: Brill, 1998), p. 36.

60. R. C. Famiglietti, *Royal Intrigue: Crisis at the Court of Charles VI (1392–1420)* (New York: AMS Press, 1986), p. 91.

61. Willard, "Allegorized Psalms," p. 321.

62. Famiglietti, *Royal Intrigue,* p. 253, n. 56, and p. 245, n. 29, which includes the following comment: "The alliance with Duke John did, in fact, open the royal coffers to the king of Navarre."

63. See the citation from *Charles V,* as quoted by Willard, "Allegorized Psalms," p. 322.

64. Willard, "Allegorized Psalms," p. 322.

65. Famiglietti, *Royal Intrigue,* p. 253, n. 56, notes that Charles the Noble did not pay his creditors before leaving Paris this final time.
66. Carruthers, *The Book of Memory,* pp. 264–65.
67. Kuczynski, "The Psalms and Social Action," p. 202.
68. Reno and Dulac, *L'Advision,* p. 9.
69. *Charles V* 1.29, "Où il est question de la pureté des moeurs du roi Charles V" [Where it is a question of the purity of the morals of King Charles V].
70. Rains, *SPA,* p. 69.
71. This devotional book is now housed in the Cleveland Museum of Art. See P. M. De Winter, "Art, Devotion, and Satire: The Book of Hours of Charles III, the Noble, King of Navarre, at the Cleveland Museum of Art," *Gamut, a Journal of Ideas and Information* 1 (1981): 42–59.
72. Willard, "Allegorized Psalms," p. 320.
73. See Deborah McGrady, "What Is a Patron? Benefactors and Authorship in Harley 4431, Christine de Pizan's Collected Works," in Desmond, ed., *Christine de Pizan and the Categories of Difference,* pp. 195–214, at p. 198.
74. For studies on Christine as a political writer, see in particular Sandra Hindman, *Christine de Pizan's 'Epitre Othéa': Painting and Politics at the Court of Charles VI* (Toronto: Pontifical Institute of Mediaeval Studies, 1986), and the essays in Brabant, ed., *Politics, Gender, and Genre.* Political aims can be discerned even in one of her earliest works, her *Cent Ballades* of 1399. See Lori J. Walters, "Chivalry and the (En)Gendered Poetic Self: Petrarchan Models in the *Cent balades,*" in *The City of Scholars: New Approaches to Christine de Pizan,* eds. Margarete Zimmermann and Dina De Rentiis (Berlin: Walter de Gruyter, 1994), pp. 43–66, on Christine's subversion of her patrons' attempt to have her compose light courtly entertainment.
75. See Spiegel, *The Past as Text,* pp. 100–10, on the status and role of prophecy in the thought of the time.
76. R. S. Janken, *Jehan Lome y la escultura gótica en Navarra* (Pamplona, 1977); J. R. Castro, *Carlos III el Noble rey de Navarra* (Pamplona, 1967), and De Winter, "Art, Devotion, and Satire."
77. Rains, *SPA,* p. 137, n. 63. Rains also incorporates information from Gabriel Chappuys, *L'histoire du royaume de Navarre . . .* (Paris: N. Gilles, 1596), pp. 389–91.
78. Louis G. Kelly, "Medieval Psalm Translation and Literality," in Jeanette Beer, ed., *Translation Theory and Practice in the Middle Ages* (Kalamazoo: Medieval Institute Publications, 1997), pp. 161–72, at p. 161.
79. This view was adopted by all the commentators on the psalms who came after Augustine. Kuczynski, "The Psalms and Social Action," p. 194.
80. In *Charles V* Christine had described that king's effort to enlarge the notion of the monarchy to include scholars at the University of Paris and members of the council of cardinals whose job was to elect the pope and to help run the papacy. Christine's enumeration of members of these groups in her address in the *SPA* constitutes part of the courtly audience

for her psalms, whether or not all the individuals mentioned were present in the flesh or only in spirit at such a reading.

81. Kuczynski, "The Psalms and Social Action," pp. 198–202.

82. Although at first cautioning that a public reading of psalms in the vernacular would be unusual in an early fifteenth-century context, Roger S. Wieck later granted that my hypothesis was justified given the evidence. He then helped me in determining the probable context for such a reading. I thank him warmly for his insightful comments on this paper (see also p. 165, below).

83. Carruthers, *The Book of Memory*, p. 88. See also the articles in van Deusen, ed., *The Place of the Psalms in Medieval Culture.*

84. Penitential Psalm 129 is the famous "De profundis," "Out of the depths I have cried to thee, O Lord."

85. These lines are present in B, but lacking in P.

86. For their assistance in translating these lines, I thank Nadia Margolis, Peter Marshall, Hans-Friedrich Mueller, and a monk (who wished to remain anonymous) who heard the paper on Christine's use and knowledge of Latin in a session on Christine's religious works that I presented at Kalamazoo in 2000.

87. I thank Nadia Margolis for bringing this point to my attention.

88. Christine also uses the term *fruis* twice in lines in 142.14 that I have not cited.

89. Solente, *Charles V,* 1:6.

90. My thanks to Nadia Margolis and Peter Marshall for correcting the Latin of Solente's edition.

91. On Christine's evocation of the commonplaces of the liturgy as an element of her vernacular humanism, see Margolis, "La progression polémique," and my remarks in "Metamorphoses of the Self: Christine de Pizan, the Saint's Life and Perpetua," in *Sur le chemin de longue étude: Actes du colloque d'Orléans, juillet 1995,* ed. Bernard Ribémont (Paris: Champion, 1998), pp. 161–62. The list of works cited, which was omitted by the publisher of that volume, can be restored by referring to the footnotes in my related article, "Fortune's Double Face: Gender and the Transformatons of Christine de Pizan, Augustine, and Perpetua," *Fifteenth-Century Studies* 25 (2000): 97–114.

92. See my "*Translatio studii:* Christine de Pizan's Self-Portrayal in Two Lyric Poems and in the *Livre de la mutacion de Fortune,*" in *Christine de Pizan and Medieval French Lyric,* ed. Earl Jeffrey Richards (Gainesville: University Press of Florida, 1998), pp. 155–67.

93. Paul Meyer (*Romania* 6 [1885]: 19, quoted by Bonnard, *Les traductions,* p. 139) claims that French translations in verse of the penitential psalms "se retrouvent dans une infinité de manuscrits du xiiie au xvie siècle"; the situation appears to be similar for the prose translations.

94. Christine echoes St. Augustine's quotation, taken from Psalm 86.3, that appears in *Civitas* 2.21, 10.7, and 11.1. My thanks to Nadia Margolis for pointing this out to me.

95. See Patrick Geary (trans. by Odile Demange), "Mémoire," *Dictionnaire raisonné de l'Occident médiéval*, eds. Jacques Le Goff and Jean-Claude Schmitt (Paris: Fayard, 1999), pp. 684–98.

96. In *Civitas* 11.1, St. Augustine claims that the Scriptures surpass "the writings of all nations in their divine authority." Augustine borrows the title of his work from a quotation from the psalms because he wants to associate his treatise with Scriptural authority. Punctuated by the refrain "natus est," Psalm 86 expresses the idea that the righteous cities of the world have their source in Zion (Jerusalem), the city of God. The birth imagery found in the two Latin verses of Christine's litanies would seem to echo that appearing in Psalm 86, the psalm from which St. Augustine borrows the title of his *Civitas*. It thus provides further fuel for my contention that Christine composed the Latin verses at the end of the litanies.

97. On the nature of the City of God, see Walters, "La réécriture de saint Augustin."

98. For further discussion of Christine's reliance on the *GCF*, see Walters, "Constructing Reputations."

99. Jules Viard, ed., *Les grandes chroniques de France,* 10 vols. (Paris: 1920–1953), 1:5–6. All subsequent references to the *GCF* will be taken from the prologue, 1:1–6.

100. Hedeman, *The Royal Image,* p. 106.

101. Ibid., p. 139.

102. Pierre Nora, "Between Memory and History: *Les Lieux de Mémoire,*" *Representations* 26 (spring 1989): 7–24, at p. 21.

103. Both oral and written accounts provide sources for Christine's biography of Charles V.

104. Jeffrey Kittay and Wlad Godzich, *The Emergence of Prose: An Essay in Prosaics* (Minneapolis: University of Minnesota Press, 1987), pp. 194–202.

105. In the Old Testament, most books are Jerome's translations made from the Hebrew; but the Psalter is an Old Latin text that was corrected by Jerome to agree with the Greek text of Origen's Hexapla, while some books (Wisdom, Ecclesiasticus, Baruch, and Maccabees) are pure Old Latin and untouched by Jerome. In the New Testament, all books have an Old-Latin base; but this base has been revised in the light of the Greek with varying degrees of thoroughness (*Vulgate,* p. xx).

106. See George Steiner, *After Babel: Aspects of Language and Translation* (New York: Oxford University Press, 1975): "*inside or between languages, human communication equals translation*" (p. 47, his italics). See also Bloch, *Etymologies and Genealogies,* pp. 35, 39, 42, 146.

107. On translation theory and practice in the Middle Ages, see the contributions in the collections edited by Jeanette Beer: *Medieval Translators and Their Craft* (Kalamazoo: Medieval Institute Publications, 1989); *Translation and the Transmission of Culture between 1300 and 1600,* ed. with Kenneth Lloyd-Jones (Kalamazoo: Medieval Institute Publications, 1995); and *Translation Theory and Practice.* See also Steiner, *After Babel.*

108. Lusignan, *Parler Vulgairement,* pp. 51–77; Hebrew was seen as the language spoken before the confusion of Babel (p. 53); "l'hébreu est la langue de la manifestation de Dieu" (p. 59), and thus one of the sacred languages along with Greek and Latin.

109. It is important to note that Christine interprets the words of the Old Testament prophet David in light of the New Testament, in other words, as typology that explains the manifest destiny of the Christian people of France. Of the two views of the Jews in medieval literature delineated by Nadia Margolis—the people of sagacious Old Testament rulers and prophets and Christ's crucifiers, condemned to wander the earth as punishment for their sins—Christine in the *SPA* clearly appeals to the former. Christine's attitudes toward contemporary Jews were more ambivalent. See Nadia Margolis, "Christine de Pizan and the Jews," in Brabant, ed., *Politics, Gender, and Genre,* pp. 53–73. Margolis, p. 62, notes that Christine did describe Charles V's unprecedented protection of the civil rights of Jews in her biography of the king.

110. Copeland, *Rhetoric, Hermeneutics and Translation,* p. 44.

111. Ibid., p. 45.

112. Lefèvre, *DLF,* p. 285.

113. See my forthcoming "Christine de Pizan as Translator."

114. Isidore of Seville (ca. 570–636) called Hebrew "the mother of all tongues"; John of Salisbury (late twelfth century) described it as the language "mother nature gave our first parents"; Brunetto Latini (ca. 1220–1295) deemed it to be the "original natural tongue." Bloch, *Etymologies and Genealogies,* p. 39.

115. See the discussion by Michelle A. Freeman, "Chrétien de Troyes' *Cligés:* A Close Reading of the Prologue," *Romanic Review* 67 (1976): 89–101.

116. In light of this discussion, Christine's question, posed rhetorically in *Cité* 1.10, "Ne fu saint Augustin, le glorieux docteur de l'Eglise, convertis a la foy pour cause des larmes de sa mere?" [Wasn't St. Augustine, the glorious Church Father, converted to the faith by his mother's tears?], seems particularly germane.

117. See Thierry Lassabatère, "La personnification de la France dans la littérature du bas Moyen Age. Autour d'Eustache Deschamps et Christine de Pizan," in *Contexts and Continuities: Proceedings of the IVth International Colloquium on Christine de Pizan* (Glasgow, 21–27 July 2000), published in honor of Liliane Dulac, 3 vols., ed. Angus J. Kennedy et al. (Glasgow: University of Glasgow Press, 2002) 2: 483–504. Lassabatère discusses how the personification of France helped define "les contours juridiques et mentaux de la nation." See my discussion of Christine's use of the term "noble nacion françoise" in *Charles V* 1.5 in Walters, "Constructing Reputations."

GERMAN AND FLEMISH

CHAPTER 8

CAN GOD SPEAK IN THE VERNACULAR?
ON BEATRICE OF NAZARETH'S FLEMISH
EXPOSITION OF THE LOVE FOR GOD

Else Marie Wiberg Pedersen

Toward a New Paradigm

It has taken a long time for scholars—historians, literary historians, and theologians alike—to acknowledge that the texts, mostly *vitae,* composed by or about religious women of the twelfth, thirteenth, and fourteenth centuries could, or rather should, be viewed as theological treatises. These texts, particularly the ones written in the vernacular, have generally been considered literature of an extremely personal character, revealing strongly subjective, emotional, and often pathological affinities. This conviction was characteristic of the German scholars studying the so-called *Frauenfrage,* who saw the treatises as either biographies or autobiographies.[1] This method of reading texts concerning religious women, that is, reading them as literal transcriptions of more or less exotic lifestyles, can be found even today in the analyses of some historians, pious monks, and psychiatrists.[2] It is also evident that scholars, whether feminist or traditional in their "scientific objectivity," have really tried to answer their own questions (the former by tending to concentrate on the negative stereotyping of women's sexuality and lack of power, and the latter by tending to use a particular male religiosity as a model for assessing texts),[3] instead of letting the texts speak out of their true setting. This setting is the cloister as a community of professional Christians who both transmit and transform their Christian tradition of faith, a setting that includes beguines and anchoresses, all of whom, whether integrated in a formal order or not, practiced their beliefs and their theology as professionals.

When carefully studied in their contexts, texts by and on such *mulieres religiosae,* as they are often called, first and foremost reveal a variety of theological messages on different levels, including the transmission of old and new liturgical practices, confessional doctrines of the church,[4] and, simultaneously, more or less explicit critiques of abusive practices of the church establishment. As we shall see in the case of Beatrice of Nazareth, their *vitae* not only generally furnish evidence of a stylization of the role of the religious woman as a mystic, but they also demonstrate that women's so-called mystical experiences were closely linked to the Eucharist and the humanity of Christ. It is of paramount importance to see such texts not only within the context of the tradition but also within the context of their immediate time. Thus, the Eucharist and the humanity of Christ were considered as *doctrinae stantis et cadentis ecclesiae* against the Albigensian "heretics" in southern France, and there is evidence of this in texts by and about *mulieres religiosae.*[5]

Vitae should not, therefore, be read as mere biographies of so-called mystics or visionary women; neither should they be read as transmittals of some form of experiential mysticism, a reading commonly found in the conservative school of scholarship on German mysticism.[6] Instead of viewing the visions and auditions of medieval women, transmitted in their *vitae,* as some expression of direct experience opposed to a speculative, and higher, form of mysticism represented by men, one should see them as literary texts written by authors recognized as such.[7] The visions and auditions are expressions of theology, of doctrine on and about God. They are literature containing particular themes, first and foremost the theme of a God-given knowledge of God, but they are not unmediated experiences. How can a text ever be that? In a tradition so determined by rhetorical and hermeneutical practices, by systems of signification and theories,[8] why should texts so forceful as *vitae* suddenly fall outside of this tradition of which they are a specific mode of expression in a certain period of Christian history? Thus, in my view, there is every reason to leave a psychological-experiential reading of these texts as "innocent" and "immediate" and to concentrate instead on a thematic reading of their message,[9] conveyed as it is in a specific tradition at a specific time and in a specific style.

Literary scholars have stated that our knowledge of *vitae* as a genre is still incomplete and mostly based on guesses. The truth is that we know too little about the origins and undertakings of the genre, as even the works handed down are still inadequately examined. Some of them exist only in editions of varying, sometimes questionable, quality, and some of them have not been critically prepared and are consequently generally inaccessible. *Vitae* and related genres are still largely *terra incognita.*[10] Many of the assumptions and hypotheses about them build on the modeling and standard formulations of hagiographers, who normally composed their works after the women died. As a comparison of a number of *vitae* reveals, these works were composed not as biography, but as well-textured narrations, shaped as individual versions of "salvation history" that should function as soteriological models, as exempla.[11]

Furthermore, not only should the contexts of the main characters of *vitae* be studied, but, because contexts illuminate texts, the contexts of the texts themselves should also be carefully studied, including the histories of textual transmission. The texts typically used by scholars are edited versions, often conveyed in multiple manuscripts from different periods. There is a tendency to forget about the continuity of transmission; few scholars have taken this aspect into consideration. It is vital, though, that we scrutinize the question of transmission of texts of the High Middle Ages into the late Middle Ages and further on, precisely because each period had its own way of editing according to the focus and conventions of the time.[12] In this light, it is my argument that texts by and about the religious women of the thirteenth century should be read as theology, as a particular new paradigm for the writing on and transmission of Christian doctrine, very often written in vernacular language in order to meet its audience within a Germanic setting.

Vernacularity: Embodying the Message

Herbert Grundmann, in his well-grounded and now classic work on religious movements in the Middle Ages, broke with the traditional view of medieval "religious women" as hysterical or heretical.[13] Grundmann put forward the original thesis that "a new stratum" between the clergy and the laity was formed in the thirteenth century by religious women who wanted to read and write theology, especially in Germany and the Low Countries. Alongside this movement arose the earliest vernacular prose writings, written for women by male scribes or by women themselves. Grundmann further observed that, indeed, these women writers were not lesser spirits than Eckhart, Seuse, Tauler, and Ruysbroeck but rather forerunners of them, and that Eckhart actually formulated his thought and language in order to communicate with and guide religious women. Vernacular theology arose out of a strong necessity, Grundmann stresses. Thus, "the language and literature of 'German Mysticism' did not arise as a protest against an alien language, nor as a whim which found no more pleasure in the dead language of theology or saw it as an unsuited means to express a living religious experience. Rather, the new literature arose as a reflection of the religious movement of the thirteenth century, conditioned and promoted by its relationships and the special forms of religious life which developed out of it."[14] Siegfried Ringler, who does not want to talk about religious women's inspiration of Eckhart or Eckhart's inspiration of religious women, manifestly states that the religious expressions of medieval nuns, as well as the similar ones of Eckhart, Ruysbroeck, Seuse, and Tauler, were "part of a discourse on a new form of divine experience" ("Teil . . . eines Diskurses, an dem die Nonnen aktiv beteiligt waren").[15] Latin remained the language of Holy Scripture and liturgy, a fact to which every male theologian would subscribe, and vernacular speech and writing were only a necessary aid.[16] As stated earlier, this new discourse or paradigm was, not least of all, a strategy to combat heterodox movements of the time, and it is Grundmann's incontestable achievement that he has shown the *mulieres sanctae* "movement" to be an expression of orthodox strategies rather than of heterodoxy. Grundmann thereby broke the ice for new ways of understanding and viewing religious women, freeing them from some of the persistent stereotypes (for instance, that they have lesser spirits and are more prone to deviance and heretical tendencies).[17]

As I have already briefly mentioned, literary historians have shown that vernacularity was a veritable cultural movement that swept over Europe, and that it actually covered a whole range of literature: translations of and commentaries on ancient works like Ovid's poetry, prose like Dante's *Convivio,* and poetry originally composed in vernacular languages. On the whole, as Alastair J. Minnis states, during the twelfth and thirteenth centuries, "literary authority moved from Latin works to works in the various vernaculars."[18] The movement took place primarily as a transformation of the commentary tradition from Latin to vernacular, a transformation that was coined on the model of *translatio studii* but that actually was a process of *translatio auctoritatis.* Minnis points to a "'reverent' and moral interpretation," an imperative for commentary *auctores* in which "the authoritative text under consideration had to be shown as pertaining to ethics or some even higher science." It was characteristic of this tradition to be just as prescriptive as it was descriptive; therefore, the tradition by no means reflects neutral methods for extracting the single definitive meaning of a text.[19]

Sharon A. Farmer has shown how the church, as a part of this cultural movement, discovered the art of persuasion.[20] There was a paradigm shift from perceiving oral language as an expression of a lower and evil nature to perceiving it as an expression of a higher and good nature. Much as Grundmann does, Farmer treats this strategy of persuasion as the response of the established church to heterodox movements and trends, which could also be found among the clergy. The church discovered orality as a political force of persuasion by observing what power married religious women had over their husbands.[21] Thus, a new epistemology, including a clear upgrading of the empirical and material world, is already discernable in the writings of Bernard of Clairvaux and William of St. Thierry. With the forceful *dictum* "a great speaker does not simply convey a disembodied message," Farmer persuasively shows how orality and materiality cohere, because clerical authorities realized that if the Church's message, doctrines, and values were to reach and persuade the laity, they simply had to make the abstract concrete. As Bernard of Clairvaux so straightforwardly states in his *De diligendo Deo*, the recognition of the concrete existence should lead everyone to the love of God.[22] With Bernard thus began a veritable humanization of the conception of God, who was no longer simply a *rex tremendae maiestatis* but the "personification" of love who could be approached and to whom one could direct certain spiritual expectations.[23] In accordance with such humanization, the new vernacular religious literature displays a broad spectrum of genres and a corresponding diversity of functions, encompassing both salvation history and secular history, in order to meet concrete needs. On the one hand, this new literature arises from a demand for education of laity, originating in the contest between spiritual and secular power in the investiture controversy of the eleventh century with its subsequent self-awareness of the secular ruling class. On the other hand, the new literature bears witness to the willingness of the clergy to meet this need.[24]

In general, there was a conviction that one could control, rationalize, and order the spoken word to the same extent as the written word, and the vernacular languages were central to this development. To defeat heresy, an intensive effort was made by itinerant preachers, both Franciscans and Dominicans, and the church as an institution to interact between the Latin world of the clergy and the vernacular world of the laity.[25] The strategy entailed the composition of manuals for preachers and confessors (written in Latin), which converted complex theological themes into practical and moral teaching. The preachers who read these manuals in turn converted their ideas into vernacular sermons and dialogues with unlearned laypersons. In this way, mendicant orders, whose most important tasks were those of preaching in the vernacular and of hearing confessions, canalized the force of the vernacular sermon to serve the purpose of the church, and the manuals without question secured the reciprocity between the spoken and the written doctrines.[26] Religious women were part of this whole missionary strategy, not as its objects but indeed as its subjects.

In addition, the literature written by women, including the *vitae* both by and (mainly) about women, similarly served to canalize orthodox doctrine for the laity, including such professional Christians as the nuns, who were frequently, although not exclusively, directed or advised by Dominican monks. The vernacular *vitae* present the life of an extraordinary person,[27] who is both the incarnation of virtues in a world of vices and, at one and the same time, an imperfect human being, in order to function as a piece of strategic edification for the laity. In their presentation both of an extraordinary exemplum for which a lay reader should strive and of a representation of ordinary imperfections with which the reader could identify and against which she or he should struggle, the *vitae* were a magnificent tool for the church's mission. They are a specific genre rooted in their time, part of a range of rhetorical and persuasive literature; the texts by the *mulieres religiosae* may thus very well be categorized as expressions of narrative theology and narrative pedagogy,[28] often characterized by a highly intelligent composition.

Vita Beatricis: From "Verba vulgaria" to "Latino"

I turn now to a very unusual vernacular text, *Seven manieren van heiliger Minnen* (hereafter SM), written by Beatrice of Nazareth (1200–1268), who from 1236 was the prioress of the Cistercian convent of Nazareth, close to Lier. This Middle Flemish treatise has a long history, and it was not until 1925, after a fairly complicated process, that Beatrice was identified, by L. Reypens, as its author through a comparison with the fifty-first chapter of *Vita Beatricis* (hereafter VB), "De caritate dei et septem eius gradibus."[29] The treatise is a very significant document, both because it is considered to be the oldest surviving manuscript in Middle Flemish and because it is considered to have had quite an influence on the development of the mystics, even of speculative affinity, in Brabant and the Rhineland through the fourteenth century.[30]

Before we take a closer look at the Middle Flemish treatise and the theology and spirituality it reflects as an integral part of the new paradigm sketched above, some remarks should be made on *Vita Beatricis*. This *vita* was composed in Latin by an anonymous monk some years after Beatrice died, purportedly as a "translation" from a notebook (*cedula*) composed in the vernacular. Thus, the hagiographer or "translator" of the *Vita Beatricis* states in the prologue that he, who never met Beatrice, wrote the *vita* on the basis of information from other sisters and her vanished notes (*cedula oblata*). He very clearly emphasizes that his contribution has been restricted to that of translating and coloring the story, so he puts it, from "verba vulgaria" into "latino."[31] Nobody knows if these notes ever existed, which, quite understandably, has made some scholars question the existence of any *cedula*.[32] Our only knowledge of such a notebook is the anonymous hagiographer's reference to it, and although some have done so, it would be wrong to draw any definite conclusions from this brief reference. What is certain, as the solid research by Reypens demonstrates, is that the Middle Flemish treatise composed by Beatrice of Nazareth was translated into

Latin by her hagiographer to form part of the *vita* he wrote. Notwith-standing, it may be correct to assume that we can actually discern some other short texts written by Beatrice in VB. There are texts that clearly dif-fer from the hagiographer's heavy style and moral tone,[33] being extensively more theological or spiritual in content and pedagogical in their approach and so revealing the hand of Beatrice the *magistra*. If it is the case that both SM and some other short texts by Beatrice actually are recompiled in VB, the hagiographer was indeed working from Beatrice's notes, consisting of theological reflections and spiritual exercises, notes that do not, however, form the substance of VB *in extenso*.[34]

Due to various speculations as to the nature of the purportedly van-ished notes, it is important to stress that if an actual *cedula* did exist, we do not know how and why it vanished. Thus, De Ganck and Kroll as late as 1986 advanced the hypothesis that Beatrice's *cedula oblata* might have con-tained some heterodox statements, most likely some expression of panthe-ism (the most commonly claimed heresy) in relation to her reflections on the Trinity.[35] De Ganck and Kroll's hypothesis is based solely on the fact that her hagiographer, in the conclusion of the *vita,* calls attention to the fact that he has abbreviated the vanished, purportedly original, *cedula* writ-ten by Beatrice herself. However, the reason given by the hagiographer for his omissions is merely that the omitted passages were of such subtlety that they would be beyond the simple reader and would, subsequently, make the hagiographer himself "sweat" more than necessary. Furthermore, they were not passages on the Trinity but on the believer's relation to God and neighbor ("de dei proximique caritate"), as the hagiographer emphasizes. These things Beatrice discussed with such a subtlety that only the wise (*sapientis*) would understand them[36]—quite a paradoxical statement from someone who is translating a vernacular text into Latin. On the other hand, he has transmitted these things for the wise, albeit in abbreviation,[37] and inserted "other things" for the edification of the reader, though only that which the Lord has inspired him to insert; therefore, the work should be ascribed to the Lord, not the hagiographer.[38] Accordingly, the hagiog-rapher explains how he, not trusting his own competence, has utilized the eloquence of other accounts of saints in his coloring of the narrative that the convent requested him to write.[39] Especially because the insertions are not indicated in the text, but only explained as an inspiration from God, they must call us on the alert. Indeed, while they are an essential guide to the reading and interpretation of the text, they must not make us jump to hasty conclusions and retain old stereotypes of women, which are, in fact, mostly based on the rhetoric of the time.

Although VB's immediate history is atypical in the sense that we have not one but two versions, both a Latin and a vernacular, of the same text,

much of its reception history has been quite typical. Thus, it is not surprising that Beatrice's vernacular treatise for some decades was classified
as a German sermon before it was interpreted as a text similar to those
of the mystics; it was even compared to the texts of Ruysbroeck.[40]
Equally typical is the fact that when it was eventually identified to be a
text written by Beatrice of Nazareth, a woman, its esteem immediately
fell in the eyes of its readers. The text, which for some decades had been
classified as a sermon and then for some time as a text by a mystic on the
level of Ruysbroeck, suddenly was deemed less poetical and intelligent
than, for instance, the prose and poetry written by another famous Flemish author, namely the beguine Hadewijch (around 1250), from whose
prose and poetry Ruysbroeck did borrow *verbatim*.[41] Similarly, Beatrice
has been accused of having paramystical experiences[42] and the aforementioned heterodox affinities.[43] Thus, Beatrice, in the sparse literature
about her, has fallen victim to the stereotypes of (medieval) women with
their long-lived cultural tradition, stereotypes also reflected in the
rhetoric of the *vita* genre.[44]

The main theme of VB is the example (exemplum) of Beatrice,[45] exposed as a drama in three main acts played in a number of different scenes
with the convent as its stage. Through the three acts, *status inchoantium* (VB
I), *status proficientium* (VB II), and *status perfectionis* (VB III), the hagiographer tells of a unique child *(puer senex)* elected by God to lead a special life,
who, "through many struggles" *(per multas tribulationes,* VB I, 34), finally
reaches perfection, though only eternally so after this earthly life. While it
may seem peculiar that the hagiographer, in an account of the spiritual life
of a contemplative nun and prioress, vividly and repeatedly describes def-
initely physical matters, we must consider the rhetoric of the time. The hagiographer, in keeping with the standards of the genre, has included a
number of bodily struggles fought by Beatrice in the form of temptations
and illnesses. Her female weakness, paralleled by her spiritual strength, is
heavily emphasized. Thus a doubleness runs through VB. On the one hand,
Beatrice is pictured as the nun inspired and elected by God; on the other
hand, she is pictured in all her corporeality as being especially exposed to
temptations, illnesses, and extreme mortification.[46] This duality expresses
itself explicitly when one compares Beatrice's own version of *Seven
manieren* with that of the hagiographer.[47] The hagiographer's incarnation
of Beatrice's spiritual and theological reflections recurs repeatedly in VB
and is already indicated by the selected subject. In Beatrice's own treatise
the subject is the impersonal soul *(die siele)*, which can be applied in general to any contemplative person, whereas the subject in VB is a clear physical portrait of Beatrice herself. A thorough comparison, furthermore,
shows that his account draws heavily on SM. When we take a closer look

at the treatise written by Beatrice herself, it becomes obvious that we are dealing with a very sober, "unemotional," and, indeed, orthodox nun, not prone to excessive practices.[48] It also becomes evident that we are dealing with a theologian whose main aim is to transmit or teach theology, in line with Bernard of Clairvaux, as a discourse on the God who is love itself.

The Vernacular Theology of Beatrice

Seven manieren van heiliger Minnen is a unique text, partly because it is the earliest surviving Flemish prose work, partly because it is written by Beatrice herself, and partly because it forms part of her *vita*. A careful study shows that the well-known stereotypes of holy women fail in regard to this text. What we find instead is thoroughly dialectical and pedagogical prose describing the meandering of a Christian's spiritual development. The constitutive feature of her theology is—as in Bernard's writings—the firm belief in the creation of man in the image and likeness of God. Her anthropology is—also as in Bernard's writings—theological, seen from the God relation, and she, accordingly, constantly emphasizes the origin of man (*die siele*, the soul) from God. Well grounded in her Cistercian tradition, Beatrice views creation itself and man, created by God, as originally good.

As the title of her treatise indicates, the direct relationship with God, love per se, is of vital importance. Beatrice discusses the seven different ways (*manieren*) of love (*minne*) that the soul, that is, the Christian believer, must go through on its way to the much longed for union with God, who is love per se. In fact, she opens the treatise by stating that "there are seven manners of loving which come down from the highest place and which return again to the summit from which they came."[49] Furthermore, these different *manieren* have a common characteristic, namely love (*minne*). As God is love itself, every *maniere* is expounded as the revelation of the divine, because this is its very cause and meaning, and Beatrice quite clearly seeks to create a treatise based on the love of God. Thus she places the key word *minne* between *maniere* and *hoegsten* or *ouersten,* a term designating God. From the very opening of her text, she captures her reader. The reader knows what love is and also knows that the seven manners of loving are characteristic manifestations of divine love. What she then wants to demonstrate is that it is possible to distinguish between these manifestations, these aspects of divine love through which God reveals God-self to humanity and through which man/the soul (*die siele*) can unite with God.[50]

The image of the circulation of love that we find in Beatrice's treatise is at the core of Bernardine theology, which also reflects Johanine theology: "love is of God; and every one that loves is born of God, and knows

God" (1 John 4:7). The utmost concern of Bernardine theology is that of expressing love as God's immanence in all aspects of life, both intellectually and emotionally. 1 John 4:16 continues, "God is love; and the one that dwells in love dwells in God, and God in him." In Bernardine spirituality this relationship is understood in such a way that the love of human beings is the very revelation or manifestation of divine love, and the unity between God and humanity comes into existence in the response to love.[51]

Beatrice correspondingly explains the first manner of love to be "an active longing which proceeds from love . . . arising from love;"[52] through the rule of love, the soul will eventually expel all opposition so that the believer will attain the image and likeness of God, his or her creator.[53] She describes this form of love with the triad "purity, liberty, and nobility," that is to say, the most pure, free, and noble form of love, the disinterested love (amor castus) that is purely spiritual and congruent with the will of God.[54] Love thus must be fostered by God in the human being, and its aim must be that of attaining likeness to God. Having posited humanity's godliness, Beatrice defines the soul's desire for perfection and knowledge of God as it reflects the possibility of love (21–24). To cement that God is love per se, she strongly stresses that such a desire is determined by love for God's purity and sublimity, not by fear of eternal punishment or temporal sufferings (52–63), again echoing 1 John.[55] In keeping with her Augustinian-Cistercian tradition, Beatrice thus is emphatically propounding a theology of love, a theologia caritatis.

The exposition of this theology continues in the discussion of the second manner of love, in which Beatrice emphasizes perfectly disinterested love, the love that wills only God's love and serves love (II, 6–10).[56] Love is Christ, God incarnated, who operates in the soul (14–20). In the account of the third manner, love's radical quality and paradoxical dialectics are expressed, whereas the description of the fourth manner emphasizes the infusion of love abundant. In the section concerning the fifth manner of love, Beatrice introduces the concept of vehement love or "stormy love" (orwoed), which rages within the soul; the explication of the sixth manner depicts the victory of love, the stage at which the soul has reached angelic life on earth as an anticipation of heavenly life and has obtained freedom from the desire (concupiscentia) that destroyed its very likeness to God.

Finally, in the discussion of the seventh manner of love, Beatrice depicts eternal love as God triune. This is the totally divine love beyond human understanding and reach, beyond time and space. It is in this section about the seventh manner that we find two significant passages (omitted by the hagiographer in his version) on God's omnipotence and sublime triunity as the comfortable dwelling place of the soul, which is capable of transcending its own nature. The most concise description of Beatrice from her own view is that of the contemplative nun—the professional Christian—who constantly works with her belief in the God who created man and who has been incarnated for the salvation of man (SM II). In accordance with the Christian Augustinian tradition, it is the belief in the triune God that determines her image of herself and man (SM VII, 45–49).[57] Additionally, as a Cistercian, she has learned that self-knowledge is congruent with God-knowledge (SM I, 22–31). The metaphors in her texts show clearly that empiricism, the experienced life,[58] and theology are inseparable in this universe. Theology and matters of faith are not passed on like a number of theses and abstracts, but rather are transmitted allegorically by means of metaphors from everyday life. Beatrice thus describes the soul having attained love's dignity as a housewife (*gelijc ere husvrouwen*) who has an organized household (SM VI). And if we examine other, shorter, texts, in general differing in style and tone from VB, we find that the work of faith is described through the metaphor of the garden that has to be looked after (VB II, 118–19), and the metaphor of the spiritual monastery, where reason is the abbess, wisdom the prioress, intelligence the vice-prioress, etc. (VB II,101–104). The eternal love between Christ and the soul is described by the often quoted metaphors of a fish in the water and a bird in the air (VB II,161–64).

What should be vigorously emphasized is that although Beatrice takes metaphors from everyday life to which the reader can easily relate, her imagery is never bound to her gender. Although she was not unaware of her gender, as can be seen from her allegory on the spiritual monastery, she has no literal interest in gender categories and does not see herself as a weak woman, a stance for which there may be good reasons. Theologically, gender does not play any part with regard to salvation, which is her major theme; also, being a scribe, she had, after all, been copying men's theological treatises for the convent's library before she, according to VB, began writing books necessary for her church.[59] Furthermore, during the greater part of her life, Beatrice lived in female communities, and one cannot exclude the possibility that this way of life may have endowed her with some kind of emancipation, albeit not in the modern sense of the term. It may therefore be no coincidence that Beatrice, like the other nuns I have studied, never comments on, or even mentions, the stories of Adam and Eve, the second Creation account (Genesis 2), and the narrative about the Fall (Genesis 3), so often interpreted and misused as God's sanctioning of female inferiority, in her *imago* theology and exposition of the creation of man as *imago Dei*. What is at the core of Beatrice's theology is the equality of individuals with regard to creation and salvation; and all individuals are, as human beings, inferior, having certain weaknesses in relation to God, love (*minne*) per se.

Vernacular Theology:
Can God Speak the Vernacular?

If we buy the hagiographer's claim that Beatrice wrote a manuscript in the vernacular (*vulgario*) with great subtlety, and if we believe that one must "be insane to think that [she] would proffer or write something false or fabricated by herself,"[60] why then might a purportedly vernacular original manuscript be translated and then supposedly disposed of? There have been several theories. Kurt Ruh lists four reasons why Latin versions of vernacular texts by *mulieres religiosae* actually were written in spite of the church's development of a new paradigm.[61] Firstly, Latin versions could function as "safety devices" against suspicions of heterodoxy and overly free spiritual dissipations, since the sacred language, Latin, through paraphrasing and abbreviation, had the ability to tone down various expressions. In his first explanation, Ruh thus adheres to the stereotype of the heretical woman, and it is always difficult to determine whether this is a suspicion held by the modern scholars themselves or by the church of the time. As another reason for the existence of a Latin version, Ruh mentions the fact that Latin first and foremost defies people who are not scholars. Thirdly, the Latin version is easier to translate into other vernacular languages, an explanation that runs counter to the second and which would thus support the church's new paradigm. Ruh's fourth proposal is that the Latin version could be seen as a scholarly acknowledgement of the texts. Ruh's list of reasons, in other words, entails both limitations and acknowledgement of the intentions of the Latin versions.

Herbert Grundmann presents us with a fifth reason for the Latinizing of vernacular texts that are subsequently destroyed, one that is more or less counter to his observation that the *mulieres religiosae* were part of the new discourse of the church's mission.[62] Like Ruh, he focuses on the idea that there were a number of "vernacular narratives and religious essays," like the treatises of Beatrice of Nazareth, that provided the basis for the activity of "other women of the first decades of the thirteenth century;" the existence of these narratives and essays can only be supposed, though, since none of these texts has been preserved.[63] Generally, the situation was rather confused during the thirteenth century, and there is no doubt that whilst the church followed a strategy of spreading its message, deliberately choosing the persuasive function of vernacular, it was at the same time (with its excessive fear of heretics) opposed to this very strategy. Thus the fear of heretics and the vernacular seem to go hand in hand in the thirteenth century, as the synod of Paris in 1210 clearly reveals. This synod not only condemned the natural philosophy of Aristotle, believed to lead to pantheism (even though Aristotle's philosophical texts were, from about 1238, ac-

knowledged, read, and commented on by the most learned), but it also condemned the students of Amalric (himself condemned, rather obscurely, for
being "neo-platonic"), who had encouraged the writing of books in the
vernacular; it additionally issued a ban against "theological books" (*libris theologicae*) in French. Anyone who did not, within a certain period of respite,
hand in such a book to the bishop would be considered a heretic. The ban
included translations of the creed and the Lord's prayer, whereas legends of
saints were excepted.[64] As the ban reads that all books confiscated were to
be burned, it is quite clear that the fear of the church was extensive. But as
the quality of these *libris theologicae* is never described in any detail, Grundmann assumes that they are related to the trial against heretical clerics who
had carried out their mission "primarily among religious women, mislead-
ing the people, especially women." He thus commits the typical fallacy of
assuming something from nothing. Grundmann, as a *contradictio in adjectu,*
states that both in Liège and in Paris there were "books of theological content of which we unfortunately know nothing more."[65]

Although I have pointed to a new paradigm of the church, that is, deliberate and persuasive ecclesiastical use of the vernacular as its instrument
against heretics, the institutional church simultaneously fought vernacularity vehemently, often condemning as heretical the same vernacular theology found so useful in other contexts. Robert le Bougre, an overzealous
inquisitor, lived at precisely the same time and place as Beatrice, and he was
succeeded by a no less zealous inquisitor. As De Ganck puts it, "anybody,
orthodox or heterodox, might become suspect . . . ,"[66] and there is evidence
that very orthodox *laici* were interrogated and, as a result, either severely
criticized or, frequently, executed. Thus Hadewijch reports that Robert, between 1233 and 1245, had a beguine executed "because of the righteous
minne," and later, in 1271, a learned layman, Van Maerlant, was criticized by
the authorities for having published a vernacular Bible in rhyme (*Rijmbij-
bel*). The authorities saw it as utterly problematic that such delicate matters
as the biblical message had been exposed "to simple people," the very people for whom Beatrice's hagiographer, curiously enough, writes *in latino.*

Thus there is evidence that the fear of letting *laici* have access to theological texts, be they Holy Scriptures (which was a "dangerous" book in the
wrong hands) or sermons and prayers, became even stronger when these
laici were women. In 1210, Innocent III had discovered, to his horror, that
women were exercising a very direct "clerical" authority by preaching,
reading the Gospel, giving blessings, and taking confessions, and he took
steps to prevent such activities.[67] In Bernard of Parma's commentary (ca.
1245), which became the *glossa ordinaria* on Gregory X's collections of dec-
retals, the range of liturgical functions prohibited to women is extended.
The gloss on Innocent's *Nova quaedam* emphasizes that notwithstanding

earlier practices, women cannot read the gospel, teach, preach, touch sacred vessels, veil nuns, give absolution, or exercise judgment, and that "in general, the office of a man is forbidden to women."[68] Likewise, the steps taken by the Dominican order in 1242 are noteworthy. That year the general chapter of the Dominicans forbade all friars to translate any writings with religious content, especially sermons and collations, from Latin to the vernacular, and on the whole the order refrained from "fostering the development of a vernacular devotional literature." This decree was followed by a general chapter meeting at Trier in 1249, forbidding Dominicans to have nuns or other women copy psalters and other books for them.[69]

There is little doubt that the church had two strategies for its mission within Europe, depending on the persons in charge. One of them was the strategy of love and openness expressed in the new discourse: the spread of the Christian message to all people of God (the *laici* included) in their own languages. This is the strategy of a church giving room and space for God, keeping his spirit free to work out of love. The other strategy was that of fear, rigid uniformity, and strict control of the Christian message in the hands of the clergy (the *clerici*), who allowed only Latin as the language of God. For this latter strategy, the vernacular was a threat to clerical monopoly of administering and transmitting theology and reading the Scriptures—the monopoly on which the post-Gregorian church built its universal theocracy centrally ruled through a strong and rigid hierarchy.[70] It seems that the ecclesial hierarchy did fear vernacular texts that thematized theology and spirituality because they were not as controllable as Latin texts; Latin texts had the ability of transcending any language barrier and any frontier. A Latin text would be understood by the clergy, independent of mother tongue, whereas, on the other hand, it would never be understood by the unlearned. The clergy, however, would not be able to control vernacular texts, either their content or their readers, a state of affairs that was extremely undesirable for an institution that wanted to safeguard God against his people and that envisioned God's kingdom as a reflection of the feudal society. By and by, however, the new paradigm of persuasion and education enacted in vernacular theology broke through, to the extent that it later was one of the major issues of the Reformation. By the end of the thirteenth century the Dominican order, which, as mentioned above, had been "launched" to preach for *laici* by the Lateran Council of 1215, broke its restrictions and fully accepted its organizational responsibility.[71]

Conclusion

In conclusion, it is evident that medieval reflection on the questions of women and the vernacular did not develop in a straightforward manner. A clear ambiguity toward both can be traced, and the opinions of the clergy and the institutional church varied greatly. Different historical situations provoked different ecclesiastical strategies, and what we witness in the cases of Beatrice of Nazareth and other thirteenth-century *mulieres religiosae* is that they operated in a specific historical situation in which the church saw itself forced to change its missionary strategy. On the other hand, the church had some difficulties in doing so and in adapting to a new set of circumstances in which a considerable number of women, at different levels, joined the church as professional Christians and claimed to be respected and accepted as such. It almost goes without saying that it was not difficult for the church to accept the vernacular as a useful instrument in spreading its moral teaching and its coherent persuasion of *laici,* including nuns, to lead a moral and disciplined life according to the restrictions of the church establishment. What was difficult for the church establishment was to lose control of its theology and of defining orthodoxy; women, who were not even *litteratae* but performed their theology in the vernacular and claimed an authority equal to that of the ordained male clergy, had to be curtailed one way or another.

However, faced with restrictions, the *mulieres religiosae* also found strategies for speaking and writing theology for which they were otherwise granted no chair. One strategy was that of writing visions, thereby claiming that their words were actually spoken by God; their theology was therefore not only talking about God but God's own talking. They were the chosen mouthpieces of God's own talking about God. The same can be said of the *vita* genre, of which the style is almost the message. Writing *vitae* was a strategy developed to spread the theology of religious women. These texts provided a narrative pedagogy and theology that transmitted, through a rich imagery and dialogue, a teaching lived by the women. As Ringler correctly states, it was a nonauthoritarian theology in accordance with its nonauthoritarian image of God taught by means of a nonauthoritarian pedagogy;[72] when one takes into consideration that these women lived in a highly authoritarian feudal society and were professed within a highly hierarchical theocratic church, maybe we should stop wondering why their strategy never became a success throughout this very church, although it did enjoy small windows of success.

Notes

1. Thus A. Hauber, treating German manuscripts from the late Middle Ages, exclaimed that "Frauen neigen ja überhaupt mehr zu Ueberschwenglichkeiten und folgen eher ihrem unmittelbaren Empfinden, ihren eigenen subjektiven Anschauungen, in Wissen sowohl wie Religion" [On

the whole, women have a tendency to exaggerate and follow their immediate feelings, their subjective considerations, both in science and religion],
in "Deutsche Handschriften in Frauenklöstern des späteren Mittelalters,"
Zentralblatt für Bibliothekswesen 31.8 (1914): 341–73, especially 342–43. Karl
Bihlmeyer, in an essay written nineteen years earlier, additionally warns
scholars to be cautious regarding autobiographies because they might give
a false picture of the writer: "Zurückhaltung empfiehlt sich um so mehr,
wenn, wie nicht selten bei mittelalterlichen Mystikerinnen, neben from-
men und Anziehendem auch Bedenkliches und Unhaltbares, selbst Pathol-
ogisches und Krankhaftes sich in ihren Offenbarungen findet," ("Die
Selbstbiographie in der deutschen Mystik des Mittelalters," *Theologische
Quartalsschrift* 114 [1933]: 504–44, especially 508–509).

2. See *inter alia* Caroline Walker Bynum, *Holy Feast and Holy Fast* (Berkeley
and Los Angeles: University of California Press, 1987), in which Bynum,
despite her groundbreaking perception of *mulieres sanctae,* sometimes reads
their *vitae* as literal transcriptions of ascetic and self-abnegating feats of
bodily suffering. Barbara Newman, in her essay "Devout Women and De-
moniacs," in Juliette Dor, Lesley Johnson, and Jocelyn Wogan-Browne,
eds., *New Trends in Feminine Spirituality: The Holy Women of Liège and their
Impact* (Liège: Brepols, 1999), discusses the *vita* of Christina the Astonish-
ing (1150–1224) as a source for fuller understanding of the constructs of
her life by stopping "to bracket the question and interpret her life as if
Thomas (of Cantimpré) had created it from thin air" (p. 52); Newman acknowledges, though, that this *vita* is more impervious to biographical
queries than most, thereby echoing the reservations of Simone Roisin,
Herbert Thurston, and Margot King. Most explicitly, Peter Dinzelbacher,
among historians of mentalities, in spite of all modifications and incorporation of insights from feminist research, seems literally to transcribe the
topoi of Christian tradition. See his *Mittelalterliche Frauenmystik* (Paderborn:
Ferdinand Schöningh, 1993), especially p. 321. Following this line of his-
toricization of medieval *vitae* and psychologization of their protagonists
(cf. Hauber and Bihlmeyer mentioned above), the Cistercian monk Roger
De Ganck and the psychiatrist Jerome Kroll wrote articles on the specific
psychology and psychiatric perspectives of Beatrice of Nazareth, in "Beatrice of Nazareth: Psychiatric Perspectives on a Medieval Mystic," *Cistercian
Studies* 24 (1989): 301–23, and "The Adolescence of a Thirteenth-Century
Visionary Nun," *Psychological Medicine* 16 (1986): 745–56. Similarly, a number of scholars have written on the supposed anorexia of holy women.
Each period seems, however, to have had its trend of reading these texts,
with certain general and tenacious traits. For the fusion of historian
(scholar), reader, and historical subject, see Kathleen Biddick, "Genders,
Bodies, Borders: Technologies of the Visible," *Speculum* 68.2 (1993):
389–418, in which she delivers a critique to Bynum's *Holy Feast and Holy
Fast* quite in accordance with mine, although not with the same intention;
see particularly pp. 416–18.

3. Bynum points to this specific problem (*Holy Feast,* p. 29). However, as I have indicated above (note 2), she herself not only ends up historicizing the food metaphors of the *vitae* into actual eating habits but, indeed, by focusing on food the way she does as a specific aspect of women's experience (p. 30), she herself becomes part of the picture.

4. Almost all texts reflect on essential Christian teaching, and not in the least the mysteries of salvation, namely the mysteries of the Incarnation and the Trinity, both part of the doctrine of the Old Church. Likewise, the fairly new doctrine of transubstantiation and Christ's real presence in Holy Communion, confirmed by the Lateran Council in 1215, is reflected in several *vitae* from the thirteenth century. See Miri Rubin, "The Eucharist and the Construction of Medieval Identities," *Culture and History 1350–1600: Essays on English Communities, Identities and Writing,* ed. David Aers (Detroit: Wayne State University Press, 1992), pp. 43–63.

5. See Anke Passenier, "'Women on the Loose': Stereotypes of Women in the Story of the Medieval Beguines," in *Female Stereotypes in Religious Traditions,* eds. Ria Kloppenborg and Wouter J. Hanegraaff (Leiden: Brill, 1995), pp. 61–88; Passenier points to the *vita* of Mary of Oignies as the example par excellence. According to the prologue of this *vita,* it was deliberately devised as a piece of propaganda to advance the interests of religious women on the one hand and to combat heresy (the main target being the Albigensians) on the other. The *vita* would also serve Bishop Fulk of Toulouse, who had been driven away from his diocese by the heretics in 1212, in his preaching against them (pp. 83–84).

6. I agree with Steven Katz, who, in the chapter "The 'Conservative' Character of Mystical Experience" in his book *Mysticism and Religious Traditions* (Oxford: Oxford University Press, 1983), points to the fact that most of our knowledge of "mystical literature" stems from "mystical literature" that is conservative in that it reflects specific confessions and traditions rather than an identifiable, universal experience (pp. 3–60). But furthermore, it reflects a controversy amongst German scholars who have led a hard, albeit futile, discussion on the classification of mysticism, each one struggling to have his candidate as the better kind of a mystic. See further Siegfried Ringler, "Gnadenviten aus süddeutschen Frauenklöstern des 14. Jahrhunderts–Vitenschreibung als mystische Lehre," in *Minnichlichiu gotes erkennusse. Studien zur frühen abendländischen Mystiktradition. Heidelberger Mystiksymposium vom 16. Januar 1989* (Stuttgart-Bad Cannstatt: Frommann-Holzboog, 1990).

7. See also Andrew Weeks, *German Mysticism from Hildegard of Bingen to Ludwig Wittgenstein: A Literary and Intellectual History* (Albany: State University of New York Press, 1993), pp. 3–39.

8. For the significance of rhetoric within the Christian tradition from the time and teaching of Augustine and onward, see Rita Copeland, *Rhetoric, Hermeneutics, and Translation in the Middle Ages: Academic Traditions and Vernacular Texts* (Cambridge: Cambridge University Press, 1991); and Walter

Haug, *Vernacular Literary Theory in the Middle Ages: The German Tradition, 800–1300, in its European Context* (Cambridge: Cambridge University Press, 1997).

9. See Weeks, *German Mysticism,* pp. 5–9. Whereas it is Weeks's conviction that the so-called mystic literature should be read only as literature, I strongly hold the view that it should be read as theology, exactly because what is transmitted are confessional and traditional expressions of Christian doctrine. In many respects, Weeks also seems to understand this literature as such, as reflected in his literary analysis of the themes. Hence, he highlights the reconciliation of synthesis of divine and human, the Christocentric nature, the doctrinal expositions (especially on the Eucharist), the symbolically rendered dialectics of religious transcendence and immanence, and the texts' aim of teaching pluralistic tolerance to their audience. The latter goes hand in hand with their challenging the central authorities of the church.

10. Ringler, "Gnadenviten," pp. 4 and 353.

11. See for example Jean-Claude Schmitt, "La fabrique des saints," *Religion et société* (1983/84): 294; Michael Goodich, *Vita perfecta: The Ideal of Sainthood in the Thirteenth Century,* Monographien zur Geschichte des Mittelalters 25 (Stuttgart: Hiersemann, 1982), and Simone Roisin, *L'hagiographie cistercienne dans le diocèse de Liège au XIIIe siècle* (Brussels: Editions Universitaires, 1947). Roisin, in her fine work, claims that the various monastic orders had their own models and standards according to which a *vita* or Nonnenbuch was shaped. Thus to the Cistercians humility plays such an important part that it shapes the way they model the genre.

12. See *The Medieval Text: Editors and Critics. A Symposium,* eds. Marianne Boerch, Andreas Haarder, and Julia McGrew (Odense, Denmark: Odense University Press, 1990), p. 101. See further Ingeborg Glier, "Texts and Their Contexts," *The Medieval Text,* pp. 31–44.

13. Herbert Grundmann, *Religiöse Bewegungen im Mittelalter* (1935), which has now been translated into English by Steven Rowan: *Religious Movements in the Middle Ages: The Historical Links between Heresy, the Mendicant Orders, and the Women's Religious Movement in the Twelfth and Thirteenth Century, with the Historical Foundations of German Mysticism* (Notre Dame: University of Notre Dame Press, 1995). This latter edition contains a fine introduction by Robert E. Lerner.

14. Rowan, trans., *Religious Movements,* p. 200.

15. Ringler, "Gnadenviten," 103.

16. Ibid., 200–201.

17. Passenier, however, finds that Grundmann, in his view of the beguines, still posits the stereotype of "women on the loose," pointing to non-organized beguines as more liable to moral deviations and heretical tendencies (Passenier, "'Women on the Loose,'" 65). This long-lived claim has, though, never been proven; compare the claim that Beatrice of Nazareth might have exhibited heretical tendencies, leading to the disposal of her notebook, as I discuss below.

18. See Alastair J. Minnis, "Commentary as Criticism: A Chapter in the History of Medieval Literary Theory," *The Medieval Text*, pp. 13–31. Dante Alighieri (1265–1321), while banished from Florence (from 1301 onward), wrote a Latin work, *De vulgari eloquentia*, between 1301 and 1307, on the situation of the vernaculars in Italy; the *Divina commedia* (from between 1305 and 1307), however, was composed in Italian.

19. Minnis, "Commentary," p. 18.

20. Sharon A. Farmer, "Softening the Hearts of Men: Women, Embodiment, and Persuasion in the Thirteenth Century," in Paula M. Cooey, Sharon A. Farmer, and Mary Ellen Ross, eds., *Embodied Love: Sensuality and Relationship as Feminist Values* (San Francisco: Harper & Row, 1987), pp. 115–35.

21. Farmer, "Softening," p. 119. See also Bernard of Clairvaux's letters to pious queens and duchesses, in which he urges these women to persuade their husbands to act according to what Bernard would consider to be a sensible ecclesiastical policy.

22. Bernard of Clairvaux, *De diligendo Deo* 2,2; 6; 8,23–25; 15,38–40.

23. Weeks, *German Mysticism*, p. 40.

24. See Haug, *Vernacular Literary Theory*, pp. 46–47. Haug also points to the new attitude toward nature and history reopened in the vernacular.

25. See Brian Stock, *The Implications of Literacy: Written Language and Models of Interpretation in the Eleventh and Twelfth Centuries* (Princeton: Princeton University Press, 1983), pp. 3–87; and Marie-Luise Ehrenschwendtner, "The Vernacular in the Dominican Convents," in *Medieval Women in their Communities*, ed. Diane Watt (Toronto: Toronto University Press, 1997), pp. 49–71; Ehrenschwendtner explains the difference in approach between Dominican nuns, who were mainly *puellae litteratae*, meaning that they could manage liturgical duties in Latin although not manage Latin scholarly works, and Dominican monks, who were *litterati* in the full sense of the word.

26. This is the very point made by Lester K. Little, *Religious Poverty and the Profit Economy in Medieval Europe* (London: Elek, 1978), pp. 146–96. For the origin of the mendicant orders that were almost "launched" by the Lateran Council in 1215, see Kajetan Esser, O.F.M., *Anfänge und ursprüngliche Zielsetzungen des Ordens der Minderbrüder* (Leiden: Brill, 1966).

27. There are few exceptions like the *Schwesternbuch* of Unterlinden and *Vita Beatricis*, the latter of which I shall treat in more detail in this paper.

28. For hagiography as rhetoric and persuasion, see further André Vauchez, "Saints admirables et saints imitables: Les fonctions de l'hagiographie ont-elles changé aux derniers siècles du moyen âge?" in *Les fonctions des saints dans le monde occidental (IIIe-XIIIe siècle), Actes du colloque organisé par l'École française de Rome avec le concours de l'Université de Rome "La Sapienza"* 149 (Rome: École Française de Rome, 1991), p. 167. Siegfried Ringler, basing his arguments on studies of Friedrich Sunder and Christine Ebner, without hesitation designates the genre of *vita* as "eine narrative Theologie" ("Gnadenviten," 104).

29. This he published in 1926 together with his former professor; see Leonce Reypens and Jozef Van Mierlo, *Beatrijs van Nazareth*. *Seven Manieren van Minne* (Leuven: DeVlaamsche Boekenhalle, 1926). A modern version of the *vita* was not published until 1964 (L. Reypens, *Vita Beatricis De autobiografie van de Z. Beatrijs van Tienen O. Cist. 1200—1268,* Studien en Tekstuitgaven van Ons Geestelijk Erf 15 [Antwerp: Het Ruusbroec-Genootschap, 1964]). It should be noted that this edition is created on the basis of three copies, one from about 1320, a second from the fifteenth century, and a third from the seventeenth century. As can be seen from the latter title, Reypens, and indeed his former collaborator J. Van Mierlo, conceded to the general assumption of the time that what was transmitted was actually an autobiography. However, one wonders that he does not seem to consider the groundbreaking research of the German literary scholars such as Georg Kunze, who, in his "Habilitations"-work, *Studien zu den Nonnenviten des deutschen Mittelalters: Ein Beitrag zur religiösen Literatur im Mittelalter* (Ph.D. dissertation, University of Hamburg, 1953), was the first to categorize *vitae* as *genre,* or Walter Blank's follow-up in his unique dissertation published as *Die Nonnenviten des 14. Jahrhunderts. Eine Studie zur hagiographischen Literatur des Mittelalters unter besonderer Berücksichtigung der Visionen und ihrer Lichtphänomene* (Freiburg: Müller, 1962).

30. See, for instance, Stephanus Axters, *Geschiedenis van de Vroomheid in de Nederlanden.* 1 (Antwerp: De Sikkel, 1950).

31. "Me solum huius operis translatorem existere non auctorem . . . oblata verba vulgaria latino tantum eloquio coloravi . . ." (VB, Prologus 4).

32. Ursula Peters has expressed her strong doubts as to the existence of any *cedula.* See her *Religiöse Erfahrung als literarisches Faktum. Zur Vorgeschichte und Genese frauenmystischer Texte des 13. und 14. Jahrhunderts* (Tübingen: Niemeyer, 1988), pp. 4–8 and 32–33.

33. Beatrice had the *officio magistralis* according to VB II, 86. Texts that differ in style and tone and reflect a greater extent of "Beatricity" are specifically 1) some allegorical writings: VB II, 101–104 on the two cells of the heart; VB II 105–110 on the five mirrors of the heart; VB II, 111–117 on the spiritual monastery; VB II, 118–119 on the garden of the heart; and VB II, 120–124 on the endeavors for self-recognition; 2) summaries of short treatises: VB I, 42–44 on meditations; VB II, 87–90 on use of time; and VB II, 91–98 on spiritual emotions; 3) accounts of visions, VB III, 213–18 (cf. SM VII) on the Trinity and VB III, 192–95 and 238–39 on the Eucharist and the doctrine of the real presence.

34. This is assumed by Van Mierlo, "Beatrice de Nazareth," *Dictionnaire de spiritualité 1* (Paris: Gabriel Beauchesnne, 1936): 1312, columns 1314–1314; Axters, *Geschiedenis,* pp. 227–30; Roisin, *L'Hagiographie cistercienne,* p. 65; and implicitly by Herman Vekemann, "Vita Beatricis en seven manieren van Minne: Een vergelijkende studie," *Ons Geestelijk Erf* 46 (1972).

35. De Ganck, "Beatrice of Nazareth," and Kroll, "Adolescence."

36. "Ne ergo multa que in libro suo . . . de dei proximique caritate sutilissima ratione disseruit . . . et sic magnam partem voluminis dicerer detruncasse; vel, econtrario, cuncta, prout ea susceperam oblata, describens, superfluis quam necessarijs potuis insudasse" (VB III, 276).

37. "Quamquam non modicam partem, in [plerisque] locis, omiserim eorium que sui minia profunditate lectoris sonsum effugere potuissent; que quidem, et-si perfectioribus intelligibilia:, minus tamen exercitatos in huiusmodi habentibus intellectus, magis tedio quam edificationi., magis dampno quam lucro forsitan extitissent . . . ad edificationem tuam insererem" (VB III, 275). (This edition preserves the medieval scribal punctuation and adds a second system of modern interpretative punctuation.)

38. "non michi sed domino gratias referens si quid in eo profeceris; qui scribentis stilum ad finem usque perduxit, et quod ad edificationem tuam insererem, ubi et quomodo voluit, inspiravit " (VB III, 275).

39. " . . . varios sanctorum triumphos, hystorica narratione depictos . . . perlegerim . . . quippe cui, nichil penitus de propijs viribus confidenti, nunc vsque potius aliene decorem eloquentie mirari libuit . . ." (VB, Prologus 2).

40. For this, see my article "The In-Carnation of Beatrice of Nazareth's Theology," New Trends in Feminine Spirituality: The Holy Women of Liège and their Impact (Liège: Brepols, 1999), p. 61.

41. This according to J. Van Mierlo, who together with L. Reypens published SM in 1926. Van Mierlo, in another article on the new discovery that the long-known text had Beatrice as its author, states that the prose by Hadewijch is "more noble, more poetical and more intelligent" than that of Beatrice. See L. Reypens and J. Van Mierlo, "Een nieuwe schrijfster uit de eerste helft der dertiende eeuw. De gelukzalige Beatrijs van Nazareth," Dietsche Warande en Belfort 25 (1925): 352–67. Although Hadewijch, like Beatrice, today is acknowledged to have made major contributions to the development of spirituality and religious literature in the vernacular, of course this view of Van Mierlo's was most likely due to the fact that Hadewijch was his own "discovery," and he actually never succeeds in substantiating his statement. Cf. J. Van Mierlo, De visionen Hadewijch, Leuvense Studiën en tekstuitgaven. 1 (Louvain: S. V. de Vlaamsche Boekenhalle, 1924). Cf. Paul Mommaers, Hadewijch: The Complete Works, The Classics of Western Spirituality (New York: Paulist Press, 1980), pp. 14–15.

42. So Reypens comments on the "raptures" and "visions" narrated by the hagiographer in VB: 61–62. It is noteworthy that "visionary" men are not labeled in this way. Ringler observes that Friedrich Sunder, chaplain in the convent Engelthal, in his life narrates a vision where he sees Christ, just received in communion, turn into a child sucking his filled breasts, followed by a scene where he sees himself as the bride kissing his bridegroom, the infant Jesus. He provocatively states that most will take Sunder's "visions" to be rhetoric, a mode of speaking of the unspeakable (Ringler, "Gnadenviten," 91–92). However, if a thirty-year-old nun describes the same, then she is immediately taken to have really had the experience.

43. See David Herlihy, "Alienation in Medieval Culture and Society," in *Alienation: Concept, Term and Meanings,* ed. Frank Johnson (New York: Seminar Press, 1973), pp. 125–40. Herlihy, using demographic research, concludes that heretical movements were primarily women's movements. He states, quite uncritically adopting orthodox inquisitors' language, "These were often denied the chance of marrying, urged to leave their homes, or even abandoned to the heretics" (p. 139).

44. Regarding Beatrice, there is an unfortunate alliance between psychology and research on so-called mysticism: what scholars of mysticism deem an example of decline in relation to the spiritual zenith of mysticism, the psychologists deem testimony to neurotic obsessions. See Siegfried Ringler, *Viten- und Offenbarungsliteratur in Frauenklöster des Mittelalters,* Quellen und Studien (Zurich: Artemis Verlag, 1980), pp. 5, 353. This alliance is very explicit in the aforementioned works by De Ganck and Kroll, who in many ways simply echo the stereotypes launched by the old German school as we find in Oskar Pfister, "Hysterie und Mystik bie Margaretha Ebner (1291–1351), *Zentralblatt für Psychoanalyse–Medizinische Monatsschrift für Seelenkunde* 1 (1910–1911): 468–85.

45. VB Prologus 1; I, 22; III, 273 and III, 274.

46. See VB I, 60–69, and the first devilish temptation inserted immediately after the first account of a vision of the Trinity in VB I, 54–59, which seems to be more the hagiographer's account of Beatrice's conversion; additionally, in VB II, 130–40, immediately after a section of small treatises (very likely from Beatrice's own hand), and likewise before another "vision" of God's love in Jesus incarnated in VB II, 145–50, which is followed by another group of temptations by Satan. Finally in VB III, 209–13, he has inserted a temptation of *insania,* immediately before her fuller account of a "vision" of the Trinity in VB III, 213–218. See Goodich, who sees this doubleness, so characteristic of most hagiography, as a traditional misogynist tendency (*Vita perfecta,* p. 208). Thus many saints, in fighting carnal temptations, warned their disciples against the snares of women. Ringler, on the other hand, notes that it is a matter of tradition whether a *vita* is characterized by Eucharistic piety or a piety of passion and suffering; thus, he has found mortification to be accentuated in the *vita* on Christine Ebner but hardly present in the *Gnadenleben* on Friedrich Sunder ("Gnadenviten," 98). Beatrice, however, clearly participates in *minne* and Eucharistic piety, which does not seem to apply to her afterlife.

47. For a more detailed comparison, see my article "The In-carnation," where I demonstrate how the hagiographer constantly in-carnates Beatrice's spiritual and theological reflections.

48. See my article "The In-Carnation," where I compare VB and SM, concluding that the hagiographer in-carnates Beatrice's theology, thus minimizing her as a theologian and maximizing her as a holy woman in whom God acts.

49. "Seuen manieren sijn van minnen, die comen uten hoegsten ende keren weder ten ouersten" (SM I, 3–5). The translations are taken from Roger

De Ganck, *The Life of Beatrice of Nazareth* (Kalamazoo: Cistercian Publications, 1991), pp. 289–331. The comments, however, will be based on the Flemish edition by L. Reypens and J. Van Mierlo.

50. See Vekeman, "'Minne' in Seven manieren van minne van Beatrijs van Nazareth," *Citeaux. Comm. Cist.* 4 (1968): 284–315.

51. This understanding runs through all of Bernard's writings. See, for instance, *De diligendo Deo* or *Sermones super Cantica canticorum. Sancti Bernardi Opera,* vols. 2 and 3.

52. "ene begerte die comt werkende uter minnen . . . comt uter minnen . . ." (SM I, 5–10).

53. "te wesene in die puerheit. Ende in die vriheit ende in die edelheit daer si in ghemaket es van haren sceppere na sijn beelde ende na sijn ghelikenesse, dat hart es te minnene" (SM I, 15–18).

54. Cf. Bernard, *De diligendo Deo* 8 (*Opera* 3: 138–39). Cf. Paul in 1 Corinthians 13:5.

55. 1 John 4:18, "There is no fear in love; but perfect love casts out fear; because fear has torment. He that fears is not made perfect in love." I cite from the Bible, Authorized King James Version, but have taken the liberty of modernizing the verbs.

56. "also begert si met minnen te dienne der minnen . . ." (SM II, 10–11).

57. Cf. VB II, 94, which seems to be the hagiographer's "recycling" of SM. According to Augustine, man is an imperfect image of the Trinity (*imago trinitatis*) by soul/reason/spirit/intellect. See, for example, *De trinitate* 7,12.

58. Cf. Bernard of Clairvaux, *De diligendo* 2, 2; 6; 8, 23–25; 15, 39–40, where acknowledgement of the concrete existence is underlined as leading the individual to love God.

59. VB actually and uniquely stresses her professions and education, both in the *artes liberals,* which she began in a beguine school in Léau (VB I, 21), and as a scribe in the monastery Rameia: "ubi scribendi facultatem addisceret., quam postmodum in scribendis libris sue necessarijs ecclesie frequentaret" (VB I, 50). Notice how the writing of her own books is stressed as an ecclesial profession: She wrote them for her church!

60. VB, Prologus 5. The hagiographer continues by stating that Beatrice "read and learned from the book of experience," a locus classicus taken from Bernard's works: "Today the text we are to study is our own book of experience. You must therefore turn your attention inward, each one must take note of his own particular awareness of the thing I am about to discuss" (*The Works of Bernard of Clairvaux,* vol. 1, *On the Song of Songs,* trans. Kilian Walsh [Kalamazoo: Cistercian Publications, 1981], p. 16—the opening of sermon 3).

61. Kurt Ruh, "Vorbemerkungen zu einer neuen Geschichte der abendländischen Mystik im Mittelalter," *Sitzungsberichte der R. Akademie der Wissenschaften zu München,* heft 7 (1982): 26. Ruh points to the fact that texts by mystics were often translated from Latin into the vernacular, but finds the opposite process of translation from the vernacular into Latin more interesting.

62. Rowan, trans., *Religious Movements,* pp. 193–94.

63. Grundmann points out that the *vita* of Juliane of Cornillon (died 1258) was first written in French or Walloon, but is preserved only in a Latin version. See *AA.SS.,* April I: 444. However, according to Barthélemy Fisen, *Flores ecclesiæ Leodiensis* (Lyon, 1647), the Walloon *vita* still survived in the seventeenth century in the library of the house of Cornillon, where Juliane was prioress. See Rowan, trans., *Religious Movements,* p. 392, note 41.Thus it is not quite the same as VB, of which part of a vernacular original, namely SM, has survived until now.

64. Rowan, trans., *Religious Movements,* p. 194.

65. Ibid., p. 195.

66. See De Ganck, *The Life of Beatrice of Nazareth,* p. xxix. In this publication, De Ganck gives a much more nuanced picture of Beatrice and her context than he does elsewhere.The following is paraphrased from De Ganck, *Life,* pp. xxviii-xxxi.

67. Innocent III, *Nova quaedam nuper,* PL 216, 356 A-C. See further Ernest W. McDonnell, *The Beguines and Beghards in Medieval Culture with Special Emphasis on the Belgian Scene* (New York: Octagon Books, 1969), p. 343.

68. See Francine Cardman, "The Medieval Question of Women and Orders," *The Thomist* 42 (1978): 596.

69. For these two decrees, see Rowan, trans., *Religious Movements,* pp. 196–97.

70. The tightening of the papal church's supremacy, the "Gregorian reform" for celibacy and against simony (started by the Cluniac movement), is named after Gregory VII (1073–1085).The ideal is a realization of the kingdom of God here on earth under the guidance of the pope as *vicarius Christi,* with the unlimited right to hold both ecclesial and secular power. See Yves Congar, "Modèle monastique et modèle sacerdotal en Occident de Grégoire VII (1073–1085) à Innocent III (1198)," *Études de civilisation médiévale (IXe—XIIe siècles),* Mélanages offerts à Edmond-René Labande (Poitiers: Centre d'Études Supérieures de Civilisation Médiévale, 1973): 159.

71. Cf. above on the new paradigm.

72. Ringler bases his observations on the lives of Friedrich Sunder and Christine Ebner ("Gnadenviten," 104).

CHAPTER 9

THIEVES AND CARNIVALS:
GENDER IN GERMAN DOMINICAN
LITERATURE OF THE FOURTEENTH CENTURY

Ulrike Wiethaus

> *"vernacular. adj [L.* vernaculus, *belonging to homeborn slaves, indigenous < verna, a homeborn slave]*
> *Using the native language of a country or place."*
>
> —Webster's New Old Dictionary

> *"Am I to go on saying*
> *for myself, for her*
> This is my body,
> Take and destroy it?"
>
> —*Adrienne Rich,* Dreams of a Common Language

Introduction: Parameters of Vernacularity

As the Latin meaning of *vernaculus* cited above indicates, languages denote not only a sense of place, but also of relations of power.[1] These relations include gender and thus gender-specific usage of language as a category of economic, cultural, and social discrimination.[2] In terms of medieval literacy, the rise of vernacular religious literacy and literatures has often been traced to the contributions of female Christian authors.[3] Barred from the study of Latin at universities and often also in monasteries, religious women took refuge in writing in their mother tongues and produced works of remarkable originality and depth.[4] Male-authored spiritual writings in the vernacular followed suit with some delay and were frequently written for an often explicitly female religious audience.[5]

The relationship between Latin and vernacular devotional literatures reflects to no small degree gendered social relationships, but also complex negotiations between a transregional, and highly expansive, social structure (the Church) and geographically specific and locally bound Christian communities. If Latin was the *lingua franca* of medieval Christian Europe, it was not free for every medieval group to use: Access to Latin was carefully monitored by male elites.[6] Nonetheless, as I will argue below, women, apart from developing the vernacular as their own language of the sacred, also appropriated liturgical and devotional Latin to suit their particular psycho-spiritual needs, and thus effectively counteracted men's hegemonic linguistic claims.[7] Furthermore, the increased use of the vernacular by male authors did not lead, as one might expect, to a gender-neutral development of vernacular spirituality. My reading of Heinrich Seuse's didactic autobiography suggests that at least in his case, the vernacular as women's sacred language was deftly turned into a tool of undermining women's growing literary independence.

In the following essay, the triangular relationship between locality, language, and gender within the Christian community will be examined through the highly original and innovative vernacular autobiographies by two German Dominicans, the *Revelations* of Margarete Ebner (ca. 1291–1351) and the *Life of the Servant* by Heinrich Seuse (1295–1366).[8]

Dominican writings in the fourteenth century offer a particularly interesting perspective, since both vernacular *and* women's devotional writings dramatically increased within just a few decades, no doubt in part owing to the rapid growth of female houses that eventually outnumbered male houses by roughly 2 to 1.[9] Generally, Dominican men in charge of the pastoral care of nuns were itinerant rather than permanently attached to a single female monastery. Since most nuns did not systematically learn to speak, read, and write Latin, the preachers' letters and treatises had to be composed in the vernacular.[10]

When placed into a geographical context, men's as well as women's increased vernacular writing can be explained as a necessary effort to maintain pastoral care across a large multiregional expanse and the often significant lapse of time between visits.[11] For example, Ebner's *Revelations* were composed in response to the demands of her absent confessor and spiritual guide, Heinrich of Nördlingen, whom she met in person less than ten times in nineteen years. The journeys could be difficult; the preacher-priest-confessors' arrival thus was often delayed substantially. As Seuse vividly described it in his autobiography, the trips were filled with discomforts of all kinds, from the dangers of violent assaults to bad weather, treacherous roads, lack of food supplies, and unsavory company.

Once the itinerant preachers encouraged women to write to maintain their pastoral relationships, however, women's literary production took on a life of its own and became difficult to control. It is not accidental that Heinrich Seuse began his autobiography with a description of burning the unauthorized writings of a woman under his pastoral charge, Elsbeth Stagel. With increasing autonomy, women's writings in turn began to incorporate criticism of male confessors' inadequacies.[12]

Over the years, scholars have vulcanized the remarkable fact of Dominican women's extensive literary production in the vernacular into a rarely challenged formula. The formula employs a certain circular logic that reinscribes gendered power relations into the divisions between Latinate and vernacular devotional literature. Although encouraged to become literate, not in the least to avoid heresy—so conventional scholarly wisdom—Dominican women were nonetheless barred from learning Latin.[13] Applying the Procrustean yardstick of Latinate literary styles, their spirituality as much as their textual production then was judged to be less sophisticated than that of Latinate authors, that is, it was labeled "practical" and "simple."[14]

I find it more productive, however, to see women's vernacular writings as autonomous literary efforts that need to be judged *sui generis*. Women's vernacular texts, unlike Latinate male-authored writing, were situated in predominantly female traditions of religious practice and belief. They reflected women's experiences, needs, and professional functions in their community, as I will argue below, and were much closer to oral traditions than Latin texts.[15]

In contrast to traditional scholarship, recent feminist studies, on the other hand, frequently recast women's literary "simplicity" more positively as an example of "body-centered" spirituality, which explores the increasing medieval emphasis on Christ's humanity and the Eucharist. Whereas "simplicity" connotes inferiority for pre-feminist scholars, "embodiedness" now becomes the marker of medieval female autonomy.[16] Whereas "inferior" vernacular female "simplicity" was previously juxtaposed to the "superior complexity" of male abstract theological thought, "holistic" and empathic female embodiedness now become contrasted to ultimately alienated male patriarchal logic. The hermeneutic battle has been straightforward: One interpretive model tries to prove the superiority of male authorship, the other that of female authorship.

To some degree, my own reading is indebted to the feminist stance. I suggest, however, that medieval Christianity, with its undeniably misogynist, anti-Judaic, militaristic, homophobic, and xenophobic elements, severely diluted any "subversive" (feminist) or "civilizatory" (in the sense of Western claims to global cultural supremacy) impact that either of the two interpretive stances might wish to demonstrate or defend.[17] I am not persuaded that self-imposed starvation and mutilation in the name of an "embodied spirituality" advanced the cause of women in patriarchy, nor am I convinced that the development of complex theological thought has benefited the lot of anybody not belonging to sociocultural elites. Rather, medieval male and female Christian spiritualities were two sides of the same cultural coin, developing on intertwined tracks in parallel motion, keeping each other in check, to be sure, yet without abandoning their commonly held hegemonic core, orthodox Christianity. I wish to thus suspend aesthetic or political qualitative judgment and instead approach women's and men's vernacular spiritualities as only different, but not as "superior" or "inferior" from either a feminist or canonical partisan point of view. In other words, I wish to understand their function within their respective subcultures, whether subaltern or dominant, *and* the larger social context rather than their relative merit according to narrowly defined interpretive standards.

My reasoning is based on the fact that medieval Christian men and women, no doubt unequal in their relationship to each other, stood united when it came to the persecution and destruction of the inferior Other: Jews, infidels, heretics, persons engaged in same-sex erotic activity, and so forth. Vernacular as much as Latinate literary activity in medieval Christianity thus simultaneously inscribed degrees of difference (religious, geographic, gendered, sexual) within the cultural system, but reinforced sameness (to be one in Christ) at the system's boundaries against a posited Other. A poignant story in Ebner's text illustrates my point. Before we claim her all too hastily as a champion for women or as oppressed by patriarchy, we need to understand what she told in the following story, a narrative teeming with intensely punitive encoding of female embodiment:

> In the summer before, a lamentable thing had happened. A woman from the village of Medingen, at the counsel of the evil enemy and with a Christian heart led astray, went into our church at Stettin, where our Lady shows herself to be especially gracious. The woman took two unconsecrated hosts from the pix and carried them into the city of Lauingen near to our monastery. She offered them for sale or in pledge for money to the Jews. A Christian woman saw this, and since the Jews wanted to give that woman nothing for them, she informed the court of the theft. The woman was apprehended. When she was sentenced to death, a child was cut away from her. It was baptized and then they were burned. Because of this, I was so filled with sadness at such dishonor to God that I was unable to look from my window toward the place where it happened. Throughout the summer I could neither listen to anything about it nor speak about it. I could not endure it if anyone felt sorry for her, because I thought that anyone who had

dishonored a dear friend could not expect mercy from the one who had
been dishonored. Often I tried to pray for her diligently, but I have been unable even to desire to pray to God for her as yet.[18]

The story contains numerous demarcations of social space, boundaries
drawn tightly between insiders and outsiders through geographic and religious markers. Ebner, like so many other women mystics, centered much
of her piety on the ritual of the Eucharistic meal. We see here, though, that
normative responses to the Eucharist were taught and reinforced through
violence deemed excessively brutal even by medieval eyewitnesses.[19] The
story suggests that in Ebner's religious environment, conformity to Eucharistic teachings implied submission to secular and ecclesiastical authorities rather than an expression of female spiritual autonomy or even
subversion. Tellingly, religious and secular values confluence in Ebner's explanation of what constituted the offense punished so severely: The crime
was framed as a secular violation of family honor. Although other people
showed compassion for the woman's suffering and the death of her innocent child, Ebner was unable to do so. Of high social standing, she counted
herself as literally belonging to the family of Christ and thus sided with
local authorities, underscoring her choice through the mystical experience
of blocked prayers.

Finally, we note the unusual precision with which Ebner cited localities
and the actions of the Jewish community. The pregnant woman, perhaps
driven by poverty more than by any religious intentions, in Ebner's view
transgressed not only her proper religious role as passive recipient of the
Eucharist. By moving from village to village and by engaging in trade with
Jews, the unnamed victim trespassed her socially dictated spatial confine-
ment as a woman as well as the charged boundaries of her Christian
ghetto. Like a man, the solitary unknown thief traded and traveled from
village to church to city. Clearly, Ebner's telling of a story about another
woman is evidence that women's devotional use of the vernacular was not
free from inscriptions of willingly accepted patriarchal authority, and did
not per se represent an opportunity for female solidarity or some kind of
proto-feminist subjectivity. Margarete Ebner identified with Christian orthodoxy, enforced through brutal punishments, and her own social group
values (family honor, avoiding Jews, enclosure for women) rather than
with women as a group in their own right.

Dominicans in Fourteenth-Century Germany

Urbane, with a relaxed lifestyle that allowed for the *vita privata* (private
ownership), and an emphasis on high mobility and exceptional educational

standards, the German Dominican order of the fourteenth century found itself in closer proximity to the dynamic centers of medieval culture than perhaps any other order, including the Franciscans. Apart from their innovative role as educators, preachers, and papal inquisitors, Dominicans also fostered changes in spiritual practices. They brought into focus a slowly developing trend within late medieval monastic spirituality: private and increasingly personalized devotional practices. In addition to the *lectio divina* and communal choir duties they shared with older orders such as the Benedictines and Cistercians, Dominicans of both sexes spent also significant time in private prayer.[20] It is therefore not surprising that the order produced innovative textual creations centering on individual holiness. This trend is epitomized on the male side by Heinrich Seuse's book collection *The Exemplar*, which contains a highly unusual autobiography or autohagiography; and among women by the *Sisterbooks*, collections of nuns' lives composed individually or co-authored by several Dominican nuns. Among these authors numbered Elsbeth Stagel. A recognized holy woman, she entertained close contacts with Seuse. Significant for our study, her biography of Seuse constitutes the basis for his autobiography.[21]

Despite the Dominican order's avant-garde status, educational and social opportunities for female and male branches differed, as noted above. The rule of strict enclosure for women severely curtailed the nuns' access to scholastic training and their participation in ecclesiastical politics. In studying the interactions between male and female members of the order, usually subsumed under the issue of *cura monialum,* the typical question of whether and how much Dominican spiritual counselors[22] taught the women and how much individual women supported individual men, has generated only a limited understanding of the gendered character of Dominican spirituality. It has been ignored that medieval Dominican women *qua* women were also part of a larger secular women's culture. Their writings reflect typically female concerns such as family relationships, children's upbringing, and care of the sick and elderly and the linguistic practices that shaped and gave expression to these concerns.[23]

To recognize these gendered sociospiritual systems as *equally* adaptive and meaningful to their respective communities without a bias against the women's texts has been an almost impossible task for most scholars. Karl Bihlmeyer's interpretation of the impact of the Dominican male mystics Meister Eckhart and his students Johannes Tauler and Seuse is paradigmatic of such scholarly traditions. "Thanks to Dominican mysticism, it was in the fourteenth century that men finally caught up with women in [the area of mysticism] and even by far surpassed their achievements, not in terms of experiential intensity but in the ability to intellectually grasp what was seen and reflect upon it theoretically in the context of theology."[24] We might find such a statement amusing today, but Bihlmeyer implicitly raised two issues of interest: the distinction between a masculine and feminine form of Christian religiosity and the dynamics of a male anxiety of influence and contact with a socially inferior feminine Other. In Bihlmeyer's view, masculine religiosity equals rationality and the skill of abstraction, whereas religious femininity stands for experiential depth; the two genders are perceived as separate and in competition (although it is not made clear for what). In an unexpected metaphorical turn, the scholarly narrative spans three imaginary moments of a gendered race between seeming equals: first, the female advance, then a male catching up, surpassing, and finally, winning the race.[25]

Yet Bihlmeyer is correct in at least one instance. Resembling other intensely masculinized literate religions such as Islam, Hinduism, and Judaism, the Christian honing of abstract cognition and intellectual analysis falls indeed predominantly into masculine rather than feminine religious spheres of activity. Two key factors might have influenced this development. Within the context of an androcentric social hierarchy, the confluence of exclusive masculine languages (Sanskrit, Hebrew, Latin, etc.) with newly emerging forms of thought and scriptural analysis can be understood as a type of highly prized social capital. It functioned as compensation for the abrogation of violence to determine masculine identity among male religious elites. The socially negotiated alternative determination of male status necessitated new language games. Privileged access to public rituals and Latinate language competency needed to be regularly exhibited on occasions such as mass. In order to protect male status defined by such precarious and immaterial criteria, women were denied access to places where the new skills could be learned for many centuries to come.

Barred from bearing arms and engaging in acts of violence, the only alternative to the socially sanctioned creation of abstraction and access to exclusionary language as definition of religious masculinity would have been the feminization of religious men.[26] Hence the seemingly irrational anxiety over medieval women's and nonliterate/non-Latinate secular men's aspirations to theological and biblical knowledge, often labeled as heresy, and persecuted rigorously. It is only with the rise of a third medieval model of masculinity, that of trader and merchant, that the Church's grip on Latin as sole marker of religious male identity begins to relax. When Dominican men begin to write in the vernacular and travel in an increasingly urban setting, their spiritual vocabulary abounds with mercantile idiom.[27]

Apart from issues of social status, geography appears to have influenced the formation of abstract religious discourse as well. Abstract or ametaphorical theological modes of thinking seem to be cultivated by religions that become, for one reason or another, dissociated from their original ties to a locality. Localized religiosity provides an abundance of religious knowledge and practice based on geographic, often agriculturally based, orally transmitted information symbolically communicated and commemorated through geographic sites and the tangible patterns of community life.[28] Missionary mandates, the exodus from a homeland, following in the trails of expansionist empires: These factors profoundly influence the intellectual formation of all globally spread religions. The local has to be rejected for the universal, the concrete for the abstract so that a religion can convey meaning beyond regional idioms.[29]

To return to fourteenth-century Germany: I argue that not only because of their connection to female worlds of ritual and work, but also because of their lesser mobility, Dominican nuns' vernacular spirituality by necessity reflected their immediate social world, that is, the impact of the local, the concrete, a consciousness of cyclical temporality: a world within feminized enclosures, rich in detail, with a complexity lost to those who look for the abstraction of a spirituality literally lived on the road.[30] The gendered tension between a spirituality of female enclosures and a spirituality of masculinized open spaces, however, is in my view circumstantial, historically determined, but not essentialist. For the fourteenth century, the ever so restless author Margery Kempe's autobiography represents the usurpation of masculinized space; the enclosed anchoress Julian of Norwich's sophisticated theology the usurpation of masculinized modes of thought. It is also important to bear in mind that both "female" and "male" types, despite their differences, remained fundamentally aligned to the same centers of religious and secular authority. I will now turn to two vernacular autobiographical texts to make my point.

Heinrich Seuse's *Life of the Servant:* Copyrighting Spiritual Dominance in the Vernacular

The Dominican author Heinrich Seuse (1295–1366) began his successful but controversial career as a spiritual author with a brave tractate in defense of his teacher Meister Eckhart, then moved on to compose one of the most widely copied and published spiritual manuals during the late Middle Ages, the *Büchlein der Ewigen Wahrheit,* the *Little Book of Eternal Wisdom,* a practical devotional manual that includes descriptions of heaven and hell, a concise *ars moriendi* "how-to" booklet, and a set of a hundred conveniently short meditations that could be used for daily meditation. In his role as a spiritual teacher to nuns (a *lebemeister*), Seuse mediated the realms of male and female Dominican lives.

Apprehensive about the *Little Book*'s scholarly reputation, he felt compelled to translate it from German into Latin, and expanded it under the title of *Horologium Sapientiae*.[31] Late in his life, while in exile, he expanded and then partially reworked the German auto/biographical text, *The Life of a Servant*. It is perhaps a sign of intense authorial anxiety that of the four books contained in *The Exemplar*, it is *The Life of the Servant* that evoked the most explanations in Seuse's prologue. The text is haunted by the presence and absence of a female writer, the Dominican nun Elsbeth Stagel, whom Seuse named as author of some of the passages.[32] Not only appears thus the issue of authorship to be oddly androgynous, but also Seuse's spirituality as such. For example, his piety has been noted to be remarkably "feminine—if we use the term feminine, as historians of spirituality have done, to mean affective, exuberant, lyrical, and filled with images."[33]

Clearly, of all his writings, the *Life* is his most innovative, but also most problematic, work. In my view, its literary achievement is complex. It offers not only an audacious modernization of the spirituality of the Desert Fathers and a remarkable appropriation of secular literary genres such as romances, but also a sustained critique and reformulation of Dominican women's community-oriented spirituality. In regard to the latter, Seuse's auto/biography represents a curious, brilliantly composed merging of feminine and masculine modes of Dominican spirituality. Despite its lengthy preambles, it is ironic that the text found only little interest among medieval audiences. Was that perhaps due to its innovative narrative devices?

Scholars have been divided about how to approach the text's autobiographical framework. Is it a literally true autobiography?[34] a partly fictional *confessio* modeled after Augustine's autobiography, with some pastoral goal in mind?[35] or is it meant to be an autohagiography? I suggest that the book is perhaps best understood as a thoroughly stylized didactic device in the service of nuns' spiritual formation, based on a critique of the strengths and weaknesses of Dominican women's spirituality. The critique, however, is not a wholehearted rejection, but, more subtly, a carefully circumscribed act of subordination.[36]

Given its didactic intent, the boundary between factually "true" and "false" autobiographical events must no doubt be permeable, at least according to contemporary standards of factuality; Seuse intentionally developed a composite personality; part fact, part metaphor.[37] Nonetheless, the truth of certain unpleasant biographical incidents, such as the accusation of having fathered the child of his female servant, demanded inclusion and explanation.

My argument that Seuse used his own life as a corrective model for Dominican nuns' spiritual lives is based on a close reading of the book's internal structure. Part 1 and part 2 represent the same message of spiritual progress in two different keys. Whereas part 1 does so historically (mirroring the Old Testament and the biblical hermeneutic level of literal meaning), part 2 repeats the same message abstractly and spiritually, expressing the biblical hermeneutic level of mystical meaning, but also mirroring the function of the "New" Testament as fulfillment of the promise of the Old Testament. Dominican women are to Dominican men as Seuse's physical acts of penance are to his later, "mature," and highly apophatic spirituality as concretion is to abstraction, perhaps even as the "literal" Jews are to the "spiritual" Christians.

Part 1, with chapters divided into the symbolic number of thirty-two, represents Christ's life span on earth. It can thus be read metaphorically as spiritual practice that is embodied, localized, concrete. Clad in narrative form, this level of spiritual understanding is mapped out by severe acts of penance and specific incidents in Seuse's life as a spiritual seeker.[38] Chapter 33 begins the second part, numerically representing Christ's death at the age of thirty-three and thus the death of His/the body. It comprises twenty-one, that is, three times seven, chapters, indicating completion and perfection.[39]

The narrative at the beginning of part 2 shifts back to the beginning of the first book and repeats the events described at the beginning of part 1, albeit in a different key. Elsbeth Stagel's authorial efforts are praised here rather than condemned. Instead of resisting his authority, Stagel is now presented as fully obedient to Seuse. Feminine spirituality marked as feminine insubordination has been overcome. The rest of the second part then shifts from biographical, embodied episodes to increasingly abstract teachings. In chapter 35, we finally get the key to properly understanding the book's overall pedagogical program. Here, Seuse inserts a long list of sayings of the Desert Fathers. Their teachings clearly serve as commentaries to events Seuse describes in part 1 of his autobiography, thus revealing their hidden meaning and purpose. All sayings focus on the themes of self-mortification, humility, calmness in difficult and trying situations, and the endurance of suffering in all its forms.[40]

Part 2 ends with a description of the final spiritual stage, entering the abyss. In the "wild mountain region of the 'where' beyond God there is an abyss full of play and feeling for all pure spirits, and the spirit enters into this secret namelessness and into this wild, foreign terrain. . . ." Seuse advised his students to "do this by a pure transport of the unfathomable, simple, and pure spirit into the brilliant radiance of the divine darkness. Here one is released from all bonds, all things are left behind."[41]

The book's two parts thus represent two clearly identifiable stages of spiritual growth. In my view, both stages are profoundly gendered: "Feminine" spirituality is represented by Seuse's adventures and mishaps recorded in part 1. They take place in the material world and are marked by spiritual practices that we find abundantly in the *Sisterbooks:* severe asceticism, illness, interactions with the dead, supernatural experiences during the liturgy, and involvement in human relationships. Superior "masculine" spirituality, however, expresses itself in intense intellectualization, a turning away from the "world" and human relationships. Seuse describes the shift from the "feminine" embodied to the "masculine" intellectualized mode in graphic terms by using racial categories and images of darkness. In contrast, his advanced stage is characterized by light and white clothing. He commented on the preliminary/feminine stage of spiritual progress as follows. "Noble daughter, now note that all these images I have developed, and these thoughts distorted by images I have explained, are as far removed from the truth, which is beyond images and as unlike them, as a black Moor is unlike the beautiful sun. And this arises because of the truth's simplicity [*einvaltekeit*], which is beyond ideas and knowledge."[42]

What should happen on the spiritual level—the erasure of the feminine—is repeated on the auto/biography's literal level. The book ends not with reflections on Seuse's life, but, oddly and tellingly, with Elsbeth Stagel's death. Seuse is granted a vision of her purified, that is, decontextualized, spirit, clad "in garments white as snow: she was well adorned with luminous brilliance and was full of heavenly joys" (chapter 53).[43] It is significant that in Seuse's skillful hands it is his teachings, and not the spiritual rigors of her community, that cause her ascent to heaven. In effect, Seuse has paradigmatically severed Stagel's ties to other women and their spirituality and thus tightened his control over the whole of her life.

This battle over the legitimacy of women's autonomous spirituality is repeated in several vignettes throughout the book. For example, Seuse recounts a story that is intended to amuse and instruct a nun in his pastoral care. In the story, Heinrich Seuse is granted a vision of a celestial carnival, during which Christ offers a cup of wine to three women sitting at a table. Drinking from the cup, the first woman "sank down faint. The second also became a bit weak. The third, however, paid no attention to him. And he [Christ] explained to the servant [Seuse] the difference between a person beginning a spiritual life and one progressing and one who is perfect, and how they differ in their response to divine goodness."[44]

In effect, this teaching story encapsulates Seuse's efforts to discipline, to rename, and reappropriate religious experiences typically associated with women. In the vision, several strategies of domination disguised as pastoral care intersect. Within the narrative, the women are deprived of speech, their responses visible only through muted changes in body posture. A not so subtle shaming takes place in that ecstatic nuns are identified with drunken—that is, loose—women attending a raucous carnival, who accept alcohol from a man. The laughs are on them. In this visionary language game, the secular (the carnival) is to the sacred (Christ) as female (drunken women, nuns) is to male (confessor father, Christ), as disorder (female beginners) is to order (male perfection), and as body (women) is to speech (man).

Although *The Life of the Servant* has provoked numerous scholarly analyses, it was hardly ever problematized that Seuse's literary self-representation arose from the ashes of a woman's writings. Like Margarete Ebner's story, this too is a story of a female thief. In an unprecedented act of masculine self-assertion and female subordination in the history of medieval devotional literature, Seuse describes in detail how he burned Stagel's biography. We immediately notice the tension between the ease of cross-gender oral communications in the vernacular and female transgressions into literary productions without male approval. It is precisely on these foundations that Seuse constructed his model biography:

> There was a Friar Preacher in Germany, a Swabian by birth. . . . He became acquainted with a holy enlightened person who was beset with hardship and suffering in this world. This person asked of him that he tell her from his own experience something about his sufferings so that her own stricken heart might take strength from it, and she kept after him for a long time. When he would visit her, she would draw him out with personal questions about his beginning and progress, about some of his practices and the sufferings he had experienced. He told her about these things in spiritual confidence. Because she found comfort and guidance in these things, she wrote it all down as help for her and for others as well; but she did this surreptitiously so that he would know nothing about it. Sometime later, when he became aware of this spiritual theft, he reproached her for it and she had to hand it over to him. He took and burned everything he got hold of at that time. When he got the rest of it and was about to do the same with it, this was hindered by a celestial message from God, which prevented it. Thus what follows remained unburned, as she wrote most of it with her own hand. A bit of good instruction was added by him in her person after her death.[45]

The burning of Stagel's biography is a reenactment of a ritual reserved for heretical texts. Just a few decades earlier, the German beguine Mechthild of Magdeburg (1212–1282) was threatened with the burning of her writings. She wrote, "I was warned of this book and was told that if it wouldn't be buried, it should be burned."[46] Mechthild's works were known in Seuse's Dominican circles through Heinrich of Nördlingen, a fellow Dominican preacher and friend, who later turned away from Seuse. In 1310, the beguine Marguerite Porete, a major influence on Meister Eckhart, was burned in Paris, together with her books, an event that surely must have been known to Seuse. Finally, both Meister Eckhart and Seuse were themselves suspected of heresy.

Placed in a biblical context, Seuse's act (whether literally true or rhetorically devised) of destroying his spiritual daughter's writings and then being stopped by a heavenly message recalls Abraham's interrupted sacrifice of Isaac. Perhaps Seuse intended the biblical allusion, because it could cast him into the pleasant role of a venerable patriarch and exonerate him from possible taints of authorial emasculation by a female pen. After all, Stagel would have been the first religious woman author to generate the biography of a living, well-known male religious figure: a historical first and an act of undue insubordination in the world of religious language games. It was men's prerogative to make holy women the object of their writing, not vice versa.[47]

Not only books were burning, however. To a medieval reader, Seuse's description of burning Stagel's writings must have evoked memories of burning Jews and heretics and their books. In the spring of 1348, a large series of pogroms spread from France to Germany, reaching Konstanz in January of 1349. In Konstanz during the month of March of the same year, 330 Jews were burned in a house built to that purpose. More burnings followed in September. The Jews were accused of poisoning wells.[48] Certainly Seuse knew the degree of pain and suffering the act of burning to death implied. In a story about his betrayal by a lay brother, Seuse described his fear when he himself was threatened with burning by a mob: "The hapless servant listened to this, quivering bitterly and sighing deeply, so that in his fear large tears ran down his face. All who were standing around and looking at him began to weep bitterly."[49] Stagel's transgressive act of unauthorized biographical writing is expiated by an act that associates her with a defamed Other. Burning her book reestablishes male prerogative.[50]

This gendered story of authorial usurpation is retold in a very different vein at the beginning of the second, more theoretical/masculine, part of *The Life of the Servant*. As in the first part, Stagel is depicted as the raison d'être for the autobiography. Whereas her writing moved her dangerously close to the marginality of Jews and heretics in part 1, she is now posited as an obedient and subordinate pupil eager to learn. Her act of writing, now presented in a different relational context, gains the flair of mystical secrets. Recounting an occasion during which he lectured Stagel on religious matters, Seuse writes:

> With these and other similar pious stories the conversation was at an end. The nun secretly wrote it all down and sent it somewhere to have it kept hidden in a locked chest. Once a good sister came to the one keeping it and asked, 'Dear sister, what kind of divine marvels do you have in that chest? I dreamed last night that there was a young boy from heaven in your chest. He had a delightful stringed instrument in his hand that is called a rebec.

And he played spiritual melodies on it that were so charming that many drew spiritual pleasure and joy from it. I ask you, take out what you have locked up so that the rest can read it, too.' The other sister remained silent and did not want to tell her anything about it because she had been forbidden to do so.[51]

Two stories tell of the same event, one canceling out the other, yet both intended to present Stagel's voice and authorial authority as inferior, private, enclosed (the locked chest), and mystical rather than intellectual. In the second stage, however, Stagel, as a model for and warning to his female audience, finally learns to obey Seuse and to abstain from disseminating her own writings in her own authority.

The *Revelations* of Margarete Ebner: Spiritual Autonomy, Community, and the Vernacular

Margarete Ebner fared better than Elsbeth Stagel. Unlike Seuse, Margarete's confessor Heinrich of Nördlingen encouraged rather than destroyed the writings of the woman in his spiritual care. In contrast to Elsbeth Stagel's central role in Seuse's narrative, Heinrich of Nördlingen as well as other confessors or secular male characters appear only at the margins of Ebner's autobiography: Masculine presence, although valued, is not central to her narrative. Much was made of Heinrich's first two visits; his one pivotal act of spiritual guidance, however, occurred in relation to Ebner's intense feelings for another woman. He was to relieve Ebner of the unremitting burden of grief over the death of a beloved sister, in whom, Ebner wrote, "I had had that peace, humility, and love, and real truthfulness that I desired."[52] The story of Heinrich's pastoral gift is well told:

They [her fellow nuns] asked me to go to him, but I went unwillingly because I still visited with no one and did not want to change [in my grief]. . . . By God's grace this well-prepared servant of God said to me, "Give me your sister." And I asked him, "Do you want her soul as well?" He answered, "What good is a body to me without a soul?" Then I received grace from his words so that the death of my sister was never again as unbearable as it had been.[53]

Ebner's strongest attachments, whether positive or negative, clearly were to the nuns of her community. Her literary works reflect these attachments. Apart from her *Revelations,* Margarete composed and reproduced vernacular sacred texts for her community's devotional use, especially a set of prayers named the *Pater Noster.* She commented with great pleasure on their ritual efficacy. "My Lord [Christ] knows well that to me there is nothing more desirable and delightful to write than the admonitions and desires of my *Pater Noster* because of the great grace that I have received and felt from them."[54]

The other type of vernacular writing caused her substantially more difficulty, perhaps because she was asked to renegotiate the distance between text and devotional practice and, concomitantly, authorial self-definition. When Heinrich of Nördlingen requests her religious life to be turned into a text, Margarete reacts with great unease:

> I was asked by the true Friend of God whom He had given me for my entire life as a great consolation to write down for him what God had given me. It was my opinion that he himself should be the author, but that could not be. He said that I should begin it and write whatever God gave me. It was difficult for me, and I began reluctantly. When I wanted to begin, I feared and dreaded it.[55]

Unlike the authors of the *Sisterbooks,* who composed *vitae* of other nuns, but very much like Seuse, Ebner eventually became her own hagiographer, and devised a narrative structure that would "accomplish much good."[56] Ebner's life is circumscribed by liturgical patterns that become aligned to women's concerns about illness and healing, the living and the dead. Despite her text's unusual status as self-authored female *vita* in Dominican convent literature, Ebner's *Revelations* share aspects of women's spiritual practices as described by other Dominican female authors, especially the emphasis on suffering, asceticism, and care for the ill and the dead.[57] Giving their devotional practices greater permanence and a wider geographic reach by writing them down in the vernacular represents a further step toward female spiritual autonomy within the parameters of Christian orthodoxy.

We already catch a glimpse of such female efficacy in Seuse's autobiography. Seuse recounted how the holy woman Anna received visions on his behalf, affirming his mission, and communicated with the dead to gather information relevant to the living.[58] Ebner's cult, which is still thriving today, shows to an extraordinary degree how deeply the connection between a nun's suffering and her qualification as a healer and caretaker of souls in purgatory could run. Frequently confined to her bed and unable to participate in the regular tasks of the choir nuns, she was still of service to her community:

> The whole time I lay in bed I longed for even greater suffering because I was not able to live according to the observances of my Order. . . . I had a great yearning to pray for the Poor Souls. In turn, they were very comforting to me in all my affairs and revealed to me the things that I wanted to know about myself and also about the souls. . . . I always rejoiced on All

Souls' Day, because I had received special consolation from the Poor Souls. Sometimes they sent a Soul to me, who had been a sister of our monastery, and she thanked me for what I had done for them. . . . Many Souls whom I did not know also visited me. They revealed their lives to me and asked me to keep them in mind.[59]

Ebner's intense focus on her suffering is pastoral: It serves as proof for her argument that God heals even when human efforts are unsuccessful. It is through intense and graphic realism and a focus on her individuality that Ebner attempts to convince her audience: As such, she is as modern as Seuse. The spiritual is to be found in daily activity. Material life is to be read as a book. Its language is the vernacular.

Whereas his literary and theological training determined Seuse's authorial stance, Ebner's authority is derived from communal observation and interpretation of her string of illnesses. Since no human medical treatment brought success ("during the first year I sought a cure through human means [medication], but it only got worse, especially during Lent and Holy Week, when the pain was greatest"),[60] Ebner and her community eventually interpreted her sickness as divine action. Even so, her discourse does not abandon a focus on concrete, time-and-place-bound phenomena. Note the "clinical" description of her symptoms in the following quotation.

God afflicted me with a grave and mysterious illness. . . . My illness began strangely with a great, unbearable pain, which gripped my heart so that I could not easily breathe. My breathing could be heard even from far away. The pain then went to my eyes so that I could not see, and this continued throughout the illness. Then it went to my hands, and I could not move them. It affected my whole body except for my hearing, which I never lost. I endured this pain for three years and, during that time, had no control over myself. Whenever it went to my head I laughed or cried continuously for four days at a time or longer.[61]

The nuns collaborated with Ebner in the creation of spiritual meaning and located it in communally shared ritual experiences. In Ebner's words, "On Palm Sunday, I cried out again at such great length during Matins that the entire community despaired of my life. They thought that I would die, and I thought so, too." Later on, "When I went into choir at Matins on the holy feast of Easter, the whole community was overjoyed and everyone marveled at the merciful works of the Lord."[62]

Eventually, Margarete and her community define Ebner's illness as reenactment of Christ's suffering. The symptoms wax and wane in accordance with the liturgical year.

During Lent of the next year I was given this: when I heard the Holy Passion of my Lord during the preaching or reading, or when I heard it mentioned otherwise, my heart was shot through powerfully and this spread throughout my whole body. I was grasped and bound inwardly and outwardly, and could not move. This lasted sometimes half the day. I could not speak, nor could I suffer anyone to touch me, and I preferred to be alone. One night I was given the sight of the five holy signs of love on me—on my hands and feet and heart. And I felt the greatest grace when I thought about it.[63]

As the community reinterprets liturgical events to fit their needs, so does it appropriate Latin to its own purposes. Latin, which the sisters rarely learned systematically, changed its role as carrier of complex theological and biblical teachings to efficacious sign used in women's daily routines. On the most practical level, Latin terms marked liturgical sequence and measured the flow of time. Secondly, Latin words could become triggers for ecstatic experiences, functioning as magical formulae that would lose their power if translated into the vernacular. Ebner used Latin terms in both ways, as the following samples from her autobiography illustrate. "I read the psalter and heard mass. During the Passion I had the same great sweetness and grace that I have during my *Pater Noster.* This continued until *Sanctus, agios* was sung. . . . Then, during the *Gloria in excelsis* the greatest power flooded into me with the greatest grace."[64]

Despite the importance of Latin to mark liturgical time and the patterns of altered states of consciousness, Ebner relied on vernacular rather than Latin texts to deepen devotional understanding. As the following incident illustrates, not only her set of original prayers, the *Pater Noster,* but even the use of biblical texts in translation was negotiated according to communal logic determined by the give and take among the sisters. Ebner described in detail how she persuaded another nun to read to her: "I went into the refectory and ate bread and drank water. Afterward the greatest desire came over me to hear the Passion read in German. I asked a sister to do it for me, but she did not want to do it. Then I told her how much good the Passion had done me during the mass, and so she read it to me."[65]

In Ebner's monastery at least, Latinate and vernacular literacies thus seem to have coexisted seamlessly, albeit with community-appropriate functions. The quotation traces their situational, spatial, and behavioral framework: The same text that is spoken by a priest in Latin during mass becomes performed again in an exclusively female space, in the vernacular, with the priest's role appropriated by a woman, and the Eucharist replaced by a meal devoid of priestly markings. This deceptively simple incident might indeed be of paradigmatic significance for Dominican women's linguistic deftness. What we find is not extinction of one kind of literacy for the sake of the other, but reflections on key Christian teachings embedded in ritualized changes of stage and tongue, complementary literacies necessitated by the *gestalt* of female monastic spirituality.

Conclusion

Seuse's text is structured as two-tiered progress toward correct mystical cognition of the abyss. Ebner's autobiography, on the other hand, is ordered by the ever-repeating liturgical cycles of the year, circular and atemporal in its narrative flow, punctuated only by infrequently occurring extraordinary events, whether of personal or larger social significance. These events include the few visits by Heinrich of Nördlingen, her health taking another turn for the worse or the better, the death of a sister, or the evacuation of her monastic community. Her autobiography is cumulative rather than carefully syncopated, as is typical of oral communication patterns.

Seuse used the vernacular to discipline and contain women under his pastoral care and to demarcate female spirituality as inferior to his own. Seuse, like Meister Eckhart and others, redefined communally situated, embodied spirituality as a beginner's phase in spiritual development. Ebner, like the authors of the *Sisterbooks,* seemed to have been oblivious of the fact that her spirituality could have been seen as less valid than scholastically oriented mysticism. Her autobiography is a spiritual manual much like Seuse's, but it works to enhance the power of the sisters' daily routine, dictated by the offices of the liturgical year. Margarete Ebner literally reenacted liturgical meaning in a mimesis that both she and her sisters declared to be sacred, and extended its efficacy to the vagaries of human life in her community, the crises brought on by illness and death. The fact that her cult is still active today pays tribute to the appeal of the very local vernacular model she and her fellow nuns created, carnivals and thieves notwithstanding.

Notes

1. The case has been made most recently by Elizabeth Hill Boone and Walter D. Mignolo, eds., *Writing Without Words: Alternative Literacies in Mesoamerica and the Andes* (Durham, NC: Duke University Press, 1994). See also Walter Mignolo, "Globalization, Civilization Processes, and the Relocation of Languages and Cultures," in Fredric Jameson and Masao Miyoshi, eds., *The Cultures of Globalization* (Durham, NC: Duke University Press, 1998), pp. 32–54.
2. It is crucial to remember that medieval "literacy" and "illiteracy" embraced a more varied spectrum of reading and writing skills than the terms denote today. For a survey of these issues in regard to medieval German cul-

ture, see, inter alia, D. H. Green, *Medieval Listening and Reading: The Primary Reception of German Literature, 800–1300* (Cambridge: Cambridge University Press, 1994), and Horst Wenzel, *Hören und Lesen, Schrift und Bild: Kultur und Gedächtnis im Mittelalter* (Munich: C. H. Beck, 1995). On the relationship between language use and gender, see Alette Olin Hill, *Mother Tongue, Father Time: A Decade of Linguistic Revolt* (Bloomington: Indiana University Press, 1986), and Deborah Tannen, *Gender & Discourse* (Oxford: Oxford University Press, 1994).

3. The locus classicus for this assessment is Herbert Grundmann, *Religiöse Bewegungen im Mittelalter: Untersuchungen über die geschichtlichen Zusammenhänge zwischen der Ketzerei, den Bettelorden und der religiösen Frauenbewegung im 12. und 13. Jahrhundert* (Historische Studien, 267. Berlin: Olms Verlag, 1935), chapter 8. See also Herbert Grundmann, "Die Frauen und die Literatur im Mittelalter," in *Archiv für Kulturgeschichte* 26 (1936): 129–61. For the Italian context, see Katherine Gill, "Women and the Production of Religious Literature in the Vernacular, 1300–1500," in *Creative Women in Medieval and Early Modern Italy: A Religious and Artistic Renaissance*, eds. E. Ann Matter and John Coakley (Philadelphia: University of Pennsylvania Press, 1994), pp. 64–105. The distribution of gender is dramatically different for the rise of secular vernacularity. For an overview on the rise of German vernacular literacy, unfortunately without attention paid to gender, see D. H. Green, *Medieval Listening*.

4. For Germanic languages, the case can be made for Hadewijch, Mechthild of Magdeburg, and Beatrice of Nazareth. On the history and complexity of the terms *latinitas, rustica lingua,* etc. and the fact that they only roughly coincide with the parameters of the use of Latin in medieval western Europe, see Karl D. Uitti, "Women Saints, the Vernacular, and History," in *Images of Sainthood in Medieval Europe*, eds. Renate Blumenfeld-Kosinski and Timea Szell (Ithaca and London: Cornell University Press, 1991), pp. 247–68. On the linguistic practices of Dominican nuns, see Marie-Luise Ehrenschwendtner, "*Puellae litteratae:* The Use of the Vernacular in the Dominican Convents of Southern Germany," in *Medieval Women in Their Communities*, ed. Diane Watt (Toronto and Buffalo: University of Toronto Press, 1997), pp. 50–71. Ehrenschwendtner argues that the nuns used the vernacular for devotional literature from the beginning, and that as a consequence, Latin quickly lost significance outside of the liturgy. My study supports her thesis.

5. See the essays in *Meister Eckhart and the Beguine Mystics Hadewijch of Brabant, Mechthild of Magdeburg, and Marguerite Porete,* ed. Bernard McGinn (New York: Continuum, 1994).

6. For an overview of the impact of Latin and vernacular languages on medieval Western civilization, see Marcia L. Colish, *Medieval Foundations of the Western Intellectual Tradition, 400–1400* (New Haven and London: Yale University Press, 1997). Colish does not discuss the issue of gendered access to Latin, however.

7. For one example of these dynamics of reappropriation, see Karen Glente, "Mystikerinnenviten aus männlicher und weiblicher Sicht: Ein Vergleich zwischen Thomas von Cantimpré und Katharina von Unterlinden," in *Religiöse Frauenbewegung und mystische Frömmigkeit im Mittelalter,* eds. Peter Dinzelbacher and Dieter R. Bauer (Wien: Böhlau Verlag, 1988), pp. 251–65. Glente argues that Dominican women's spirituality developed as a countermovement to scholastic (Latinate) theology and science.

8. The writings constitute the "second wave" of German vernacularity. The first wave occurred between 750 and 1050. See Marion E. Gibbs and Sidney M. Johnson, *Medieval German Literature: A Companion* (New York and London: Garland Publishing, 1997), part II. The best overview on Ebner's work and context is offered by Manfred Weitlauff, "'dein got redender munt machet mich redenlosz . . . ' Margareta Ebner und Heinrich von Nördlingen," in *Religiöse Frauenbewegung,* ed. Peter Dinzelbacher, pp. 303–53. I will quote from the following critical edition of Ebner's *Revelations* and its edited translation into English: Philipp Strauch, *Margaretha Ebner und Heinrich von Nördlingen. Ein Beitrag zur Geschichte der Deutschen Mystik* (Amsterdam: Verlag P. Schippers N.V., 1966); and *Margaret Ebner: Major Works,* trans. and ed. Leonard Hindsley (New York: Paulist Press, 1993). Ebner's book did not survive as original manuscript. The *Revelations* must have been based at least in part on earlier letters written by Ebner (all but one lost to us), and were composed in collaboration with another nun, Elsbeth Schepach. Weitlauff is probably correct in assuming that Heinrich of Nördlingen might have put final touches on the text. See Weitlauff, "Margareta Ebner," n. 3 on textual production; Strauch, *Margaretha Ebner,* on the earliest extant manuscript in Medingen, copied after Ebner's death in 1353, and other primary sources, pp. xiii–xxxi. However, Heinrich promised Ebner to not make any additions or changes, whether in German or Latin, without her approval. "Ich wage auch nicht, etwas dazuzutun oder wegzunehmen, weder lateinisch noch deutsch, bis ich es mit Dir überlese und aus Deinem Munde und aus Deinem Herzen in neuer Wahrheit verstehe," in *Deutsche Mystikerbriefe des Mittelalters, 1100–1500,* ed. Wilhelm Oehl (reprint of 1931 edition. Darmstadt: Wissenschaftliche Buchgesellschaft, 1972), p. 327. The extent of secondary literature on Heinrich Seuse (in the English version of his name, Henry Suso) is too voluminous to be cited here. For a recent assessment, see the essays in *Heinrich Seuse. Diener der Ewigen Wahrheit,* ed. Jacobus Kaffanke (Tagungsberichte der Katholischen Akademie der Erzdiözese Freiburg. Freiburg: Katholische Akademie, 1998). A short biographical survey is offered in *Henry Suso: The Exemplar, with Two German Sermons,* trans. and ed. Frank Tobin (New York: Paulist Press, 1989). The following quotations in translation will be based on this edition. For a critical edition of German primary sources, I have used Karl Bihlmeyer, *Heinrich Seuse. Deutsche Schriften* (Stuttgart: Kohlhammer Verlag, 1907). I wish to thank Frank Tobin for his thoughtful comments on my essay, for which I am very grateful.

9. On German Dominican women's spirituality, see the magisterial studies by Gertrud Jaron Lewis, *By Women for Women about Women: The Sisterbooks of Fourteenth Century Germany* (Toronto: Pontifical Institute of Mediaeval Studies, 1996), and Rosemary Hale, *Imitatio Mariae: Motherhood Motifs in Late Medieval German Spirituality,* diss., Harvard University, typescript, 1992. For an art-historical perspective, see Jeffrey F. Hamburger, *The Visual and the Visionary: Art and Female Spirituality in Late Medieval Germany* (New York: Zone Books, 1998).

10. On evidence in the *Sisterbooks* regarding Dominican nuns' varied access to and use of Latin, see Jaron Lewis, *Sisterbooks,* chapter 8, "Love of Learning"; also Ehrenschwendtner, *"Puellae litteratae."* On the remarkable production of letters, see the still-unsurpassed collection by Oehl, *Deutsche Mystikerbriefe.* For a stimulating discussion of the creative adaptation of the epistolary genre in German vernacular spirituality, see Paul Mommaers and Frank Willaert, "Mystisches Erleben und sprachliche Vermittlung in den Briefen Hadewijchs," in Dinzelbacher, ed., *Religiöse Frauenbewegung,* pp. 117–53.

11. Green makes this point generally about the advantages of literacy (Green, *Medieval Listening,* p. 8). Another means to maintain relationships across spatial and temporal divides was the frequent exchange of gifts that could even stand in for the absentee. Heinrich von Nördlingen, for example, requested Margarete Ebner's used nightgown for his comfort (Margarete claimed that she had not bathed for thirty years), and Seuse and his circle of female admirers engaged in a lively trade in small patches of cloth that he had first placed on his bare chest. Less physically charged objects of exchange included little knives, loaves of cheese, cloth, candles, and small ivories. See Oehl, *Deutsche Mystikerbriefe,* pp. 297–397.

12. On nuns' critical attitudes toward friars, see Jaron Lewis, *Sisterbooks,* pp. 190 ff.

13. On aspects of the *cura monialium,* the Dominican order's care for its female wing, see especially Otto Langer, *Mystische Erfahrung und spirituelle Theologie. Zu Meister Eckharts Auseinandersetzung mit der Frauenfrömmigkeit seiner Zeit* (München: Artemis Verlag, 1987), part 1, section 1. On the male order's emphasis on education, see Alois Haas, "Die deutsche Mystik im Spannungsbereich von Theologie und Spiritualität," in Haas, *Gottleiden-Gottlieben. Zur volkssprachlichen Mystik im Mittelalter* (Frankfurt/Main: Insel Verlag, 1989), pp. 59–97.

14. For a survey of these attitudes, but also more sympathetic readings in recent scholarship, see Jaron Lewis, *Sisterbooks,* chapter 3; for a typical reading based on the position outlined above, see Alois Haas, "Traum und Traumvision in der deutschen Mystik," in Haas, *Gottleiden-Gottlieben,* pp. 109–27, especially pp. 115 ff.

15. See the lucid article on the confluence of orality and the vernacular in women's writings by Evelyn Birge Vitz, "From the Oral to the Written in Medieval and Renaissance Saints' Lives," in *Images of Sainthood in Medieval Europe,* eds. Renate Blumenfeld-Kosinski and Timea Szell, pp. 97–115. My

theoretical perspective is informed by Susan Starr Sered's seminal study, *Priestess, Mother, Sacred Sister: Religions Dominated By Women* (New York and Oxford: Oxford University Press, 1994). Starr Sered argues that in traditional societies women's concerns center on healing, birthing, and care for the dead, as well as family relationships as they relate to the human life cycle.

16. For a recent critical analysis, see Julie B. Miller, "Eroticized Violence in Medieval Women's Mystical Literature: A Call for a Feminist Critique," *Journal of Feminist Studies in Religion* 15:2 (1999): 25–50.

17. On the endorsement of misogynist and anti-Judaic violence in Latin devotional texts, see Thomas H. Bestul, *Texts of the Passion: Latin Devotional Literature and Medieval Society* (Philadelphia: University of Pennsylvania Press, 1996).

18. Quotation based on the translation by Hindsley, *Margaret Ebner* (see n. 8), pp. 148–49.

> Ez geschach da vor in dem summer ain kleglich ding. Ein frowe von dorf Medingen von dem rat des bösen vindez und von ainem verkerten cristenlichen herzen kom in ain unser kirchen, da unser frowe sunderlich genedig ist, und haisset zu Steten, und nam uz der bühse zwo ungesegnet oblata und truog si in ain stat nahen bi unserm closter, diu haisset Lougingen, und bot si vail den juden oder daz si dar uf gelihen heten phenning. Und daz sach ain cristen frawe und do der jude nihtz da zuo tuon wolt, do rüeget si sie dem gerihte und daz fieng sie. Und do si verurtailet wart zem tode, do snaide man ain kint vor von ir, daz wart getaufet, und verbrant si do. Dar umb wart ich so voller grosser trurket umb die unere gotez, daz ich ze minen betevenstern an die stat nimer moht gesehen, da daz geschehen was. Allen den sumer moht ich nihtz da von gehörn noch da von gesprechen. Ich moht ouch nit wohl liden, wer barmherzeket über si het, wan ich gedaht, wem man sinen lieben fruint also geunert het, er möht sich nit über den erbarmen. Ich versuoch auch dik mit flizze [für si zu betten] und ku nde kain begirde zuo got für si noch nie gehaben.

Strauch, *Margaretha Ebner*, pp. 116–17. A short reference to the incident is also recorded in a letter by Abbot Ulrich von Kaisheim to Ebner. See *Deutsche Mystikerbriefe*, ed. Oehl, p. 338. Although Ebner firmly denies any interest in the case in her autobiography, the letter indicates that she asked Ulrich for further details.

19. On the polemical association of Jews with the Eucharist as taught in medieval sermons, see Joan Young Gregg, *Devils, Women, and Jews: Reflections of the Other in Medieval Sermon Stories* (Albany: State University of New York Press, 1997), chapter 4; Miri Rubin, "Imagining the Jew: the Late Medieval Eucharistic Discourse," in *In and Out of the Ghetto: Jewish-Gentile Relations in Late Medieval and Early Modern Germany*, eds. R. P. Hsia and H. Lehmann

(Washington, D.C., and Cambridge: Cambridge University Press, 1994): pp. 177–208. On persecutions of Jews during Ebner's time, see Alfred Haverkamp, "Die Judenverfolgungen zur Zeit des Schwarzen Todes," in Haverkamp, ed., *Zur Geschichte der Juden im Deutschland des späten Mittelalters und der frühen Neuzeit* (Stuttgart: Anton Hiersemann, 1981), pp. 27–94.

20. In regard to Seuse's training in the Dominican order, see P. Isnard M. Frank, "Zur Studienorganisation der Dominikanerprovinz Teutonia in der ersten Hälfte des 14. Jahrhunderts und zum Studiengang des seligen Heinrich Seuse OP," and P. Ephrem M. Filthaut OP, "Heinrich Seuse in dominikanisch-priesterlich-seelsorgerlicher Sicht," both in *Heinrich Seuse. Studien zum 600. Todestag. 1366–1966,* ed. Filthaut (Köln: Albertus Magnus Verlag, 1966), pp. 39–69 and pp. 267–305 respectively.

21. On the felicitous term "autohagiography" and medieval women's writings, see Kate Greenspan, "Autohagiography and Medieval Women's Spiritual Autobiography," in Jane Chance, ed., *Gender and Text in the Later Middle Ages* (Gainesville: University Press of Florida, 1996), pp. 216–36.

22. The serendipitous German vernacular term is *lebemeister,* a master teacher of how to live life well, a spiritual psychologist.

23. Given that Dominican women entered the monasteries later in life than Benedictine oblates, they would bring more secular knowledge and concerns to their spiritual responsibilities. Because of the monasteries' urban setting, the nuns, like beguines, would also remain in comparatively greater contact with the lay communities around them. It would therefore be worthwhile to develop theoretical models of female devotional cultures across the (porous) boundaries of religious and lay female communities; a useful beginning could be made, for example, by comparing Rosemary Hale's work on Dominican motherhood spirituality with scholarship on the cult of St. Anne, which was widespread by the fourteenth century. On the cult of St. Anne, see Kathleen Ashley and Pamela Sheingorn, *Interpreting Cultural Symbols: Saint Anne in Late Medieval Society* (Athens and London: The University of Georgia Press, 1990).

24. "Erst im 14. Jahrhundert wurde durch die Dominikanermystik der bisherige Vorsprung der Frau auf diesem Gebiete vom Manne eingeholt und ihre Leistung dann allerdings weit übertroffen, freilich nicht an Innigkeit des Erlebens, aber an der Fähigkeit, das Geschaute mit dem Intellekt zu erfassen und im Zusammenhang des theologischen Systems spekulativ zu verarbeiten." Karl Bihlmeyer, "Die Selbstbiographie in der deutschen Mystik," *Theologische Quartalschrift* 114 (1933): 504–44, at 513. Translation mine.

25. The Western association of women's intellect with experience and emotion and men's intellect with reason and abstraction is well documented. See, *inter alia,* Martha Lee Osborne, *Woman in Western Thought* (New York: Random House, 1979).

26. This constitutes one reason for the widespread embrace of misogyny among religious men. For Judaism, see Daniel Boyarin, *Unheroic Conduct. The Rise of Heterosexuality and the Invention of the Jewish Man* (Berkeley and

Los Angeles: University of California Press, 1997). Boyarin argues the exception that proves the rule. Due to the Jewish minority's precarious historical situation, abstraction, literacy, and male effeminacy went hand in hand. Similar studies are unfortunately still lacking for Christianity, Islam, and Hinduism. World religions' ambivalence toward violence can be studied as a crisis in masculine identity, and should be tied to the cultivation of abstract thought as "masculine" privilege that can substitute for violence as measurement of masculinity. We need to take seriously the sociopsychological finding that modes of thought are culturally conditioned, which also includes gender socialization. See Bruce Bower, "Cultures of Reason: Thinking Styles May Take Eastern and Western Routes," *Science News* 157 (January 22, 2000): 56–58.

27. See John van Engen, "Dominic and the Brothers: *Vitae* as Life-Forming *Exempla* in the Order of Preachers," in *Christ among the Medieval Dominicans,* eds. Kent Emery, Jr., and Joseph Wawrykow (Notre Dame: University of Notre Dame Press, 1998), pp. 7–26.

28. Regarding Latin and its impact on abstraction, Walter J. Ong writes pointedly, "because of its base in academia, which was totally male—with exceptions so utterly rare as to be quite negligible—Learned Latin had another feature in common with rhetoric besides its classical provenance. For well over a thousand years, it was sex-linked, a language written and spoken only by males, *learned outside the home in a tribal setting which was in effect a male puberty rite setting. . . . Learned Latin was a striking exemplification of the power of writing for isolating discourse and of the unparalleled productivity of such isolation . . . thus reducing interference from the human lifeworld"* (italics mine) (Ong, *Orality and Literacy: The Technologizing of the Word* [London and New York: Routledge, repr. 1999], pp. 113–14). On medieval culture generally, see Ong, "Orality, Literacy and Medieval Textualization," *New Literary History* 16 (1984–1985): 1–12.

29. My point redefines the old debate about religious transcendence and immanence. Georges Bataille grasped the connection in his own way in *Theory of Religion* (translated by Robert Hurley. New York: Zone Books, 1989): "The moment of change is given in a passage: the intelligible sphere is revealed in a transport, in a sudden movement of transcendence, where tangible matter is surpassed. The intellect or the concept, situated outside time, is defined as a sovereign order, to which the world of things is subordinated, just as it subordinated the gods of mythology" (p. 73). For a contemporary analysis, see Eric Zencey, "The Rootless Professors," in *Rooted in the Land: Essays on Community and Place,* eds. William Vitek and Wes Jackson (New Haven and London: Yale University Press, 1996), pp. 15–20.

30. On ways to interpret medieval religious women's experiences of space, especially architectural space, see Roberta Gilchrist, *Gender and Material Culture. The Archeology of Religious Women* (London and New York: Routledge, 1994).

31. On Seuse's use of German, see Maria Bindschedler, "Seuses Auffassung von der deutschen Sprache," in Filthaut, *Heinrich Seuse,* pp. 71–75. The author

argues that for Seuse, authorial tension existed not between Latinate and vernacular languages, but between oral ("alive") and written ("dead") communication. It is instructive to see the distinction between "life" and "death" as symbolic of pastoral presence and absence, and as such as symbolic of the tension inherent in an itinerant Dominican preacher's difficulties to maintain close ties with individual female communities.

32. I am offering a feminist twist to Frank Tobin's thoughtful discussion of the issue in his recent essay, "Henry Suso and Elsbeth Stagel: Was the *Vita* a Cooperative Effort?" in *Gendered Voices: Medieval Saints and their Interpreters,* ed. Catherine M. Mooney (Philadelphia: University of Pennsylvania Press, 1999), pp. 118–36. I am in fundamental agreement with Tobin's conclusion that *The Life of the Servant* is a highly stylized text whose carefully designed structure forbids any identification of Stagel's contributions.

33. Caroline Walker Bynum, *Holy Feast and Holy Fast: The Religious Significance of Food to Medieval Women* (Berkeley and Los Angeles: University of California Press, 1987), p. 105. This definition needs to be corrected, since Seuse himself sees his use of images as inferior to his abstractions: "feminine" spirituality, indeed, but only as a beginner's first steps toward spiritual progress.

34. This question is rather anachronistic anyhow. As Ruth Morse points out, medieval auto/biographies were intent on depicting people as "instances of unchanging types," not as unique individuals. Morse, *Truth and Convention in the Middle Ages: Rhetoric, Representation, and Reality* (Cambridge: Cambridge University Press, 1991), chapter 3, "Let Us Now Praise Famous Men," p. 173.

35. Julius Schwietering, "Zur Autorschaft von Seuses Vita," in *Altdeutsche und altniederländische Mystik,* ed. Kurt Ruh (Darmstadt: Wissenschaftliche Buchgesellschaft, 1964), pp. 309–23.

36. Seuse presents himself throughout as extremely polite toward women; furthermore, most of his stories center on women, which also may indicate that *The Life of the Servant* was intentionally composed for a female audience. In chapter 18, Seuse underscores his good intentions by telling a story of courteous behavior toward a woman of lower social status, recording his words as 0well as the woman's response.

"Dear woman, it is my custom to show freely politeness and honor to all women for the sake of the gentle Mother of God in heaven." She raised her eyes and hands to heaven and said, "I shall ask this same esteemed Lady that you not depart from this world without her granting you some special grace, since you show her honor through all of us women" ["Ey, liebu frowe, min gewonheit ist, daz ich allen frowen gern zuht und ere but dur der zarten gotes muter willen von himelreich." Si hub of iru ogen und ir hende gen dem himel und sprach also: "Nu bit ich die selben erenwirdigen frowen, daz ir von diser welt niemer geschediet, uch bescheh

etwas sunder gnaden von ir, die ir an uns allen frowen erent"].
(Tobin, Bihlmeyer, chapter 18 [see n. 8]).

How "true" is this incident? Viewed typologically, it retells a story in St.
Elisabeth of Thuringia's *vita,* in which the saintly princess encounters a
poor old woman while on a walk.

37. I find Kate Greenspan's comments on autohagiography most pertinent
here. She suggests that the genre, "rather than serving as a peephole for curious onlookers onto someone else's exclusive experience, . . . compre-
hends the reader, and all possible readers, expressing that which is potential
in all of us," in Chance, *Gender and Text,* p. 233, n. 3.

38. To my knowledge, nobody has as yet catalogued the many parallels between Seuse's acts of self-mortification and the stories told in the *Sisterbooks,* such as carving letters into one's chest, fastening oneself to a life-size
crucifix, wearing belts studded with nails that pierced the skin, etc. To do
so would exceed the limits of this essay; because of these many parallels,
however, it is conceivable that Seuse invented or "autobiographized" many
of these ascetic exercises for himself. On examples of self-disciplining in
the *Sisterbooks,* see Peter Ochsenbein, "Leidensmystik in dominikanischen
Frauenklöstern des 14. Jahrhunderts am Beispiel der Elsbeth von Oye," in
Dinzelbacher, ed., *Religiöse Frauenbewegung,* pp. 353–73.

39. On the symbolism of these numbers, see Ernst Curtius, *European Literature
and the Latin Middle Ages* (New York: Harper & Row, 1953), pp. 503–505.

40. Richard Kieckhefer's insights into fourteenth-century spirituality are helpful here to create a cultural context. He suggests that the key values espoused by fourteenth-century saints were patience, devotion to the Passion,
penitence, and rapture. Kieckhefer, *Unquiet Souls: Fourteenth Century Saints
and Their Religious Milieu* (Chicago: University of Chicago Press, 1984).

41. The abyss, or *abgrunt,* is a well-used mystical topos, especially in Hadewijch, Eckhart, and Tauler. It indicates both the deity beyond divinity and a
space of oneness of human and divine reality. See Michael Sells, *Mystical
Languages of Unsaying* (Chicago: University of Chicago Press, 1994), especially chapters 5, 6, and 7. "In disem wilden gebirge des ubergotlichen wa
ist ein enpfintlichu vorspilendu allen reinen geisten abgruntlichkeit, und da
kunt si in die togenlichen ungenantheit und in daz wild
enpfromdekeit . . ."; " . . . in die solt du dringen unwussende, in daz
swigenm daz do ob allen wesen ist . . . mit einem blossen abzuge des
grundlosen, einvaltigen, reinen gemutes, hin in den uberweslichen wider-
glast der gotlichen vinstri." Bihlmeyer, Tobin, chapter 52. Unlike Tobin, I
do not see the experience of the abyss as a place where gender inequality
becomes erased and reconciled, because women arrive at this stage through
subordination and the abnegation of their own models of spiritual growth.

42. "Fro tohter, nu merk eben, daz disu ellu entworfnu bild und disu us-
geleiten verbildetu wort sind der bildlosen warheit als verr und als un-
gelich, als ein swarzer mor der schonen sunnen, und kunt daz von der

selben warheit formlosen, unbekanten einvaltekeit." Bihlmeyer, Tobin, chapter 53.

43. " . . . und luhte in schnewisser wat wol gezieret mit liehtricher klarheit vol himelscher froden." Ibid.

44. "du erst seig da nider kraftlos, du ander ward och enklein swach, aber du drit ahtet sin niht. Und seit im do den underscheid eins anvahenden, zunehmenden und volkomen menschen, wie sich die misslich haltent in gotlicher sussekeit." Bihlmeyer, Tobin, chapter 36.

45. "Es waz ein brediger in tutschen lande, von geburt ein Swabe, dez nam geschriben sie an dem lebenden buch. Der hat begird, daz er wurde und hiesse ein diener der ewigen wisheit. Er gewan kuntsami eins heiligen erluhten menschen, der ein vil erbetseliger lidender mensch waz in diser welt. Der mensch begert von im, daz er ir etwas seiti von lidene usser eigenr enpfindunge, dar abe ir lidendes herz ein kraft mohti nemen; und daz treib si vil zites mit ime. Wenn er zu ir kom, do zoch si im us mit heinlichen fragen die wise sines anvanges und furgangs und etlich ubunge und liden, die er hat gehabt, du seit er ir in gotlicher heimlichi. Do si von den dingen trost und wisung bevand, do schreib si es alles an, ir selb und och andren menschen ze einem behelfen, und tet daz verstoln vor ime, daz er nut dur von wuste. Dar na neiswen, do er diser geischlichen dupstal innen ward, do straft er si darumbe, und muste im es her us geben. Er nam es und verbrand es alles, daz im do ward. Do ime daz ander teil ward und er in glicher wise och also wolt han getan, do ward es understanden mit himelscher botschaft von got, du im do geschah, du daz wante. Und also bleib E dis nagende unverbrennet, als si es den meren teil mit ir selbes handen hate geschriben. Etwaz guter lere wart och na ir tode in ir person von im dur zu geleit." (Bihlmeyer, Tobin, chapter 1)

46. "Ich wart vor disem buche gewarnet, und wart von menschen also gesaget: Wolte man es nit bewaren, da mohte ein brant uber varen." Book II: 26: 1, 2; Mechthild of Magdeburg, *Das fliessende Licht der Gottheit,* ed. Hans Neumann (München and Zürich: Artemis Verlag, 1990), p. 68.

47. Exceptions prove the rule. See Hugeburc of Heidenheim, *Vita Willibaldi Episcopi Eichstetensis;* Hrotsvit of Gandersheim's numerous legends and plays about male saints; and finally, Hildegard of Bingen's *Vita Sancti Disibodi* and *Vita Sancti Ruperti.* Cited in Andrew Kadel, *Matrology. A Bibliography of Writings by Christian Women from the First to the Fifteenth Centuries* (New York: Continuum, 1995).

48. See *Die Juden in ihrer mittelalterlichen Umwelt,* ed. Alfred Ebenbauer and Klaus Zatloukal (Wien: Böhlau Verlag, 1991). Seuse himself was accused of poisoning wells. *Life,* chapter 25.

49. "daz horte der ellend diener mit mengem bitern schreken und mit erholten sufzen, daz im von angst die grossen trehen uber daz antlut ab runnen. Ellu du menschen, du umb den ring stunden und in sahen, wurden biterlich weinende." Bihlmeyer, Tobin, chapter 25.

50. Thus the story falls squarely into Nancy Jay's analysis of the dynamics of sacrifice in patriarchal cultures. Jay, *Throughout Your Generations Forever: Sacrifice, Religion, and Paternity* (Chicago: University of Chicago Press, 1992).

51. "Mit disem und derley gotlichen kosene nam du red ein ende. Si screib es alles an heinlich und sante es neiswa hin ze gehalten und ze verbergen in ein beschlossen lade. Eins males do kom ein gutu swester zu der, du es behalten hate, und sprach also: 'eya, liebu swoster, was hast du verborgens gotliches wunders in diner lad? Lug, mir waz hinaht vor in einem trome, daz ein junger himelscher knab stunde in diner lade, und hate der ein susses seitenspil in sinen handen, daz man nemmet ein robobli, und da machet er uf geischlich reyen, die waren als reislich, daz menlich dur von geischlichen lust und frod nam. Ich bit dich, gib es her us, daz du beschlossen hast, daz wir endru es och lesen.' Si sweig und wolte ir nit dur von sagen, wan es ir waz verboten." (Bihlmeyer, Tobin, chapter 36)

52. "wan ich het an ir, wes ich begert: daz was fride, demüetikait, minne und rehtiu warhait." Strauch, p. 15; Hindsley, p. 92 (see n. 8).

53. "do baten sie mich dar ze gaun. Daz tet ich niht gern, wan ich dennoht zuo niemen gieng noch wandel het . . . nun sprach der aller wol beraitest diener mit der gnaud gotes zuo mir: 'gebent mir iwer swester.' Ich sprach zuo im:'wend ir die sel dar zuo aun?' Er antwurt:'waz sol mir ain lib aun sel?' do enphieng ich die gnaud da von sinen worten, daz mir der tod miner swester nimmer mer als unlidig was als er was gewesen." Strauch, p. 16; Hindsley, p. 93.

54. "ez waizze daz min herre wol, daz mir kain dink begirlicher und lustlicher wer ze scriben denn diu manunge und die begirde miner paternoster von der grossen genade, der ich dar uz enphangen und enphunden han." Strauch, p. 83; Hindsley, p. 130.

55. "Item ich wart gebeten von dem warhaften friund gotez, den er mir ze grossem trost geben hatt allem minen leben, daz ich ime scribe, waz mir got gebe. Do was min mainunge, daz er selber der scriber wer, daz maht nit gesin." Strauch, pp. 83–84; Hindsley, p. 130.

56. " . . . und gelopt mir vil dar umb ze tuon guotes," Strauch, p. 84; Hindsley, p. 131.

57. There is no need to highlight why these concerns were especially urgent in the fourteenth century considering the impact of the Black Plague, the great famine of northern Europe in the first half of the century, and the decline of traditional institutions. On the return to intense mysticism during the fourteenth century, see Michael Goodich, *Violence and Miracle in the Fourteenth Century: Private Grief and Public Salvation* (Chicago: University of Chicago Press, 1995), and Kieckhefer, *Unquiet Souls*. On the consequences of these crises for minorities, see David Nirenberg, *Communities of Violence: Persecution of Minorities in the Middle Ages* (Princeton: Princeton University Press, 1996).

58. Anna is referred to by name in chapters 11, 13, 34, and 37. For a discussion of Anna's function in the autohagiography as "exemplary eyewitness

to Suso's visions," who complements Stagel as "exemplary imitator and interpreter of Suso's text," see Jeffrey Hamburger, "Medieval Self-Fashioning: Authorship, Authority, and Autobiography in Suso's *Exemplar,*" in Hamburger, *The Visual and the Visionary: Art and Female Spirituality in Late Medieval Germany* (New York: Zone Books, 1998), chapter 5, p. 243.

59. "Ich het auch begird, die wil ich ze bette lage, daz ich noch grözzern wetagen gern het gehebt da von daz ich minen orden niht geleben maht. . . . Ich het grozz begird den selen ze beten; und die warn mir gar trostlichen in allen sachen und ofenten mir diu ding diu ich gern west von mir selber und auch von den selen . . . ich fräwet mich alle zit uf aller selen tag, so het ich sundern trost von in. sie santen etwen zuo mir ain sel, diu ain swester unsers coventz was, diu mir dankte waz ich in ze guot tät . . . mich suochten auch vil sel, der ich niht kant, und gauben mir ir leben ze erkennen und baten mich daz ich ir gedehte." Strauch, pp. 5–7.

60. "Aber in dem ersten jar do suoht ich mensclich ertzni und ward ie siecher und siecher und sunderlichen alle vasten und die jungsten wochen so was min wetag aller gröst." Strauch, p. 2.

61. "Do erzaiget mir got sin grozz vätterlich triu . . . und gab mir grozzen siechtagen und unkunden. . . . Des ersten huob sich wunderlich min siechtag. Mit grossem unlidigem wetagen gieng ez mir in daz hertz, daz ich niht wol den auten maht han, daz man mich verre hört autmen. So gieng ez mir dann in diu augen, daz ich niht gesehen maht alle die wil ez mir da was. So was ez mir dann in den henden, daz ich sie niht kund geregen. Also gieng es mir über allen minen lib aun allain die gehörd, diu ging mir nie ab. Und den wetagen het ich biz in daz trit jar, daz ich min selbs ungeweltig was. Und wen ez mir in daz haupt gieng, so lachet ich oder wainet vier tag oder mer emsclichen." Strauch, pp. 1–2.

62. "Und do an dem balmtag under der metin do schrai ich aber as lang, daz aller covent an mir verzaget und wanden, ich wölt azo sterben, und waunde ich ez selber auch." Strauch, p. 55, Hindsley, p. 115. "Und do an dem hailigen ostertag gienk ich ze metin in den cor. Do wart aller min covent gefräwet, und namen alle wunder ab den barmhertzigen werken unsers herren." Strauch, p. 57; Hindsley, p. 116.

63. "Dar nach in der nehsten vasten wart mir geben, wenn ich daz hailig liden mins hereen hört am bredigen oder an lesen oder so ich ez hört nennen, so schosse ez mir in min hertz as kreftiklichen und tailet sich denn in älliu miniu lider, und wird denne gefangen und gebunden inwendik und uswendik und mag mich niena geregen, und daz wert etwenn ainen halben tag. Ich mag auch ain wort nit gesprechen und mag nit geliden, daz mich ieman an rege, und bin gerne aine. Item ze der zit wart mir geben aines nahtes, daz ich an mir sach die hailigen fünf minnzaichen in henden, an füezzen und in hertzen, und da gewan ich die aller grösten genade von, wenn ich dar an gedaht." Strauch, pp. 49–50.

64. " . . . und las den salter und hört daz ampt. Aber under dem passion het ich die aller grössten süessekeit und genade, die ich under minen paternoster

han, und daz wert an mir biz daz man sank Sanctus ayos." Strauch, p. 53.
Hindsley, p. 114–15: " . . . do ez nu kom under dem Gloria in excelsis, do
gienk mir diu aller gröst kraft zuo mit der süezzesten genade . . ." Strauch,
p. 56; Hindsley, p. 115.

65. "Do kom ich do in daz reventer und az wasser und brot. Dar nach kom
   mir der gröst lust ine, daz ich den passion solt hörn tiuschen, und bat ain
   frawen, daz siu mir in tuti. Daz wolt siu nit tuon. Do set ich ir, daz er mir
   under dem ampt as wol getan het. Azo las siu mir'n." Strauch, pp. 53–54;
   Hindsley p. 114.

CHAPTER 10

THE EROSION OF A MONOPOLY:
GERMAN RELIGIOUS LITERATURE
IN THE FIFTEENTH CENTURY

Werner Williams-Krapp

In the fifteenth century the production and reception of vernacular literature in the German-speaking world veritably exploded. The primary factor for this revolutionary development was the desire of the *simplices* (the unlearned and semi-learned) for religious literature for independent reading. More than 80 percent of all extant manuscripts written in German and Dutch contain religious literature; a similar percentage applies to the production of the printers. Approximately three thousand authors and anonymous works offering spiritual literature belong to the fifteenth and early sixteenth centuries.[1] In the context of social history the great popularity of religious writing is hardly surprising. At no other time were the peoples of the Holy Roman Empire so acutely focused on their personal salvation, so intensely interested in religious matters, and at no other time was the lay elite so strongly supportive of church reform. This, in turn, generated the production of works with a clear instructional character and unequivocal lessons for a pious life. Since at the same time general education and literacy were increasingly valued and even considered prestigious by the laity, especially in an urban milieu, there was a growing hunger among these newly educated for a more thorough knowledge regarding questions of faith. There are testimonies, for example, that laypersons actually borrowed books from monasteries, such as the Charterhouse at Basle, or used the libraries in the monasteries themselves; an example is the Benedictine monastery of St. Ulrich and St. Afra in Augsburg where the commotion caused by lay readers seriously disturbed the normal life in the cloister.[2]

The establishment of church- and city-run schools in late medieval towns, which educated the children of the middle class—even private tutors are frequently mentioned as teachers—created the fertile ground that led to the reception of more demanding spiritual writings, a reception that transcended class boundaries. Even the poorer craftsmen are reported to have made great sacrifices in order to make at least elementary education possible for their offspring. Looking at the vast data concerning the transmission of the most widely disseminated works of religious literature, we find that those who could read and could afford to be book owners— nuns, the semireligious and prosperous laypersons—essentially read the same works. Books written on paper, which was enormously cheaper than vellum, were in the price range even craftsmen could now afford.

A special aspect of the literary production in this period was the fact that highly learned men as well as high-ranking church officials, both in the north and in the south, could be counted among the most important vernacular authors. They were members of the secular and regular clergy who devoted themselves with immense vigor to a wide-ranging reform of the church *in capite et in membris* and subscribed to a new direction in theology, which Berndt Hamm has called "theology of piety"[3] and Georg Steer "practical scholastics."[4] This theology had primarily a practical/pastoral orientation and was propagated especially by Jean Gerson (1363–1429), a pioneer of conciliar thought and radical church reform. It sought to breach the huge gap between sterile late scholasticism and the concerns of everyday piety; it put aside the purely academic "pulpit theology" and committed itself to adapting university knowledge to the everyday needs of those who had chosen to live pious lives, and thus aimed to achieve a truly pastoral theology.

The decisive turn of the learned to pastoral concerns led to innovative strategies in educating and edifying the faithful, the most revolutionary being the implementation of vernacular literature on a broad scale as the most important medium for the programmatic conveyance of this "theology of piety" to the—in the medieval sense—semieducated. The theological legitimization of the hitherto forbidden independent reading of religious literature in the vernacular on the part of semiliterate *simplices* broke down the rigid educational barriers characteristic of the Christian Middle Ages. Even German translations of the Bible, still to a large extent completely forbidden by most church authorities in the fifteenth century, were, for example, benignly tolerated in cloisters of the reformed female orders.[5]

As was to be expected, some rigorists, alarmed by the erosion of the clerical monopoly on religious education, fought relentlessly in the hope of stemming the tide. But in the end, any call to suppress the immense diffusion of vernacular literature was a futile attempt at stopping what had long become irreversible reality. The lament of a hopeless Catholic traditionalist, Friedrich Staphylus, in 1562, that "nowadays everyone wants to read, . . . even such books as the Bible [in the vernacular]"[6] is a clear indication of the revolutionary changes that had transpired in general education within the German-speaking world by the time of the Reformation.

Especially the reformed clergy clearly recognized the dynamics of this revolution in education and acted upon it. Traditionally the church had had great reservations against the private reading of vernacular spiritual literature on the part of the *illiterati,* but now the reformers actively supported the use of religious writings, seeing it as an extremely useful tool in monastic as well as in lay pastoral care. As early as the 1420s there is evidence that urban laypersons were explicitly encouraged from the pulpit to immerse themselves seriously and independently in spiritual works.

In the *niderlant,* comprising the German-speaking north and the present-day Benelux countries, the spiritual reform movement of the *Devotio moderna,* originating in the Netherlands and immensely popular among the clergy as well as the laity, propagated new and highly influential forms of spirituality and fundamental church reform. As in the south, the rejection of forms of scholasticism not concretely dealing with the needs of the faithful was of prime importance for this movement. The devout were encouraged to search for a simple path toward God within their own souls by turning to their own experience, activating their affective powers, and practicing individual meditation. The central tenet of their piety was to follow in the footsteps of Christ's humility.[7] The movement's most influential work, the *Imitatio Christi* by Thomas a Kempis, which deals in depth with these concepts, became one of the most widely disseminated works in all of Christian literature.

The production and dissemination of religious texts in the vernacular played a central role in the *Devotio moderna.* Since the majority of the writings of the *Devotio moderna* originated in the Netherlands, it was primarily Dutch spiritual literature that was read in the areas under the influence of this movement, including all of Middle Franconia and northern Germany. Copying religious texts for others was one of the most important sources of income for the adherents of the *Devotio moderna,* since this activity was also considered to be an ideal spiritual exercise. Remarkably, the southern German-speaking regions were little affected by this movement.[8]

In order to further its religious educational initiatives in the south, the reformed clergy composed appropriate texts and also promoted older works considered to be in line with the program of reform. Thus a number of texts originating in the circles of thirteenth- and fourteenth-century "German mysticism" were disseminated widely, particularly in the monastic milieu.

Examples are the works of Heinrich Seuse, Johannes Tauler, and Marquard of Lindau as well as the *Alemannische Vitaspatrum*.[9] Seuse's *Büchlein der ewigen Weisheit* [Little Book of Eternal Wisdom], a compendium of spiritual guidance as well as a sort of guideline for the contemplation of suffering in imitation of the tortured Christ, experienced a wider manuscript diffusion than any other medieval German text (approximately 400 extant manuscripts).

Among the works composed by the reformed clergy we find above all translations of works that had hitherto been reserved for the learned clergy, but also an impressive body of original works written in the vernacular. Belonging to the group of "theologians of piety" in the late fourteenth and fifteenth centuries were such important authors as Heinrich of Langenstein, Nikolaus of Dinkelsbühl, Johannes Nider, and Geiler of Kaysersberg. They created either Latin models meant for translation into the vernacular or composed works directly in German. Their patrons often were laypersons.

One of the most important projects of the reformed clergy was the (sometimes forced) return to a strict adherence to monastic rules within both men's and women's convents, a movement that extended to almost all of the monastic orders. This project had far-reaching consequences for the production and transregional dissemination of religious literature in the vernacular. A particularly strong literary engagement could be found among the Dominicans, Benedictines, and Franciscans in the south, and in the north among the semireligious Brothers and Sisters of the Common Life, Augustinian canons and canonesses, Franciscan Tertiaries, and other minor orders, who were all inspired by the *Devotio moderna*. The establishment of libraries in reformed convents was generally one of the first points on the reform agenda. Through a network of reformed monastic houses, religious works then found their way from town to town, from region to region, to end up finally also in the libraries of laypersons.[10]

The goals of the "theology of piety" and the reformed clergy were clearly of a very conservative and restorative nature. The divulgence of the secrets of the learned world to the semieducated in a pastoral context should not however be understood as a propagation of a gradual softening of the concept of a very strict hierarchy within the church. Just the opposite is the case. The reform of the church was aimed at restrengthening the essential immutability and integrity of the church's hierarchical structure. Especially in catechetical literature it was generally stressed that absolute trust in qualified members of the clergy was a major element in the quest for salvation. For this reason the majority of the German spiritual works composed in the fifteenth century transmit primarily elementary religious knowledge. The reception of vernacular literature was clearly not to be misunderstood as a means of actually becoming independent of the authority of the clergy.

Catechetical Writings

Although the reformed clergy strove to satisfy the desire for theological knowledge among the laity with a truly remarkable zeal, there could be no question that as far as the quality and extent of the transmitted theological knowledge were concerned, a definite distance between the clergy and the *simplices* was to be maintained. This applied particularly to everything dealing with the Bible. The independent reading of the Scriptures on the part of the unlearned was not only considered pointless—since they lacked the education for understanding them properly—but also potentially dangerous to the faith and the church, as many heresies that relied on an erroneous understanding of the Scriptures, or in any case a reading limited to the literal sense, had demonstrated again and again. In spite of interdictions, such as the one by the archbishop of Mainz forbidding the production and proliferation of vernacular Bibles in 1485, many manuscripts and twelve different printings of German Bible translations from the fourteenth century circulated widely, though they were not among the great bestsellers of the fifteenth and early sixteenth centuries. Apparently even laypersons came to the conclusion that it was not absolutely necessary to read the Bible independently in order to acquire true faith and piety.[11]

Ideal readings for the unlearned were rather those widely diffused works that offered an introduction to the basic tenets of the faith and their correct perception in everyday life. These included elucidations of the Credo, Paternoster, Ave Maria, the secrets of the mass and the Eucharist, as well as teachings on sin or the preparation for death, clear instructions for confession, and similar texts.[12] Thus the influential Dominican reformer Johannes Nider contrasted the *spitzigen subtilen buchern* (that is, books concerned with subtle theological questions, especially from mystical circles) with those works he considered ideal for lay reading, *die von den zechen gebott sagen oder des gelich* (which deal with the Ten Commandments or similar topics).[13]

A good illustration of the far-reaching consequences of ecclesiastical reform initiatives and of the victorious campaign of the theology of piety for the production and diffusion of vernacular religious literature can be found in the writings of the so-called Viennese School.[14] The spiritual center of this school, which was a relatively clearly defined group of translators and authors of vernacular religious literature, was the University of Vienna, reorganized in 1384 by the famous theologian Heinrich of Langenstein (d. 1397), whom Duke Albrecht III had lured away from the Sorbonne and who quickly led the university to great scholarly renown. As a foundation of the Habsburgs, the university was under special ducal protection. The Habsburgs therefore considered the university their own, basked in its glory, and sometimes used it for their own political goals. An academic-courtly culture was thus created in Vienna that could compete with the court of the Luxemburgs in Prague. This culture led to literary experiments within the program of the theology of piety and encouraged new impulses for lay education.

Vienna was also at the origin of a vital Benedictine reform movement, centered around the monastery of Melk. The driving force here was Heinrich of Langenstein's famous student Nikolaus of Dinkelsbühl. In the framework of this reform, texts in German played an important role, especially since Benedictine sisters and lay brothers, generally charged with manual labor, also had to be supplied with catechetical and edifying works in line with the new strict observance.

At the Viennese court, religious zeal combined with the desire to become better acquainted with the curriculum of the university. It seems that these interests were satisfied eagerly by local academics who composed a large number of works explicitly conceptualized for laypeople. An impressive number of predominantly catechetical works were created at the suggestion of or commissioned by the court or members of the ducal council. In these texts, instruction in the basic questions of the faith went hand in hand with the conveyance of simplified scholastic teachings.

The most successful representative of these efforts was the widely disseminated treatise on sin and contrition *Erchantnuzz der sünd* [The Recognition of Sin], attributed to Heinrich of Langenstein and preserved in more than eighty manuscripts. While many manuscripts testify to Heinrich's authorship, it remains unclear whether this applies to a lost Latin original, the German text, or both. One of the later manuscripts, originating in northern Bavaria, designates the Viennese professor and later bishop of Constance, Marquard of Randeck, as the text's translator.[15]

With this work, dedicated to Duke Albrecht, Heinrich inaugurates the Viennese School and at the same time offers a conceptual model for lay education within the program of the theology of piety. The work is filled with quotes from eminent theologians. On the one hand this demonstrates that the semi-learned were taken somewhat seriously intellectually; on the other hand, in view of the work's clear didactic character, this profusion of quotes also demonstrates to the reader the unbridgeable gap between the highly learned teacher and the semiliterate pupil. This didactic strategy is a distinctive feature of religious instructional literature in the fifteenth century, although the mania for excessive quotations typical of the Viennese School did not catch on everywhere.

The fifteenth-century desire to form *summae* and to assemble knowledge encyclopedically transcended spiritual literature and, in particular, influenced the catechetical literature produced in Vienna. The monumental catechetical *summa* produced for the court by Ulrich of Pottenstein (ca. 1360–1416–1417), fills approximately twelve hundred densely covered folio sheets. It contains extensive commentaries on the Paternoster, Ave Maria, Credo, Magnificat, and Decalogue, interspersed with many digressions, some of them offering interpretations from the perspective of ecclesiastical law. With this work Ulrich strives to offer meaningful readings to laypersons and at the same time divert their literary interests away from the very popular secular epics.[16]

Ulrich's "encyclopedia" dealing with questions of faith and morals is much more than a handbook for everyday religious life. It does not restrict itself to simple explanations of basic questions of faith but treats in detail such topics as the sacraments; the education of confessors; heretics; and abuses in monasteries as well as within the secular clergy and the nobility. Ulrich supports his arguments with masses of learned quotations. For instance, in his elucidation of the first commandment alone, he makes use of three thousand quotes. The limited diffusion of Ulrich's work (eleven manuscripts restricted to the Austrian territories) suggests that it did not respond to a true need, or perhaps that it was aimed from the outset at a very limited and relatively sophisticated target audience.

Ulrich's stylistic and linguistic reflections are quite remarkable: He forgoes the German used in elitist circles (*aygen dewtsch*), closely linked to Latin, and instead writes in everyday language (*nach des lanndes gewonhait*) because he hopes for a wide reception of his works.[17]

Another Viennese writer, Thomas Peuntner,[18] was also aiming for catechetical completeness in his *œuvre,* though not with the intention of creating a *summa.* Peuntner, a student of Nikolaus of Dinkelsbühl, was a priest and preacher at the ducal court in Vienna. He was the author of disquisitions on the Paternoster and Ave Maria, of a confessional tract including an exegesis of the Decalogue, and a treatise on the *ars moriendi* (art of dying), as well as didactic works for the faithful, combining several catechetical treatises. His most widely diffused work is the *Büchlein von der Liebhabung Gottes* [Little Book on Loving God], extant in seventy-two manuscripts and nine printed versions, which explains how and why human beings should love God, a fundamental theme in almost all of Peuntner's works. The works of his teacher, Nikolaus, who in his written sermons strove to transpose catechetical subjects into edifying ones, formed the basis for Peuntner's writings. Peuntner also used commentaries on the basic tenets of the faith as points of departure for his more general teachings on a pious life.

The last phase of activity of the Viennese School produced Stephan of Landskron's *Himmelstrass* [The Road to Heaven], a catechetical compendium, that features transcriptions (many of them word for word) of several authors. This work was considerably easier to handle than the voluminous *summa* of Ulrich of Pottenstein and it was probably for that reason that it was much more widely diffused, especially in printed form. An extensive table of contents with brief descriptions of each chapter facilitated its use as a reference work. Stephan, like other Viennese authors, aimed for a broader audience; he wanted his text to serve as a convenient book of advice and self-help for all those who searched for the path to salvation. Only a thorough knowledge of the faith can prepare these seekers for proper action.

The writings of the Viennese School represent but one, if very important, segment of the large quantity of similarly conceived catechetical literature of the late fourteenth and fifteenth centuries. Like the works just discussed, this literature also pursues the far-reaching goal of convincing its readers, through extensive introductions to the fundamental tenets of the faith, that they can search for the salvation of their souls only within the church, within its dogmas and moral teachings. Undoubtedly, this attitude implied a strengthening of the clerics' role, a significant goal of the reformers.

Collections of Sermons for Reading

Closely related to catechetical treatises are treatises in the form of sermons, one of the reformed clergy's most often used genres for the pastoral care of the semiliterate.[19] The sermons typical for the fifteenth century generally offer elucidations of basic religious issues or contain practical teachings attuned to the everyday lives of their audience. Topics such as marriage, the education of children, and the desire for wealth are discussed, with the lessons generally supported by quotes from canonical authors, and almost always linked to clear instructions for proper Christian behavior. Some of the often voluminous cycles were written by very prominent authors and frequently reflect sermons they had actually preached from the pulpit.

Since in the area of written sermons we are confronted by an immense amount of manuscripts that even today have only been partially catalogued and analyzed by scholars, we will consider only three of the most important fifteenth-century cycles: the model sermons by Nikolaus of Dinkelsbühl, originally written in Latin and translated into German by one of his students, the *Twenty-Four Golden Harps* by Johannes Nider, and the sermon texts of Johann Geiler of Kaysersberg. Nikolaus and Geiler were both secular clerics, heavily invested in church reform; the Dominican Nider was one of the most influential personages in fifteenth-century church politics.

Within the framework of his reform efforts Nikolaus of Dinkelsbühl (ca. 1360–1433) composed several voluminous collections of model sermons, meant to provide suggestions and exemplary texts for the clergy's preparation of their preaching on Sundays and holidays. The Latin works circulated widely and were even printed, due to their author's great reputation. Around 1420, perhaps in collaboration with Nikolaus, a student[20] translated and adapted the "Sermons for the Year" and the "Tractatus octo," probably for priests, since the language often alternates between German and Latin. But these works were also read by the nobility and in male and female monasteries, despite their size of four hundred to five hundred folio leaves.

In the two German cycles, the true Christian way of life is extensively described, explained, and illustrated by means of examples (*exempel*). Linked to this is the use of a vast number of quotations from the canonical authors, meant on the one hand to illuminate specific cases and on the other to provide didactic or mnemonic formulas that would help readers to commit the catechetical teachings to their memories.

Of special interest is the inclusion of a sermon in praise of the University of Vienna, probably not authored by Nikolaus. In this text, the Nikolaus-redactor, as he is called, takes as a point of departure the story of Jesus in the temple (Lk 2:33–40) and thus tries to make transparent to the *simplices* the usefulness of the university and its reform program. The scholars know only too well "how much damage has been done to people by the error of the papal schism. . . . The harmful divisions . . . , which have damaged holy Christendom for so many years, were so awful that one did not dare describe them to the people."[21]

Of course, the sermon claims, the university is important for the education of the clergy: Only the university permits a truly substantial study of the Bible (*soliche ding vindt man nicht da haim in den chlain schuelen* [such things can not be found at home in the small schools]), providing a weapon in the fight against heresy (*von wiclefisten vnd den hussonyten* [against the Wycliffites and Hussites]). In addition, at the university, scholars plan "how to reform the monasteries and to bring them back from their foolish lives to the blessed lives of old, as established by the holy fathers" (*wie man die chlöster solt reformieren vnd widerbringen von irm toräten leben auf das alt selig leben, das die heiligen veter aufgesetzt haben*).

Since this is a model sermon, the whole text is put into the mouth of a simple priest (*ainuoltigen priester*), who constantly bewails his incompetence when it comes to more learned questions. He for his part puts his entire confidence into the university and thanks God that "the well-born dukes of Austria have brought this school here and are protecting it" (*die hochgeborenen fürsten von Osterreich . . . die schuol herpracht haben vnd noch beschirmen*).

The work of another writer from the Viennese school, the *Twenty-Four Harps* by the Dominican Johannes Nider (ca. 1380–1428)[22] became a big success in monastic as well as in lay circles. Nider received his doctorate as a student of Franz of Retz in Vienna and had two stints as a professor there.

His extensive engagement in church politics was primarily devoted to the reform of his order—a goal he pursued tirelessly—but he was also one of the most prominent organizers of the Council of Basel, where he was entrusted with negotiations with the Hussites. Nider's activities transcended those of an activist in church politics; he composed a wide-ranging Latin and German *œuvre,* which made him into one of the most frequently cited authorities in fifteenth-century Germany. In this light we can consider Nider as a kind of ideal model of the new practice-oriented reform theologian who, besides his scholarly activities, eagerly engaged in the religious education of the *simplices.* Even more than Nikolaus of Dinkelsbühl, then, who wrote only in Latin, Nider, through his vast original compositions in German, can be seen as a member of the reform movement who is profoundly committed to the improvement of lay literacy.

The bases for the *Harps,* which were disseminated (remarkably mostly without any indication of their author) as a cycle of treatises, were a series of sermons given by Nider in Nuremberg in the 1420s, probably before a broad audience. Serial sermons were popular with the reformed clergy; they permitted a preacher to present a compact program of religious education not necessarily related to the liturgy and passed on within a limited time frame. Nider's twenty-four sermons are not based on biblical themes but on the sayings of the Desert Fathers, which Nider took from Cassian's *Twenty-Four Conlationes,* one of the central works of the monastic movement. This is remarkable because Nider was not addressing an exclusively monastic audience; but considering the spirit of Nider's teachings, this choice is not surprising.

Nider's religious views of the world are marked by a rigorous severity; his goal is to bring the monastic and lay ways of life closer together. In Nider's "monasticized" lay world, people should, for instance, do without comfortable beds and clothes, because they induce lust; laypeople should be willing to practice more severe forms of asceticism, and married couples should commit themselves to a chaste marriage after having produced their offspring. It goes without saying that the soul's salvation can be achieved only through the faithful's absolute subordination to qualified pastors.

The *Harps* was among the most popular didactic writings in the fifteenth century: It was transmitted in an impressive number of manuscripts and nine different printings. The library of Emperor Maximilian I contained no fewer than four copies of this text.

One of the most famous preachers of this pre-Reformation century was the secular priest Johann Geiler of Kaysersberg (1445–1510), active at the Strassburg cathedral. Like Nider, who incidentally was one of Geiler's models, he was a relentless advocate of profound church reform as well as a severe critic of clerical abuses. His extraordinary rhetorical and didactic talents gripped his audience; his performances were so impressive that his listeners often transcribed what he said or took his personal notes as a basis for transcriptions. Only a part of the many works attributed to Geiler, generally printed, was actually authorized by him.

Geiler was not an especially independent theological thinker—despite his initially promising university career—but rather committed himself to teaching the modern theology of others to the faithful. He was especially intent on bringing the works of Jean Gerson to his audience's attention; he translated them and used them as a basis for many of his sermons. Nider's *Formicarius* [The Ant Hill] and Sebastian Brant's *Narrenschiff* [Ship of Fools] also served as bases for his serial sermons *Die Emeis* [The Ants] and *Doctor Keiserspergs Narrenschiff* [Doctor Keisersperg's Ship of Fools].

A perfect example of Geiler's adaptation of Gerson are the serial sermons of the *Berg des Schauens* [Mountain of Contemplation], which Geiler presented before a rapt audience during a visit to Augsburg in 1488.[23] For about three months, he preached almost daily in Augsburg (*predigt er fast all tag ze Augspurg*), as the chaplain of the Augsburg bishop noted. His principal source is Gerson's *De monte contemplacionis,* a treatise on perfection, composed by the Parisian chancellor for a community of semireligious women, which plots the soul's ascent up to the very rare—but possible— mystical union. Geiler follows his model very faithfully as far as the substance of its teachings is concerned, but he illustrates Gerson's arguments with a language that can sometimes be quite crude, as well as with lively images and a multitude of examples.

The moral rigor of charismatic reformers like Geiler was often expressed in public criticism of his fellow clerics or important figures in the church hierarchy. This stance probably contributed to the church's loss of authority in lay circles and to the strengthening of laypeople's independence in religious matters, especially in the cities. From this perspective, influential moral authorities like Geiler were important precursors of the success of another "reformed cleric," Martin Luther.

Narrative Edifying Literature

Among the numerous religious narratives that were widely disseminated in the fifteenth century (such as collections of exemplary stories and fables), saints' lives and legendaries stand out,[24] primarily because the veneration of the saints reached its absolute medieval peak in this era. Saints were primarily seen as accessible mediators before God's throne; they were venerated as models and especially as intercessors in various spheres of life where they became patrons of just about any ailment, any everyday situation or professional group. As outcroppings of this vastly exaggerated veneration of the saints and their relics almost every child received a saint's name, the days of the year were counted by the saints' feast days, etc. The interest in relics often reached absurd levels.

The immense popularity of saints' lives in the fifteenth century was also due to intense promotional activities on the part of the church. Saints' lives, which conveyed unequivocal messages, were seen as the ideal type of narrative literature for the *simplices,* far more suitable than the Bible. This helps to explain why legends were transmitted much more widely than translations of the Bible. Approximately three thousand manuscripts from the fourteenth and fifteenth centuries containing legends prove very clearly that this genre surpassed all other narrative literature of the time in popularity.

In the context of the saints' lives we can once again observe particularly well the preference of the late Middle Ages for the compiling of *summae.* The most common form of the fifteenth-century legend is that of a simple prose text, reduced to a narrative minimum and concise style, and organized in large legendaries; an appendix of miracles, often considerably longer than the life itself, is a standard part of the text. The *Legenda aurea* [Golden Legend] by Jacobus of Voragine, by far the most popular legendary of the Middle Ages, is also of special significance for German hagiography. This extremely successful work, extant in over one thousand manuscripts, was translated into German more or less completely eight times and twice into Dutch. Two of these translations, the *Alsatian Legenda aurea* and the *Southern Netherlandish Legenda aurea,* experienced an immense diffusion through the networks of the monastic reform movement in the Alemannic regions and those areas where the *Devotio moderna* flourished, including the German north. It can be said that every reformed convent library possessed at least one legendary; any layperson who owned books was certain to possess a collection of saints' lives.

By the fifteenth century the contents of the *Legenda aurea* translations frequently offered insufficient material for the daily readings at mealtimes in the female convents, which were considered essential for the success of any reform. In addition, the absence of German saints in the original *Legenda aurea*—which had a clear bias toward the Mediterranean saints—was considered a major drawback. For this reason and as a contribution to the reform effort within his order, a Dominican from Nuremberg composed at the beginning of the fifteenth century *Der Heiligen Leben* [The Lives of the Saints], the most widely diffused vernacular legendary in all of medieval Europe.[25] Among the two hundred fifty-one legends were numerous lives of saints from central Europe and especially from southern Germany. It was only the Reformation and in particular a polemical tract by Luther, directed against this very legendary, that put a stop to its popularity. By then, it was circulating in innumerable manuscripts (over two hundred are extant) and forty-one High and Low German printed editions. These numbers allow a safe estimate of thirty to forty thousand copies circulating in the fifteenth and sixteenth centuries. The areas reached by this absolute bestseller extended beyond the German-speaking world to the Netherlands as well as to Scandinavia (even to Iceland), where it was sold by merchants from Lübeck. There was basically no serious competition for *Der Heiligen Leben* when it came to the spreading of hagiographic knowledge to the *illiterati* in the era of printing.

In *Der Heiligen Leben* the legends were shaped in the context of the cult of the saints as was typical for the late medieval period: On the one hand, they propagate an emotional intimacy with the saints by attributing to them a constant availability for assistance and comfort. On the other hand, the saints are not portrayed as figures that can be understood from a human perspective: Rather than being seen primarily as pious models, as intended by theology, they appear as miracle workers, far removed from humanity, and while they demonstrate God's omnipotence and goodness, they are mostly depicted as self-sufficient superhuman beings. It is also less a question of seeing the saints as mediators between human beings and God but rather as independent agents who can perform even spectacular miracles and promise protection and safety. As a result, the version of a given saint's life in legendaries like *Der Heiligen Leben* not only responded to the need of determining a clearly specified area of competence for a saint, but also propagated through its wide diffusion among the *illiterati* an image of the saint as a personal and extremely effective helper. In the appendices of miracles the "mechanism of request heard and request granted"[26] is clearly demonstrated to the reader. At the same time, in *Der Heiligen Leben* we also observe an avoidance of the kind of theological commentaries as well as of any reservations about the "truth" of episodes in a given life or of certain miracles, which can often be found in the *Legenda aurea*.

This was exactly the type of veneration of the saints rejected by the sixteenth-century reformers. For this reason the legendaries became special and rewarding targets: Luther considered the Catholic cult of the saints as a form of idolatry, strongly promoted through the "liegends" (*lügenden*), as he called them. And indeed, in the vernacular didactic literature of the fifteenth century there are basically no reservations against the excesses of the veneration of saints and relics criticized by Luther. Undoubtedly he was justified in using of all things a legend from *Der Heiligen Leben,* which for him was a prime example of the way the church had misled the faithful, in order to support his biting criticism in 1535.

Contemplative and Mystical Texts

About 80 percent of the manuscripts containing the works of Meister Eckhart, Heinrich Seuse (Suso), Johannes Tauler, and other fourteenth-century authors of mystical or mystagogical literature date from the fifteenth century; for the *Sisterbooks* the only manuscripts we have date from this period. This finding does not mean that at this time there was a renewed flourishing of the female religious movement characterized by the desire for mystical experiences—quite the contrary. The reformed clergy propagating the diffusion of these texts made every effort not to give new life to the spiritual excesses of the previous century.[27] But we should not be surprised that Seuse and the other Dominican "life masters" (*lebmeister*) were among the most widely disseminated authors in monastic circles. For, contrary to common scholarly opinion, these authors did not support the striving for mystical experiences among women, but rather used their didactic skills and careful arguments to effect a removal of elements of (pseudo-mystical) fantasy and harsh ascesis from spirituality. In the context of the *Devotio moderna* we encounter a similarly skeptical attitude toward mystical spirituality.[28]

Reformers like Nider, an ardent admirer of Seuse, did not consider the works of his Dominican brethren a danger to women but rather furthered their dissemination. But when it came to the works authored by the female Dominican mystics themselves, the reformed clergy favored the *Sisterbooks,* which did not highlight so much individual experiences—as did, for example, the lives of Christina and Margarete Ebner, Elsbeth of Oye, and others—but rather divine demonstrations of Godly grace, which had been accorded to those women who, in the early days of their convents, had led exemplary lives, totally devoted to their monastic community.

The Dominican chronicler of monastic life Johannes Meyer (1422–1485) even reedited some of the *Sisterbooks* (those of Katharinental, Töss, and Oetenbach) but warned explicitly that one should not put too much faith into the divine acts of grace described therein. Two reasons, he says, prevented him from writing too much about *gesicht* (visions) and *offenbarung* (revelations): firstly, because it is more edifying to write about the virtues than about *offenbarungen, trömen, und erschinungen* (revelations, dreams, and apparitions), and secondly, because the danger of being deceived by the devil in these kinds of experiences is immense. He further states that the religious egocentricity of female ecstatics diverts attention from the great task of reform, is a sign of arrogance, and leads to personal unhappiness.[29] Meyer himself composed a "chronicle" of the Alsatian Dominican convent in Schönensteinbach, the first reformed female house, and he did so exactly in the style of the *Sisterbooks.*

The reformed Dominican Eberhard Mardach from Nuremberg targets the risks for the salvation of the soul posed by meditation on the Passion in his *Sendbrief von wahrer Andacht* (Missive on True Devotion) of 1422. He believes that a misguided immersion into the *passio Cristi* leads to women being enraptured, to see the figure of Christ hanging on the cross and to be under the impression that He speaks with them from there.[30] Mardach's attitude toward mystical spirituality can be seen as typical for the reformed clergy. For him, exaggerated asceticism and the striving for mystical union are an evil poison for a thriving monastic communal life; he condemns any form of egocentric spirituality. In particular, he considers the concentration on Christ's Passion, so central to Dominican mysticism, to be one of the most important sources of spiritual danger.

There were numerous, often very detailed, treatises on the Passion—of which the *Extendit manum* (He extends His Hand; Gn 22:10) tractate by Heinrich of St. Gallen was the most widely diffused (over two hundred extant manuscripts)—that strove to direct the meditation on the Passion into acceptable channels and to prevent the straying of the mind to private fantasies.

As in the literature dealing with the discernment of spirits, in the Dominican missives the devil is often accused of being at the origin of supernatural experiences. This is not surprising, as the "dealings of the devil" was a highly popular topic in the fifteenth century. In the *Sendbrief vom Betrug teuflischer Erscheinungen* [Missive on the Deception Caused by Devilish Apparitions], a Dominican, perhaps from Nuremberg, qualifies mystical experiences as dangerous mischief, which must be met with decisive dissuasion and sometimes with even more concrete measures. Ecstatic women should be lifted up and brought out of their trances and then be instructed on their errors.[31] According to him, the devil is always the instigator of visions and auditions, something the author documents through case histories from the diocese of Bamberg, to which Nuremberg belongs.

It is not certain if the missive refers to the laywoman Katharina Tucher from Neumarkt (near Nuremberg), who for three years (1418–1420) kept a sort of diary recording her mystical experiences.[32] This unique document gives us insights into how mystical literature could influence experience— Katharina is inspired by various fourteenth-century works—as well as into the way mystical spirituality could help in dealing with an obviously troubled life. In one mystical experience, for instance, Christ orders her to stop drinking.

Johannes Nider as well was deeply concerned with the more extreme forms of female piety. In his famous Latin treatise, the aforementioned *Formicarius,* he comments on the case of a mother and daughter who were both inclined toward mystical piety. The mother, Margareta of Kenzingen, always entrusted herself to the advice of her pastors and led an exemplary "reformed" monastic life. Her special state of grace never disturbed the communal daily life. It was quite different with her daughter, Magdalena of Freiburg: She showed early on a preference for extreme asceticism and the capacity of having visions, but she never sought the advice of proven pastors. One day she even predicted her own death, but did not succeed in performing this miracle in front of the assembled town notables. Nider has no doubt that this was the devil's work.[33]

The Dominican campaign against mystical piety is somewhat surprising, since the initiator of the reform movement within the order was herself a mystic: Catherine of Siena. But it is important to remember that authors like Nider do not deny mystical piety completely but simply believe that true divinely sent grace is an extremely rare phenomenon. In addition, Catherine's lifelong efforts were—according to Raymond of Capua—not devoted to her own elevation but to the abolition of the Great Schism and the reform of her order.

Among the few known fifteenth-century mystical women, Elsbeth Achler stands out. She had a reputation for sanctity in her time; to this day there are pilgrimages to her grave in Reute near Lake Constance. Her confessor Konrad Kügelin, an ardent adherent of the reform movement, composed a *vita* for Elsbeth that helped establish her cult and that was modeled heavily on the Life of Catherine of Siena.[34] Kügelin stylizes Elsbeth as a "reform mystic," that is, a German Catherine of Siena, with the goal of mobilizing the forces of renewal. Kügelin was certainly convinced of Elsbeth's putative sanctity and therefore considered rather generous hagiographic borrowings as totally legitimate. After all, Elsbeth lived an exemplary monastic life, actually overfulfilling the ideals espoused by the Dominican reform movement, which Catherine had initiated. She was completely obedient and humble at all times and, of course, always followed the advice of her male spiritual mentor. In other words, she is portrayed as being quite the opposite of the German women mystics of the thirteenth and fourteenth centuries.

The life of Ursula Haider, a member of the order of St. Clare in Villingen in the Black Forest, illustrates the spirit of reform particularly well. Ursula was reputed to have been a pupil of Elsbeth Achler and, after her successful work in another convent, was asked by the city council of Villingen to reform the local house, the Bickenkloster. Ursula wanted to keep silent about her spiritual life, which fit the image of a selfless reformer. Her goal was to create a communal life without piety competitions that could disturb its harmony. Ursula's extraordinary devotion to the observance movement was probably the main reason for the mystic's hagiographic transfiguration on the part of her biographer Juliana Ernestin (1637–1638). In the *Chronik des Bickenklosters* [Chronicle of the Bicken Convent], a work based on some serious misunderstandings, the mystical experiences of both Elsbeth and Ursula are shown to be not only the result of extraordinary piety but also a divine reward for their exemplary reformist activities.[35] "True" piety, the kind that leads to true perfection, was predicated on the eager observance of rules and norms. This view was shared by most reformers. As a consequence, a "true"—or divinely sanctioned—state of grace was only possible in a milieu infused with the spirit of reform.

Religious Education as a Prerequisite for the Reformation

By the end of the fifteenth century the use of the vernacular was widespread in practically all areas of knowledge, public discourse, and administration. This had led to a certain democratization of knowledge, thereby slowly eroding the absolute authority of the clergy in the eyes of the urban semiliterate. The rise of humanism in the latter part of the fifteenth century, with members of the laity often belonging to its most prominent adherents, is definite evidence of this erosion. Laypersons were often far better educated than the local clergy. This gradual process of emancipation from rigorous church domination of all learning, coupled with the enormous possibilities for public discourse that the invention of modern printing techniques made available, set the stage for the Reformation. An intensely pious and well-read laity had become critical and extremely watchful of deficiencies in the church. In most cases, powerful members of the urban laity had demanded of the various orders that they reform their local convents. Apologetical digressions by learned authors aimed at dispelling popular doubts concerning certain aspects of church teaching can frequently be found in vernacular literature, thereby showing that the laity was no longer blindly accepting all works written by the clergy. Martin Luther could rely on a rather well-read and critical urban readership among the urban elites as he began his quest for church reform, a readership that had educated itself to a large extent through its independent study of religious literature in the vernacular.[36]

Notes

1. See Kurt Ruh, "Geistliche Prosa," in Willi Erzgräber, ed., *Europäisches Spätmittelalter*, Neues Handbuch der Literaturwissenschaft 8 (Wiesbaden: Athenaion, 1978), pp. 565–605, and the volume edited by Ruh, Überlieferungsgeschichtliche Prosaforschung (Tübingen: Niemeyer, 1985). Also see Werner Williams-Krapp, "Fifteenth Century German Religious Literature in its Social Context," *Etudes germano-africaines* (Dakar, Senegal) 15/16 (1997–1998): 113–120, and Williams-Krapp, "'Alles volck will in yetziger zit lesen vnd schriben'. Zur literarischen Laienunterweisung im 15. und frühen 16. Jahrhundert," in *Rottenburger Jahrbuch für Kirchengeschichte* 16 (Sigmaringen: Thorbecke, 1997), pp. 11–22. Of course, in the context of this article only a very small but representative sample of this enormous body of literature can be considered.

2. See Kurt Ruh, "Versuch einer Begriffsbestimmung von 'städtischer Literatur' im deutschen Spätmittelalter," in Ruh, *Kleine Schriften*, vol. 1 (Berlin/New York: de Gruyter 1984), pp. 214–33, and the volume edited by Johannes Janota and Werner Williams-Krapp, *Literarisches Leben in Augsburg während des 15. Jahrhunderts*. Studia Augustana 7 (Tübingen: Niemeyer1995).

3. See Berndt Hamm, *Frömmigkeitstheologie am Anfang des 16. Jahrhunderts: Studien zu Johannes von Paltz und seinem Umkreis*. Beiträge zur historischen Theologie 65 (Tübingen: Mohr 1982).

4. See Georg Steer, "Geistliche Prosa," in Ingeborg Glier, ed., *Die deutsche Literatur im späten Mittelalter, 1250–1370* (Munich: Beck, 1987), pp. 306–70.

5. See Werner Williams-Krapp, "Observanzbewegungen, monastische Spiritualität und geistliche Literatur im 15. Jahrhundert," *Internationales Archiv für die Sozialgeschichte der deutschen Literatur* 20 (1995): 1–15; p. 4, n. 11.

6. Williams-Krapp, "Alles volck" (as in n. 1), p. 11.

7. See Erwin Iserloh's article on the Devotio moderna in *Lexikon des Mittelalters*, vol. 3 (Munich/Zurich: Artemis, 1980–1998), cols. 928–30. See also the volume edited by Thom Mertens, *Boeken voor de eeuwigheid. Middelnederlands geestelijk proza* (Amsterdam: Prometheus, 1993).

8. For the circulation of the literature of the Devotio moderna in the south see Kristina Freienhagen-Baumgardt, Hendrik Herps '*Spieghel der Volcomenheit*' *in oberdeutscher Überlieferung. Ein Beitrag zur Rezeptionsgeschichte niederländischer Mystik im oberdeutschen Raum*. Miscellanea Neerlandica XVII (Leuven: Peeters, 1998); for the role of literature within the institutions of the Devotio moderna, see Thomas Kock, *Die Buchkultur der Devotio moderna. Handschriftenproduktion, Literaturversorgung und Bibliotheksaufbau im Zeitalter des Medienwechsels. Tradition—Reform—Innovation*. Studien zur Modernität des Mittelalters 2 (Frankfurt: Lang, 1999).

9. Seuse's German works were the most popular of all "mystical" texts. They are transmitted in over five hundred medieval manuscripts and eight early prints. For the circulation of Seuse's works, see Rüdiger Blumrich, "Die Überlieferung der deutschen Schriften Seuses. Ein Forschungsbericht," in Blumrich and Philipp Kaiser, eds., *Heinrich Seuses Philosophia spiritualis. Quellen, Konzept, Formen und Rezeption. Tagung Eichstätt, 2.–4. Oct., 1991*. Wissensliteratur im Mittelalter 17 (Wiesbaden: Reichert, 1994), pp. 189–201. Surprisingly, the German Vitaspatrum, a truly monastic work, were read in the homes of many laypersons; see Ulla Williams, *Die 'Alemannischen Vitaspatrum.' Untersuchungen und Edition*. Texte und Textgeschichte 45 (Tübingen: Niemeyer, 1996).

10. See Werner Williams-Krapp, "Ordensreform und Literatur im 15. Jahrhundert," *Jahrbuch der Oswald von Wolkenstein-Gesellschaft* 4 (1986–87): 41–51, and Klaus Graf, "Ordensreform und Literatur in Augsburg während des 15. Jahrhunderts," in Janota and Williams-Krapp, eds., *Literarisches Leben in Augsburg* (as in n. 2), pp. 100–159.

11. See Klaus Schreiner, "Laienbildung als Herausforderung für Kirche und Gesellschaft. Religiöse Vorbehalte und soziale Widerstände gegen die Verbreitung von Wissen im späten Mittelalter und in der Reformation," *Zeitschrift für historische Forschung* 11 (1984): 207–354, esp. pp. 287–325; and Schreiner, "Laienfrömmigkeit—Frömmigkeit von Eliten oder Frömmigkeit des Volkes? Zur sozialen Verfasstheit laikaler Frömmigkeitspraxis im späten Mittelalter," in Schreiner, ed., *Laienfrömmigkeit im späten Mittelalter. Formen, Funktionen, politisch-historische Zusammenhänge.* Schriften des Historischen Kollegs. Kolloquien 20 (Munich: Oldenbourg, 1992), pp. 1–78; esp. pp. 72–74.

12. See Egino Weidenhiller, *Untersuchungen zur deutschsprachigen katechetischen Literatur des späten Mittelalters.* Münchener Texte und Untersuchungen 10 (Munich: Beck, 1965); Robert James Bast, *Honor Your Fathers. Catechisms and the Emergence of a Patriarchal Ideology in Germany 1400–1600.* Studies in Medieval and Reformation Thought 63 (Leiden, New York, Cologne: Brill, 1997).

13. See Margit Brand, *Studien zu Johannes Niders deutschen Schriften.* Dissertationes historicae XXIII (Rome: Istituto Storico Domenicano, 1998).

14. See Thomas Hohmann, "'Die recht gelerten maister.' Bemerkungen zur Übersetzungsliteratur der Wiener Schule des Spätmittelalters," in H. Zeman, ed., *Die österreichische Literatur. Ihr Profil von den Anfängen im Mittelalter bis ins 18. Jahrhundert (1050–1750),* vol. 1 (Graz: Adeva, 1986), pp. 349–65.

15. On the authorship of this text see Peter Wiesinger, "Zur Autorschaft und Entstehung des Heinrich von Langenstein zugeschriebenen Traktats 'Erkenntnis der Sünde,'" *Zeitschrift für deutsche Philologie* 97 (1978): 42–60.

16. See Gabriele Baptist-Hlawatsch, ed., *Ulrich von Pottenstein. Dekalog-Auslegung. Das erste Gebot. Text und Quellen.* Texte und Textgeschichte 43 (Tübingen: Niemeyer, 1995), p. 2.

17. Ibid., p. 2.

18. See Bernhard Schnell, *Thomas Peuntner: 'Büchlein von der Liebhabung Gottes.' Edition und Untersuchungen.* Münchener Texte und Untersuchungen 81 (Munich/Zurich: Artemis, 1984).

19. There is no comprehensive study of German sermons in the fifteenth century. A list of edited sermons can be found in Karin Morvay and Dagmar Grube, *Bibliographie der deutschen Predigt im Mittelalter.* Münchener Texte und Untersuchungen 47 (Munich: Beck, 1974). A four-volume catalogue of sermon manuscripts in the Staatsbibliothek Berlin is due to appear soon: Hans-Jochen Schiewer and Volker Mertens, eds., *Repertorium der ungedruckten deutschsprachigen Predigten des Mittelaters* (Tübingen: Niemeyer 2001).

20. See Thomas Hohmann, "Nikolaus-von-Dinkelsbühl, Redaktor," in Kurt Ruh et al., eds., *Die deutsche Literatur des Mittelalters. Verfasserlexikon. 2.,* völlig neu bearbeitete Auflage (Berlin/New York: de Gruyter, 1978-), vol. 6, cols. 1059–62.

21. Was schaden den lewt chömen ist von den irrsals vnd von der zwaiung der päbst [. . .] Di schedleichen prechen . . ., die die heilig christenhait so vil manig iar verderbt hat . . . (were so awful), das man es dem volck nicht torst sagen. Quoted from the manuscript Stockholm, Kungliga Biblioteket, cod. A 190, 41rb–47rb.

22. On Nider's German writings, see Brand, Studien, and Ulla Williams, "'Schul der Weisheit.' Spirituelle artes-Auslegung bei Johannes Nider. Mit Edition der '14. Harfe,'" in Konrad Kunze et al., eds., *Überlieferungsgeschichtliche Editionen und Studien zur deutschen Literatur des Mittelalters. Kurt Ruh zum 75. Geburtstag.* Texte und Textgeschichte 31 (Tübingen: Niemeyer, 1989), pp. 365–90.

23. On Geiler's adaptations of Gerson, see Heribert Kraume, *Die Gerson-Übersetzungen des Geiler von Kaysersberg. Studien zur deutschsprachigen Gerson Rezeption.* Münchener Texte und Untersuchungen 71 (Munich and Zurich: Artemis, 1980) and Werner Williams-Krapp, "Johann Geiler von Kaysersberg in Augsburg. Zum Predigtzyklus 'Berg des Schauens'," in Janota and Williams-Krapp, ed., *Literarisches Leben in Augsburg,* pp. 265–80.

24. See Werner Williams-Krapp, *Die deutschen und niederländischen Legendare des Mittelalters. Studien zu ihrer Überlieferungs-, Text- und Wirkungsgeschichte.* Texte und Textgeschichte 20 (Tübingen: Niemeyer, 1986); Williams-Krapp, "Deutschsprachige Hagiographie von ca. 1350 bis ca. 1550," in Guy Philippart, ed., *Hagiographies. Histoire internationale de la littérature hagiographique latine et vernaculaire en Occident des origines à 1550,* vol. 1. Corpus Christianorum. Hagiographies I (Turnhout: Brepols, 1994), pp. 267–88; and Edith Feistner, *Historische Typologie der deutschen Heiligenlegende des Mittelalters von der Mitte des 12. Jahrhunderts bis zur Reformation.* Wissensliteratur im Mittelalter 20 (Wiesbaden: Reichert, 1995).

25. The first volume of the edition appeared in 1996: Margit Brand, Kristina Freienhagen-Baumgardt, Ruth Meyer, and Werner Williams-Krapp eds., *Der Heiligen Leben. Bd. I: Der Sommerteil.* Texte und Textgeschichte 44 (Tübingen: Niemeyer 1996); vol. 2 will appear in 2001.

26. See Feistner, *Historische Typologie,* p. 281.

27. See Werner Williams-Krapp, "'Dise ding sint dennoch nit ware zeichen der heiligkeit.' Zur Bewertung mystischer Erfahrungen im 15. Jahrhundert," *Zeitschrift für Literatur und Linguistik* 80 (1991): 61–71, and Williams-Krapp, "Frauenmystik und Ordensreform im 15. Jahrhundert," in J. Heinzle et al., eds., *Literarische Interessenbildung im Mittelalter. DFG Symposion 1991.* Germanistische Symposien. Berichtsbände 14 (Stuttgart: Metzler 1993), pp. 310–13.

28. On these points, see Thom Mertens, "Mystieke cultuur en literatuur in de late middeleeuwen," in Frits van Oostrom et al., eds., *Grote lijnen: syntheses over Middelnederlandse letterkunde* (Amsterdam: Prometheus, 1995), pp. 117–135, 205–217; Wybren Scheepsma, "'Verzamelt de overgebleven brokken, opdat niets verloren ga.' Over Latijnse en Middelnederlandse levenbeschrijvingen uit de sfeer van de Moderne Devotie," in P. Wackers et

al., eds., *Verraders en bruggenbouwers. Verkenningen naar de relatie tussen Latinitas en de Middelnederlands letterkunde* (Amsterdam: Prometheus, 1996), pp. 211–38, 334–46.

29. For the women mystics discussed here, see Werner Williams-Krapp, "Frauenmystik und Ordensreform im 15. Jahrhundert," in Joachim Heinzle et al., eds. *Literarische Interessenbildung im Mittelalter. DFG-Symposion 1991.* Germanistische Symposien, Berichtsbände 14 (Stuttgart/Weimar: Metzler, 1993), pp. 301–313.

30. See Williams-Krapp, "'Dise ding,'" p. 64.

31. For the Missive's detailed instructions for dealing with would-be mystics see Williams-Krapp, "'Dise ding,'" p. 69.

32. *Die 'Offenbarungen' der Katharina Tucher,* ed. Ulla Williams and Werner Williams-Krapp. Untersuchungen zur deutschen Literaturgeschichte 98 (Tübingen: Niemeyer, 1998).

33. See Werner Tschacher, *Der Formicarius des Johannes Nider von 1437/38. Studien zu den Anfängen der europäischen Hexenverfolgung im Spätmittelalter* (Aachen: Shaker, 2000), esp. pp. 206–213, 510–12.

34. Williams-Krapp, "Frauenmystik," pp. 308–10.

35. Ibid., pp. 310–12.

36. See Ludger Grenzmann and Karl Stackmann, eds., *Literatur und Laienbildung im Spätmittelalter und in der Reformationszeit. Symposion Wolfenbüttel 1981.* Germanistische Symposien. Berichtsbände 5 (Stuttgart: Metzler, 1984).

SPANISH

CHAPTER 11

FEMALE PATRONAGE OF VERNACULAR RELIGIOUS WORKS IN FIFTEENTH-CENTURY CASTILE: ARISTOCRATIC WOMEN AND THEIR CONFESSORS

Ronald E. Surtz

As Walter J. Ong has argued, the study of Latin was gendered masculine in the Renaissance, for its study by young males signaled their separation from the vernacular-speaking, maternal space of the home and their entry into the Latin-speaking and Latin-writing public sphere.[1] Although some medieval Spanish women did study Latin—Queen Isabella of Castile among them—one has the impression that even for that minority, only a few felt truly "at home" in the language. Tarsicio de Azcona observes, for example, that the queen was probably capable of understanding simple Latin prose, but not longer, more complicated texts.[2] The dichotomy between the vernacular and Latin extended beyond women as consumers of texts to involve female patronage as well. Queen Isabella herself seems to have recognized the Latin vs. vernacular, male vs. female division when she asked the humanist Antonio de Nebrija to publish his *Introductiones latinae* in a bilingual edition (ca. 1488). The *Introductiones,* a textbook for learning Latin, which had been previously published in two Latin-only editions (1481 and 1485, each with several reprints), was now to be directed also to nuns so that they could learn Latin on their own without needing to have contact with men.[3] In other cases, it was the author himself—or his translator—who saw the question of Latin vs. romance as involving two different audiences. Pedro Montes dedicated the original Castilian version of his *Opusculum de Conceptione Virginis* to Queen Isabella, but it was the Latin translation by G. Ayora, apparently the only version published, that came out in Milan in 1492, its dedication to the queen intact.[4]

Religious practice was likewise in a sense gendered, for Spain's intellectual cheerleaders saw the success of the military campaign against the Muslims of Granada as the result of the happy combination of Ferdinand's military prowess and Isabella's prayers and good works.[5] The anonymous prologuist of a Castilian life of Mary Magdalene originally commissioned by Queen Isabella establishes a similar gendered division of duties between the queen and her husband, declaring that while to Ferdinand fell the task of governing and extending Spain's dominions, to Isabella fell the task of looking after the salvation of the souls of her subjects. To that end, Isabella sponsored the translation of saints' lives, which functioned as mirrors in which the queen's subjects could recognize their sinful behavior and then mend their ways.[6] The constellation of female patronage, religious texts, and the use of the vernacular is not unique to Spain, for in the rest of Europe a preponderance of late medieval devotional works was sponsored by women.[7] This essay will consider two instances of female patronage of vernacular religious texts in late medieval Castile, concentrating on the writer-maecenas relation revealed by the prologues, if not the works themselves. In both cases the inevitably male writer is also the patron's confessor, with the result that the production of vernacular devotional texts becomes a site for establishing hierarchies of estate and gender.[8]

Isabella the Catholic's royal propagandists did an effective job of creating the image of a humble, maternal, and pious queen, who was also a model wife.[9] Although Ferdinand and Isabella funded the printing of many religious works, works whose authors expressed their gratitude in dedications to both monarchs,[10] in fact Isabella was not as actively involved in the patronage of devotional texts as her carefully crafted image might have led us to believe.[11] Or, to put it another way, she was as interested—and maybe even more interested—in commissioning chronicles that projected a positive image of her queenship as she was of patronizing books of spiritual guidance.[12] Perhaps Isabella's religiosity was more practical than contemplative.[13] However, at least at the beginning of her reign, Isabella did call upon her confessor, Hernando de Talavera, to write two devotional treatises for her, and it is those commissions I will consider here.[14]

Some time in late 1475, Queen Isabella asked Hernando de Talavera for a copy of the sermon he had delivered on the first Sunday of Advent to his fellow monks at the Hieronymite monastery of Santa María del Prado in Valladolid. Thus, strictly speaking, the *Colación de cómo se deben renovar en las ánimas todos los fieles cristianos en el tiempo de adviento* [Sermon on How All

Faithful Christians Must Be Renewed in Their Souls during Advent] had not originally been commissioned by Isabella. However, in recycling a work formerly intended for another audience, Talavera revised his text, and this rewritten version, the only one that is extant, can be considered a new work in and of itself.[15] Talavera also added a prologue in which he dedicates the work to Isabella, and it is that prologue I would like to discuss first of all.

At first it appears that Talavera is going to withhold his treatise from his royal penitent, for he begins by observing that that which is directed to clerics in order to refine and purify their holy conversation is not in keeping with what lay people should hear. Indeed, Christ himself taught some things to his disciples and other things involving less spiritual perfection to the masses of believers.[16] However, the queen's confessor, to the extent that he is aware of his penitent's sharp mind and devout wishes, is willing to communicate his sermon to her. Nonetheless, Talavera almost teasingly postpones passing to the work proper and, in a display of his knowledge of Holy Scripture, belabors the question of his penitent's worthiness to receive his tract by citing biblical episodes analogous to the situation in which the queen and her confessor now find themselves.

Talavera declares that he could well say to Isabella what Christ said to Saint Peter in Matthew 16:17 when Peter recognized Christ as the Messiah: "Your spirit is blessed, for it inquired about that which human dullness could not reveal to it, but which inspired it to ask for some ray of divine light, which, although it touches and illuminates everyone who comes into this world, especially touches and illuminates royal hearts."[17] On the other hand, Talavera will not say to Isabella what Christ said to the mother of the apostles James and John, who knew not what she asked (Matthew 20:22), but rather that which is written concerning Solomon, a king chosen by God, whose request was found pleasing to the Lord, for he asked for neither a long life nor measureless wealth nor the death of his enemies, but rather an understanding heart to judge his people and discern between good and evil (3 Kings 3:9–11). Talavera will further respond what Christ answered to his disciples when they asked him to explain the parable of the sower: "Because to you it is given to know the mysteries of the kingdom of heaven, but to them it is not given" (Matthew 13:11).[18] The queen has requested what she ought to request, concludes Talavera, for since the sermon argues that all must renew themselves like the eagle during Advent and since the eagle is the queen of all the birds, the work's subject is more hers than his.[19]

At first glance it would appear that such passages from Talavera's prologue are intended as a compliment to the sovereign: Isabella is worthy of receiving her confessor's sermon because her piety and intelligence distinguish her from the mass of believers.[20] However, when Talavera's scriptural quotations and allusions are placed in their biblical context, his praise of Isabella becomes problematic, and there emerges a barely hidden political agenda involving the hierarchical relation between male confessor and female penitent, between Church and state. Talavera embellishes Christ's words to Saint Peter by observing that the ray of divine light "especially touches and illuminates royal hearts," thus adding a clear allusion to Isabella's royal status as well as signaling the *Colación*'s political dimension. This political connection is underscored by the fact that the biblical verse that immediately follows Matthew 16:17 contains the celebrated phrase "thou art Peter, and upon this rock I will build my church." By appropriating Christ's words from Matthew's gospel, Talavera ends up casting himself in a role analogous to that of Christ, while Isabella's role corresponds to that of Peter. In this way, Talavera refers to the situation at hand—Isabella's worthiness to receive his sermon—and simultaneously to the wider issue of the hierarchy of Church and state: Peter may have had authority over the Church, but Christ had authority over Peter; Isabella may have temporal authority over Castile, but Talavera, as her confessor, has spiritual authority over his queen.

With regard to Talavera's quotation of Matthew 20:22, the cleric is ostensibly declaring that Isabella is not like the mother of John and James, who made an inappropriate request when she asked that her sons sit next to Christ in his kingdom. Talavera could have alluded to Mark 10:38, in which it is James and John themselves who ask to sit on Christ's right and left hands, thus demonstrating that it is they who have misunderstood the nature of Christ's kingdom.[21] Is it accidental that, given two biblical texts that contain the same phrase, Talavera chooses Matthew's account of this incident, an account that involves a woman, rather than males, of limited understanding? Thus, Talavera ends up saying by not saying. Although he denies that the verse in question is applicable to Isabella, in a sense the damage is done, for the queen, by the very fact of her feminine gender, can be construed to be guilty by association with a misguided woman in need of correction, the mother of James and John. In any case, Talavera goes on to compare Isabella to Solomon, who did make a wise request. Talavera's remark that Solomon was chosen king by God is likewise another parallel with Isabella, for the queen's propagandists expressed similar messianic notions regarding her accession to the throne of Castile.[22] However, despite Talavera's approval of Solomon's choice, the cleric interjects a phrase in which he alludes to the king's sinful behavior by observing that no one knows if Solomon was later saved or damned.[23] Is this to be understood as a warning to Isabella from her confessor? Severe moralist that he was, Talavera was obsessive in his desire to control the queen's behavior. In a letter written nearly twenty years later (September 28, 1493), he criticized

Isabella for what he deemed to be certain excesses during a reception in Barcelona in honor of the French ambassadors. He censures, among other problems, the cost of new garments, the dancing, and the fact that French gentlemen sat with Castilian ladies during the banquet.[24] Perhaps Talavera's veiled warning to Isabella in the *Colación*'s prologue is an attempt to control preemptively the minutiae of her behavior, lest she end up as morally ambiguous a figure as Solomon.

Talavera's appropriation of Christ's words to his disciples when he was about to explicate for them the parable of the sower once again seems to flatter Isabella: Just as the apostles were privileged to hear Christ's own exposition of the parable, while the crowds were left to glimpse something of Christ's meaning from the parable itself, Isabella is worthy to receive the biblical commentary contained in Talavera's sermon. Traditional interpretations of the parable identify the sower as Christ or, more broadly, as all those who preach the word of God.[25] To the extent that Isabella has asked for a copy of one of Talavera's sermons, the quotation of a biblical text that foregrounds preaching and scriptural exegesis underscores Talavera's role as a stand-in for Christ and establishes Isabella's role as passive receiver of her confessor's doctrine. Because only ecclesiastics were permitted to preach and ecclesiastics were males, the allusion to the parable of the sower calls attention to the gendered hierarchical relation between cleric and penitent: Isabella is a passive female who is to read and heed the words of her superior, an active male divinely empowered to preach and explicate Holy Writ.[26]

The ensuing treatise on the necessity of renewing oneself during Advent is theoretically a commentary on the first part of Psalm 102, but Talavera concentrates on verse 5 ("thy youth shall be renewed like the eagle's"), and the greater part of the text consists of the exposition of the spiritual meaning of the habits of the eagle and of how pious Christians should imitate those traits. Nonetheless, because the sermon was initially directed to ecclesiastics and is now being redirected to the writer's sovereign, the revised work's inscribed audience consists of both spiritual and secular leaders. It seems likely that the original version of the sermon either did not contain the advice to secular rulers or that those teachings were expanded in the version revised for the queen. In any case, the sermon proper reiterates the concepts of hierarchy and control introduced in the prologue. For example, Talavera expounds the notion that earthly sovereigns are God's vicars on earth and that they must do the will of God (546, 549). Indeed, the correct behavior of secular rulers is crucial, for those who rule well will win a crown of precious stones in heaven, while those who are negligent and give themselves over to temporal delights and pleasures will be punished in hell (546). This is not the only passage in which Talavera anticipates the puritanical notions expressed in his aforementioned letter to the queen, for later in the *Colación* he cautions that good rulers should never engage in games and jests (551). Although Talavera usually uses the inclusive masculine form of nouns and adjectives to refer to secular sovereigns of both sexes, when he begins to rail against idleness, he notes that especially queens and highborn ladies should always keep busy, as Solomon requires of the valiant woman (551).[27] In light of patriarchal conceptions of women as inherently sexual beings, female idleness was viewed as especially dangerous, for an idle woman was likely to be a wanton woman. If woman's natural sexual voracity made female sexuality dangerous and if idleness offered an opportunity for the manifestation of that sexuality, then female otiosity was to be avoided at all costs.[28] Isabella may be the queen of Castile, but for her confessor, she is a woman and, as such, subject to all the frailties of her sex.

By far the longest chapter of the treatise concerns the need to read the stories of exemplary figures so as better to imitate their virtues. Once again, Talavera violates his pattern of using the masculine form to refer inclusively to both male and female rulers. He begins with a list of mostly Old Testament male leaders whose virtues are worthy of imitation by temporal kings and nobles: the faith, obedience, and goodness of Noah, the long-sufferance and patience of Jacob, the justice of Saul, and so on (553).[29] There follows a list of negative biblical examples whose behavior is to be avoided: Nemrod's pride, Pharaoh's obstinacy, Jephthah's rashness, etc. (555). Finally, Talavera exhorts queens, princesses, and noblewomen to imitate the women of the Old and New Testaments. However, since he views his female readers not primarily as secular authorities but rather in terms of their biological functions as mothers and nurturers of their children,[30] the virtues that distinguish his biblical women are not the same as those of their male counterparts who were in positions of leadership, but rather correspond to traditional models of feminine behavior: Sarah's chastity, Rebecca's modesty and humility, Rachel's devotion, etc. (557). As he did for his male leaders and readers, Talavera also adds a list of biblical figures whose behavior is to be avoided: Eve's idleness, loquaciousness, and credulity, Dinah's gallivanting, Hagar's pride, etc. (557). Even when Talavera has the theoretical opportunity to propose feminine models more akin to those he offers to his male readers, he avoids that option. In the case of Judith, for example, he fails to mention her miraculous empowerment to perform the "masculine" deed of killing Holofernes and chooses instead to present her as a model of chastity and maturity, who is notable only because she spent her widowhood enclosed in her dwelling (557).[31]

Juan Bautista Avalle-Arce claims that Talavera became Isabella's confessor in 1474.[32] If this is so, Talavera had not occupied that position for long when his penitent asked him for a copy of the *Colación,* and, much as in the anecdote recorded by Sigüenza, he may have seized the opportunity to use an instance of patronage to affirm his authority from the very beginning. While both Isabella and Talavera are God's vicars on earth, the prelate seeks to call attention to the hierarchical difference between them in order to establish his control over his penitent. The *Colación* is not a one-size-fits-all devotional tract but very much a work directed *ad hominem,* or rather, *ad feminam,* for Talavera never loses sight of his patron. For Talavera, Isabella's status as confessant overshadows her status as queen, and thus he views her as a generic woman who must be shown her place. The submission to the will of God that he preaches is to be identified with submission to Talavera.

The Advent sermon pleased the queen so much that she almost immediately commissioned another work, on the perfections of Saint John the Evangelist, who had been mentioned but in passing in the *Colación* and to whom Isabella was particularly devoted.[33] In the prologue to his *Tractado de loores de sant Juan evangelista* [Treatise in Praise of Saint John the Evangelist], Talavera claims that since the queen's palate had grown accustomed to the flavor and sweetness she found in the sermon, she commanded him to write another work in praise of Saint John the Evangelist.[34] Continuing his alimentary metaphor, Talavera reminds the queen that she should be thankful that God has given her a devout turn of mind so that she can taste His sweetness. Such devotion is very necessary for someone who is to act as God's vicar, for otherwise her will might deviate slightly from the will of God. Furthermore, Isabella should also be grateful that, being of a youthful age more given to worldly pleasures, she desires to read devout books that will illuminate her and inspire her to know and carry out God's will.[35]

Of course, as the queen's confessor, Talavera was the person in charge of judging Isabella's conformity to God's will. Although I will not discuss the *Tractado* in detail, I would like to call attention to a later section of the treatise proper in which Talavera returns to the matter of rulers as God's vicars and their conformity to the divine will. In the passage in question, the author relates the harmony of the human will with God's will to the hypostatic union and the respective roles of man and wife in marriage:

Lo qual deve vuestra alteza mucho notar para saber cómo ha de ser una y se ha de conformar en todo y por todo lo bueno con el sereníssimo marido y muy cathólico vicario suyo que tenéys en su lugar. Ca el estado matrimonial en que vos El quiso ayuntar sacramento es que representa aquella suma unión y muy perfecta conformidad (fol. 71rv).

[Which your highness should note well in order to know how she must be one and in conformity in everything and for all that is good with your most serene husband and most Catholic vicar of His that you have in His place, for the state of matrimony in which He wished to join you is a sacrament that represents that highest union and most perfect conformity.]

Male anxiety over the fact of a female sovereign must have been widespread after Isabella's succession to the throne of Castile in 1474.[36] Isabella had been married to Ferdinand of Aragón since 1469, but by the terms of the agreement drawn up in Segovia in January of 1475, to Isabella alone fell the proprietorship of the crown of Castile.[37] Thus, Ferdinand, against centuries of patriarchal tradition, was theoretically subordinated to Isabella. Perhaps Talavera, who writes his *Tractado* the very year of the Segovia agreement, is seeking to counteract the political accord by insisting that as a married woman Isabella must subordinate herself to her husband.[38]

Isabella the Catholic was not the only strong woman whose confessor sought to tame her through the patron-writer relationship. Whether because of the advanced age of her husband or the relatively free range of action enjoyed by aristocratic women of her time, the countess of Plasencia, Leonor Pimentel, played a notable role in Castilian politics in the last years of the reign of Henry IV and the first years of that of Ferdinand and Isabella. Ignoring more worthy candidates, Leonor used her influence with Henry IV and the pope to secure the grand mastership of the Order of Alcántara for her canonically underage son, Juan de Zúñiga. Her influence with the pope likewise enabled her to obtain the deanship of Plasencia for her retainer Diego de Jerez. Although Leonor and her husband originally belonged to the political party opposed to the Catholic Monarchs, when they decided to switch loyalties, it was Leonor who took the initiative in seeking the first contacts with Ferdinand and Isabella through the offices of her stepson, Pedro de Zúñiga.[39]

Leonor Pimentel had Juan López, her Dominican confessor, compose a series of works for her, of which only two, the *Historias que comprenden toda la vida de Nuestra Señora* [Histories that Include the Entire Life of Our Lady] and the *Evangelios moralizados* [The Gospels Sermonized], are extant.[40] In light of Leonor Pimentel's personal initiative and independence from male control, Juan López may have felt that his penitent should be reined in, and his concern for channeling her behavior into more traditional models of humility and subservience may explain his preaching of traditional feminine virtues in the works he wrote under her commission.

Historias is a Mariological treatise structured around the principal feasts of the Blessed Virgin. In his prologue, López declares that in order to foment his penitent's devotion, the text will take the form of a dialogue between two women, one of whom (the Countess) will ask questions like a student anxious to learn, while the other (Mary herself) will answer like a master anxious to teach.[41] As Leonor's confessor, both extratextually and intratextually Juan López plays the role of teacher. Since intratextually the Virgin Mary is the interlocutor who instructs, that role must necessarily fall to Juan López, who in a sense has to disguise himself as a woman in order to enter, as teacher, the fictitious dialogue he is creating. In any case, the intra-textual distribution of roles maintains the extratextual hierarchy through which Juan López, as Leonor's confessor, exercises a spiritual jurisdiction over her. Of course, in reality the friar *en travesti* plays both roles, teacher and pupil, because he is the author of the dialogue. For her part, as she reads the work the Countess plays the role of herself, that is, the role of disciple, but her words are determined by the preexisting script composed by her confessor. In this way, Leonor does not speak in her own voice, but rather her confessor ventriloquizes his words through her.[42] Thus, Juan López establishes, so to speak, the rules of game from the very beginning of his treatise, assigning roles according to a strict hierarchy of gender and estate.[43]

Although the Blessed Virgin addresses Lady Leonor by her title of "Countess," the literary persona that Juan López creates for his patron is characterized by profound humility and even abjection. In the prayers inscribed in the text, the Countess is made to refer to herself as "handmaiden," "slave," and "servant" (14), and later as the Virgin's "ash-covered slave" (58). That persona adopts an attitude of total passivity before the Queen of Angels:

> Tú me guía cómo ande, Tú me enseña cómo fable, Tú me doctrina cómo piense. Dame regla cómo rija mi corazón, cómo mesure mi razón, cómo ordene mi conversación. . . . Lo que me aconsejares, eso escogeré. Lo que Tú mandares, todo lo compliré (10).

> [Guide how I should walk, teach me to speak, instruct me how I should think. Give me a rule for governing my heart, tempering my intellect, regulating my speech. . . . I will choose to do whatever you counsel me. I will carry out whatever you command.]

The Virgin answers with a series of commands:

> Lanza de tu corazón pensamientos curiosos. Arriedra de tu ánimo pensamientos maliciosos. Alanza de tu alma pensamientos deliciosos. Como los vieres venir empiézalos a resistir. Cierra tus entrañas, no los quieras rescebir, ni que entren consentir. . . . Desdeñe tu voluntad deseos seglares. Aborrezca tu voluntad apetitos carnales. Esquiva con todas fuerzas deleites corporales. . . . [44] Fable tu lengua loores de Dios. . . . Guarda tu lengua de murmuraciones de mal testimonio e infamaciones (10–11).

> [Cast all inquisitive thoughts from your heart. Drive all malicious thoughts from your mind. Cast all pleasurable thoughts from your soul. As soon as you see them approach, start to resist them. Close your innermost parts, refuse to accept such thoughts. Do not allow them to enter. . . . Let your will disdain all worldly desires. Let your will detest carnal appetites. Avoid bodily delights

with all your strength . . . Let your tongue speak the praises of God. . . .
Keep your tongue from defamatory gossip and slander.]

Moreover, the very fact that the Countess is cast in the role of the disciple
underscores her ignorance in the face of the Virgin's wisdom. Indeed, at
one point Lady Leonor is made to exclaim to Mary: "Although I have
heard your words, by no means did I understand them."[45] The Countess,
by means of the prayers and speeches her confessor ventriloquizes through
her, is to become her literary image: a woman who is suitably humble and
in need of guidance.

In addition to being a glossed life of Mary and a collection of prayers
directed to her, *Historias* is also a treatise for married women who are to
model their behavior on that of the Virgin. To that end Juan López has the
Virgin pronounce diatribes against the use of cosmetics (87) and wigs
(97). Mary also observes that as a young girl, she never laughed or shouted
(260), and that as an adult, her ears were always "ready and disposed and
inclined to hear divine laws and precepts and good counsel and healthy
instruction."[46] Once again, the message is clear. Juan López provides Lady
Leonor with a model of obedience and attempts to control her behavior,
paying special attention to regulating her female sexuality, which could
become especially dangerous and alluring if enhanced by cosmetics and
false tresses.

Medieval didactic texts that consist of a dialogue between a teacher and
a disciple have a built-in intellectual hierarchy, for the teacher is clearly the
superior interlocutor. This is the case in *Historias* to the extent that the
Countess is the disciple who asks the questions and the Virgin Mary is the
teacher who answers them; but since both interlocutors are women, there
is no hierarchy with regard to the gender of the participants.[47] However,
so intent is Juan López to establish his extratextual control and to incul-
cate notions of hierarchy that he undercuts the Virgin's intratextual authority and thereby the very authority he had allotted to himself by
ventriloquizing through Mary. To the extent that the Virgin is also a
woman, for Juan López she can not be autonomous but must be made to
assert her subjection to male superiority. Thus, in the course of her exegesis of the qualities of the star prophesied in Numbers 24:17, López has the
Virgin observe:

Mira, Condesa, que en toda mi vida nunca en grado ni medio me moví a
mi propia voluntad, mas siempre presta e aparejada para muy aína coste-
mente [*sic*] obedescer a la voluntad de mi mayor, que fue el Espíritu Santo,
por el cual los fijos de Dios son reglados e gobernados, aderezados e bien
regidos, como son las estrellas movidas del fundamento (253).

[Behold, Countess, that never to any degree in my entire life did I act according to my own will; rather, I was ever ready and prepared to obey very quickly the will of my superior, who was the Holy Spirit, by whom the children of God are ruled and governed, put on the right path and well guided, even as the stars are moved by the firmament.]

The Countess answers the Virgin in the following speech:

Agora veo veramente el Espíritu Santo ser vuestro Perlado, a cuyo obedescistes; ca el Espíritu Santo sobre Vos vino para que fuese vuestro abad; ca do iba el rebate del Espíritu Santo, allá íbades prestamente. (Ay!)e qué será de nosotros? E otra vez digo: ¿qué será de nosotros, que somos estrellas erráticas, que nos movemos sólo como queremos, ora retrogradando, agora descendiendo, agora montando? Y más contrarios al movimiento de nuestros mayores; lo que peor es, al contrario de Dios e de sus preceptos (253).

[Now I truly see that the Holy Spirit, whose will you obeyed, is your superior, for the Holy Spirit came over you so that he might be your abbot; wherever the impetus of the Holy Spirit went, there you went speedily. Alas! What will become of us? And I ask again: What will become of us who are wandering stars and move only as we wish, now retrograding, now descending, now rising, and contrary to the motion of our superiors, and, what is worse, contrary to God and his laws?]

The lesson of obedience versus disobedience inscribed in the preceding exchange could not be clearer. The intratextual inconsistency in the authority of the Virgin serves to bolster the extratextual hierarchy between confessor and penitent: The Countess is to imitate the model provided by the Virgin Mary by obeying her own prelate, her own abbot, that is to say, her confessor Juan López.

The other work that Juan López wrote for Leonor Pimentel, the *Evangelios moralizados,* is a commentary on the Gospels of the liturgical year. Each chapter is articulated with the scholastic divisions and rhymed formulae typical of late medieval sermons. López also novelizes the Scriptures in the tradition of the thirteenth-century *Meditationes vitae Christi* and other texts that filled in the Gospel narratives with dialogue and invented episodes. Although I will not consider the *Evangelios* in detail here, it should be noted that in addition to edifying passages directed to the general reader, other parts seem addressed to such specific groups of readers as ecclesiastics or women. For example, when Saint Joseph realizes that his spouse is pregnant, he lists the seven signs of the unfaithful wife in order to determine if Mary has been untrue to him. Such signs include excess in her clothing, loquacity, immodesty in her glance, idleness, and disdain for her husband. Needless to say, Joseph thereupon observes that the Virgin is the exact opposite, for she is modestly dressed, keeps silent, does not raise her eyes from the ground, is always busy sewing and embroidering, and honors her husband.[48] The Eve/Mary dichotomy is very much in evidence here, as the text addresses its female readers, if not the Countess herself, specifically contrasting two models of feminine behavior, one to be imitated, the other to be avoided.

Both Leonor Pimentel and Isabella the Catholic appear to have been pleased by the works they commissioned, for one instance of patronage led to another. Both Talavera and López were suitably rewarded for their services, and the sermonizing of their highborn female patrons did not harm their ecclesiastical careers. Although Juan López did not live to see the building completed, he was instrumental in Leonor Pimentel's founding of a Dominican monastery in Plasencia,[49] and the new foundation can be seen as both an example of López' control over Leonor and a reward for the services he rendered to her. Hernando de Talavera went on to become one of Isabella's most trusted advisers and was eventually rewarded by being named the first archbishop of the newly reconquered city of Granada. Leonor Pimentel's continued independent lifestyle suggests that Juan López' efforts to tame her were ultimately ineffectual. Likewise, one can well debate the extent to which Isabella heeded Talavera's advice on the question of humility and subordination, for she continued to take an active role in politics and never relinquished the proprietorship of the throne of Castile to Ferdinand. However grateful the two women may have been for the advice proffered them in the works they had commissioned, both Leonor and Isabella seem to have blithely ignored their confessors' ideological pressure to conform to more traditional models of female behavior, and neither of them retired from public life to spin and have babies.

Notes

1. For the concept of Latin as a sex-linked male language, see Walter J. Ong, S. J., "Latin Language Study as a Renaissance Puberty Rite," in *Rhetoric, Romance, and Technology: Studies in the Interaction of Expression and Culture* (Ithaca and London: Cornell University Press, 1977), pp. 119–120.

2. Tarsicio de Azcona, *Isabel la Católica: Estudio crítico de su vida y su reinado,* third edition (Madrid: Biblioteca de Autores Cristianos, 1993), p. 373. For learned women at the court of Queen Isabella, many of whom had mastered Latin, see María Dolores Gómez Molleda, "La cultura femenina en la época de Isabel la Católica," *Revista de Archivos, Bibliotecas y Museos* 61 (1955): 176–184.

3. Antonio de Nebrija, *Introduciones latinas contrapuesto el romance al latín (c. 1488)*, ed. Miguel Angel Esparza and Vicente Calvo (Münster: Nodus Publikationen, 1996), p. 6. The dedication of the bilingual edition to Isabella is new, for the previous Latin-only editions of 1481 and 1485 had been dedicated to Cardinal Pedro González de Mendoza (the archbishop of Toledo) and Gutierre de Toledo (the rector of the University of Salamanca), respectively (viii).

4. "Petri Montis philosophi, ad serenissimam illustrissimamque Elisabeth Hispaniarum Reginam benemeritam in opusculum de Conceptione Virginis praefatio, interprete G. Ayora cordubensi," in *Monumenta Antiqua Immaculatae Conceptionis Sacratissimae Virginis Mariae,* ed. Pedro de Alva y Astorga, 2 vols. (Louvain, 1664), 2: 319.

5. In a letter addressed to Ferdinand the Catholic in 1485, congratulating the king on the reconquest of the city of Ronda, Diego de Valera observes that Isabella fought with her alms and prayers no less than the king did with his lance: "La qual [Isabella] no menos pelea con sus muchas limosnas e devotas oraciones, e dando hórden a las cosas de la guerra, que vos, Señor, con la lança en la mano" ("Epístola XXIV," in *Prosistas castellanos del siglo XV, I,* ed. Mario Penna, Biblioteca de Autores Españoles, vol. 116 [Madrid: Atlas, 1959], p. 31).

6. *Vida de Santa María Magdalena e cómo sirvió a la Virgen María Nuestra Señora* [Burgos, 1514], sig. a 2rv. Female patronage was essential to the composition and publication of this life of the Magdalen. Queen Isabella commissioned a cleric to write the first version of the text. Then, after the queen's death (1504), another unnamed female patron commissioned a second author to expand and revise the text for publication (sig. a 3r).

7. On female patronage of works in the vernacular in the Middle Ages, see Susan Groag Bell, "Medieval Women Book Owners: Arbiters of Lay Piety and Ambassadors of Culture," *Signs* 7 (1982): 759–60; Katherine Gill, "Women and the Production of Religious Literature in the Vernacular, 1300–1500," in *Creative Women in Medieval and Early Modern Italy: A Religious and Artistic Renaissance,* eds. E. Ann Matter and John Coakley (Philadelphia: University of Pennsylvania Press, 1994), pp. 64–104; Carol M. Meale, "' . . . alle the bokes that I haue of latyn, englisch, and frensch': Laywomen and Their Books in Late Medieval England," in *Women and Literature in Britain, 1150–1500,* ed. Carol M. Meale, 2nd ed. (Cambridge: Cambridge University Press, 1996), pp. 128–58; and *The Cultural Patronage of Medieval Women,* ed. June Hall McCash (Athens and London: University of Georgia Press, 1996).

8. I know of no specific study of the relation between aristocratic women and their confessors in late medieval Castile. For the penitent-confessor relationship in other contexts, see Rudolph M. Bell, "Telling Her Sins: Male Confessors and Female Penitents in Catholic Reformation Italy," in *That Gentle Strength: Historical Perspectives on Women in Christianity,* ed. Lynda L. Coon et al. (Charlottesville and London: University Press of Virginia,

1990), pp. 118–33; Jodi Bilinkoff, "Confessors, Penitents, and the Construction of Identities in Early Modern Avila," in *Culture and Identity in Early Modern Europe (1500–1800)*, eds. Barbara B. Diefendorf and Carla Hesse (Ann Arbor: University of Michigan Press, 1993), pp. 83–100; and Darcy Donahue, "Writing Lives: Nuns and Confessors as Auto/Biographers in Early Modern Spain," *Journal of Hispanic Philology* 13 (1989): 230–39.

9. Isabella's success in projecting a carefully constructed image of herself extended even to future generations of historiographers. Alonso de Santa Cruz, writing in the early 1550s, extols Isabella's chastity, piety, and loyalty to her husband: "Fue fiel amiga, sujeta y muy amada a su marido, favorecedora de las mujeres bien casadas y de lo contrario muy enemiga. Católica y cristianísima, fidelísima a Dios. Madre muy piadosa a sus súbditos, y reina muy justa a sus vasallos. Hera dada a contemplación. Ocupávase continuamente en los oficios divinos. Fue religiosa y devota, y tenía gran caridad con todas las religiones" (*Crónica de los Reyes Católicos*, ed. Juan de Mata Carriazo, 2 vols. [Sevilla: Escuela de Estudios Hispano-Americanos de Sevilla, 1951], 1:304–305).

10. Representative examples of religious works dedicated jointly to Ferdinand and Isabella include Pedro Jiménez de Préxano's *Lucero de la vida humana* (1493), Andrés de Li's *Tesoro de la Pasión* (Zaragoza, 1494), and Sancho Pérez Machuca's *Memoria de nuestra redención* (1497).

11. Although the library Isabella inherited from her father John II contained Castilian translations of many classical works and although the queen herself saw to it that her children received a humanist education, Isabella was nonetheless disinterested in patronizing classical translations. For the education of the royal children, see Peggy K. Liss, *Isabel the Queen: Life and Times* (New York and Oxford: Oxford University Press, 1992), pp. 251–53. For the observation that John II's royal library formed the core of Isabella's library, see J. N. H. Lawrance, "The Spread of Lay Literacy in Late Medieval Castile," *Bulletin of Hispanic Studies* 62 (1985): 93 n. 44.

12. Since Henry IV had passed over his putative daughter Juana and named his sister Isabella as his successor, Isabella used the royal chroniclers in her pay to bolster her questionable claim to the throne by having them exaggerate the negative aspects of her brother's reign and project an impeccable image of her. For example, it appears that Diego Enríquez del Castillo, otherwise favorable to Henry IV, painted a more negative portrait of the king in the later revised version of his chronicle, perhaps in an effort to ingratiate himself with Isabella. See Julio Puyol, "Los cronistas de Enrique IV," *Boletín de la Real Academia de la Historia* 78 (1921): 413–14. Hernando del Pulgar, either at his own initiative or at the bidding of his patron, states that his chronicle is intended to justify Isabella's right to the throne of Castile: " . . . la fidelidad nos obliga a recontar algunas cosas de las que en verdad pasaron sobre esta materia, especialmente algunas de aquéllas que muestran claramente el derecho que esta princesa doña Isabel tovo a la subcesión destos

reynos" (*Crónica de los Reyes Católicos,* ed. Juan de Mata Carriazo, 2 vols. [Madrid: Espasa-Calpe, 1943], 1:20). Moreover, as Pulgar penned his chronicle, he seems to have submitted what he had written to Queen Isabella for her approval: "Yo iré a vuestra alteza segund me lo enbía a mandar e leuaré lo escrito fasta aquí para que lo mande examinar" ("Letra XI," in Fernando del Pulgar, *Letras. Glosa a las "Coplas de Mingo Revulgo,"* ed. J. Domínguez Bordona, Clásicos Castellanos, 99 [Madrid: Espasa-Calpe, 1958], p. 53).

13. The active and even activist orientation of Isabella's religiosity can be seen in her efforts to reform the Spanish clergy and in the works she commissioned to further that project. Both Antonio de Nebrija's *Introduciones latinas* (ca. 1488) and Alfonso de Palencia's *Universal vocabulario en latín y en romance* (1490) were dedicated to Isabella and were at least partially intended to raise the intellectual level of the clergy by encouraging greater proficiency in Latin. Similarly, Rodrigo de Santaella's *Vocabularium ecclesiasticum* (1499), likewise dedicated to Isabella, is a Latin-Castilian dictionary of ecclesiastical terms intended for clerics whose Latin is weak. For Ferdinand and Isabella's support of clerical reform, see José García Oro, *La reforma de los religiosos españoles en tiempo de los Reyes Católicos* (Valladolid: Instituto Isabel la Católica, 1969), and the same author's *Cisneros y la reforma del clero español en tiempo de los Reyes Católicos* (Madrid: CSIC, 1971).

14. In addition to patronizing such original works, Isabella supported the translation of at least two devotional texts. It appears that it was the queen who commissioned a Castilian translation of Ludolph of Saxony's *Vita Christi.* In a letter to Hernando de Talavera dated December 4, 1493, the queen expresses her impatience that a certain Logroño is not working fast enough: "y mandad a Logroño que no alze la mano del cartujano ansí con su romanze y el latín juntamente, como yo le dixe, hasta acabarlos, y aun querría que entanto me embiase lo que tiene hecho" (Diego Clemencín, *Elogio de la reina católica Doña Isabel* [Madrid: Sancha, 1821], p. 378). Logroño appears to be the copyist of Ambrosio Montesino's translation of the *Vita Christi,* which would eventually be published in 1502. The queen also commissioned Alfonso Ortiz to do a Castilian translation of Ubertino da Casale's *Arbor vitae crucifixae.* See Oscar Lilao Franca and Carmen Castrillo González, *Catálogo de manuscritos de la Biblioteca Universitaria de Salamanca, I: Manuscritos 1–1679bis* (Salamanca: Ediciones Universidad de Salamanca, 1997), pp. 260–61.

15. José Amador de los Ríos notes that the margins of the manuscript of the *Colación* are filled with corrections and additions (*Historia crítica de la literatura española,* 7 vols. [Madrid, 1861–1865], 7:541).

16. "Y como quier que lo que a los religiosos se dirige para más cendrar y purificar su sancta conuersación, no es conforme a lo que los seglares deuen oyr; ca segund la diuersidad y diuersa profession y capaçidad de los oydores deuen ser proporçionados los sermones; por lo qual nuestro Redemptor y Maestro Jhesu Xpo, Dios y hombre uerdadero, unas cosas enseñaua a sus

prinçipales discípulos y otras de menor perfection al pueblo" (Amador de los Ríos, *Historia crítica*, 7:544). Subsequent quotations from this edition will be indicated by the page number in parentheses.

17. "Que es bienauenturado uuestro spíritu, que demandó lo que la rudesa humanal no le pudo reuelar; mas lo que le inspiró a demandar algund rayo de la lumbre diuinal, la qual, como quier que alumbre a todo honbre que uiene en este mundo; pero espeçialmente toca y esclaresçe el coraçon real, que por ella más que otra se ha de regir y gouernar" (544). Actually, Talavera paraphrases Matthew 16:17 ("Blessed art thou, Simon Bar-Jona: because flesh and blood hath not revealed it to thee, but my Father who is in heaven") and interpolates part of John 1:9 ("That was the true light, which enlighteneth every man that cometh into this world").

18. Cf. Mark 4:11 and Luke 8:10.

19. Elizabeth A. Lehfeldt connects the theme of religious renovation with the text's political agenda and discusses the political implications of Isabella's identification with the eagle: Talavera is addressing simultaneously the question of personal spiritual renovation and the collective political renovation of Spain. See "Ruling Sexuality: The Political Legitimacy of Isabel of Castile," *Renaissance Quarterly* 53 (2000): 39. Peggy K. Liss observes that "Talavera offered Isabel not simply an inspirational tract for a devout queen, but a politically astute guide to royal morality and devotion, indeed a vision of herself within the divine scheme" (*Isabel the Queen*, p. 122).

20. But the queen is not so distinguished as to receive credit as a participant in the genesis of the treatise, for Talavera crossed out a passage from the *Colación* in which he revealed that his notions on the habits of the eagle had been culled from a copy of Bartholomeus Anglicus' *De proprietatibus rerum* that Isabella had given him. See Elisa Ruiz García, "El poder de la escritura y la escritura del poder," in *Orígenes de la monarquía hispánica: propaganda y legitimación (ca. 1400–1520)*, ed. José Manuel Nieto Soria (Madrid: Dykinson, 1999), p. 291 n. 45. By crossing out the passage in question, Talavera erased any notion of the queen's intellectual collaboration in the writing process.

21. Cf. Matthew 19:28.

22. See Américo Castro, *Aspectos del vivir hispánico* (1949; Madrid: Alianza, 1970), pp. 13–45, and José Cepeda Adán, "El providencialismo en los cronistas de los Reyes Católicos," *Arbor* 17 (1950): 177–190.

23. In his *Tractado de loores de sant Juan evangelista*, Talavera praises Solomon for his humility and sense of justice at the beginning of his reign, but then censures him for his later debauchery and idolatry: "Quán justo y quán humilde quando començó a reinar. Quán limpio y quán devoto edificó a Dios aquel templo que no fue visto ni oído tal. Después de pocos años, quán loco y dissoluto. Quán idolatia [*sic*] y quán perverso en todo linaje de mal" (Biblioteca Lázaro Galdiano, Madrid, MS 332, fol. 59r).

24. For the text of Talavera's letter to the queen, see Clemencín, *Elogio*, pp. 359–71. For an analysis of both Talavera's letter and Isabella's response, see

Barbara Weissberger, "'Me atrevo a escribir así': Confessional Politics in the Letters of Isabel I and Hernando de Talavera," in *Women at Work in Spain: From the Middle Ages to Early Modern Times*, ed. Marilyn Stone and Carmen Benito-Vessels (New York: Peter Lang, 1998), pp. 147–69.

25. Stephen L. Wailes, *Medieval Allegories of Jesus' Parables* (Berkeley and Los Angeles: University of California Press, 1987), p. 98.

26. In a celebrated anecdote recorded by José de Sigüenza, the first time Isabella confessed to Talavera, the queen knelt, while her confessor sat. When the queen insisted that both confessor and penitent should kneel, Talavera answered that he should remain seated because he was God's earthly representative: "porque este es el tribunal de Dios, y hago aquí sus vezes" (*Historia de la Orden de San Jerónimo,* ed. Juan Catalina García, 2 vols., Nueva Biblioteca de Autores Españoles, vols. 8 and 12 [Madrid: Bailly-Baillière, 1907–1909], 2:295). Weissberger observes that the anecdote records the "taming of a female monarch by the patriarchal law of the Church and family" ("'Me atrevo a escribir así,'" p. 149).

27. Cf. Proverbs 31:10–27.

28. Sewing and spinning were the quintessential means for women to avoid idleness. In his *De institutione feminae christianae* of 1523, the self-exiled Valencian humanist Juan Luis Vives recalled with approval that not only Queen Isabella herself, but also her daughters the *infantas* were taught how to spin, sew, and embroider: "Queen Isabella, wife of Ferdinand, wished her four daughters to be expert in spinning, sewing and needlepoint. Of these two were queens of Portugal, the third we see is queen of Spain and mother of the Emperor Charles, the fourth is the saintly wife of Henry VIII of England" (*De institutione feminae christianae,* eds. C. Fantazzi and C. Matheeussen, trans. C. Fantazzi, 2 vols., in *Selected Works of J. L. Vives,* vols. 6–7 [Leiden and New York: Brill, 1996–1998], 1:23). If a busy woman was a chaste woman, then a woman who refused to spin and sew was thought to be sexually promiscuous. Writing in the late fourteenth century, the Catalan writer Francesc Eiximenis quotes an anecdote ascribed to Cicero about a wanton Roman woman who refused to spin, while the empress herself did so. The empress barred her recalcitrant subject from the palace and decreed that any woman who refused to spin should be exiled from Rome and placed with those who do not spin, that is to say, the prostitutes: "[La emperadriu] . . . féu fer crida que dona qui en Roma no volgués filar, que fos gitada de Roma e collocada ab aquelles qui no filen, qui estan al bordeyll" (*Lo libre de les dones,* ed. Frank Naccarato, 2 vols. [Barcelona: Universitat de Barcelona and Curial Edicions Catalanes, 1981], 1:33–34).

29. Lehfeldt observes that this part of Talavera's tract makes little mention of bellicose and forceful virtues: "The emphasis is on more passive attributes. A recounting of important, but gentler, virtues may be intended to avoid attributing any 'manly' features to Isabel" ("Ruling Sexuality," p. 41).

30. "Por essa mesma manera las reynas, prinçessas y todas las grandes y pequeñas dueñas deuen haser cama, estrado y assyento para parir y criar sus

hijos y hijas de sus buenas obras, y nobles costumbres, en la buena uida y sancta conuersaçion de las dueñas que la Escriptura loa y aprueua por buenas" (556).

31. Others were less reticent to adduce the example of Judith. A certain Basque diplomat, for example, stated that Isabella was greater than Esther or Judith, who killed Holofernes to liberate her people (Liss, *Isabel the Queen*, p. 199).

32. "Sobre Fray Hernando de Talavera," in *Temas hispánicos medievales* (Madrid: Gredos, 1974), p. 266.

33. For Isabella's devotion to Saint John the Evangelist, see Liss, *Isabel the Queen*, pp. 136–37, 155–56.

34. For medieval alimentary metaphors, see Ernst Robert Curtius, *European Literature and the Latin Middle Ages,* trans. Willard R. Trask (1953; New York: Harper and Row, 1963), pp. 134–36. While such food metaphors are traditional, they function somewhat differently in cases where the writer is a man and the patron is a woman, for writer and patron can be said to reverse gender roles as the male author is cast in "female" role of nurturer and provider of food. For the use of such maternal imagery in the Middle Ages, see Caroline Walker Bynum, *Jesus as Mother: Studies in the Spirituality of the High Middle Ages* (Berkeley and Los Angeles: University of California Press, 1982), pp. 110–69.

35. "Byen ueo yo que es de haser muchas grasias a nuestro Señor que commo a su vicaria y grand commissaria uos da spíritu de deuotión, con que por esta uía gostes quan suaue es esse mesmo señor. Lo qual es mucho menester para bien executar sus veces y conplir su comisyón, ca de otra guisa, ligeramente discreparía uuestra uoluntad de la suya" (quoted in Juan Meseguer Fernández, O.F.M., "Isabel la Católica y los franciscanos (1451–1476)," *Archivo Ibero-Americano* 30 [1970]: 267).

36. For example, Barbara Weissberger observes a certain ambiguity in the royal chronicler Alfonso de Palencia's denigration of Henry IV and efforts to give legitimacy to Isabella herself: "I suggest that the discourse of effeminacy that Palencia aims at Enrique for the purpose of promoting Isabel's political legitimacy and authority also plays a more personal role in his work. It expresses and contains the sexual and political anxiety that her anomalous power arouses in the ambitious intellectual, and, we may assume, in the equally ambitious nobles and courtiers that would have formed his readership" ("'A tierra, puto!': Alfonso de Palencia's Discourse of Effeminacy," in *Queer Iberia: Sexualities, Cultures, and Crossings from the Middle Ages to the Renaissance,* eds. Josiah Blackmore and Gregory S. Hutcheson [Durham and London: Duke University Press, 1999], p. 307). Weissberger goes on to note: "What we witness in Palencia's growing discomfort with the virile queen whose image he helped to create is his gradual, dismayed realization that it is in reality Isabel and not Fernando who rules supreme in Castile" (p. 310).

37. Liss, *Isabel the Queen*, pp. 106–7.

38. For the differences of opinion among their contemporaries regarding the respective roles of Ferdinand and Isabella in the government of Castile, see María Isabel del Val Valdivieso, "Fernando II de Aragón, rey de Castilla," in *Fernando II de Aragón, el Rey Católico,* ed. Esteban Sarasa (Zaragoza: Institución "Fernando el Católico," 1996), pp. 29–46.

39. See Francisco de Rades y Andrada, *Chrónica de las tres Ordenes de Santiago, Calatrava y Alcántara* (Toledo, 1572; facsimile edition Barcelona: El Albir, 1980), *Chrónica de Alcántara,* fols. 49v–50r; Domingo Sánchez Loro, *Historias placentinas inéditas, Primera Parte: volumen C* (Cáceres: Diputación Provincial de Cáceres, 1985), p. 93; and Alonso de Palencia, *Crónica de Enrique IV,* II, trans. A. Paz y Melia, Biblioteca de Autores Españoles, 258 (Madrid: Ediciones Atlas, 1975), p. 255.

40. The inventory of the possessions of Leonor's husband, Alvaro de Zúñiga, drawn up in 1468 lists several other works as having been written by Juan López under commission from Leonor. These include a two-volume manuscript entitled *Sol de justicia* [The Sun of Justice] and the *Libro de la casta niña* [Book of the Chaste Maiden] (Liciniano Sáez, *Demostración histórica del verdadero valor de todas las monedas que corrían en Castilla durante el reynado del señor don Enrique IV* [Madrid, 1805], p. 543). The inventory also lists a manuscript whose binding shows "cómo la duquesa aparta de sí todos los instrumentos y placeres" (p. 543), an illustration that seems to correspond to the rubric of the first chapter of *Historias:* "Cómo la Condesa aparta de sí todos estruendos que le pueden empedir su intento" (Juan López, *Concepción y Nascencia de la Virgen,* ed. Luis G. A. Getino [Madrid: Tipografía de la *Revista de Archivos,* 1924], p. 4). If that is the case, then the 1468 inventory offers a *terminus ad quem* for the composition of the work. Since Leonor did not become Countess of Plasencia until she married Alvaro de Zúñiga in 1458, that year would be the text's *terminus a quo.* Getino edited only the first half of *Historias,* whence the title he gives to his edition. Future quotations from Getino's edition will be indicated by the page number in parentheses. Lawrance observes that Leonor, as a book collector and patron, followed in the steps of her father, the noted bibliophile Count of Benavente ("Lay Literacy," 83–84).

41. "Será la escripta lectura por manera de fabla entre dos personas de sexu feminino, de las cuales la una pregunta como discípula afectuosa de aprender; la otra, como maestra ganosa de enseñar y responder" (3).

42. The interlocutors in Spanish dialogues of the fifteenth century, whether they speak in Latin or in Castilian, are almost invariably male. One exception is the anonymous *Libro de la consolación de España,* in which two female speakers, Spain and Grace, discuss the evils of the times. However, unlike Lady Leonor and the Blessed Virgin in *Historias,* the interlocutors in the *Libro de la consolación de España* are allegorical figures, their female gender being determined by the grammatical gender of the abstractions they represent.

43. Here and elsewhere I draw upon notions expressed in my "Fray Juan López en travestí: sus *Historias que comprenden toda la vida de Nuestra Señora,*"

in *Studia Hispanica Medievalia IV,* ed. Azucena Adelina Fraboschi et al. (Buenos Aires: Pontificia Universidad Católica Argentina, 1999), pp. 248–55.

44. All these phrases end in either assonant or consonant rhyme, perhaps as a mnemonic device.

45. "Aunque oí vuestras palabras, en ninguna guisa las entendí" (191).

46. "Dispuestas y ordenadas y inclinadas para oír a las leyes y preceptos divinales e a los buenos consejos e sanos documentos" (94).

47. The use of the vernacular in fifteenth-century dialogues is not gendered, for several of the most well-known texts in Spanish involve male interlocutors and are presumably directed to a masculine audience. However, such works can involve notions of hierarchy. For example, Juan de Lucena's *Libro de vita beata* (1463) purports to be a dialogue between three noted figures who were already deceased by the time of its composition: Alonso de Cartagena, the bishop of Burgos; the nobleman and poet Iñigo López de Mendoza; and the poet Juan de Mena. In the course of a discussion of the possibility of obtaining happiness in this life, both Mendoza and Mena defer to Cartagena's superior age and wisdom.

48. *Libro de los evangelios moralizados* (Zamora, 1490), sig. d 3v.

49. It is said that Leonor's son Juan was miraculously brought back from the dead after Juan López suggested that the countess pray to the recently canonized (1455) Dominican preacher, Saint Vincent Ferrer. In gratitude, Lady Leonor promised to build a Dominican monastery in Plasencia that would be named after the saint whose powers she had so successfully invoked. The friars moved into the new building in 1486, seven years after López' death in 1479. For the founding of San Vicente de Plasencia, see Manuel de los Hoyos, O.P., *Registro historial de la Provincia de España,* 3 vols. (Madrid: Librería OPE, 1966–1968), 1:94–96. A letter that Leonor wrote to the Dominican prior in Plasencia after López' death confirms her confessor's significant role in the planning and design of the new monastery: "quise e fue mi voluntad y es dar e traspasar en Vos el dicho monesterio con todos sus bienes e declarar e manifestar todo lo que çerca del dicho monesterio, asi en el edifiçio como en lo spiritual e temporal e cosas a el neçesarias deseo se hagan e cumplan, segund que mas por estenso en vra. presençia conferimos e determinamos yo y el reverendo maestro frey Juan Lopez mi Padre Spiritual antes que falleçiesse" (Crescencio Palomo Iglesias, O.P., "Carta inédita de la Duquesa de Plasencia, doña Leonor Pimentel, donando a los Dominicos el convento de San Vicente Ferrer de la ciudad de Plasencia [22 de agosto y 10 de octubre de 1484]," *Revista de Estudios Extremeños* 31 [1975]: 50).

CHAPTER 12

CISNEROS AND THE TRANSLATION
OF WOMEN'S SPIRITUALITY

Elizabeth Teresa Howe

In 1495, Fray Francisco Jiménez de Cisneros was appointed archbishop of Toledo and thus primate of Spain. It was a remarkable achievement for a man who had turned his back on an ambitious ecclesiastical career in midlife by taking the habit of a Franciscan monk of the strict Observantine Congregation. While serving as provincial, he had been chosen by Queen Isabella the Catholic in 1492 to be royal confessor.[1] The combination of his austere piety and his commitment to reform attracted the like-minded queen to Cisneros. As primate (and later regent of Castile), he did not disappoint her, for in these diverse offices he devoted himself to a number of endeavors that would have profound repercussions on the spiritual and intellectual future of the nation.

Reform of the clergy and monasteries of Spain began under Ferdinand and Isabella with the approbation of a papal bull in 1494. With the appointment of Cisneros it received added impetus.[2] As part of his commitment to reform, the archbishop (later cardinal) undertook the foundation of a university at Alcalá de Henares that would advance the study of theology, canon law, and, initially at least, the new humanism.[3] Cisneros gathered an impressive group of scholars at the new institution and set them the task of preparing a Polyglot edition of the Bible. In order to facilitate publication of the final edition of this monumental work, he also established a press at Alcalá under the direction of the German printer Arnao Guillén de Brocar.

In addition to the large and complicated job of printing the Complutense Polyglot, Cisneros also decided to use the press to further other worthy aims of his episcopate. Among these was the encouragement of piety among both the clergy and the laity. To accomplish this goal, the primate sponsored the translation and publication of a number of devotional texts from other countries, including the *Vita Christi* of Ludolph of Saxony (1501–1502), usually referred to as the Cartujano in Spain; the *Scala paradisis* of John Climacus (1504); a biography of Thomas a Kempis (1506); as well as works devoted to the life of Angela of Foligno;[4] and the letters and prayers of Catherine of Siena.[5] In the case of Angela of Foligno and Catherine of Siena, some five editions were published under the aegis of Cisneros. These included a Latin version entitled *Liber qui dicitur Angela de Fulginio* (Toledo, 1505), and translations from the Italian of the same (*Libro de la bienaventurada sancta Angela de Fulgino* [Toledo, 1510]); as well as the *Vida de la bienaventurada sancta Catarina de Sena* (Alcalá, 1511), based on the work of Raymond of Capua; *Obra de las epístolas y oraciones de . . . Sa. Catarina de Sena* (Alcalá, 1512); and another edition of the *Vida de Sa. Caterina* (Alcalá, 1511) that also provided lives of Sor Joana de Orbieto and Sor Margarita de Castello (Alcalá, 1511).[6] While these works served as guides to devotional practices, they also suggest a growing literacy among women readers more likely to know the vernacular than Latin. Given the fact that the editions used for the Spanish translations were, in some cases, those published in Italian, the spread of vernacular versions made access to reading by women possible.[7]

One of the cardinal's stated intentions in these endeavors was to ensure that the nuns of his archdiocese had suitable spiritual reading "so that they might read in the choir and in the refectory and that they might fulfill their obligations and avoid idleness."[8] Direct and indirect citation of these works by subsequent generations of nuns suggests that his wishes were fulfilled.[9]

An ancillary benefit also accrued to others besides those whom the primate first targeted. By fostering translation and publication of devotional works, Cisneros also hoped to provide an alternative to the romances of chivalry that "women and ignorant men read for amusement."[10] Although chivalric romances continued to entertain readers throughout the sixteenth and seventeenth centuries, nevertheless, devotional texts more than held their own in popularity, as the inventories of private libraries attest.[11]

Cisneros not only manifested his interest in reform through his patronage of publishing but also in his attraction to affective spirituality, especially as practiced by the nuns of his archdiocese. The lives and works of such visionaries as Angela of Foligno and Catherine of Siena provided examples of prayer and practice to those drawn to the mystical life. At the same time they validated the teachings of women, as the prologue to the Spanish translation of the life of Angela of Foligno suggests: "It appears that this strong woman clearly reveals what was hidden even from very educated men, who, nevertheless, were blinded by their carnal displays and understanding."[12]

While acquired knowledge is the province of males privileged to study at the university, infused knowledge characterizes that of women.[13] The means to disseminate the latter resided in part in the printing press.

The dual interests of Cisneros in publishing and in encouraging affective spirituality coalesced in his involvement with two visionary women of his own archdiocese, Sor María de Santo Domingo (popularly known as the Beata de Piedrahita) and Madre Juana de la Cruz, abbess of the Franciscan convent of Santa María de la Cruz. In the circumstances of their lives and their literary production, they represent the power of "translation" in text and action set in motion by Cisneros.

Sor María de Santo Domingo, an illiterate peasant woman, entered the Dominican convent of her native Piedrahita as a lay sister, or *beata*. In 1504 she moved to another convent in nearby Avila, then, in 1507, she transferred yet again. Later in the same year she moved once more with a band of followers to Toledo. The group was intent on reforming the Spanish Dominicans along the lines laid out by Savonarola and Catherine of Siena. One of the beata's followers, Antonio de la Peña, was also the translator of the works of Catherine.[14] In Sor María, all of her followers believed that they had found a leader equal to the eminent Sienese mystic and stigmatic.[15]

The basis for their belief resided in more than her pious utterances while in an ecstatic state. Just as both Catherine of Siena and Angela of Foligno had done, Sor María manifested one of the signs of stigmata (the wound in the side). She also abstained from food for long periods of time.[16] She could neither read nor write, so that, like Catherine, she depended on others to transcribe what she said while in a trancelike state.[17] Although she was unable to read the works of the two Italian visionaries, as Mary Giles points out, "it is not far-fetched to suppose that she knew about them through her friend, Antonio de la Peña, who had translated the life of Catherine at the order of Cisneros."[18]

Controversy surrounding the beata's utterances brought her to the attention of the Inquisition and then the cardinal and the king. Cisneros was in a powerful position to either silence her or protect her. He chose the latter course, claiming as he did that he "had never seen living doctrine except from this Sister María."[19] Part of his motivation seems to have been his interest in reforming the Dominicans along the lines of his own order. In the beata he perceived a nucleus around which to build a reform movement.[20] At his behest, Fray Diego de Vitoria compiled her utterances into a work entitled the *Book of Prayer* [Libro de oración]. In the prologue, the editor likens her to Christ and, implicitly, to Catherine of Siena, because of "the miracle that occurs each year on the day of the Passion when her right side opens, pouring forth blood from the same place where the lance wounded the side of Christ."[21]

Although unlettered as was Catherine, according to Fray Diego, Sor María's teaching is nonetheless valid. Invoking the authority of Augustine, he defends her right to teach: "The unlettered rise up and grasp heaven while we with our learning sink into Hell."[22] Turning the tables on men and their university education, he argues further that "the unlettered are those with acquired learning [that is, men] and that in terms of infused learning, the Holy Spirit bestowed as much on this His Handmaid as on any other."[23]

The prologue imputes more sinister motives to her detractors in a subtle evocation of her *limpieza de sangre* as a *cristiana vieja,* in contrast to their more suspect lineage.[24] The editor remarks that she is the daughter of poor parents and, therefore, of pure or Old Christian blood. In contrast, her "persecutors are . . . either of the lineage of Our Lord's [*sic*] [that is, Jewish] or persons of scant prudence, devotion and humility or changeable people who are ruled by their passions."[25] It was an argument sure to resonate with the suspicions prevalent in the court of Queen Isabella.[26]

Before the Inquisition, others made even greater claims, such as Fray Antonio de la Peña's testimony that "when the said Sor María speaks in ecstatic rapture she seems to have . . . a different way of speaking, one more exalted, elegant and excellent than when she speaks ordinarily."[27] Equally impressive to those who witnessed her raptures was her ability to answer questions on theology and Sacred Scripture put to her by learned men.[28]

Contemporaneously with the case of Sor María de Santo Domingo, Cisneros also became involved in that of another visionary nun, Madre Juana de la Cruz. Like Sor María, she, too, exhibited an inclination to asceticism and contemplative prayer at an early age. At thirteen she defied parental authority and entered the Franciscan convent of Santa María de la Cruz in Cubas, where, unlike the Beata de Piedrahita, she remained for the rest of her life. She rose quickly through a number of conventual offices and eventually served as abbess.[29]

The convent of Santa María de la Cruz had become cloistered under the auspices of Cisnerian reforms and had adopted the rule of the Regular Third Order of Saint Francis.[30] Among the texts found in the conventual library were the lives of the Franciscan visionaries Angela of Foligno and Clare of Assisi,[31] as well as the works of Catherine of Siena, Bernard of Clairvaux, Bonaventure, and the Cartujano;[32] in short, works made available by the press at Alcalá. Given Madre Juana's position as abbess, it is likely that she could read them. What she synthesized from her mystical predecessors informs the composition of her own *Book of Consolation* [Libro del conorte].

As was the case with Catherine of Siena and Sor María de Santo Domingo, Madre Juana de la Cruz did not actually set pen to paper in producing her book. Due to a series of illnesses, paralysis rendered her incapable of doing so. Rather, over the course of some thirteen years, she preached sermons to her nuns consisting of novelized Gospel events and allegorical interpretations of heavenly pageants. Her companions transcribed some of these into the *Book of Consolation*.[33]

Strictly speaking, Madre Juana never claimed authorship of what she said but, rather, she credited God with using her as an oracle through which he transmitted his messages to mankind.[34] Hence, she assumes a position similar to that assigned by Fray Diego de Vitoria to Sor María de Santo Domingo, who stipulated that God could elect to speak through women's voices as readily as through men's. Catherine of Siena had assumed a similar role.

Madre Juana's assertion both empowered her to assume a masculine role as preacher even as it validated what she said. In what Surtz describes as a "brilliant display of circular reasoning, Juana argues that if writing is an act of obedience and of submission, then obedience and submission empower her to write."[35] In fact, she maintains that God is indifferent to whether a man or woman speaks, citing the biblical examples of Mary Magdalene and Elizabeth as worthy witnesses to important events in the life of Christ.[36]

Joining the debate over acquired and infused learning, she argues in another sermon that God deliberately hides divine secrets from the learned only to reveal them to "the simple and despised and humble" ("los sinples y despreçiados e humildes"), among whom she clearly includes herself.[37] In his annotations to her book, Fray Francisco Torres takes up the same argument, convinced that God had selected her in order to humble "the proud and ambitious and puffed up learned men of this time." He maintains that she embodies "'infused knowledge,' infused by God and not acquired by 'human industry or study,'"[38] ultimately identifying her as a great theologian.[39] Yet, paradoxically, he also describes her as both "a very ignorant woman" ("idiotíssima mujer") and a "very wise virgin" ("sapientíssima virgen"). Torres renders these epithets laudatory and admirable when he identifies in her book a prophetic voice "taught by God" ("enseñada de Dios").[40]

Juana justified her appropriation of a traditionally male role by citing the unusual circumstances of her conception and birth. Her *Vida* asserts that she was originally conceived as male but was miraculously changed into a female while in the womb.[41] The prominence of her Adam's apple provided a physiological justification for this remarkable claim. At the same time, it made her a "mujer varonil" (a manly woman) in more than the metaphoric sense. Her physical appearance manifested the masculine qualities that she believed ratified her role as preacher.

Unlike the *Book of Prayer* of Sor María de Santo Domingo, Juana's *Book of Consolation* was not published in her lifetime. Indeed, not until the twentieth century was an abridged edition of the *Libro de conorte* published, and some of the sermons translated.[42] The original manuscript of the *Libro* eventually became part of Philip II's collection at the Escorial, where it was annotated by two different priests. Frémaux-Crouzet speculates that the first to gloss her work was the Franciscan Francisco Ortiz Yáñez. The second, more favorable, gloss was the work of Francisco Torres in 1567–68.[43] Both men ultimately faced the scrutiny of the Inquisition for their association with other visionaries.

Presumably, Cisneros was aware of the existence of the *Conorte,* but during 1509 when the sermons were transcribed he was in Oran on a military expedition. After his return, he was in communication with Juana concerning the exercise of her abbatial powers.[44] At the same time, his attention was also focused on assisting the king in governing the country until his grandson, Charles, came of age. Clearly, after Cisneros' death in 1517, the Holy Office began to take a harder line with all visionaries, especially women, whom they condemned as *alumbrados.*[45]

Both Sor María de Santo Domingo and Madre Juana de la Cruz share more than passing resemblance to such forebears as Catherine of Siena and Angela of Foligno. Because of their humble beginnings and lack of formal education, all of these women translate their visions to the printed page through the medium of others. In doing so they assert, however indirectly, their right to teach. Equally significant, they implicitly reject the application of the Pauline dictum "mulieres in ecclesia taceant," usually invoked to silence women like them.[46]

Although excluded from higher education by reason of their sex, nevertheless, they gained a modicum of legitimacy by embracing the interiorized spirituality characteristic of the *devotio moderna.* Still, the dichotomy between their lack of formal education and the importance attached to their teaching polarized male opinion. While some men invested their utterances with oracular significance, others dismissed each of them as a "mujer idiota y sin letras"—that is, an ignorant and illiterate woman.[47]

It remained for Cisneros to ratify their teaching, first by extending his ecclesiastical protection to them and then by setting in motion publication of works such as that of Sor María de Santo Domingo.[48] His actions reflect the contradictions of his own varied interests. On the one hand, he supported university scholarship that produced the Complutensian Polyglot Bible by employing learned men who oftentimes scorned the likes of Sor María de Santo Domingo and Madre Juana de la Cruz. On the other, he encouraged new, affective forms of spirituality among clergy and laity alike, forms especially attractive to those without access to higher education.[49] Concomitantly, in his establishment of the press at Alcalá he assured publication of the Polyglot and of devotional works by women from Catherine to María de Santo Domingo. Cisneros thus translated the debate between infused and acquired learning to concrete form through his many enterprises.

In doing so, he prepared the way for a subsequent generation of women writers who would add immeasurably to the fund of spiritual literature. By validating the ecstatic utterances of Sor María de Santo Domingo and Madre Juana de la Cruz, he created a climate conducive to other "enlightened" women drawn to affective spirituality. By arranging for translation and publication of the works of European visionaries as well as those of Spanish writers, he ensured a library of texts for others to consult. Among those who would benefit profoundly from these endeavors were Saint Teresa of Avila and the nuns of the Carmelite reform, who acknowledged their familiarity with the works of Catherine, Bonaventure, and the Cartujano even as they embraced the life of contemplation described by these writers. What began as a literal translation from one language to another at Cisneros' insistence thus became a figurative movement of ideas and actions from person to person and, potentially, from generation to generation.

With the rise of Protestantism and the death of the cardinal, however, conservative forces within Spain eventually silenced this promising beginning. The Index of Forbidden Books produced in 1559 by the inquisitor Valdés at Valladolid and later revised and elaborated by Gaspar de Quiroga in 1583 prohibited the publication of many of these texts and virtually all devotional literature in the vernacular.[50] As a consequence, this promising movement at the beginning of the sixteenth century, which benefited women both spiritually and educationally, had, by its close, come to an abrupt end.

Notes

1. Marcel Bataillon, *Erasmo y España,* 2nd ed. (Mexico-Buenos Aires: Fondo de Cultura Económica, 1966), p. 1, considers Cisneros' early reforms of the monastic orders in Spain one of the reasons that Protestant reformers had little success later in the century. He considers Cisneros a pivotal figure in the eventual Spanish reaction to the Protestant Reformation, which occured after his death. There are a number of works chronicling the life and works of Cisneros, many based on that of his first biographer, Alvar Gómez de Castro, *De las hazañas de Francisco Jiménez de Cisneros,* ed. and trans. José Oroz Reta (Madrid: Fundación Universitaria Española, 1984). Some have compared Cisneros to France's Cardinal Richelieu, among them M. Brion, *Le cardinal François Ximenes: Le Richelieu de l'Espagne* (Paris: Éd. Franciscaines, 1948); and José Bañares y Magan, *Cisneros y Richelieu: Ensayo de un*

paralelo entre ambos Cardenales y su tiempo (Pontevedra: 1911). J. B. Trend, *Alfonso the Sage and Other Spanish Essays* (London: Constable, 1926), pp. 24–25, is far more critical of the part he played in reform in Spain. For more on the contacts between Cisneros and the Catholic Monarchs, see Jean Hippolyte Mariejol, *The Spain of Ferdinand and Isabella,* trans. Benjamin Keen (New Brunswick, NJ: Rutgers University Press, 1961).

2. Marcel Bataillon, *Erasmo y España,* p. 5. Mary Giles, introduction to *The Book of Prayer of Sor María de Santo Domingo* (Albany: State University of New York Press, 1990), p. 40, points out that in 1495 the Catholic Monarchs commissioned Cisneros to begin reforms in the women's monasteries.

3. For more on the University of Alcalá, see J. Ignacio Tellechea, "La création de l'université d'Alcalá et sa signification dans la Renaissance espagnole," in *Pédagogues et juristes,* ed. Pierre Mesnard (Paris: Vrin, 1963), pp. 137–47; and J. Fernández Montaña, *Rasgos principales del cardenal Cisneros, Arzobispo de Toledo más otras sobre la inquisición con apéndice vindicativo de Felipe II y las descalzas reales de Madrid* (Madrid: Helenica, 1921), who lists the endowed chairs and their occupants.

4. Ronald Surtz, *The Guitar of God: Gender, Power, and Authority in the Visionary World of Mother Juana de la Cruz (1481–1534)* (Philadelphia: University of Pennsylvania Press, 1990), p. 2, notes that Cisneros commissioned the translation and published this book bearing his coat of arms.

5. Marcel Bataillon, *Erasmo y España,* pp. 44, 49. Eusebio Martínez de Velasco, *El cardenal Jiménez de Cisneros (1492–1517)* (Madrid: Dirección y administración, 1883), pp. 171–72, lists other titles. José García Oro, *El cardenal Cisneros. Vida y empresas,* 2 vols. (Madrid: Editorial Católica, 1993), 2:486, notes the popularity of these and other authors, including Saint Bonaventure, Jean Gerson and Savonarola, among the European devout. Saint Teresa of Avila was familiar with the works of Catherine of Siena and the *Vita Christi,* as was Sor Juana Inés de la Cruz. The rule proposed by Archbishop Talavera (a later primate of Spain) for nuns as well as his advice to married women included these and other titles. See O. González Hernandez, "Fray Hernando de Talavera. Un aspecto nuevo de su personalidad," *Hispania sacra* 13 (1960): 143–74, and Fray Hernando de Talavera, "De cómo se ha de ordenar el tiempo para que sea bien expendido. Avisación a la . . . muy noble señora Doña María Pacheco, Condesa de Benavente," in *Escritores místicos españoles,* vol. 16 of Nueva Biblioteca de Autores Españoles (Madrid: Bailly/Baillière, 1911), 1:93–103.

6. Pedro Sainz Rodríguez, *La siembra mística del cardenal Cisneros y las reformas en la iglesia* (Madrid: Fundación Universitaria Española, 1979), pp. 43–44, lists these editions as does James Lyell, *Cardinal Ximenes* (London: Grafton & Co., 1917), pp. 113–14. The latter also indicates two editions of John Climacus' *Scala paradisis.*

7. V. Beltrán de Heredia, *Miscelánea Beltrán de Heredia* (Salamanca: Dominicos de las Provincias de España, 1972), 3:527–528, points out that Antonio de la Peña translated the *Vida* of Catherine from the Latin original and the

Epístolas from the Italian or *toscano* version. García Oro, *El cardenal Cisneros,* 1:246–247, notes the Italian edition as the basis of the Spanish translation of the letters. He also credits de la Peña with translating the *Exposición del salmo Miserere* of Savonarola and the *Vida* of Catherine of Siena.

8. "Para que se leyesen en el coro y en el refectorio, y ellas atendiesen a su obligación y desterasen la ociosidad." Cited by Julian Martín Abad, *La imprenta en Alcalá de Henares (1502–1600)* (Madrid: Editorial Arco Libros, 1991)

9. Saint Teresa of Avila among others refers to the works of Catherine of Siena, while a number of other participants in the Carmelite reform intimate a similar knowledge of these works.

10. According to Valentin Esprit Fléchier, *Histoire du cardinal Ximenès* (Paris: 1693), n.p., the object of their publication was "pour empêcher les femmes et les ignorans de s'amuser à lire des romans." Quoted by Reginald Merton, *Cardinal Ximenes and the Making of Spain* (London: Kegan Paul, Trench, Trubner & Co., 1934), p. 139. Ludwig Pfandl, *Juana la Loca* (Madrid: Austral, 1955), pp. 33–34, offers similar reasons for Cisneros' decision. Ronald Surtz, *Writing Women in Late Medieval and Early Modern Spain* (Philadelphia: University of Pennsylvania Press, 1995), p. 11, points out that "when Cisneros sponsored the printing of a Castilian translation of Saint Vincent Ferrer's *Tractatus de vita spirituali,* the translation omitted the chapters in which the saint warned against the temptation to seek after visions and revelations. Significantly, the vernacular version of the *Tractatus* was appended to the Cisneros-sponsored Castilian translation of the *Book* of the female mystic, Angela of Foligno."

11. Harvey J. Graff, *The Legacies of Literacy* (Bloomington and Indianapolis: Indiana University Press, 1987), p. 121, states that "the literary face of a sixteenth-century reader was qualitatively different from that of his or her fourteenth-century predecessor." See also Sara T. Nalle, "Literacy and Culture in Early Modern Spain," *Past & Present,* 125 (1989): 86. Martín Abad, *La imprenta en Alcalá de Henares,* describes in detail the editions published in Alcalá under Cisneros and his successors.

12. "[P]aresce que en esta muger fuerte claramente se muestra lo que estava abscondido aun a los varones muy especulativos, pero ciegos con sus carnales exposiciones y entendimientos." Cited in Surtz, *Guitar,* p. 10, n. 9.

13. See Anne Frémaux-Crouzet, "L'Antiféminisme comme théologie du pouvoir chez Melchor Cano," in *Hommage à Louise Bertrand (1921–1979): Études ibériques et latino américaines* (Paris: Les Belles Lettres, 1983), p. 148; Otger Steggink, "Teresa de Jesús, mujer y mística ante la teología y los teólogos," *Carmelus* 29 (1982) :113; and Surtz, *Guitar,* p. 2, who comment on the tensions between the two approaches to spirituality and learning. Felipe Fernández Armesto, "Cardinal Cisneros as a Patron of Printing," in *God and Man in Medieval Spain: Essays in Honour of J. R. L. Highfield,* eds. Derek W. Lomax and David Mackenzie (Warminster, England: Aris and Phillips, 1989), p. 166, criticizes Cisneros' "notorious susceptibility to excesses of spinsterly piety," while Sainz Rodríguez, *La siembra mística,* pp.

35–36, defends the cardinal's predilection by noting that Cisneros "did no more than agree with an atmosphere that was evolving throughout the prolonged crisis . . . that provoked the necessity for reform" [no hacía más que coincidir con un ambiente que venía desarrollandose a lo largo de la prolongada crisis . . . que provocó la necesidad de la reforma].

14. Beltrán de Heredia, *Miscelánea,* pp. 449–50, provides background on Antonio de la Peña, who enjoyed the confidence of both Cisneros and the Isabelline court. According to Beltrán, he was "the most active promotor of Savonarola's thought in Spain" [el más activo promotor del savonarolismo en España].

15. Sor María (ed. Giles), *The Book of Prayer,* p. 135. See also, Vicente Beltrán de Heredia, "Directrices de la espiritualidad dominicana en Castilla durante las primeras décadas del siglo XVI," in *Corrientes espirituales en la España del siglo XVI: Trabajos* (Barcelona: Juan Flors, 1963), p. 200.

16. Sor María (ed. Giles), *The Book of Prayer,* p. 55. In her stigmata as well as her fasting, Sor María resembles Saint Catherine of Siena, as Caroline Walker Bynum, *Holy Feast and Holy Fast* (Berkeley and Los Angeles: University of California Press, 1987), p. 166, describes her.

17. In Sor María (ed. Giles), *The Book of Prayer,* pp. 55, 91–92, Giles comments on "composition" vs. "writing" in both cases.

18. Sor María (ed. Giles), *The Book of Prayer,* p. 55.

19. "Nunca había visto doctrina viva sino desta soror María." Quoted by José Manuel Blecua, "Estudio," in *Libro de la oración de Sor María de Santo Domingo* (Madrid: Hauser y Menet, 1948), n.p., n. 10. Blecua does not paginate his edition. Henry Charles Lea, *Chapters from the Religious History of Spain Connected with the Inquisition* (New York: Burt Franklin, repr., 1967), p. 220, repeats Cisneros' opinion.

20. See Frémaux-Crouzet, "Antiféminisme," 144; García Oro, *El cardenal Cisneros,* 1:241; and Jodi Bilinkoff, "Charisma and Controversy: The Case of María de Santo Domingo," *Archivo Dominicano* 10 (1989): 32; all of whom interpret his motivation in this manner.

21. Sor María (ed. Giles), *The Book of Prayer,* p. 23; Blecua, "Estudio," a.Ir.

22. In Sor María (ed. Giles), *The Book of Prayer,* p. 130, Fray Diego comments on Sor María's obedience.

23. Ibid., p. 124. See Ernest W. McDonnell, *The Beguines and Beghards in Medieval Culture* (New Brunswick: Rutgers University Press, 1954), p. 376, who comments on the penchant among biographers of women visionaries to "underline inspiration rather than learning . . . [since] such a source of knowledge or information immediately assigns to writings, *dictante Spiritu sancto,* an authority that defies criticism."

24. *Limpieza de sangre,* or purity of blood, referred to a lineage free from Jewish or Moorish ancestry. *Cristianos viejos* or "Old Christians" were those who traced their lineage to wholly Christian roots, as opposed to the so-called *cristianos nuevos* or "New Christians," whose families had converted from Judaism or Islam.

25. Sor María (ed. Giles), *The Book of Prayer*, p. 132; Blecua, "Estudio," iiii–v. See Surtz, *Writing Women*, p. 103, who interprets a similar passage equating her with Mary Magdalene.

26. During the reign of Isabella the expulsion of the Jews in 1492 marked the culmination of the queen's almost morbid religiosity and her equation of national identity with Christian faith. She also saw to the establishment of the Spanish Inquisition as a means of enforcing orthodoxy. The uprising of the Alpujarra Muslims early in the sixteenth century led to a similar decree demanding their conversion or expulsion in February of 1502.

27. "Cuando la dicha soror María habla en raptu parece tener . . . otro stilo de hablar muy más alto, elegante y excelente que cuando habla extra raptu." Cited in Blecua, "Estudio," as number 19 of the points made in the second defense of Sor María.

28. Sor María (ed. Giles), *The Book of Prayer*, p. 22. See also *Defensas* in Blecua, "Estudio." Ronald Surtz, "La Madre Juana de la Cruz (1481–1534) y la cuestión de la autoridad religiosa femenina," *Nueva revista de filología hispánica* 33 (1984): 488, remarks that "the idea that God reveals his mysteries to the humble and among them to women was taken seriously in Cisneros' Spain" [la idea de que Dios revela sus misterios a los humildes, y entre ellos a las mujeres, se tomaba en serio en la España de Cisneros]. He also comments on this "strategy" in *Writing Women*, p. 6. Alison Weber, *Teresa of Avila and the Rhetoric of Femininity* (Princeton: Princeton University Press, 1990), p. 26, states that "in the eyes of Cisneros and his followers a woman's humble ignorance was no obstacle to spiritual knowledge—ignorance could even give a woman the moral advantage." Jodi Bilinkoff, "A Spanish Prophetess and Her Patrons: The Case of Sor María de Santo Domingo," *Sixteenth Century Journal* 23 (1992): 33, argues that Sor María's prophecies "gave needed rhetorical and spiritual support to Cisneros's public policies as monastic reformer, inquisitor, and missionary-crusader." Angela Selke, "El iluminismo de los conversos y la Inquisición. Cristianismo interior de los alumbrados: Resentimiento y sublimación," in *La Inquisición española: Nueva visión, nuevos horizontes*, ed. Joaquín Pérez Villanueva (Madrid: Siglos veintiuno, 1980), p. 617, goes so far as to state that "Illuminism begins to appear in Spain at the end of the fifteenth century, undoubtedly encouraged by Cisneros's reforms" [el iluminismo empieza a brotar en España a fines del siglo XV, fomentado sin duda por las reformas de Cisneros].

29. Anne Frémaux-Crouzet, "Alegato en favor de 'las mujeres e idiotas': aspectos del franciscanismo feminista en la *Glosa* de Francisco de Torres a *El conorte* (1567–68) de Juana de la Cruz," in *Homenaje a José Antonio Maravall*, 3 vols. (Madrid: Centro de Investigaciones Sociológicas, 1985), 2:103.

30. Surtz, *Guitar*, p. 3. Frémaux-Crouzet, "Alegato," p. 103, also provides a brief history of this convent.

31. One of the sermons of Madre Juana focuses on the feast of Saint Clare.

32. Frémaux-Crouzet, "Alegato," p. 105.

33. Surtz, *Guitar,* p. 6. Manuel Serrano y Sanz, *Apuntes para una biblioteca de Escritoras Españolas,* 4 vols. (Madrid: Biblioteca de Autores Españoles, 1903), 2:2.651, comments that "composition of the *Libro del conorte* was completed in 1509 and it seems to be the original manuscript" [se acabó de escribir (el *Libro del conorte*) en 1509, y parece ser manuscrito original]. Later, he recognized that the nuns of the community actually wrote the manuscript. See, also, García Oro, *El cardenal Cisneros,* 1:253, who mentions a biography of her written by one of the nuns.

34. Surtz, *Guitar,* p. 24.

35. Ibid., p. 123.

36. *Conorte,* fol. 76v.

37. Ibid., fol. 369v.

38. "[L]os soberbios y ambiciosos e hinchados letrados de este tiempo" (fol. 38a); "la 'ciencia infusa' infundida por Dios y no adquirida 'por industria humana ni ciencia'" (fol. 85a). Cited in Frémaux-Crouzet, "Alegato," p. 112. See also "L'Antiféminisme" 146–47.

39. *Conorte,* fol. 353b.

40. Ibid., fol. 134b; Frémaux-Crouzet, "Alegato," p. 110.

41. Surtz, *Guitar,* p. 6.

42. Surtz published some of the *Conorte* in the appendices of his *Guitar of God.*

43. Frémaux-Crouzet, "Alegato," pp. 100–101. In addition to the glosses, a life of Juana is also in the Escorial. *Vida y fin de la bienaventurada virgen sancta Juana de la Cruz,* MSS. K-III-13, is cited in Frémaux-Crouzet, "Alegato," p. 100, n. 5, and Surtz, "La madre Juana," 485, n. 9.

44. Surtz, "La madre Juana," 484, refers to two *rescriptos* that Cisneros wrote in 1510 regarding the chaplaincy at Cubas.

45. The term means "enlightened," but in Spain it was associated with heterodox religious practices and thus became grounds for investigation by the Inquisition.

46. Surtz, *Guitar,* pp. 24–25; 66.

47. In his *Censura* of Archbishop Carranza, Melchor Cano is especially critical of "*mugercillas ignorantes*" and "*mugercillas ociosas,*" that is, uneducated women who dared to teach others. See, Frémaux-Crouzet, "L'Antiféminisme" 149–50, 157, for more on this theme. In spite of the admiration of others, Cajetan and the Dominicans eventually reined in Sor María de Santo Domingo and her followers, as Bilinkoff, "Charisma and Controversy," 66, points out. The silencing of the reformers met with Beltrán's approval (*Miscelánea,* p. 410): "Finally good sense was imposed and, with the prompt reintegration of the dissidents into the province, all danger of division was eliminated" [Al fin se impuso el buen sentido y, con la pronta reincorporación de los disidentes a la provincia, quedó conjurado todo peligro de división].

48. Sor María (ed. Giles), *The Book of Prayer,* p. 77, explains Cisneros' involvement in the transcription of the text after the examination of Sor María

concluded in 1510. As she points out, "1518 is the probable date of publication" of the *Book;* that is, a year after Cisneros' death.

49. For example, see Jodi Bilinkoff, *The Avila of Saint Teresa* (Ithaca: Cornell University Press, 1989), pp. 140–41; and Weber, *Teresa of Avila,* pp. 21–22.

50. Both Bataillon and Lea discuss in some detail the evolution of the Index and its effect on the publication of devotional literature, especially in the vernacular. In her *Vida* 26.6, Saint Teresa laments the proscription of many of the works that had assisted her in advancing in mystical prayer.

CHAPTER 13

"ESTE GRAN DIOS DE LAS CAVALLERÍAS"
[THIS GREAT GOD OF CHIVALRIC DEEDS]:
ST. TERESA'S PERFORMANCES OF
THE NOVELS OF CHIVALRY

Carole A. Slade

Teresa of Avila is often represented book in hand. The book is not one she is reading, but one she is writing, with the Holy Spirit hovering over her quill pen to demonstrate that the words are not her own. Teresa (1515–1582) was in fact quite bookish, and quite well read for a sixteenth-century Spanish woman. In the words of Joel Saugnieux, author of an important study of popular and high culture in early modern Spain, "The entire existence of St. Teresa is organized around, depends upon, and proceeds from books."[1]

Throughout her autobiographical writings Teresa represents many of her most significant experiences as scenes of reading, that is, as scenes of engagement with written texts.[2] Always a very imaginative person, and unusually impressionable in childhood, Teresa read subjectively, searching for explanations of her life, projecting herself into various narrative contexts, and very often acting out the parts of one or more characters. In this surrender of self to the world of the text, Teresa resembled the majority of lay readers of her time: Bruce Wardropper attributes this practice of blurring the distinction between self and text to *devotio moderna,* which trained worshipers to insert themselves empathetically into visual and verbal texts, while Juan Manuel Cacho Blecua ascribes it to a need for new role models in the wake of the Middle Ages and, I would add, in the aftermath of the Reconquest.[3]

For some or all of these reasons, as well as for her lifelong engagement with books, Teresa narrates the long, tortuous path to her unequivocal dedication to a monastic vocation as a series of scenes of reading. When she was about seven, Teresa and her older brother Rodrigo ran away from home to follow in the footsteps of the martyrs whose lives they had read (or listened to) from the *Flos sanctorum,* the Spanish translation of Jacobus de Voragine's *Golden Legend* (ca. 1260). That project having been thwarted by a relative who is said to have retrieved the youngsters just outside the walls of Avila, they tried out another type of saintly life, that of the hermit, with no more success: "En una huerta que havía en casa procurávamos, como podíamos, hacer ermitas, puniendo unas pedrecillas, que luego se nos caían" [In a garden that we had in our house we tried as we could to make hermitages piling up some little stones, which afterward would quickly fall down again] (*El libro de la vida* 1.5; hereafter *Vida*).[4] At eighteen, still undecided about her future, Teresa visited a paternal uncle, Pedro Sánchez de Cepeda, who was preparing for the priesthood by reading religious and devotional books *en romance* (in Spanish). At the time, she had no interest whatever in religious books: "Hacíame le leyese, y aunque no era amiga de ellos, mostrava que sí" [He asked me to read these books to him; and although I did not like them, I pretended to] (*Vida* 3.4). Nevertheless, this scene of reading to him apparently modified her literary tastes, for later that year her reading of the *Letters of St. Jerome* gave her the courage to tell her father that, in defiance of his wishes, she had decided to join a convent (*Vida* 3.7).[5] Early one morning in 1536 she ran away from home to the Carmelite convent of the Encarnación, where she took vows in 1537. She withheld full emotional commitment to the religious life until her final conversion experience in 1554, which she narrates in part as a scene of reading of Augustine's *Confessions.*[6] Only then did she correct the course she ascribes in large part to a scene of reading staged by her mother nearly thirty years earlier, a clandestine reading of novels of chivalry. Teresa's conversion, among other reversals, entailed translating her participation in chivalric narratives from the carnal to the spiritual register, where she could perform both the feminine and masculine roles.

Teresa does not say how she learned to read; indeed, she seems to take for granted her own literacy and that of her parents, siblings, and relatives. Her descriptions of her childhood home emphasize religious instruction through rituals and readings, which in the typical family would have been given by the mother. Although her maternal grandmother was illiterate, Teresa's mother, Beatriz de Ahumada (ca. 1495–1528), read fluently enough to derive pleasure as well as instruction from reading. How and when Beatriz learned to read is not known, but she must have profited from educational opportunities provided to women in the late fifteenth century by Queen Isabella as part of the Catholic Monarchs' campaign to unite the Spanish nation religiously as well as politically and geographically. In *Tiempo y vida de Santa Teresa,* the most comprehensive biography of Teresa, Efrén de la Madre de Dios and Otger Steggink surmise that Beatriz taught the children to read and that a tutor helped teach them to write.[7] Teresa's observation that her mother's nearly continual childbearing, of ten children in nineteen years, had given her mother the aspect of an old woman by the age of thirty, suggests that tutors probably contributed to the children's instruction in reading.

When Teresa was twelve or thirteen, her mother initiated her into the reading of novels of chivalry. Based on French translations of medieval Arthurian materials, these novels attained widespread popularity in sixteenth-century Spain. More accurately called books of chivalric deeds, the novels are prose narratives of the adventures of a legendary or fictional knight who performs heroic deeds in a series of combat situations, including wars, duels, jousts, and tournaments.[8] Unlike the epic hero, the Arthurian knight of chivalry has no homeland (hence his designation as *caballero andante* [knight errant]). Often he is an orphan or foundling who as the story opens does not know his birthright, which is subsequently revealed to be noble or royal.[9] His currency is his courage, and with it he wins honor and glory, which in turn, together with his fidelity and courtesy, earn him the love of a beautiful lady, often the daughter of a king. Although some authors claim historicity for these novels, they make no more than vague reference to any actual time or place. Garci Rodríguez de Montalvo, who inaugurated the Spanish novel of chivalry with the first five books of the *Amadís de Gaula* series, defined the genre in his prologue as *historia fengida* [imagined history].[10] Montalvo's novels of chivalry share with the literature of courtly love the prolonged separations of knight and lady, agonizing for both, but especially for the knight, who must fight his way back to her. Unlike the lady of courtly love poetry, this lady is not married. Private vows between the lovers suffice to legitimate sexual consummation, which is often narrated in detail that, if not explicit by modern standards, was considered licentious at the time.

Notwithstanding the obligatory censure of the novels of chivalry, which by the time she wrote the *Vida* (1561–1565) had been unofficially condemned by the Church, Teresa's scene of reading the novels radiates happiness in the memory of spending time alone with her mother and sharing this mutually enjoyable, diverting activity:

> Era aficionada a libros de cavallerías, y no tan mal tomava este pasatiempo como yo le tomé para mí, porque no perdía su lavor, sino desenvolviémonos para leer en ellos. Y por ventura lo hacía para no pensar en grandes travajos

que tenía, y ocupar sus hijos que no anduviesen en otras cosas perdidos. De esto le pesava tanto a mi padre, que se havía de tener aviso a que no lo viese. Yo comencé a quedarme en costumbre de leerlos, y aquella pequeña falta que en ella vi me comenzó a enfriar los deseos y comenzar a faltar en lo demás; y parecíame no era malo, con gastar muchas horas de el día y de la noche en tan vano ejercicio, aunque ascondida de mi padre.

[She loved books of chivalry. But this pastime didn't hurt her the way it did me, for she did not fail to do her duties; and we used to read them together in our free time. Perhaps she did this reading to escape thinking of the great trials she had to bear and to busy her children with something so that they would not turn to other things dangerous to them. Our reading such books was a matter that weighed so much upon my father that we had to be cautioned lest he see us. I began to get the habit of reading these books. And by that little fault, which I saw in my mother, I started to grow cold in my desires and to fail in everything else. I didn't think it was wrong to waste many hours of the day and night in such a useless practice, even though hidden from my father.] (*Vida* 2.1)

Although compacted and contradictory, as are many of Teresa's accounts of her early years, the passage yields a good deal of information about Teresa's development of gender identifications and constructions. Teresa's adolescent imitation of her mother in her choice of reading matter can be considered an echo of infantile language acquisition, a process in which, according to many theories of psychological development, an infant daughter identifies her language with her mother's, while the infant boy, in differentiating himself with respect to gender, also distinguishes his language from hers.[11] While lamenting the time she now considers wasted in this literary pastime, she also justifies it on various grounds: Her mother needed relief from household chores, which in any case she did not neglect, and from unspecified emotional burdens; they read in their "free time"; and her involvement with this reading may have protected her from even more "dangerous" activities. Teresa does not say why her father disapproves of the activity, and although she implies that he disapproves her shift in literary taste from the *libros buenos* in his library, the actual reasons could have extended to resentment of this pleasurable occupation that removed the two female members of his household from his control. The onset of Beatriz' terminal illness probably marked the end of this conspiratorial reading; she died in late 1528, when Teresa was thirteen. Teresa relates that she immediately required a substitute, and she chose one with whom she could envision an eternal relationship: "Como yo comencé a entender lo que havía perdido, afligida fuime a una imagen de Nuestra Señora y supliquéla fuese mi madre, con muchas lágrimas" [When I began to understand what I had lost, I went, afflicted, before an image of our Lady and besought her with many tears to be my mother (*Vida* 1.7)]. At the same time, she began to prepare herself for the rituals of courtship, in effect following her mother's footsteps toward becoming a wife.

Teresa does not name the novels they read, but critics usually assume that these included the cycle of *Amadís de Gaula* and his descendants, the most popular of the chivalric novels in Spain.[12] At least one volume was published every year beginning in 1508, and all editions considered together, they were the bestselling books of Spain's Golden Age.[13] At the time Teresa and her mother read the novels, probably between 1527 and mid-1528, they would have had several editions of *Amadís* to satisfy Teresa's insatiable appetite: "Era tan estremo lo que en esto me embevía, que si no tenía libro nuevo, no me parece tenía contento" [I was so completely taken up with this reading that I didn't think I could be happy if I didn't have a new book] (*Vida* 2.1). The first four books of *Amadís de Gaula* were published in 1508 and reprinted in 1511, 1519, 1521, and 1526, to cite only the imprints available during this span of time.[14] Printings of the fifth book, *Sergas* [*Deeds*] *de Esplandián*, the adventures of Amadis's son, were issued in 1510, 1521, 1525, and 1526; of the sixth, *Florisando*, nephew of Amadís, in 1510 and 1526; of the seventh, *Lisuarte de Grecia*, grandson of Amadís, in 1514 and 1525.[15] In addition, twelve other Spanish novels of chivalry, as well as translations from French, Portuguese, and Catalan, had been published by 1528, though in smaller numbers and to less acclaim.[16] The *Amadís* series, considered the most sentimental of the genre for a greater emphasis on romantic courtship and idealized love, not only would have been the most readily available but also very likely the most appealing to both mother and daughter.

Their apparently easy access to books seems as potentially threatening to her father as any titles Teresa and her mother may have read. The scene implies a casual relationship with books not unlike that enjoyed by consumers of the modern paperback. Teresa's father owned a library, which was inventoried in 1511 after the death of his first wife. The catalogue of this library lists some of the devotional and inspirational books Teresa mentions, and includes a selection of classical texts, such as an edition of Virgil and a compilation entitled *Proverbs of Seneca*.[17] No novel of chivalry appears on the list, even though a few editions had been published by 1511. Even if he had owned some, he might have kept them off the record due to their questionable respectability.

It is difficult to imagine Teresa's father purchasing novels of chivalry for his wife and daughter, still less giving them the money to do so, even though books were not priced beyond the means of the merchant class. The lively market in used books, as well as the custom of renting books, would have made access to the books still more affordable.[18] The novels of chivalry might well have come into the house as loans or exchanges, perhaps with the cousins she later accuses of leading her into compromising situations. The introduction of the novels, then, might have led to introductions to the friends Teresa calls "mala compañía" [bad influences] (*Vida* 2.5), illustrating Natalie Zemon Davis' observation that more readily than manuscripts, printed books served "not merely as source[s] for ideas and images, but as carrier[s] of relationships."[19] In the first biography of Teresa (1587), Diego de Yepes considers reading itself as a relationship with a "compañero muerto" [dead companion]; in the case of novels of chivalry, he asserts, such companions might have damned her for eternity but for two personal qualities: a natural hatred for dishonesty, and intense concern about her honor.[20]

   Along with an enormous readership, the novels of chivalry attracted fierce criticism. Some previously addicted readers, among them Juan de Valdés in his *Diálogo de la lengua,* regretted that they had wasted their youths on these frivolous entertainments. He and other critics also attacked the genre for the lack of verisimilitude, trivial subject matter, confusing proliferation of characters, and random serial plotting.[21] Moralists, both humanistic and ecclesiastical, expressed alarm about the influence on the numerous women readers. Juan Luis Vives, one of the most prominent humanists of the time, wrote a vituperative chapter on the novels in his pamphlet *The Education of a Christian Woman,* published in Latin in 1524.[22] Vives advocates the education of women, not as an end in itself, but as a means of preserving young women's virginity, which he links to proper governance of a Christian state.[23] In the chapter entitled "Which Writers Are to Be Read and Which Not to Be Read," Vives locates the writers of novels of chivalry firmly in the latter category; most of the books he condemns by title are novels of chivalry, including *Amadís, Esplandián,* and *Florisando.*[24] Vives decries the publication of these books "in the vernacular" because "they may be read by idle men and women." And he implies that these novels—"full of lies and stupidity," "immoral," and "obscene"— could have been written only in the vernacular because the authors— "idle, unoccupied, ignorant men, the slaves of vice and filth"—had neither the learning nor the talent to write in Latin.[25]

   Vives purports to analyze the effect of novels of chivalry on women, but he concentrates on male rather than female responses. All of the enactments he decries are male activities. The novels of chivalry, he fulminates, encourage men to participate in jousts and tournaments, thus defying the Christian proscription on handling arms except for a holy cause; the novels induce men to give undue attention to women's responses to their performances in such events; and the novels teach men "how to impress and arouse the woman [they] love if she shows some resistance." Vives asserts that the effect on women is even worse, not because they would take such actions, but because they could not. Thus, reading about warfare and competitions will harm women because they cannot take up weapons themselves: "And if she does not hold [weapons] with her own hands, she certainly participates in the spectacle with heart and mind, which is worse." He worries that the female mind thus imaginatively engaged will not have enough extra capacity to defend itself against sexual aggression, one of the male responses to the novels: "What room do these thoughts [of the sword and sinewy muscles and virile strength] leave for chastity, which is defenseless, unwarlike, and weak?"[26] Vives portrays a passive female reader whose reaction to reading about "other people's loves" is confined to "pleasant gratification in amorous reveries." Given his definition of virginity as "integrity of mind, which extends also to the body," this mental activity alone irreparably contaminates female readers: "For such girls it would have been preferable not only that they had not learned literature but that they had lost their eyes so that they could not read, and their ears so that they could not hear."[27] Vives mentions that women readers might "be spurred on to shameful conduct" or "become clever in their depravity," but he does not elaborate. In his 1546 Spanish translation of Vives' *Introduction to Wisdom*, Francisco Cervantes de Sálazar filled the vacuum with additions to the chapter of that treatise similarly devoted to books with a pernicious influence on readers. Sálazar explains that the father who "leaves in [his daughter's] hand an *Amadís*" exposes her to an influence worse than socializing with men; she develops a "longing to be just such another Oriana, courted by another Amadís; and having conceived this longing she soon attempts to gratify it."[28]

As Vives correctly observed, a woman's performance of the novels of chivalry was confined to the realm of love, and the actions Teresa attributes to reading the novels suggest that she made the identifications that Sálazar deplores. Through juxtaposition, which frequently functions as logical connective in Teresa's writings, she associates her attempts to meet the standard of female attractiveness described in the novels of chivalry, extraordinary beauty displayed to perfection by luxurious adornment, with her reading. In the passage that follows immediately upon *Vida* 2.1 (quoted above), she narrates her newfound awareness of her own sexuality:

Comencé a traer galas y a desear contentar en parecer bien, con mucho cuidado de manos y cavello, y olores y todas las vanidades que en esto podía tener, que eran hartas, por ser muy curiosa. No tenía mala intención, porque no quisiera yo que nadie ofendiera a Dios por mí. Duróme mucha curiosidad de limpieza demasiada, y cosas que me parecía a mí no eran ningún pecado, muchos años. Ahora veo cuán malo devía ser.

[I began to dress in finery and to desire to please and look pretty, taking great care of my hands and hair and about perfumes and all the empty things in which one can indulge, and which were many, for I was very vain. I had no bad intentions since I would not have wanted anyone to offend God on my account. For many years I took excessive pains about cleanliness and other things that did not seem in any way sinful. Now I see how wrong it must have been.] (*Vida* 2.2)

Preoccupied completely with virginity, Vives does not consider that the novels of chivalry, rather than threatening the social order, might contribute to keeping it in place. Teresa's mother apparently read the novels of chivalry in the same way that many women now read sentimental romances, such as those in the Harlequin series. In her study of such readers, Janice Radway concludes that by providing compensation for their unsatisfactory lives, particularly with respect to their relationships with men, the romances contributed to maintaining the status quo. No matter how distant the novelistic world in time or place, the readers in Radway's study expressed "deep-seated unwillingness to admit that the perfect union concluding the story is unattainable in life."[29] By giving them hope, even if unrealistic, for improvement, the fantasy world of the novels encouraged these readers to remain in their real-life situations.

Teresa certainly notices the deficits in her mother's life, but she begins to prepare herself for the role of wife. The only other role society permitted to young women, that of nun, had not yet held much appeal for Teresa: "Gustava mucho, cuando jugava con otras niñas, hacer monesterios, como que éramos monjas; y yo me parece deseava serlo, aunque no tanto como las cosas que he dicho" [When I played with other girls I enjoyed it when we pretended we were nuns in a monastery, and it seemed to me that I desired to be one, although not as much as I desired the other things I mentioned (martyr, hermit)] (*Vida* 1.6). She followed the lead of an older cousin in fantasizing about sex and perhaps experimenting to some extent, which cannot be ascertained from Teresa's cryptic and contradictory account in *Vida* 2.3–7. To prevent her from continuing to jeopardize the family's honor, which was intertwined with the chastity of its female members, her father sent her to be sequestered temporarily in an Augustinian convent.

Not everyone agreed with Vives' denial of spiritual or moral significance to the novels of chivalry, nor with the premise that they could be read only literally, which he implies in the assertion that the only admirers of the genre are those who "see their own morals reflected in them as in a mirror."[30] In his prologue to the *Amadís* series Montalvo directs readers to religious "enxemplos y doctrinas" [examples and doctrines] he has added in the process of editing the manuscript he describes as coming

from a hermit's tomb near Constantinople by way of a Hungarian merchant.[31] Reflecting the relative tolerance that prevailed under Ferdinand
and Isabella toward Jews and Moors who had converted to Christianity,
Montalvo recommends that instead of persecuting converts at home, kings
turn their attention to combating infidels abroad. Accordingly, Esplandián
leads crusades against the Turks, whose defeat of Constantinople in 1453
had prompted the pope to grant indulgences for waging war against them.

Montalvo occasionally halts the action with allegorical and moral interpretations of the narrative. Blown-off course onto an unfamiliar shore
in Great Britain in book 3 of *Amadís de Gaula*, King Perión and three
squires leave their ship to determine where they have landed. A short way
inland they are greeted by a beautiful maiden who invites them to take
dinner and lodging in her castle. They enjoy a lavish meal and comfortable
beds, but Montalvo warns that they should look beyond physical appearances: "A esta donzella muda, hermosa, podemos comparar el mundo en
que bivimos, que pareciéndonos hermoso, sin boca, sin lengua, halagán-
donos, lisonjándonos, nos combida con muchos deleites y plazeres" [We
can compare this beautiful mute maiden with the world in which we live;
which, appearing beautiful to us, flattering us, delighting us without
mouth or tongue, lures us with many delights and pleasures]. Even though
these knights have taken the devil's bait, the narrator assures the reader that
God will redeem them: "Y si estos cavalleros la ovieron, fue por ser ahún
en esta vida, donde ninguno por malo, por pecador que sea, deve perder la
sperança del perdón" [And if these knights had (God's great compassion),
it was because they were still in this life; in which no one, however evil and
sinful he may be, ought to lose hope of pardon].[32] This invocation of
Catholic doctrine not only guarantees readers the safety of identifying
with the protagonists but also reminds them that repentance provides a
guarantee against eternal damnation. In his later installments, beginning
with *Sergas de Esplandián*, Montalvo states the religious significance of the
action still more explicitly.

By the mid-sixteenth century, some authors of novels of chivalry had
moved beyond the occasional didactic intervention to spiritualized versions
of the genre known in Spain as *caballería a lo divino*. This technique of di-
vinizing or moralizing secular literature was applied to poetry in the early
sixteenth century, to the novel by midcentury, and finally to drama in the
early seventeenth century.[33] In his preface to *Cavallería celestial* (1554), the
most popular novel of *caballería a lo divino*, Jerónimo de San Pedro bills his
work as a replacement for the profane novels, the pernicious influence of
which he illustrates with an allusion to Francesca's fateful scene of reading
in Dante's *Inferno*. Jerónimo casts Old Testament figures as knights-errant;
and he portrays Christ as Knight of the Lion, who, with his apostles,

Knights of the Round Table, wages war against Lucifer, Knight of the Serpent.[34] In this struggle between good and evil, Christ triumphs, of course. Jerónimo's theological claims for *Cavallería celestial* brought it to the attention of the Inquisition, which placed it on the Index. Ironically, none of the secular novels of chivalry suffered such banishment.[35]

As Vives observed, men had numerous outlets for performance of the novels of chivalry, not just entertainments such as jousts and duels, but honorable holy wars. A brief comparison between Teresa's enactments of the novels and those of Ignatius of Loyola (1491–1556) is instructive on this point, both for their near contemporaneousness—their crucial scenes of reading took place in the mid-1520s—and for differences attributable to gender. In *Reminiscences,* a third-person autobiography, Ignatius relates that he cast himself in the role of chivalric knight: "Until the age of twenty-six he was a man given up to the vanities of the world, and his chief delight used to be in the exercise of arms, with a great and vain desire to gain honour."[36] During the long convalescence he required to recover from serious wounds he incurred in defending Pamplona from French assault, he could not find any "tales of chivalry" to read, so he turned to the only books available, the *Vita Christi* and a book of saints' lives. Even as he read these spiritual books he continued to imagine himself performing heroic deeds on behalf of a wellborn lady. When he noticed that thinking about chivalric deeds left him "dry and unhappy" and considering spiritual acts made him "content and happy," he decided to take up the religious life. In making this change of vocation, he continued to perform as a knight of chivalry:"Because [Ignatius] had his whole mind full of those things [exploits for love of God] from *Amadís of Gaul,* he was getting some thoughts in his head of a similar kind. Thus he decided to keep a vigil of arms for a whole night, without sitting or lying down, but sometimes standing up, sometimes on his knees, before the altar of Our Lady of Montserrat."[37] Ignatius probably refers to the vigil kept by Amadís' son Esplandián to mark his investiture as a knight. Unlike Esplandian's vigil, Ignatius' culminated in his abandoning the military life. He left his sword and dagger in the church and exchanged clothing with a poor man, and after still more wandering without clear aim, he founded "an army for God," the Jesuit order.

Constrained in earthly performance of the novels of chivalry to feminine roles that risked dishonor to herself and her family, Teresa translated her enactment of the novels of chivalry into the spiritual realm. Teresa attributes her progress toward mystical union to several texts, most of them devotional or religious, but imagery from the novels of chivalry pervades her accounts of her interior life, where she performs the roles of both knight and lady.

Teresa's most frequent use of martial imagery appears in the beginning phases of her spiritual development, which she relates in the *Vida* and the first three mansions of *El castillo interior* (1577) [The Interior Castle; hereafter *Castillo*]. These works leave the impression of an interior struggle so desperate that it can only be described as a war: "En veinte y ocho [años] que ha que comencé oración, más de los dieciocho pasé esta batalla y contienda de tratar con Dios y con el mundo. Los demás que ahora me quedan por decir, mudóse la causa de la guerra, aunque no ha sido pequeña" [For more than eighteen of the twenty-eight years since I began prayer, I suffered this battle and conflict between friendship with God and friendship with the world. During the remaining years of which I have yet to speak, the cause of the war changed, although the war was not a small one](*Vida* 8.3). (Teresa often misstates her age and spans of times by a year or two; here she probably refers to years between 1536 or 1537 and 1564.) She identifies the opposing combatants in various terms; worldly versus spiritual goods, pride against humility, self-indulgence opposed to charity. She also describes a conflict between her vows to Christ and her relationships with mortal men, which though probably not sexual, were, in the psychological terms Mary Frohlich uses to describe them, "sexually weighted."[38] The quality to which she attributes her ultimate victory is *ánimo* [courage], a word she uses twenty-four times in the *Vida* alone: "I fail to know how the Lord gives me the courage or strength to approach him" (*Vida* 38.21).

A vision of the prospect of overwhelming defeat summarizes the fear and isolation she felt until about age fifty:

Vime estando en oración, en un gran campo a solas, en rededor de mí mucha gente de diferentes maneras que me tenían rodeada; todas me parece tenían armas en las manos para ofenderme: unas, lanzas; otras, espadas; otras dagas; y otras, estoques muy largos. En fin, yo no podía salir por ninguna parte sin que me pusiese a peligro de muerte, y sola, sin persona que hallase de mi parte. Estando mi espíritu en esta aflición, que no sabía qué me hacer, alcé los ojos a el cielo y vi a Cristo, no en el cielo, sino bien alto de mí en el aire, que tendía la mano hacia mí, y desde allí me favorecía de manera, que yo no temía toda la otra gente, ni ellos, aunque querían, me podían hacer dano.

[I saw myself standing alone in prayer in a large field; surrounding me were many different types of people. All of them I think held weapons in their hands so as to harm me: Some held spears; others, swords; others, daggers; and others, very long rapiers. In sum, I couldn't escape on any side without putting myself in danger of death; I was alone, without finding a person to take my part. While my spirit was in this affliction, not knowing what to do, I lifted my eyes to heaven and saw Christ. . . . He was holding out His hand

toward me, and from there He protected me in such a way that I had no fear
of all the people, nor could they harm me even though they wanted to.]
(*Vida* 39.17)

She would surely have succumbed in this spiritual ambush but for the intervention of God, who favored her against the others.[39]

When she relates similar experiences of spiritual duress in the form of
analogies in the *Castillo,* Teresa again turns to the vocabulary of warfare. In
the courtyard and outer rooms of the castle, enemies take the form of animals she found repugnant: lizards, snakes, vipers, wild animals, vermin, and
worms, all of them poisonous and putrid. The conditions in which the soul
fights are equally difficult: mud, filth, and darkness. These enemies represent the honors and vanities of the world, but they also reflect the sinful
condition of the soul itself, a far more difficult opponent than any exterior
force. She lives in constant terror in these first three mansions: "Harto gran
miseria es vivir en vida que siempre hemos de andar como los que tienen
los enemigos a la puerta, que ni pueden dormir ni comer sin armas y siempre con sobresalto si por alguna parte pueden desportillar esta fortaleza" [It
is a great misery to have to live a life in which we must always walk like
those whose enemies are at their doorstep; they can neither sleep nor eat
without weapons and without being always frightened lest somewhere
these enemies might be able to break through this fortress"] (*Castillo*
3.1.2). From a more interior room of the castle she remembers this suffering as so debilitating that she could not even read.

Teresa characterizes her reading of the novels of chivalry as cooling her
desire to please God, but with Béatrice Didier I consider the scene of reading them with her mother (*Vida* 2.1, quoted above) to be the "birth of desire," a desire she eventually directed toward God: "If the same language is
used for love of man and God, it is because the desire is *one and the same,*
the drive of life and death toward the Other."[40] From the fourth mansion
forward, the castle becomes the domain of a lady, and it becomes progressively more beautiful, comfortable, and peaceful: "El temor que solía tener
a los trabajos ya va mas templado" [The fear (the soul) used to have of trials now seems to be tempered] (*Castillo* 4.3.9). This area is pretty well in-
sulated against the enemies, with the occasional exception of small lizards
that can poke their noses even into the fifth mansion (*Castillo* 5.1.10),
which she labels the prayer of union.

Here the soul begins to anticipate mystical marriage, which here and elsewhere Teresa describes primarily through allegorical interpretation of the
Song of Songs but also with reference to the idealized romance portrayed in
the novels of chivalry. She knows that she must wait for God to take initiative: "Esta entiendo yo es la bodega donde nos quiere meter el Señor, cuando

quiere y como quiere; mas por diligencias que nosotros hagamos, no podemos entrar" [I understand this union to be the wine cellar where the Lord wishes to place us when He desires and as He desires, but we cannot enter by any efforts of our own] (*Castillo* 5.1.11). In the meantime, prospective Bride and Bridegroom engage in the ritual of courtship:

> Por acá cuando se han de desposar dos, se trata si son conformes y que el uno y el otro quieran y aun que se vean, para que más se satisfaga el uno del otro, ansí acá; pro supuesto que el concierto está ya hecho y que esta alma muy bien informada cuán bien le está y determinada a hacer en todo la voluntad de su Esposo de todas cuantas maneras ella viere que le ha de dar contento, y Su Majestad—como quien bien entenderá si es ansí—lo está de ella.

> [Here below when two people are to be engaged, there is discussion about whether they are alike, whether they love each other, and whether they might meet together so as to be more satisfied with each other. So, too, in the case of this union with God, the agreement has been made, and this soul is well informed about the goodness of her Spouse and determined to do His will in everything and in as many ways and she sees might make Him happy. And His Majesty, as one who understands clearly whether these things about His betrothed are so, is happy with her.] (*Castillo* 5.4.4)

This image of prenuptial romance coincides not at all with her mother's experience. When her mother married, at age fourteen, the alliance was arranged to give her impoverished old Christian family the dowry that *conversos* like Teresa's father were obliged to pay. Beatriz was six months pregnant by the time he received the costly papal permission required to marry a third cousin of his deceased wife. Teresa's idealized view probably comes not from life "here below," but from fantasies derived from novels of chivalry, among other possible sources. The lovers in *Amadís de Gaula* are genuinely enamored and deeply committed solely to each other. Through many protracted separations as well as ingenious attempts by evil wizards and giants to convince Amadís and his lady, Oriana, that each has betrayed the other, they remain loyal lovers. They pass the ultimate test of true love at the Gate of the Faithful Lovers on the Firm Island, where fire and smoke prevent the unfaithful from completing the passage. Amadís and Oriana pass through the gate easily, a proof of their exceptional mutual fidelity, for which they are rewarded with the magical green sword and crown of perennially fresh flowers, respectively.[41]

In the sixth mansion, the stage of betrothal, the Bride receives engagement gifts in the form of spiritual favors, including a vision of the Trinity. Here the Bride waits, and Teresa keeps the reader waiting: The sixth mansion, with eleven chapters, is by far the longest in the *Castillo*. When God

is ready to marry, He invites the soul into the seventh, and most interior,
mansion, where he manifests Himself to her:

> A ésta de quien hablamos [Teresa] se le representó el Senor, acabando de co-
> mulgar, con forma de gran resplandor y hermosura y majestad, como des-
> pués de resucitado, y le dijo que ya era tiempo de que sus cosas tomase ella
> por suyas y Él ternía cuidado de las suyas, y otras palabras que son más para
> sentir que para decir.

> [The Lord represented Himself to her, just as He was after His resurrection,
> and told her that now it was time that she considered as her own what be-
> longed to Him and that He would take care of what was hers, and he spoke
> other words more to be heard than to be mentioned.] (*Castillo* 7.2.1)

After the ceremony of mystical marriage, she expresses the hopeful confidence of a newlywed that the couple now forms an indivisible unit.

As early as the sixth mansion, Teresa begins to formulate a postnuptial role,
one that amalgamates the knight and the lady: A Bride of Christ with the authority to preach and evangelize in the world. As she had in her initial scene
of reading the novels, she genders herself principally as feminine. Occasionally she does gender the embattled soul as *varón* [male, manly]: She urges spiritual virility on those who would follow her spiritual route through the castle:
"Sea varón y no de los que se echavan a bever de buzos cuando ivan a la
batalla no me acuerdo con quién" [Let the soul be manly and not like those
soldiers who knelt down to drink before going into battle (I don't remember with whom)] (*Castillo* 2.1.6; see also *Camino de perfección* 7.8). Aside from
using this commonplace exhortation to spiritual fortitude, Teresa does not
represent herself as masculine. This reconfiguration of gendering in the novels of chivalry implies that in retrospect, she read against the ideology of the
genre as defined by Vives, that she became a "resistant reader."[42]

To perform this role in the world, she faces opposition not from the
devil but from human males, the men who controlled the ecclesiastical and
monastic establishments:

> Se querría meter en mitad del mundo, por ver si pudiese ser parte para que
> un alma alabase más a Dios; y, si es mujer, se aflige del atamiento que le hace
> su natural, porque no puede hacer esto, y ha gran envidia a los que tienen
> libertad para dar voces publicando quién es este gran Dios de las Caballerías.
> ¡Oh pobre mariposilla, atada con tantas cadenas que no te dejan volar lo que
> querrías!

> [(After the experience of union with God) the soul would want to enter
> into the midst of the world to try to play a part in getting even one soul to

praise God more. And if it is a woman, she is afflicted by the bondage of her nature because she cannot do this, and she has great envy of those who have the liberty to cry out and proclaim who is this great God of chivalric deeds. Oh, poor little butterfly, bound with so many chains which do not let you fly where you would like!"] (*Castillo* 6.6.3–4)

This translation for "gran Dios de las cavallerías" is mine, and I think it more accurate than the usual translation, "great God of hosts." Like most editors, Efrén and Steggink consider the phrase an allusion to God's vow to the Hebrew people in Exodus 14:17: "Thus will I win glory for myself at the expense of Pharoah and his army, chariots and cavalry all together."[43] The Book of Exodus does echo through this chapter of the *Castillo,* but having more to do with Teresa's own release from the strictures of male bias than with the exodus of the Hebrew people. Teresa wrote the *Castillo* in 1577 while under house arrest and orders to cease making any more foundations of her order, the Barefoot (Discalced) Carmelites. Jodi Bilinkoff rightly judges such comments as expressions of her thwarted desire to have the freedom and power enjoyed by priests: "Teresa deeply envied male priests, who did not have to suffer, as she did, the bonds of misogynism, lack of formal education, and disqualification from office that kept her from achieving her goals."[44] The "God of chivalric deeds" Teresa summons is one who will permit her to carry out her own chivalric deeds, which she defines here and elsewhere as "bringing souls to God" through preaching and teaching.

In the second biography of Teresa (1590) Francisco de Ribera writes that Teresa "bebió aquel lenguaje y estilo, que dentro de pocos meses ella y su hermano Rodrigo de Cepeda compusieron un libro de caballerías con sus aventuras y ficciones, y salió tal, que habría harto que decir de él" [drank in their language and style with such effect that within a few months she and her brother Rodrigo composed a book of chivalry, of which a great deal could be said].[45] Ribera says no more of it, but the story gained accretions in the testimony taken for her canonization and the subsequent hagiographical tradition. A novel about a "knight of Avila" attributed to Teresa surfaced during the celebration of her canonization in 1622.[46] Considering that the saint-making process entailed preserving every residue of a candidate's life on earth, the subsequent oblivion of this novel marks it pretty clearly as a fake.

It is very unlikely that Teresa ever tried to write a novel of chivalry; she rarely wrote voluntarily except to accomplish some specific goal.[47] With regard to her own accomplishments Teresa valorized deeds over words: "Yo no soy para más de parlar, y ansí no queréis Vos, Dios mío, ponerme en obras. Todo se va en palabras y deseos cuanto he de servir, y aun para esto no tengo libertad" [I'm not much good for anything but talk, and so You don't desire, my God, to put me to work; everything adds up to just words and desires about how much I must serve, and even in this I don't have freedom] (*Vida* 21.5). From our vantage point more than four hundred years later, Teresa's accomplishments seem remarkable: the creation of a new order; the foundation of seventeen monasteries and convents throughout Spain; counsel concerning the spiritual and religious life that still provides inspiration; and remarkably extensive writings. Toward the end of her life, however, Teresa occasionally expressed doubts about her accomplishments, wondering at times whether she might not better have secured her salvation by taking the role of hermit or martyr. And despite her charisma and her talent for organization, she frequently had to operate through men, which prevented her from taking full satisfaction and credit for her work. Finally, she tired of the strenuous performance of the role of knight, and longed to confine herself again to the contemplative, feminine aspect of her identity, the role of Bride: "Ansí son las almas mostradas a estar en las corrientes de las agues de su Esposo, que sacadas de allí a ver las redes de las cosas del mundo, verdaderamente no se vive hasta tornarse a ver allí" [So it is with souls accustomed to living in the running streams of their Spouse. When taken out of them and caught up in the net of worldly things, they do not truly live until they find themselves back in those waters] (*Libro de las Fundaciones* 31.46). Soon after writing these words, she began a journey back to her first foundation, the convent in Avila, but she did not reach it. Instead, overcome with her ultimately fatal illness, she stopped in Alba de Tormes, where, in her words, she died "a daughter of the Church," which is also to say, a Bride of Christ.

Notes

I am exceedingly grateful to Jodi Bilinkoff for insightful comments on the rough draft.

1. Joel Saugnieux, "Culture féminine en Castille au XVIe siècle: Thérèse d'Avila et les livres," in *Cultures populaires et cultures savantes en Espagne du Moyen Âge aux Lumières* (Paris: Centre National de la Recherche Scientifique, 1982), pp. 45–77, at p. 45. Unless otherwise specified, all translations are mine.
2. On scenes of reading, defined as "scenes of engagement with the public discourse for meaning and agency," in the nineteenth-century novel, see Nancy Cervetti, *Scenes of Reading: Transforming Romance in Brontë, Eliot and Woolf* (New York: Peter Lang, 1998).
3. Bruce Wardropper, "The Religious Conversion of Profane Poetry," *Studies in the Continental Background of Renaissance English literature: Essays Presented to John L. Lievsay,* ed. Dale B. J. Randall and George Walton Williams

(Durham, NC: Duke University Press, 1977), pp. 203–21, at pp. 210–12; Juan Manuel Cacho Blecua, "Del gentilhombre mundano al caballero 'a lo divino': los ideales caballerescos de Ignacio de Loyola," in *Ignacio de Loyola y su tiempo,* ed. Juan Plazaola (Bilbao: Universidad de Duesto, 1992), pp. 129–59, at p. 137.

4. Efrén de la Madre de Dios and Otger Steggink, eds., *Teresa de Jesús: Obras completas* (Madrid: Biblioteca de Autores Cristianos, 1986); for the English translation I use Kieran Kavanaugh and Otilio Rodríguez, trans. and eds., *The Collected Works of St. Teresa of Avila,* 3 vols. (Washington, D.C.: Institute of Carmelite Studies, 1976–85), unless otherwise noted.

5. When she went again to this uncle during her life-threatening illness in 1538, he introduced her to Francisco de Osuna's *Tercer abecedario espiritual* [Third Spiritual Alphabet], which succeeded, where numerous other devotional books had failed, in starting her off on the path toward recollected prayer (*Vida* 4.7).

6. I analyze Teresa's interpretation of Book 8 of Augustine's *Confessions* in my *St. Teresa of Avila: Author of a Heroic Vida* (Berkeley and Los Angeles: University of California Press, 1995), pp. 34–37.

7. Efrén de la Madre de Dios and Otger Steggink, *Tiempo y vida de Santa Teresa,* 2nd revised ed. (Madrid: Biblioteca de Autores Cristianos, 1977), p. 32. The authors find signs of some training in Teresa's calligraphy, p. 32 n.19.

8. The most accurate Spanish term for the genre is *libros de caballerías,* meaning books of chivalric deeds: "books" because the sixteenth-century Spanish word *novela* referred to Italianate short stories or novellas; and *caballerías,* acts of chivalry, rather than *caballería,* the code or institution of chivalry. Daniel Eisenberg, *Romances of Chivalry in the Spanish Golden Age,* intro. Martín de Riquer (Newark, Del.: Juan Cuesta, 1982), p. xv n. 1.

9. Juan Manuel Cacho Blecua, "Introducción," *Amadís de Gaula,* by Garci Rodríguez de Montalvo, 2 vols. (Madrid: Cátedra, 1996), 1:136–37.

10. Ibid., p. 223. On this characteristic of the novels of chivalry, see James Donald Fogelquist, *El Amadís y el género de la historia fingida* (Madrid: Porrúa Turanzas, 1982).

11. David Bleich, "Gender Interests in Reading and Language," in *Gender and Reading: Essays on Readers, Texts, and Contexts,* eds. Elizabeth A. Flynn and Patrocinio P. Schweikart (Baltimore: Johns Hopkins University Press, 1986), pp. 234–66, at pp. 264–65.

12. Montalvo is thought to have revised a late-fifteenth-century manuscript by an unknown author. The earliest articles on this subject took the form of surveys of all of Teresa's reading: Albert Morel Fatío, "Les lectures de Sainte Thérèse," *Bulletin hispanique* 10 (1907): 19–67; Gaston Etchegoyen, *L'amour divine: Essai sur les sources de Sainte Thérèse* (Paris: Burdeos, 1923). More recently, Marcel Bataillon finds a verbal echo from *Sergas de Esplandián* in Teresa's *Vida* ("Santa Teresa, lectora de libros de caballerías," in *Varia lección de clásicos españoles* [Madrid: Gredos, 1964], pp. 21–23, at p. 21); Manuel Criado

de Val defines mysticism as chivalry "a lo divino" and usefully compares the novels of chivalry and the picaresque novels in "Mística frente a picaresca," in *De la edad media al Siglo de Oro* (Madrid: Publicaciones Españoles, 1965), pp. 89–105; Victor García de la Concha perceptively identifies a generalized influence of the novels of chivalry in Teresa's concept of love, balance of idealism and realism, and heroic concepts of moral obligation and action in *El arte literario de Santa Teresa* (Barcelona: Ariel, 1978), pp. 51–52; Antonio Garrosa Resina evaluates and extends the previous literature on Teresa's secular reading in "Santa Teresa y la cultura literaria de su tiempo: Referencias literarias profanas en la obra Teresiana," *Castilla* 4 (1982): 83–117; in "The Knight and the Mystical Castle," *Studies in Formative Spirituality* 4 (1983): 392–407, the most important article for my thinking about this topic, Javier Herrero argues, in broad terms, that "the main features of her imagination are dominated by the literature [of chivalry] she so passionately loved, and [that from it] not only her *Vida,* but her art took its roots." Joseph Chorpenning attributes Teresa's imagery of the garden in the *Vida* and of the castle in *El castillo interior* to her early immersion in the novels of chivalry (*The Divine Romance: Teresa of Avila's Narrative Theology* [Chicago: Loyola University Press, 1992], pp. 22–23, 62, 98, 157 n. 13).

13. Keith Whinnom, "The Problem of the 'Bestseller' in Spanish Golden-Age Literature," *Bulletin of Hispanic Studies* 52 (1980): 193. Fernando de Rojas' *La Celestina* was the bestselling single work of the era.

14. It is believed that an edition was printed in Seville in 1496, but no copy is known to have survived (Frank Pierce, *Amadís de Gaula* [Boston: Twayne, 1976], p. 16).

15. Montalvo wrote the fourth volume of *Amadís* and *Sergas de Esplandián,* while Paéz de Ribera wrote *Florisando,* and Feliciano de Silva wrote the first volume of *Lisuarte de Grecia.* Subsequent volumes in the *Amadís* series featured his descendants out to the seventh generation.

16. For titles and dates of publication, see Henry Thomas, *Spanish and Portuguese Romances of Chivalry* (1920; New York: Kraus Reprints, 1969), p. 147.

17. Victor García de la Concha, *El arte literario,* p. 17.

18. Sarah T. Nalle, "Literacy and Culture in Early Modern Castile," *Past & Present,* no. 125 (1989): 65–96; Maxime Chevalier, *Lectura y lectores de la España de los siglos XVI y XVII* (Madrid: Turner, 1976), p. 73. Nalle posits the existence of a used-book market as one way to reconcile the discrepancy between those who told the Inquisition that they had a library and the much larger number who said they had read books.

19. Natalie Zemon Davis, "Printing and the People," in *Society and Culture in Early Modern France* (Stanford: Stanford University Press, 1975), pp. 189–226, at p. 192.

20. Diego de Yepes, *Vida de Santa Teresa de Jesús,* Tesoro de místicos españoles, vol. 1 (Paris: Garnier, 1847), p. 12.

21. Eisenberg, *Romances of Chivalry,* p. 11; Fogelquist, *El Amadís,* pp. 15–17.

22. Juan Luis Vives, *The Education of a Christian Woman: A Sixteenth-Century Manual* [De Institutione Foeminae Christianae], ed. and trans. Charles Fantazzi (Chicago: University of Chicago Press, 2000). Vives dedicated the work to Queen Isabella's daughter, Catherine of Aragón, for the instruction of her daughter, Mary. Ironically, Isabella owned several sentimental novels, precursors of the novels of chivalry (Ian Michael, "'From Her Shall Read the Perfect Ways of Honour': Isabel of Castile and Chivalric Romance," in *The Age of the Catholic Monarchs, 1474–1516,* ed. Alan Deyermond and Ian Macpherson [Liverpool: Liverpool University Press, 1989], pp. 103–112, at p. 104).

23. On this point, see Valerie Wayne, "Some Sad Sentence: Vives' *Instruction of a Christian Woman,*" in *Silent but for the Word: Tudor Women as Patrons, Translators, and Writers of Religious Works,* ed. Margaret Patterson Hannay (Kent, Ohio: Kent State University Press, 1985), pp. 16–29.

24. Vives, *Education of a Christian Woman,* pp. 73–79.

25. Ibid., p. 75.

26. Ibid., p. 73.

27. Ibid., p. 74.

28. *Camino para la sabiduria . . . compuesto en latin por . . . Luys Vives, buelta en Castellano, con muchas adiciones . . . por Francisco Ceruantes de Salazar* (1546); as quoted, documented, and translated by Thomas, pp. 164–65. "Y dexanla vn amadis enlas manos . . . deseando ser otra Oriana como alli, y verse seruida de otro Amadis, tras este desseo viene luego procurarlo . . ."

29. Janice Radway, *Reading the Romance* (Chapel Hill: University of North Carolina Press, 1984), p. 193. Radway's readers noted that their reading provided a welcome release from domestic responsibilities and a refuge from insistent familial demands, the same kind of escape Teresa reports.

30. Vives, *Education of a Christian Woman,* p. 76.

31. Garci Rodríguez de Montalvo, *Amadís de Gaula,* ed. Juan Manuel Cacho Blecua, 2 vols. (Madrid: Cátedra, 1996), 1:235. For a discussion of prologues as directives for reading early books in the vernacular, see Ruth Evans, "An Afterword on the Prologue," in *The Idea of the Vernacular: An Anthology of Middle English Literary Theory, 1280–1520,* eds. Jocelyn Wogan-Browne, Nicholas Watson, Andrew Taylor, and Ruth Evans (University Park: Pennsylvania State University Press, 1999), pp. 366–78.

32. *Amadís de Gaula,* ed. Cacho Blecua, 2:3.39, p. 1055; *Amadís de Gaula,* trans. Edwin B. Place and Herbert C. Behm, vol. 2 (Lexington: University Press of Kentucky, 1975), p. 101.

33. Dámaso Alonso, *Poesía española: Ensayo de métodos y límites estilísticos,* 5th ed. (1966; Madrid: Gredos, 1987), pp. 220–27.

34. George Ticknor, *History of Spanish Literature,* 6th American ed., vol. 1 (1891; Gordian Press, 1965), pp. 257–60. Ticknor judges the allegory of *Cavallería celestial* "strange and revolting."

35. Eisenberg, *Romances of Chivalry,* pp. 45–46.

36. Saint Ignatius of Loyola, "Reminiscences," *Personal Writings,* trans. and ed. Joseph A. Munitiz and Philip Endean (Harmondsworth: Penguin, 1996), p. 13. Ignatius dictated the account in 1553 to friars who cast it in the third person.

37. Loyola, *Reminiscences,* p. 20.

38. Mary Frohlich, *The Intersubjectivity of the Mystic: A Study of Teresa of Avila's "Interior Castle"* (Atlanta: Scholars Press, 1993), p. 320.

39. This interior battle scene very likely draws on multiple sources, including stories of wars of the Reconquest, during which her city of birth came to be known as Avila de los Caballeros [Avila of the Knights], and, perhaps, the legend of an Avilan woman warrior, Jimena Blázquez, said to have mobilized a group of women who deflected a Moorish assault on the city while their husbands were away (Jodi Bilinkoff, personal communications, July 2000, and *The Avila of Saint Teresa: Religious Reform in a Sixteenth-Century City* [Ithaca: Cornell University Press, 1989], pp. 1–4).

40. Béatrice Didier, "Thérèse d'Avila et le désir de Dieu," in *L'écriture-femme* (Paris: Presses Universitaires de la France, 1981), pp. 51–70, at pp. 52, 66. Didier goes on to specify that love for man is not *like [comme]* love for God.

41. *Amadís de Gaula,* 1:2.56, pp. 798–99.

42. The term was developed by Judith Fetterly in *The Resisting Reader: A Feminist Approach to American Fiction* (Bloomington: Indiana University Press, 1978), where she argues that much of American fiction forces women to read against their gender. On women as "resistant readers" of sixteenth-century Spanish novels, see Barbara Weissberger, "Resisting Readers and Writers in the Sentimental Romances and the Problem of Female Literacy," in *Studies on the Spanish Sentimental Romance (1440–1550): Redefining a Genre,* eds. Joseph J. Gwara and E. Michael Gerli (London: Tamesis, 1997), pp. 174–90.

43. Madre de Dios and Steggink, eds., *Teresa de Jesús,* p. 544 n. 3.

44. Jodi Bilinkoff, "Woman with a Mission: Teresa of Avila and the Apostolic Model," in *Modelli di santità e modelli di comportamento: contrasti, intersezioni, complimentarità,* eds. Giulia Barone, Marina Caffiero, and Francesco Scorza Barcellona (Turin: Rosenberg & Sellier, 1994), pp. 295–305, at p. 296.

45. Francisco de Ribera, *La Vida de la Madre Teresa de Jesús, fundadora de las Descalças y Descalços,* ed. and introd. Jaime Pons (Barcelona: Gustavo Gili, 1908), p. 99.

46. Stephen Clissold, *St. Teresa of Avila* (London: Sheldon Press, 1979), p. 17. Clissold writes that "those who read it thought well of it," but does not identify those readers or detail their opinions. She has also been named as author of the first version of *Amadís* (Cacho Blecua, "Introducción," p. 57).

47. On Teresa's attitude toward her own writing, see Slade, *St. Teresa of Avila,* pp. 6, 121.

CONTRIBUTORS

RENATE BLUMENFELD-KOSINSKI is Professor of French at the University of Pittsburgh. She is the author of *Not of Woman Born: Representations of Caesarean Birth in Medieval and Renaissance Europe* (1990) and of *Reading Myth: Classical Mythology and Its Interpretation in Medieval French Literature* (1997). She also edited and translated *The Selected Writings of Christine de Pizan* (1997; with K. Brownlee) and translated the works of Margaret of Oingt (1991). She has written numerous articles on medieval French literature and coedited *Images of Sainthood in Medieval Europe* (1991), *Translatio Studii* (2000), and *The Politics of Translation in the Middle Ages and the Renaissance* (2001). She is currently working on visionary narratives at the time of the Great Schism.

MAUREEN BOULTON is Professor of French at the University of Notre Dame with particular interests in religious literature, textual criticism, and the relations between lyric poetry and medieval romance. She has edited two fourteenth-century texts, the *Old French Evangile de l'Enfance* and the Anglo-Norman *Enfaunces de Jesu Crist*. Her study of lyric quotations in thirteenth- and fourteenth-century romances, *The Song in the Story*, was published in 1993. Her most recent book (with Ruth J. Dean) is *Anglo-Norman Literature: A Guide to Texts and Manuscripts* (1999). She is currently editing a collection of essays on *Passion Narratives in Late Medieval Europe*, and is completing a study of apocryphal lives of Christ in Old and Middle French.

MOIRA FITZGIBBONS is Assistant Professor of English at Western Washington University. Her scholarly interests focus on the linguistic and social impact of late medieval works of religious instruction, including *Handlyng Synne*, Mirk's *Festial*, and *Jacob's Well*. She is working on a book about penitential texts' endorsement and/or rejection of particular kinds of learning for lay people.

ELIZABETH TERESA HOWE has been Professor of Spanish at Tufts University since 1978. She specializes in Spanish literature of the sixteenth and seventeenth centuries and has published articles on a variety of topics in this field. She is the author of *Mystical Imagery: Santa Teresa de Jesus and San Juan de la Cruz* (1988) and editor of a Spanish edition of the *Instrucción de la mujer cristiana* of Juan Luis Vives (1995). She is currently working on a study of women and education during the Spanish Golden Age.

LISA MANTER is Associate Professor at Saint Mary's College of California, where she teaches courses in medieval studies and film. "Rolle Playing" is from a larger study linking late medieval English mystical texts with post-modern theory. A portion of this work, "The Savior of Her Desire: Margery Kempe's Passionate Gaze," which addresses problems of female desire in *The Book of Margery Kempe*, has recently come out in *Exemplaria*. She is also currently working on medieval dream vision literature and on camp aesthetics.

BARBARA NEWMAN is Professor of English and Religion at Northwestern University, specializing in medieval women. She is the author of *Sister of Wisdom: St. Hildegard's Theology of the Feminine* (1987) and *From Virile Woman to WomanChrist: Studies in Medieval Religion and Literature* (1995), and editor and translator of Hildegard of Bingen's *Symphonia* (1988). Her most recent book is *Voice of the Living Light: Hildegard of Bingen and Her World* (1998). She was awarded a Guggenheim Fellowship for 2000–2001 to complete a book entitled *God and the Goddesses: Vision, Poetry, and Belief in the Middle Ages*.

MORGAN POWELL is Assistant Professor of Modern Languages at Franklin College, Switzerland. He has been a Fellow of the Institute for European History in Mainz, Germany, and currently holds a Getty Postdoctoral Fellowship in Art History and the Humanities. He has written on the correspondence of Abelard and Heloise as a text for monastic instruction, and on the *Speculum virginum*, the first major medieval treatise on female monastic life. He is completing a book with the provisional title *The Woman in the Mirror: Reading, Performance, and Vernacular Poetics*, to be published by Palgrave in 2002.

DUNCAN ROBERTSON's studies have focused on French religious writings of the twelfth and thirteenth centuries. He is the author of *The Medieval Saints' Lives: Spiritual Renewal and Old French Literature* (1995) and has published articles on related topics in *Romance Philology, Cahiers de Civilisation Médiévale, French Forum,* and other journals. He has taught at the Centre d'Etudes Supérieures de Civilisation Médiévale (Université de Poitiers), at the University of San Francisco, and at the University of Michigan. He is presently Professor of French and Spanish at Augusta State University in Georgia.

CAROLE A. SLADE teaches in the Department of English and Comparative Literature and directs the summer session at Columbia University. From 1995 to 1997 she also participated in the project on religious experience at the Rutgers Center for Historical Analysis. A comparatist and medievalist, she has published the MLA volume *Approaches to Teaching Dante's Divine Comedy* (1982) and *St. Teresa of Avila: Author of a Heroic Life* (1995). Her recent articles include "St. Teresa as a Social Reformer" (2001), "The Value of Diamonds in English Literature" (1997), and "A Definition of Mystical Autobiography" (1991).

FIONA SOMERSET is Associate Professor of Medieval English at the University of Western Ontario. Her research focuses on Middle English and Latin texts from 1100 to 1500. She is the author of *Clerical Discourses and Lay Audience in Late Medieval England* (1998) as well as a number of articles in such journals as *Studies in the Age of Chaucer, English Literary History,* and *Yearbook of Langland Studies,* and in essay collections. She is working on an edition of four Wycliffite dialogues as well as a hypertext database of vernacular and Latin resources for the study of heresy in medieval England. Current projects include articles on the chronicles of the Peasant Revolt and on *Piers Plowman.*

RONALD E. SURTZ is Professor of medieval and Golden Age Spanish literature at Princeton University. He is the author of *The Birth of a Theater: Dramatic Convention in the Spanish Theater from Juan del Encina to Lope de Vega* (1979), *The Guitar of God: Gender, Power, and Authority in the Visionary World of Mother Juana de la Cruz (1481–1534)* (1990), *Teatro castellano de la Edad Media* (1992), and *Writing Women in Late Medieval and Early Modern Spain: The Mothers of Saint Teresa of Avila* (1995).

LORI J. WALTERS is Professor of French at Florida State University in Tallahassee, Florida. She has edited *Lancelot and Guinevere: A Casebook* (1996) and coedited *The Manuscripts of Chrétien de Troyes* (1993) and *'Translatio Studii': Essays by his Students in Honor of Karl D. Uitti for His Sixty-Fifth Birthday* (1999), in addition to contributing pieces to these collections. She has also published widely on the *Romance of the Rose* and Christine de Pizan. She is currently investigating the construction of vernacular authority in texts and manuscript collections dating from the late thirteenth to the mid-fifteenth century.

NANCY BRADLEY WARREN received her B.A. in English and French from Vanderbilt University, and her Ph.D. in English from Indiana University. She is the author of *Spiritual Economies: Female Monasticism in Later Medieval England* (2001) and numerous articles on women's religion. At present she is working on a book entitled *Women of God and Men of Arms: Female Spirituality and Political Conflict 1350–1580,* which investigates the cultural work performed by manifestations of female spirituality at the intersections of the ecclesiastical, international, and civic political systems. Nancy Bradley Warren is assistant professor of English at Utah State University.

ELSE MARIE WIBERG PEDERSEN is Senior Lecturer in Dogmatics at the University of Aarhus, Denmark. She publishes on a variety of dogmatic themes within medieval and modern theology, especially on Cistercian nuns' theology and spirituality. Recent works include "Image of God— Image of Mary—Image of Woman: On the Theology and Spirituality of Beatrice of Nazareth," *Cistercian Studies Quarterly* 29 (1994), and "Gottesbild—Frauenbild—Selbstbild: Die Theologie Mechthilds von Hackeborn und Gertruds von Helfta," in *Vor dir steht die leere Schale meiner Sehnsucht. Die Mystik der Frauen von Helfta* (1998). She also contributed an essay on Beatrice to *New Trends in Feminine Spirituality: The Holy Women of Liège and Their Impact* (1999) and published *Se min Kjole,* a study of the first women priests in Denmark (1998).

ULRIKE WIETHAUS teaches at Wake Forest University. She is the author of articles and books on medieval Christian mysticism, including *Ecstatic Transformation* (1995). She edited *Maps of Flesh and Light: The Religious Experience of Medieval Women Mystics* (1993), coedited *Dear Sister: Medieval Women and the Epistolary Genre* (with Karen Cherewatuk, 1993), and has recently completed a translation of *The Life and Revelations of Agnes Blannbekin* (2001).

WERNER WILLIAMS-KRAPP is Professor of Medieval German Language and Literature at the Universität Augsburg in Germany. His primary area of research is late medieval German and Dutch religious literature, with special emphasis on hagiography, mystical literature, drama, sermons, and manuscript culture. He is the author of *Die deutschen und niederländischen Legendare des Mittelalters* (1986) and *Überlieferung und Gattung: Zur Gattung 'Spiel' im Mittelalter* (1980), and the editor of numerous medieval texts. He is currently working on a history of German literature in the fifteenth and early sixteenth centuries.

INDEX